# Communicative
# Reading  Fourth Edition

For information about this book, write or call:

Sheffield Publishing Company
P.O. Box 359
Salem, Wisconsin 53168
(414) 843-2281

ACKNOWLEDGMENTS

CHAPTER 1

"A Certain Peace" by Nikki Giovanni. Reprinted by permission of William Morrow & Co., Inc. from *My House* by Nikki Giovanni. Copyright © 1972 by Nikki Giovanni.

"The Old Bus" from *Revenge of the Lawn* by Richard Brautigan. Copyright © 1963, 1964, 1965, 1966, 1967, 1969, 1971 by Richard Brautigan. Reprinted by permission of Simon & Schuster, Inc.

"In the Lobby" © 1967 by Ruth Whitman. Reprinted from her volume *The Marriage Wig and Other Poems* by permission of Harcourt Brace Jovanovich, Inc.

"On the Death of a Student Hopelessly Failing My Course"

CHAPTER 2

"Terra-cotta Horse, First Century, A.D." by Morris Bishop. Reprinted by permission of Archaeological Institute of America.

"Naming of Parts" from *A Map of Verona* by Henry Reed. Reprinted by permission of Jonathan Cape Ltd., publishers.

"Versus at Night" from *Selected Poems* by Dannie Abse. © 1970 by Dannie Abse. Published by Oxford University Press. Reprinted by permission of Anthony Sheil Associates Limited.

Excerpt from *The Autobiography of Will Rogers.* Copyright 1949 by Roger Company. Reprinted by permission of Houghton Mifflin Company.

"Song of the Queen Bee" in *The Second Tree from the Corner* by E. B. White. Copyright, 1945 by E. B. White.

CHAPTER 3

"A Christmas Carol" from *Christmas Songs and Easter Carols* by Phillips Brooks. Published by E. P. Dutton & Co., Inc. and reprinted with their permission.

"The Spires of Oxford" from *The Spires of Oxford and Other Poems* by Winfred Letts. Copyright, 1917 by E. P. Dutton & Co., Inc.; renewal 1945 by Winifred Letts. Reprinted by permission of the publishers, E. P. Dutton & Co., Inc.

by George Cuomo. Originally published in *Saturday Review.* Copyright 1959 Saturday Review, Inc. Reprinted by permission of George Cuomo.

"Gielgud Reading Lear" by Peter Kane Dufault. Originally published in *Saturday Review.* Copyright 1959 Saturday Review, Inc. Reprinted by permission of Peter Kane Dufault.

"The Poetry Reading" copyright 1954 by Karl Shapiro. Reprinted from *Selected Poems*, by Karl Shapiro, by permission of Random House, Inc. Originally appeared in *The New Yorker.*

Originally appeared in *The New Yorker.* By permission of Harper & Row, Publishers, Inc.

Excerpt from *God Bless You, Mr. Rosewater* by Kurt Vonnegut, Jr. Copyright © by Kurt Vonnegut, Jr. Reprinted with the permission of Delacorte Press/Seymour Lawrence.

"Night" from *Selected Poems of Gabriela Mistral* (translated by Langston Hughes), Indiana University Press, 1957.

"The Dover Bitch" from *The Hard Hours* by Anthony Hecht. Copyright © 1960 by Anthony Hecht. Reprinted by permission of Atheneum Publishers. Originally appeared in *Transatlantic Review.*

"Snakecharmer" copyright © 1962 by Sylvia Plath. Reprinted from *The Colossus and Other Poems*, by Sylvia Plath, by permission of Alfred A. Knopf, Inc.

"The Death of the Ball Turret Gunner" by Randall Jarrell. Reprinted with the permission of Farrar, Straus & Giroux, Inc. from *Selected Poems* by Randall Jarrell. Copyright 1945; © renewed 1973 by Mary von Schrader Jarrell.

"Between Walls" from William Carlos Williams, *Collected Poems.* Copyright 1938 by New Directions Publishing Corporation. Reprinted by permission of New Directions Publishing Corporation.

# Communicative
# Reading Fourth Edition

## Elbert R. Bowen
*Central Michigan University*

## Otis J. Aggertt
*Indiana State University*

## William E. Rickert
*Wright State University*

Sheffield Publishing Company

Salem, Wisconsin

# Preface

Otis J. Aggertt's untimely death in 1973 brought to an end a collaboration that produced three editions of *Communicative Reading*, in 1956, 1963, and 1972. In a sense, however, the collaboration continues for the life of the book, as Otis is to be found throughout this edition also. The productivity that began at a convention luncheon in Ann Arbor, Michigan, in 1952 persists.

The invitation to William E. Rickert to join this collaboration was an exacting choice that proved to be a good one. It seemed that the book needed to be improved and updated as only a younger person could fully see the need for such alteration. On the other hand, the new edition had to maintain the philosophy of interpretation embraced by those who had adopted previous editions, namely the belief that oral interpretation is, indeed, a most dynamic approach to literature because it offers the most acute imaginative and muscular participation in the literary experience at the moment of communication. Many texts have appeared during the life-span of this one, offering many approaches to a relatively small market. That this text has received continued support when so few have prevailed is indicative of the faith its users have had in its focus. Such support by those we do and do not know is deeply appreciated.

In the present edition we have made some minor rearrangements, which we hope will facilitate study. We have revised throughout the chapters with the intention of being better teachers. We have provided a completely new textual treatment of prose fiction. We have substantially changed and expanded the range of quoted literature in order to recognize the excellence of contemporary literature. In two appendixes we have provided a selective list of texts in oral interpretation to encourage reading in other sources and a suggestive list of anthology titles for the student who is particularly hard-pressed to find something interesting to read. Finally, we hope to have improved our own communication with the reader by attempting to say things more felicitously.

Last, some personal words: I wish to thank my wife, Louise, for her many years of patience and her assistance with clerical matters, especially when deadlines became most demanding. I also wish to thank my colleague William R. Haushalter for many good suggestions, the copyright holders for their cooperation, and our long-standing editor, Lloyd C. Chilton, and the staff of Macmillan Publishing Co., Inc. for their continued confidence and guidance.

E.R.B.

# Contents

## Five

### Group Reading and Interpretative Theatre

## Appendixes

## Indexes

# One

## Exploring Interpretative Reading

# 1

# What Is
# Interpretative Reading

We are all aware of the importance of the spoken word in the traffic of practical life, but we should not overlook its significance as a vital aspect of our cultural-esthetic life. In addition to the speaker and actor, there is a third speech artist: the interpretative reader, who has been around for centuries. Originally, the reader was the poet, singing his own verses, or the wandering storyteller, communicating literary experiences long before books were written. After learning to read and to print, our ancestors still enjoyed listening to an effective interpreter weave a spell, making a story or poem *live*. In recent years we have seen a rebirth of this form of literary communication. Today authors, actors, and others are reading to us on the platform, through records, and on television. We listen enthusiastically, if they read well.

At a relatively simple level, interpretative reading is practiced in a variety of contexts, from the simple reading of a bedtime story to a child to the complex interpretation of great literature in artistic performance. Simplicity of expressional or communicative function may be very personal, as in this poem:

## A CERTAIN PEACE

NIKKI GIOVANNI

it was very pleasant
not having you around
this afternoon

not that i don't love you
and want you and need you
and love loving and wanting and needing you

but there was a certain peace
when you walked out the door
and i knew you would do something
you wanted to do
and i could run

a tub full of water
and not worry about answering the phone
for your call
and soak in bubbles
and not worry about whether you would want something
special for dinner
and rub lotion all over me
for as long as i wanted
and not worry if you had a good idea
or wanted to use the bathroom

and there was a certain excitement
when after midnight you came home
and we had coffee
and i had a day of mine
that made me as happy
as yours did you

Simplicity and directness of interpretation are called for in reading a recollection that extends beyond the individual to other persons, as in this prose excerpt:

## THE OLD BUS

### RICHARD BRAUTIGAN

I do what everybody else does: I live in San Francisco. Sometimes I am forced by Mother Nature to take the bus. Yesterday was an example. I wanted to get some place beyond the duty of my legs, far out on Clay Street, so I waited for a bus.

It was not a hardship but a nice warm autumn day and fiercely clear. An old woman waited, too. Nothing unusual about that, as they say. She had a large purse and white gloves that fit her hands like the skins of vegetables.

A Chinese fellow came by on the back of a motorcycle. It startled me. I had just never thought about the Chinese riding motorcycles before. Sometimes reality is an awfully close fit like the vegetable skins on that old woman's hands.

I was glad when the bus came. There is a certain happiness sighted when your bus comes along. It is of course a small specialized form of happiness and will never be a great thing.

I let the old woman get on first and trailed behind in classic medieval tradition with castle floors following me onto the bus.

I dropped in my fifteen cents, got my usual transfer, even though I did not need one. I always get a transfer. It gives me something to do with my hands while I am riding the bus. I *need* activity.

I sat down and looked the bus over to see who was there, and it took me about a minute to realize that there was something very wrong with that bus, and it took the other people about the same period to realize that there was something very wrong with the bus, and the thing that was wrong was me.

I was young. Everybody else on the bus, about nineteen of them, were men and women in their sixties, seventies and eighties, and I only in my twenties. They stared at me and I stared at them. We were all embarrassed and uncomfortable.

How had this happened? Why were we suddenly the players in this cruel fate and could not take our eyes off one another?

A man about seventy-eight began to clutch desperately at the lapel of his coat. A woman maybe sixty-three began to filter her hands, finger by finger, through a white handkerchief.

I felt terrible to remind them of their lost youth, their passage through slender years in such a cruel and unusual manner. Why were we tossed this way together as if we were nothing but a weird salad served on the seats of a God-damn bus?

I got off the bus at the next possibility. Everybody was glad to see me go and none of them were more glad than I.

I stood there and watched after the bus, its strange cargo now secure, growing distant in the journey of time until the bus was gone from sight.

Oral interpretation may involve flights of the imagination beyond real human relationships, such as the one described in this poem:

## IN THE LOBBY

### RUTH WHITMAN

In the lobby while people shook hands
and flashbulbs of friendship popped like smiles,
while you said hello and hello to everyone
who didn't matter and I stood sylishly by
pretending I didn't know you
suddenly
I took my machine gun and,
dressed as I was in maroon velvet,
mowed down the popular lecturer with
his witty charm and good wife,
his friends, clingers, all parasites
and passersthrough, all those related to me
by birth, marriage, and death,
until finally I could see the ceiling.

The walls were absolutely bare and solitary.
Across the tiled floor only you were left.
You smiled, took my arm, and we
began to go home together

At a much more complex level, oral interpretation occurs when the accomplished reader experiences and communicates the most intricate mental and emotional significances of the human being, delineated in a passage such as this:

## *from* HAMLET

WILLIAM SHAKESPEARE

O, that this too too solid flesh would melt,
Thaw and resolve itself into a dew!
Or that the Everlasting had not fix'd
His canon 'gainst self-slaughter! O God! God!
How weary, stale, flat and unprofitable,
Seem to me all the uses of this world!
Fie on't! ah fie! 'tis an unweeded garden,
That grows to seed; things rank and gross in nature
Possess it merely.

It is hoped that the principles expounded in this book will help you learn to experience many kinds of literature in the process of oral communication. Most of the principles discussed here apply to all forms of oral reading. Some of them go beyond the problems in reading simple expository materials and deal with the complex art of interpreting to a public audience the most challenging prose, poetry, and dramatic literature.

We hope that you will not only achieve some skill in the simple forms of oral reading, but also learn to enjoy the *art* of interpretative reading, both as a reader and as a listener.

The art of interpretative reading concerns itself with more than the mere translation of written words into sounds. It concerns itself with the communication of human *experience*. For example, consider the functions of the novelist, poet, painter, sculptor, musician, or actor, and you will find that all artists are involved in the process of communicating human experience to other human beings. We acknowledge that some artists do not seem to care whether or not others get their exact meanings, but at least they do create works that *may* communicate experience to those who make the effort to respond to them. Human experience cannot be handed from one individual to another; it is only transferred in terms of expressed meaning communicated from the artist to the viewer or hearer through some sort of symbol system: shapes, colors, sounds, or actions.

The simplest definition of *interpretative reading* would be the broad statement that it is "reading aloud." This would account for any instance in which the reader changes written symbols into oral symbols. We usually think of the reader doing this for the benefit of an audience, but we should not ignore the value of the performer's reading aloud for his *own* understanding and appreciation. In studying difficult writing, it is helpful to read it aloud and suddenly discover meanings not apparent in silent, passive contemplation of the symbols on the page. Furthermore, because a part of the value of good literature, especially poetry and drama, lies in the *speech* implicit in the symbols, reading aloud helps us participate physically, and hence more completely, in the author's language. We can feel the sounds as well as hear them. Thus, without really being at all farfetched, we can assert that a reader at times can and should read aloud to himself. Keep in mind that when we read aloud we communicate with ourselves as well as with others.

We can be more precise in constructing a definition of interpretative reading. For the time being, let us say that it is "the oral communication of ideas and feelings from the printed page to an audience, so that the listeners will understand the ideas and will experience the feelings."

This definition is not yet complete, but it will be with the addition of three concepts. The first is that we communicate both audibly and visibly. As readers, we appeal to both the ears and eyes of our listeners. Not only do we utter meaningful sounds, but we also use our entire visible personalities in meaningful ways.

The second concept pertains to the ideas and feelings that we have said are obtained from the printed page. Of course, ideas and feelings are not actually on the page: They exist only inside *human beings*. What is found on the printed page is language significantly arranged as to arouse within the reader ideas and feelings similar to those existing within the writer. Words are not actualities but only symbols. Because no one can transport thoughts from one brain to another, and because symbols are relatively poor transmitters of such intangibles, we readers really perceive only what we *think* the writer is saying. As oral interpreters, therefore, we try to the best of our ability, to validate our own experiences with the author's work.

The third and last concept needed to complete our definition of interpretative reading concerns appreciation. One of the goals of reading to others is the contagious transference of appreciation from reader to listener. For example, you may enjoy reading a certain story; therefore, you wish to share it with someone else. This desire to share appreciation is quite natural to us. We see a movie and like it; therefore, we do our best to get our friends to see it, too. (We'll even see it a second time in order to get them to go.) We like a certain recording; therefore, we insist that our friends listen to it. If they do not appreciate it, we are disappointed. Likewise, if we enjoy a story by Kurt Vonnegut, Jr. or John Updike, a poem by Gwendolyn Brooks or

Robert Frost, a play by Peter Shaffer or William Shakespeare, we wish to share it with others. Just watching them read it silently is not enough, we must *communicate* it to them and reexperience it ourselves *while* communicating. As one teacher of literature put it: " I don't know what you feel like, but when a text starts to excite me and there is somebody else in the room, I start bouncing up and down and want to jump up and read it to them and get their response to it in an active, involved kind of way."[1] And we know that we not only must communicate the ideas and feelings suggested to us by the author's symbols, but also must make our listeners appreciate the way in which the author has expressed himself.

Putting all these concepts together, we have a fairly complete definition of interpretative reading. It is " the communication of the reader's experience of the author's ideas and feelings to the eyes and ears of an audience, so that both the reader and the audience experience and appreciate the author's literary creation."

## The Changing Nature of Interpretative Reading

Like any other art form, interpretative reading is dynamic; it is constantly changing. The music of today, either classical or popular, is not the same as the music of yesterday. So it is with painting, sculpture, drama, and all the other arts. One has only to observe the reactions of one's elders to what is on the television, the movie screen, the stage, or the stereo to realize that styles in art change as the times change. This is also true of the oral interpretation of literature. A hundred years ago our forefathers, lacking the many avenues for entertainment that we have today, depended a great deal on the spoken word from orator, actor, and reader (then called an *elocutionist*) for vicarious experiences in living. In those days, the oral reader employed a style of presentation that stressed the skills of performance to such an extent that the reader often left the manner in which he read overshadow the content of the literature. Audiences often paid more attention to the performance than to the author's message. For many years this heightened, even exaggerated, style pleased audiences. The performer's bodily action and gestures were sometimes so highly arbitrary that practiced poses became substitutes for genuine physical behavior. Furthermore, his efforts to develop a powerful and expressive voice often resulted in " how now brown cow " tones and stilted diction that today would seem reminiscent of the old ham actor. Eventually, public taste so rebelled against such artificiality in the performance-oriented form of reading that elocution was

[1] Gary Esolen, "Advantages of the Oral Study of Literature," *Oral English* (Summer 1972), 2.

discarded. The terms *expression* and *interpretation* were adopted as names for a new style of performance with more realistic modes of behavior for the oral reader. In defense of elocutionists, we must say that for a time, at least, they were in tune with the tastes of listeners who also appreciated flowery oratory and ornate acting, but the "spouter," the "orator," and the "ham," all eventually went out of style.

Interpretative reading, as the name would suggest, rightfully stressed that the reader attend primarily to the substance of the literature rather than to the method of delivering it. Therefore, early in our century, oral reading sometimes became terribly tame to some and yet a most desirable revolution had taken place: The reader now studied the literature and made an effort to give to listeners not a "show," but the literature itself. Since that time, respected oral interpreters have recognized that literary analysis is as important as performance skill in their art.[2]

We are living in a rather golden period in the history of a revered art form, but the form of the art is still changing. In the first edition of this textbook, in the 1950's, we were quite concerned with obtaining recognition and respect for the revival of an old art as a distinct form clearly distinguishable from the art of acting. In our writing and teaching, most instructors were very careful to differentiate interpretative reading from acting, but today we no longer consider the difference important. It is sometimes obvious and sometimes obscure. Often it is so confusing that to explain it requires valuable instructional time better spent on more constructive matters. We shall try to establish in a later chapter that acting inclines toward portraiture and that interpreting inclines toward suggestion, but it is not really all that simple, for good actors "suggest" to the imagination, too. And who can say exactly when audible and visible cues go beyond suggestion? The manifestations of the two arts may sometimes be so similar that what labels to pin on them becomes a moot and insignificant question. Both acting and interpretative reading are honorable arts, both have their rightful functions, and if they are sometimes quite different and sometimes similar, what difference does it make?

When we were obsessed with such labels, we often made the mistake of equating physical and vocal animation in performance with "acting" and insisting that the reader accomplish his communication primarily with restrained uses of the voice and face and very little use of the body. *Movement* was out! Today interpretation is once again physically and vocally dynamic. Resting secure in the knowledge that we are concerned with having our own experiences in the literature, we are showing greater interest in learning the *means* by which we can accomplish communication of the

---

[2] Two especially useful and concise accounts of the history of interpretative reading are to be found in: Charlotte I. Lee and Frank Galati, *Oral Interpretation* (5th ed., Boston: Houghton Mifflin Company, 1977), pp. 555–62; Keith Books, Eugene Bahn, and L. LaMont Okey, *The Communicative Act of Oral Interpretation* (Boston: Allyn and Bacon, Inc., 1975), pp. 3–18. We recommend that you read one or both.

literary experiences to our audiences. It seems, then, that respecting the literature and respecting also the necessity for developing skill in communicating the literature, we are living in the happiest age of the art.

Objectives for interpretative reading vary from era to era, but they also vary among present practitioners. Some writers and teachers stress the communicative aspects of the art whereas others promote oral interpretation primarily as a means for literary study. The editors of *Oral English* resolved the divergence in their very first edition: "We are certainly not aiming to supplant traditional approaches to literature. Rather we want to bring them to completion by adding the culminating act of performance demanded by the concrete verbal nature of literature."[3]

We think the "culminating" they speak of is most vividly accomplished when the performance *communicates* to others. Communication facilitates understanding and appreciation that are worthwhile in themselves and that also provide the needed basis for more intensive *study* of literature. Interpretation is an old and honored art of communication that has taken its directives from literary study. Little wonder, then, that it has proved to be a most dynamic means of literary study itself. The extent to which an oral study of literature succeeds will be directly dependent upon the success of both the interpreter's responses to the literature and his capacity for expressing them in performance.

## INTERPRETATIVE READING IS CENTRAL

Interpretative reading is the ideal meeting ground of many persons with diverse interests and reasons for being involved with the art. To over-simplify, we can point out three basic types of students because of their distinct interests. Public speakers usually have a utilitarian role to play, a practical function to fulfill. They wish to inform audiences of something, to persuade them to some point of view or action, or to entertain with materials that will amuse or move their listeners. The rhetorical mode is direct: Public speakers face their audiences and are, at best, psychologically close to their listeners. Actors, on the other hand, perform an esthetic function. Whereas speakers are purveyors of their own messages, actors are usually part of a team effort to portray fictive experiences, sometimes informative or persuasive in intent, but always, we hope, moving! The esthetic mode is primarily indirect. Actors usually turn from their audiences toward each other, removing themselves from listeners psychologically as they assume fictional personalities in an imaginative picture. Literary students may be most interested in realizing literary meaning through their own muscular participation while expressing it orally. To literary students, the audience may seem of less importance than

---

[3] William Forrest and Neil Novelli, eds., *Oral English* (Winter 1972), 1.

it is to a speaker or actor, and yet all performers appreciate the presence—yes, even the contribution—of an audience. For it is the audience that provides the communicative opportunity to actualize the results of study and to test, confirm, or perfect their own responses. Because the materials these students read vary so greatly in literary form, and in their consequent demands for effective communication, the techniques used by the readers may differ considerably from one communicative event to another. Professor Don Geiger put it succinctly in his definition of the art: "Oral interpretation, then, is an unformulable amalgam of acting, public speaking, critical reaction, and sympathetic sharing."[4]

We would assert that Professor Geiger is not contending that oral interpretation is merely a melting pot. It is an independent art that synthesizes many arts, skills, and processes. Training in acting, public address, or literature are excellent foundations for interpretative study, and *vice versa*.

## WHY SHOULD I STUDY INTERPRETATIVE READING?

Few of the many thousands who take courses in oral interpretation expect, or even hope, to become professional performers. This goal, while admirable for the few, is undoubtedly the least significant reason of all for studying the subject. Nearly all of us need to improve our speaking skills, both public and private, for the basic techniques of expression, visible and audible, are the same.

Practice in interpretative reading should sharpen our diction, improve our voices, facilitate our use of facial expression and gesture, and improve our poise and confidence. Most of all, such study will help us develop the ability to think on our feet under stress. The person who can learn to concentrate on ideas while speaking is in possession of an immeasurable asset. Thus, oral reading is good exercise for the improvement of speaking in general.

Practice in interpretative reading is excellent training for radio, television, and the theater. In addition to developing the ability to read lines with facility and meaning, student actors sharpen their sensitivity to character, to emotion, and to fine literature. If all students of theater, television, and radio could study interpretative reading early in their training, much of the present work of instructors in those fields would be accomplished in advance.

Interpretative reading is also a form of communication that should be mastered by every public speaker. Public officials and politicians often find that they must read their speeches in order to speak precisely without fear of misinterpretation. They find that to meet the requirements of time, particularly for television appearances, they must read their speeches from

---

[4] Don Geiger, *The Sound, Sense, and Performance of Literature* (Chicago: Scott, Foresman and Company, 1963), p. 86.

manuscript. Their reading must, of course, be convincing. Furthermore, it must have the quality of spontaneity. Even the extemporaneous speaker must be able to read authoritative and statistical evidence with clarity and communicable persuasiveness.

Important to all students who study interpretative reading are the personal values that accrue from the unique association the individual has with literature when he reads it aloud. Interpretative reading is an ideal liberal arts study because it offers a fusion of literature and communication. Literature has been of prime importance in liberal education—the education of the whole person, intellectually and emotionally—throughout the history of civilized man. Effective use of the means of communication has always been an attribute of the well-rounded individual. (Of course, the oral communication of literary experience antedates written literature itself.)

In this practical, pragmatic age, we are so concerned with learning certain information and skills that will enable us to make our economic and social ways through life that we are inclined to neglect the pursuits that seem to offer no immediate or tangible benefits yet that are essential for the full life of the individual among the masses. The person who has no appreciation of the arts, who cannot listen attentively to good music, who cannot sit comfortably with a good book, who can see nothing meaningful in a great painting nor anything significant in a well-designed building, is unfortunate indeed. You, who are studying interpretative reading, are in an admirable position to develop your own responsiveness (understanding and appreciation) to good stories, speeches, essays, poems, novels, and plays. The purpose of this study is somewhat different from that of a survey course in literature. The emphasis here is on savoring good *pieces* of literature rather than on consuming volumes of it. Study here is intensive rather than extensive. Analysis of literary works will occur in both literature and interpretation courses, but here analysis is pursued not as an end in itself but as a means to the *appreciation* of the reader and his audience.

Let us put it in a slightly different frame of reference by changing that word " appreciation " to " experience," because it appears obvious that the essential element of appreciation is the experiencing of the literary work in its complete significance. A work of any art form is not meant to be glanced at or casually listened to as one might observe an occasional football play while chiefly involved in friendly conversation. Loosely, we may say that literature is meant to be *lived*. Professors Bacon and Breen suggest that the writer has tried to *embody* a life experience, actual or fictional, in his work.[5] It follows that the fullest understanding and appreciation of that work lies in the fullness of the reader's experience in—or embodiment of—the literary work.

Without undue elaboration, we have just attempted to justify interpretative

---

[5] Wallace A. Bacon and Robert S. Breen, *Literature as Experience* (New York: McGraw-Hill Book Company, Inc., 1959), Chapter 1.

reading as the most potent way for a person to be possessed of the literary experience created by a writer, namely in the act of communicating it orally either to himself or to others. For the students who already have a profound respect for literature, this should be the end of our introductory chapter.

If, however, you are one who honestly admits (to yourself, at least) that literature is not yet very important to you, we suggest that you read the following paragraphs.

Why do we read? For several reasons. We read to understand ourselves. Life can be not only difficult but perplexing as well. If we read good literature, written by persons who can interpret life, we often find solutions to our own problems through understanding other persons, fictional or real.

We read to get away from ourselves—for escape. We find that it is occasionally good—even necessary—to get away from our own troubled existence merely for the purpose of escaping; hence the popularity of motion pictures, stage plays, radio and television programs, and exciting books.

Such escape, taken in reasonable doses, is healthful. We thus read to enlarge our existence through experiencing secondhand the adventures others have but that are far removed from our own lives. We read therefore, to participate in experiences we might otherwise never have. The range of human experience is far too great for any one life to encompass. Most of us lead rather narrow, sheltered lives, but we need to know how other types of persons think and feel. We may never climb a mountain, but it is good for us to climb one vicariously, not only for the secondhand experience, but also to understand the person whose life mission seems to be the reaching of places where most of us will never go.

We read for the pleasure of experiencing beauty. Literature at its best is an art, and one of the functions of art is to communicate beauty. What is beauty? To some, beauty is found in what gives pleasure to the senses: attractive sights, sounds, smells. To appreciate a writer's skill in using words in a way that delights us constitutes one value of reading.

Beauty is often given a deeper significance than mere pleasurable sensation, however. John Keats made the poetic observation that " Beauty is truth, truth beauty. . . ." Some persons believe that beauty in nature is a representation of spiritual truth, that beauty in a work of art is also a representation of truth in nature, or truth in man, or truth in spirit. If we accept the idea that the artist can communicate truth, we find an additional value in reading beyond sensation. We find that we are intellectually and emotionally awakened by the great writer.

To learn to appreciate good writing is to learn to appreciate the effective expressions of sensitive and articulate persons who can experience and communicate ideas and feelings that most of us cannot express. To learn to read this literature aloud effectively is to intensify our own experiences and to bring these same experiences to others. To learn to read to others is to have the pleasure of eating a good meal with friends at the table rather than to eat alone.

## EXERCISES

1. Find a paragraph in a magazine, newspaper, or book that contains comparatively little emotional coloring. Study it and get a firm grasp of the ideas involved. Try communicating these ideas to a listener.

2. Find a paragraph in a story or novel that stirs you with strong emotional content. Study it and practice reading it aloud. Then read it to the class with the goal of making your listeners feel as you feel.

3. Find a paragraph or short piece of writing that you enjoy thoroughly. Read it so well that your listeners like it, too.

4. Bring to class a piece of writing that expertly expresses ideas or feelings that seem " true " to you. For example, find a paragraph that seems to you to express a fundamental " truth," which makes you say to yourself: " I've always felt that, but I've never put it into words! " The author of the following poem seems to have made a sound observation of a truth about some of today's students:


## ON THE DEATH OF A STUDENT HOPELESSLY FAILING MY COURSE

GEORGE CUOMO

He died the day before the last exam,
Leaving parents a lifetime of saying
"He could have made it, poor boy!" Poor boy, he
Could not. How little he could do in life!
He lacked whole galaxies of talents, lacked
Quickness of hand or foot or eye or mind,
Lacked will and ambition, lacked height and strength,
Lacked even hope, lacked means of being hurt.
He could swim well, he told me, and tried out,
And did not make the team, and did not mind.
Failure themed his small life, comforting him.
He died racing a fire-red sports car,
Soaring from the mountain roadway to spread
A giant arc across the still night sky.


5. Compare the effectiveness of the readers described in the following poems. Obviously, the two performers are quite different personalities using quite different techniques and are quite different in their effectiveness. Write an analysis of each performance.

## GIELGUD READING LEAR

PETER KANE DUFAULT

He comes on with a keening moan
as if all stops upon his pipe
but the last falsetto vent
were choked by grief,
and with poor grasping-empty
lingering-loosening hands delineates
dead Cordelia . . . What is she
to him that he should weep for her?—A corpse of air.
And no more there (stage left)
than say at rear right of the mezzanine
or lobby, equally empty, or
the street outside, or anywhere-
under-the-moon vacant. Yet he weeps for her,
with seeming-helpless hands conducts
a whole mighty orchestra of eyes
to weep for her . . . Something lies there—
Cordelia, Hecuba, the abstract
and distillate of loss—an element
invisible, but as real to character
as waves to fish or fire to salamanders?
He cannot face it but the blast
contorts his features to a mask
of Heracles gone mad or Oedipus . . .
Gielgud, you take the wind
out of our question: Not
"Why does he weep?" but, "Why—
since we're all fathers, sons,
daughters, to lose or to be lost—why
are we tonight only come to tears?"

## THE POETRY READING

KARL SHAPIRO

He takes the lectern in his hands
And, like a pilot at his instruments,
Checks the position of his books, the time,
The glass of water, and the slant of light;
Then, leaning forward on guy-wire nerves,
He elevates the angle of his nose
And powers his soul into the evening.

Now, if ever, he must begin to climb
To that established height
Where one hypnotically remains aloft,
But at the thought, as if an engine coughed,
He drops, barely clearing the first three rows,
Then quakes, recovers, and upwards swerves,
And hangs there on his perilous turning fans.

O for more altitude, to spin a cloud
Of crystals, as the cloud writes poetry
In nature's wintry sport!
Or for that hundred-engined voice of wings
That, rising with a turtle in its claws,
Speeds to a rock and drops it heavily,
Where it bursts open with a loud report.

O for that parchment voice of wrinkled vowels,
The voice of all the ages, polyglot,
Sailing death's boat
Past fallen towers of foreign tours—
The shrouded voice troubled with stony texts,
Voice of all souls and of sacred owls,
Darkly intoning from the tailored coat!

Or for the voice of order, witty and good,
Civilizing the ears of the young and rude,
Weaving the music of ideas and forms,
Writing encyclopedias of hope.
Or for that ever higher voice that swarms
Like a bright monkey up religion's rope
To all those vacant thrones.

But he who reads thinks as he drones his song:
What do they think, those furrows of faces,
Of a poet of the middle classes?
Is he a poet at all? His face is fat.
Can the anthologies have his birthday wrong?
He looks more like an aging bureaucrat
Or a haberdasher than a poet of eminence.

He looks more like a Poet-in-Residence. . . .

O to be *déclassé*, or low, or high,
Criminal, bastard, or aristocrat—

Anything but the norm, the in-between!
Oh, martyr him for his particular vice,
Make him conspicuous at any price,
Save him, O God, from being nice.

Whom the gods love die young. Too late for that,
Too late also to find a different job,
He is condemned to fly from room to room
And, like a parakeet, be beautiful,
Or, like a grasshopper in a grammar school,
Leap for the window that he'll never find,
And take off with a throb and come down blind.

# 2 *Communicating with the Audience*

Every form of human discourse has its conventions: forms of behavior anticipated by the audience of a given time and place. The art of interpretative reading has conventions that will be of immediate concern to you.

We have already indicated in the previous chapter that interpretative reading is not now exactly what it once was and that its nature is variable. Its conventions are not always the same. We shall try to present an eclectic description of the conventions of present-day oral interpretation; and without being unduly arbitrary, we shall indicate some minor preferences of our own because we think they promote communication. In the final analysis, however, we invite you to make your own judgments.

In the first place, only one abiding law is valid: whatever the reader does that enables him to communicate the author's meaning (as he honestly perceives it) is *good*; whatever he does that interferes with that communication is *bad*. Applying that principle, let us look at the reader in action before an audience. We shall do this by looking at three distinct facets of the experience: the interpreter's preparation for performance, the communicative performance itself, and the role of the audience.

## PREPARATION AND INTERPRETATIVE PERFORMANCE

**The Interpretative Setting.** The conventional setting of oral interpretation is characterized by its lack of adornment. For a reader to communicate literature to his audience, no special devices are needed. Theatrical settings, visual displays, or costumes would simply get in the way of the imagination. By preserving simplicity, we avoid distractions that would coax attention away from the literature.

In a classroom, the oral interpreter "sets his stage" simply by removing anything that might be a distraction. If an earlier class left mathematical equations or drawings of a dissected frog on the chalkboard, they should be erased. Movie projectors, record players, or models of the human ear should be removed. Chairs should be placed back far enough so that the interpreter is not pinned between the wall of the room and the knees of his front listeners. Doors should be closed to prevent performances in the hallway from competing with the reading. Be careful that you are not halfway through your performance when you discover that the pictorial leavings of an anatomy class are attracting more attention from the audience than you are.

**The Reading Stand.** Teachers of interpretative reading differ on the use of reading stands. Some prefer to have their students hold their reading materials in their hands so that they do not become so accustomed to having a stand that they feel naked when forced to read without one. Others permit their students to use stands at all times. And still others insist on their use. Of course, there are reasons for using them under certain circumstances: when the manuscript is too large or too heavy to handle with ease, when the reader's hands should be free for gesturing, or when the stand would add a desirable degree of psychic distance by further separating the reader from his audience. If you do employ one, let us hope that it is a thin one, so that your body can communicate emotional significance. Good readers often have to struggle valiantly behind large lecterns in order to communicate to listeners who can see only their faces. How much better they could communicate if their bodies were also visible! Whatever stand you use, do not permit it to become a leaning post or an anchor for your hands. Let your hands have an opportunity to express meanings, as hands are wont to do!

**The Manuscript.** Most present-day authorities in the field of interpretative reading contend that the reader should usually have some sort of manuscript present—whether the degree of memorization requires it or not—as a symbol of the source of the literature. They agree that the manuscript ordinarily should be there to remind both reader and audience that the experience being communicated comes from an author, not from the reader. In this respect, the reader's situation is quite different from that of either the public speaker, who may either have notes or manuscript or speak completely from ideas in his head, or the actor, to whom a manuscript would be a severe hindrance to his appearance within a fictional life on a stage.

What kind of manuscript should be used? Here, various instructors have their favorites. Some like their students to copy their literary selections into small, looseleaf notebooks; others prefer the use of typed scripts rested on a reading stand or lectern; still others contend that there is nothing so appropriate to a literary mode as for the reader to read from a *book* if the literature originally came from a book. It would seem obvious that the reader should use and handle well a manuscript appropriate to a particular selection or speaker within that selection.

Whatever the literature may be—newspaper or magazine article, story, play, novel, poem, essay—it should exist for the oral reader in a form that can be handled with ease and comfort and that will not distract attention from the act of communication. To juggle a large notebook or book or to fuss with loose sheets of paper, especially if you are already ill at ease, can only disconcert both you and your audience. Time used in preparing a usable manuscript is well spent. We recommend that you prepare your manuscript early so that you can rehearse with it frequently. In this way you will become familiar with the arrangement of the words on the page and, thereby, be able to locate the right place when you need to refer to the manuscript during the performance.

**Memorization—Familiarization.**   Students of interpretative reading often ask: "Shall I memorize?" The answer will probably depend on the teaching methods of the instructor because there are two valid approaches to the subject. A few instructors require complete memorization because they believe that this permits the reader to be free to concentrate on communicating. Complete memorization has another advantage: it enables the reader to remember worthwhile literature, perhaps for a lifetime. It is often pleasant for a person to be able to quote passages of great literature from memory. More commonly, familiarization, which is really a partial memorization gained through study and practice, is used by interpretative readers. Familiarization gained through practiced concentration on meaning seems to be a more natural method of gaining command of important phraseology than mechanical memorization. Besides, the time spent in such memorizing might well be better spent in analysis of material and attention to the communication of precise meanings. Because most teachers of the subject feel that the reader should have the manuscript as he reads, they feel that the reader ought actually to use it.

It is possible for an interpreter to read from a manuscript and yet be sufficiently free from it to communicate to an audience if he has studied and practiced *enough*; thus most readers now depend on familiarization rather than complete memorization.

We should admire the person who can do either well. If one can memorize easily and still convey literary content as he speaks, he should not be criticized for memorizing. If one can become so familiar with the manuscript that he can communicate to his audience—while, of course, participating in his material—he should not be criticized for not memorizing. The important thing is not the technique but the communication accomplished.

We cannot deny (although we do not necessarily approve) that audiences expect a reader to *read* and are sometimes disturbed by the reader who holds an unused manuscript. Perhaps they worry that he may forget and lose his place. There is no reason why the reader who memorizes easily, as some readers do, cannot *appear* to refer to the script occasionally, particularly at transitional points such as major divisions, beginnings of paragraphs, or while turning pages. It is natural to look at the page when turning it, at the phrasal unit occurring nearest the bottom of the page just before turning the page, or to see what appears at the top of the next page.

A suggestion to the memorizer: Remember always to concentrate on meaning, not on words. Mechanical memorization without mental activity always calls attention to itself.

A suggestion to the familiarizer: Do not look back at the manuscript in the middle of a thought unit; that action breaks the concentration of the audience and calls attention to the act of looking back. Familiarization is really very easy if you will only try it this way: Take a paragraph from a piece of well-written prose that lends itself to oral reading. Read it aloud. Now, read it aloud again, starting with your eyes on the material and raising your eyes toward an imaginary audience when you know you can finish speaking the first thought unit. Read to the " audience " until you have completed that thought. Go on through the paragraph doing this. Then, read the paragraph aloud a third time, raising your eyes earlier in each thought unit. By the time you have read the paragraph aloud five times, you ought to have excellent freedom to read to your *audience* rather than to your manuscript. The important part of the thought unit is the *end* of it, not the beginning. Looking back during the thought unit only breaks the concentration of your hearers. When you destroy the end of the unit, you reveal one of two things: either a lack of command of that thought or a haste to see what the *next* phrase is going to be. In fact, when you do this, your voice performs unnaturally because your mind is obviously not on the same thought that your voice is trying to express! There is plenty of time to look down at the manuscript for the next thought after this one is communicated.

**Beginning and Stopping.**    Except for informal situations in which reader and audience sit and read to each other in small groups, as in a living room or other intimate social gathering, we anticipate that the reader will do as the public speaker does: walk to the front of the room and stand while reading. All the conventional rules for behavior relating to poise, appropriate dress, and courteous manner that we anticipate from the speaker, we also expect of the reader. When the interpreter of literature behaves in ways different from these, he does so for specific reasons. Sitting on a chair, stool, or desk, is done not because of self-consciousness or laziness, but to promote informality appropriate to a particular piece of literature. The reading to follow must show the unexpected behavior to be appropriate and effective. Unanticipated methods sometimes prove effective for a given reader with a given selection of literature before a given audience on a given occasion.

The wise public speaker plans the introduction and the end of the speech carefully, so that the speech can skillfully enlist and hold the attention of the audience from the time of his appearance on the platform until he leaves. On the other hand, the poor speaker merely jumps into the argument and evaporates from the scene when the arguments are finished. Good interpreters avoid the latter's errors and provide introductions that ready listeners for the readings to follow.

What, then, should an introduction contain? Obviously, the title and author, if they have not been announced by a chairman or included on a printed program. Just as valuable are a few remarks concerning the reason you have chosen to read this particular selection to this particular audience. Is it appropriate to the times? Does it lead to an understanding or appreciation of a current happening? Do you enjoy it because of an experience it brings to mind? What needs to be said about the author, the literary form, any linguistic or stylistic peculiarities, or other significant matters to help your audience understand it? Aside from information necessary for an intellectual preparation of the audience for the literature to follow, the introduction is important to serve as a bridge from the existing mood of the audience to the mood of the literature. If the literature is dignified, your manner of introducing it should be dignified. If the material is light or casual, the introduction should also be light and casual.

The introduction should be delivered in a natural, spontaneous manner, even though you may have chosen your words carefully. The introduction is important in establishing *your relationship* with your audience; do not let it sound as if you have memorized a statement someone else has written for you to say. The introduction is your best opportunity to meet your audience personally in a conversational way. Although it may be wise to extemporize your remarks, prepare sufficiently so that you do not flounder, depend excessively on your notes, speak of inappropriate matters, or otherwise make a generally poor impression. And do be more original than to start: " The piece I want to read to you today is . . . ." Of course, we know that you are here with a literary work and that you presumably wish to read it to us!

What should an introduction do?

An introduction may be needed to prepare an audience for the message communicated by the poetry. That is obviously the case with difficult literature, but it can also be essential for light satire.

*One of our most famous verses is not a very good one. It's Joyce Kilmer's renowned "Trees." I think the worst thing about "Trees" is its specious assumption that in comparison with God's creation of Nature (the tree), the human's creation of art works (the poem) is an inferior act and worthy of fools. You'll remember that Kilmer said, " Poems are made by fools like me, but only God can make a tree." The humorist Morris Bishop answered Kilmer's logic, not by argument, but by a wry piece of light verse with a long title: "Terra–cotta Horse, First Century A.D. (Museum of Old Corinth, Greece)." Bishop is looking at a photograph of this little piece of sculpture and writes this:*

# TERRA-COTTA HORSE, FIRST CENTURY A.D. (MUSEUM AT OLD CORINTH, GREECE)

MORRIS BISHOP

What this photograph reveals
Is a little horse on wheels,
Made by some Corinthian potter;
Nero was the Imperator
(So it figures on the lists
Of the archaeologists.)

May we not suppose that this
Starts a metamorphosis?
For the horse has turned to steel.
First the leg became a wheel;
Bones developed to a chassis,
Eyes to headlights bright and glassy.
It is needless to insist on
Engine-heart and muscle-piston.
Pray continue as you please
Furnishing analogies.

While I recognize, of course,
Only God can make a horse,
It is flattering to feel
Only Man could make a wheel.

Sometimes, a biographical detail may be desirable information lending understanding and appreciation for a literary work.

*In his sonnet "On First Looking into Chapman's Homer," John Keats expressed his joy in the inspiration he received from a writer named Chapman who translated Homer's works into English. This translation was so much more exciting to Keats than other translations that after spending an entire night reading Chapman's Homer with a good friend, he wrote this tribute:*

# ON FIRST LOOKING INTO CHAPMAN'S HOMER

JOHN KEATS

Much have I travell'd in the realms of gold,
And many goodly states and kingdoms seen;
Round many western islands have I been
Which bards in fealty to Apollo hold.

Oft of one wide expanse had I been told
That deep-browed Homer ruled as his demesne;
Yet did I never breathe its pure serene
Till I heard Chapman speak out loud and bold:
Then felt I like some watcher of the skies
When a new planet swims into his ken;
Or like stout Cortez when with eagle eyes
He star'd at the Pacific—and all his men
Look'd at each other with a wild surmise—
Silent, upon a peak in Darien.

An introduction sometimes must tell the audience who the persona is (the person speaking in the poem).

*Among the thousands of war poems, one of the most interesting is Henry Reed's "Naming of Parts." Reed gives us no tag lines to inform us who is speaking, but we can tell that the poem is composed of either the outer or inner speech of two distinct personalities. Perhaps, they are a drill sergeant and a recruit, as some authorities assert. Perhaps they are two facets of the sergeant's personality. This ambiguity creates interest, but most significant is the opposition of the two attitudes toward the drill in teaching and learning the parts of a gun while Spring is blossoming.*

## NAMING OF PARTS

HENRY REED

Today we have naming of parts. Yesterday,
We had daily cleaning. And tomorrow morning,
We shall have what to do after firing. But today,
Today we have naming of parts. Japonica
Glistens like coral in all of the neighbouring gardens,
    And today we have naming of parts.

This is the lower sling swivel. And this
Is the upper sling swivel, whose use you will see,
When you are given your slings. And this is the piling swivel,
Which in your case you have not got. The branches
Hold in the gardens their silent, eloquent gestures,
    Which in our case we have not got.

This is the safety-catch, which is always released
With an easy flick of the thumb. And please do not let me
See anyone using his finger. You can do it quite easy

If you have any strength in your thumb. The blossoms
Are fragile and motionless, never letting anyone see
   Any of them using their finger.

And this you can see is the bolt. The purpose of this
Is to open the breech, as you see. We can slide it
Rapidly backwards and forwards: we call this
Easing the spring. And rapidly backwards and forwards
The early bees are assaulting and fumbling the flowers:
   They call it easing the Spring.

They call it easing the Spring: it is perfectly easy
If you have any strength in your thumb: like the bolt,
And the breech, and the cocking-piece, and the point of balance,
Which in our case we have not got; and the almond-blossom
Silent in all of the gardens and the bees going backwards and forwards,
   For today we have naming of parts.

Sometimes a poem may be so compressed that your reading of it will be completed before the audience can "get the drift" of it. An introduction that gives the listeners a headstart will be conducive to successful communication. This would certainly be true of reading Randall Jarrell's poem "The Death of the Ball Turret Gunner," quoted in chapter 3, and would also be true of any sonnet.

Sometimes a piece of literature may have an unfamiliar vocabulary or allusions that should be explained in order for your audience to comprehend it at first hearing. Such would be true of "Verses at Night" by Dannie Abse. Two anthologists felt this need for their readers, and so they provided a helpful introduction in print:

## VERSES AT NIGHT

DANNIE ABSE

*In a century when nearly all times seem to be periods between wars, poets have often attempted to render the general fears of whole nations in specific, personal, and therefore more emotional terms. Here the author uses unusual words like* metaphrast *(one who alters the sense of something) and* preterites *(words or tenses that belong to the past) as he relates a small incident in relation to the bad dream of the past and the appalling prospect of the future.*

      —JOHN MALCOLM BRINNIN AND BILL READ, *The Modern Poets*

Sleepless, by the windowpane I stare—
  black aeroplanes disturb the air.
  The ticking moon glares down aghast.
    The seven branched tree is bare.

Oh how much like Europe's gothic Past!
  This scene my nightmare's metaphrast:
  glow of the radioactive worm,
    the preterites of the Blast.

Unreal? East and West fat Neros yearn
  for other fiddled Romes to burn,
  and so dogma cancels dogma
    and heretics in their turn.

By my wife now I lie quiet as a
  thought of how moon and stars might blur,
  and miles of smoke squirm overhead
    rising to Man's arbiter;

the grey skin shrivelling from the head,
  our two skulls in the double bed,
  leukaemia in the soul of all
    flowing through the blood instead.

"No," I shout, as by her side I sprawl,
  "No," again, as I hear my small
  dear daughter whimper in her cot
    and across the darkness call.

For some audiences, the reader might also choose to explain " gothic " and " arbiter," or any significant symbolism he finds in the poem. The needs of your specific audience are not to be neglected if you wish to maximize your communication. Remember: The eye can backtrack and retrace the printed line, but your listeners' ears are limited to one hearing. In your introduction, give them all that they need in order to understand and appreciate what you read *while* you read it.

The content and style of an introduction may prepare the audience for the personality of the writer and put the listeners into the right mood for the literature.

*Most of us may be too young to have had any firsthand acquaintance with Will Rogers as a newspaper columnist, radio commentator, movie actor, or vaudeville rope-twirler, comedian, and expert gum-chewer. Only if we've seen him on the late-late show, or possibly heard an old recording, are we really acquainted with his flat, nasal, Oklahoma cowboy twang and his good-natured chuckles. Those are some of the traits that made him popular and contributed to his ability to make people love him while he really expressed some sharp criticisms of the fallacies in American political and sociological thinking. For example, my grandfather told me about something he remembered Will Rogers saying on the radio back during the Great Depression when the New Deal was trying to get farm prices up by destroying piles of oranges, slaughtering surplus pigs, and preventing surplus crops from maturing—all this at a time when people were starving right here in America. (It's an economic policy we still seem to follow.) Well, Rogers wasn't the kind of social critic to give an angry speech. He made us laugh at the absurdity of our ways. It was about this time that the Dionnes in Canada had the quintuplets. On the radio, says my granddad, Rogers put it all in a nutshell: "Humph, if they'd been born in America, we'd have to plow three of 'em under!"*

*Well, today, we're still having disarmament talks. What do they call them, the SALT talks? Way back in 1924, Rogers wrote this:*

## *from* THE AUTOBIOGRAPHY OF WILL ROGERS

December 7 [1924]:

Well, we were all last week trying to sink our greatest Battleship, the Washington.

Here is a Boat we had spent 35 millions on, and we go out and sink it. And the funny part is that it cost us more to sink it than it did to build it. We shot all the ammunition we had left over from the war into it and those big Guns on the Texas they were using, they only are good for so many shots during their lifetime. So we spoiled the Guns of our next best boat trying to sink the best one.

A great many people don't understand just how this sinking come about. You see we had a conference over here a few years ago. It was called by America. We were building a lot of Battleships and we had plenty of money to do it on, and it looked like in a couple of years we might have the largest Navy in the World. Well, the League of Nations gathering in Paris had attracted a lot of attention and got quite a lot of publicity, none of which had been shared in this country by the Democrats. So, when the Republicans got in, they conceived the idea of a publicity stunt for the Republicans. Why not then have a conference? But what would they confer about? The League of Nations had conferred about six months, and in that time had taken up about every question on the Calendar.

So Secretary Hughes happened to think of an idea: "Let us confer on sinking Battleships." Well, the idea was so original that they immediately made him the Toastmaster. You see, up to then, Battleships had always been sunk by the enemy, and when he proposed to sink them yourself it was the most original thought that had ever percolated the mind of a Statesman. So, when we communicated the idea to England and Japan that we had an idea whereby we would sink some of our own Battleships, why they come over so fast, even the Butler wasn't dressed to receive them when they arrived.

England was willing to tear her blueprints on planned building into half, Japan was willing to give up her dreams of having more ships on the seas than any nation and stop building up to 3/5 of the size of England and America, and Secretary Hughes met that with, "Now, Gentlemen, I will show you what America is prepared to do. FOR EVERY BATTLESHIP YOU FELLOWS DON'T BUILD AMERICA WILL SINK ONE."

Now they are talking of having another Naval Disarmament Conference. We can only stand one more. If they ever have a second one we will have to borrow a Boat to go to it.

You see, we don't like to ever have the start on any Nation in case of war. We figure it looks better to start late and come from behind. If we had a big Navy some Nation would just be picking on us all the time. Sinking your own Boats is a military strategy that will always remain in the sole possession of America.

A good introduction motivates listening. The introduction is a convention that does work when done well, with planning but also with spontaneity. Don't neglect it.

Furthermore, the introduction may be essential for *you*, the reader. In the first place, it is your one opportunity to meet the audience as yourself. Generally, it is advantageous for reader and audience to get to know each other before the reader becomes involved with communicating the literature, although what he actually says will almost invariably be concerned with the literature in some way. In doing such talking you get feedback from your listeners, perhaps audible but always visible; and if your speaking is effective, the establishment of personal rapport is conducive to good communication in the reading to follow. It contributes to your confidence in yourself and confidence of the audience in your capacity to communicate the literature. It is equally true that audiences enjoy such a meeting with the person of the reader alone before listening to the reader and literature speaking together.

Of course, there are exceptions to any rule. Your authors have heard expert readings preceded by no introductions whatsoever, but these were exceptional performances accomplished by experienced readers who omitted the introduction for some specific, constructive reason. A good policy may be to use an introduction on every occasion until you have very good reason not to use one.

Although the methods of introducing a reading may be fairly obvious, it is considerably more difficult for us to describe the methods for effectively ending a reading, even though it is no less valuable to do so. Because it is commonly desired that an interpretative reading provide the audience with an *experience*, it should be obvious that remarks by the reader to the audience at the close of the reading are almost invariably anticlimactic, unnecessary, unwarranted, and unwanted. To tell a reader how to stop effectively without saying to the audience "I'm stopping" is practically impossible, although any good reader is capable of demonstrating effective endings.

It will require no stretch of imagination to picture a reader who has built up strong images or feelings in listeners or has them engaged in deep thought, ruining his reading by suddenly slamming the book shut and running, striding, or slithering off the platform! Don't be in any hurry to leave at the end of your reading. Your audience is traveling behind you in its thoughts and imaginings; it is wrapped up in emotions suggested by your reading. Once you have finished, let the effect of the literature sink in for a few moments, close the manuscript unobtrusively, and pause before leaving. Once you start to move away, that act will abruptly terminate the imaginative, thoughtful, or emotional processes. Delay that termination until your audience is ready for it; give yourself a chance to feel the "right" instant.

However, even before reading the last word of your literature, you will have prepared your audience for the ending to come. Rarely should an audience be caught unaware by an unexpected ending, although some few pieces of literature may demand such a surprise. Usually, the effective reader will—and appropriately to the material—tip off his listeners to the fact that the end is coming. How is this done? Well, both visibly and audibly.

As to the visible means for indicating that the end of a piece of literature has arrived, it is of course impossible to prescribe any particular facial expression. It is certain, though, that audience contact at the end is significant. The end is no place for the reader's eyes to be locked onto a printed page; it is, rather, the most important time for the face to be projecting meanings to the audience, and with an air of finality.

As to audible means, there are several. Some are related to elements of time. A slowing rate or a slowing of the rhythmic pattern of verse, a series of pauses punctuating the final thought groups of the final sentence or lines, or a lengthening of important words somewhat beyond the duration commonly expected—all these are audible means for making clear to the ear that one is completing the ideas or images of the author's material. In addition, one can indicate approaching finality through a variation of loudness of voice, building to a loud climax where appropriate, or diminishing the degree of loudness for a quiet ending if this is called for. Furthermore, we can observe the commonly accepted intonation pattern of the voice for finality, which is the falling of the pitch in the manner we associate with completion. (A final sentence in the form of a question demanding a rising inflection, would, of course, be an exception to this.) Finally, an appropriate change in the quality of the voice consistent with the purposes of the author may be called for. Those techniques cannot be systematized or specified in any way, for the method of concluding vocally depends on a complex mixture of factors: literature, idea, mood, reader, audience, occasion—all of which cannot be reduced to a formula of any kind. The point is: Do not neglect the effect you produce at the end, for it will be the lasting one you leave with your listeners. It deserves your careful analysis, attention, and practice.

Actually, a problem that often presents itself in respect to an unsatisfactory conclusion is caused by a poor choice of a *portion* of a longer piece of literature. Sometimes, the reader will, in reading a portion of a longer work, ignore the fact that audiences like a reading to get somewhere, to arrive at some conclusion, to come to a head, to produce an experience. Even in reading a part of a scene from a play, it is possible to end with a climactic line that gives some *sense* of completion even though the play obviously goes on from there. Therefore, in choosing materials to read from longer works, give thought to the effect of the part as it stands alone.

A good selection of literature, or a well-chosen portion of a work, will establish its own sense of closure, or absence of further expectations. The body of the selection raises questions, produces tensions, builds suspense, and otherwise suggests that more is to come. Then, as questions are answered, tensions resolved, and suspense terminated, the expectations of the work are fulfilled and its end seems likely. Effective performance reflects a sensitivity to the means by which the literature achieves its closure.

**Attention.**    Because we are vitally interested in *communicative* reading, we must acknowledge that holding the attention of the audience is an essential element of our performances.

We have just used the words "holding the attention of the audience," but psychologists have discovered experimentally that it is impossible to "hold" attention. The attention span of even an interested, cooperative listener is startlingly short. We once thought that a person's attention was a result of simple will power and that a good listener could attend indefinitely. Later we realized that every listener has a very short attention span, perhaps only a few minutes in length. Then experimentation indicated that listening spans are a matter of only seconds, or fractions of a second, in duration and that even the best listener cannot attend longer without something disrupting his attention. This is a frightening prospect to the would-be speaker, but there is little reason to deny its implications. The speaker or reader is faced not with *holding* attention but with constantly *regaining* it, by performing in such a way as to bring the listener back alive as often as possible.

When William Cowper wrote " Variety's the very spice of life, / That gives it all its flavour," he gave great advice to us who would aspire to hold audiences in our hands.[1] Aside from factors in the reading situation that affect attention, such as attitudes and moods of the audience, environmental

---

[1] Benjamin Disraeli also wrote: " Variety is the mother of enjoyment," but Publilius Syrus, *c.* 42 B.C., probably said it first: " No pleasure endures unseasoned by variety."

and acoustical conditions, and factors relating to the reader's personality and choice of literature, the reader must recognize that variety in techniques of performance is of such importance as to demand study and practice.

The reader's concern must be for effective variety in both the visible and audible means of communicating. Appropriate responsive physical variety, calling for animated facial and bodily responses to literary suggestion, is essential. The inert body and the poker face rarely communicate anything of value, except certain limited forms of comedy where they may be excruciatingly funny by their very unnaturalness. Attention getting is likewise abetted by constant changes in vocal behavior—appropriate to the literature, we must again remind you. Vocal variety is achieved through the use of meaningful pauses of various lengths, changes of rate, duration, rhythm, loudness, pitch, and quality of the voice. We suggest that sensitivity on the reader's part to literary content, coupled with a lively desire to communicate that content to an audience, is likely to cause such visible and audible responsiveness in the reader's behavior as to constitute the kind of oral performance that will gain and " hold " attention.

**Audience Contact.** In speaking about familiarization, we have already indicated that the reader must have effective contact with his audience. It is always important to remember this admonition: *Never bury your nose in a book!*

You must learn to have the manuscript high enough (either in your hand or on a stand) for you to address the audience and to look at the manuscript without a gross movement of your head. (Let us have no bobbing heads or chicken-pecking!) Of course, you must have the manuscript low enough that persons in the front row can see your face, too. These matters may seem unnecessarily pedantic to you, but it is amazing how often they are mishandled by readers who just do not think about them.

The most direct form of audience contact is with the eyes of the audience members. Much literature demands this very personal form of contact. Certainly no obstacle should prevent eye contact when you read expository or narrative materials. If you are reading to a small group, establish eye contact with as many individuals as possible. If you are reading to a large audience, establish eye contact with individuals in representative sections of the audience. If you are reading on television, read to the lens. No listener likes to feel slighted. Try to make all your listeners feel that you are communicating with them personally.

On the other hand, some forms of literature will require less directness of communicative approach. Many authorities feel that much lyric poetry and dialogue may often be more effectively communicated when the reader uses a less personal form of audience contact than eye contact, which can become an intrusion at times, an obstacle to communication. Let us assume, for example, that you are to read the following sonnet:

## DEATH, BE NOT PROUD

JOHN DONNE

Death, be not proud, though some have called thee
Mighty and dreadful, for thou art not so;
For those whom thou think'st thou dost overthrow
Die not, poor Death; nor yet canst thou kill me.
From rest and sleep, which but thy pictures be,
Much pleasure; then from thee much more must flow;
And soonest our best men with thee do go—
Rest of their bones, and souls' delivery!
Thou'rt slave to fate, chance, kings, and desperate men,
And dost with poison, war, and sickness dwell;
And poppy or charms can make us sleep as well
And better than thy stroke. Why swell'st thou then?
One short sleep past, we wake eternally,
And Death shall be no more: Death, thou shalt die.

    If the reader establishes the locus of a person, scene, or thing as being on the platform and focuses there, the audience will expect to see that person, scene, or thing on the platform. Focusing toward hearers puts their imaginations to work. Once we have accepted the realm of the audience as being the place to focus, how can we decide whether to focus to eyes or to focus less directly? The answer lies in the literature. Anything the author has directed specifically to a silent reader, we would read to our listeners' eyes. This would be true of an article, a speech, an essay, narration in a story or novel, or even a poem in which the poet is speaking to his reader or in which the persona (the speaker in the poem) is speaking to a specific audience. Anything an author puts into print that he is only *thinking*, we would probably direct elsewhere, perhaps in the direction of the back wall of the room, or we might read it with unfocused eyes (a thoughtful demeanor) somewhere in the realm of the audience but not to any individual listener. This focus would be suitable for Donne's poem as well as much other lyric poetry, and especially dramatic soliloquies. Anything the speaker in the literature addresses to a specific individual or character in the literature, we would normally utter by imagining that listener's presence in the realm of the audience, perhaps slightly over the heads of the listeners.

    Interpretative reading has a convention for the handling of dialogue that is often recommended to novice readers and is also often retained by experienced ones as an aid to communication. Characters' lines (in either drama or fictional prose) are directed to different areas slightly over the heads of the listeners: Character A, slightly to the right of the center of the back wall; Character B, slightly to the left; Character C, slightly to the right of A; Character D, slightly to the left of B. Care should be taken not to direct any of these very far from the center line. Readers very seldom show a profile to their audiences. To do so is to tend to appear in the scene. When the reader is consistent with these focuses, the audience has little trouble distinguishing the characters as they speak in the scene being read. This convention is very helpful both to reader and audience; but the better the reader, the less this device needs employment for there will be other more potent ways to suggest characters' personalities.

Focus is the technique we employ to establish locus.

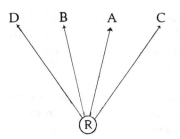

**Suggestion, Impersonation, and Psychic Distance.** It has become conventional to think of interpretative reading as being a *suggestive* rather than a *portraitive* art, that the reader suggests persons and actions to the imaginations of his hearers rather than portrays them for the audience; hence, according to the convention, the reader's functions are demonstrably different than those of the actor. We agree with this; however, we hasten to recall to you that in Chapter 1 we indicated that the old puristic dichotomy between oral interpretation and acting is apparently dying out. We believe it is true that interpretation is fundamentally a suggestive art, but we also note that those who are most vehement in this contention are sometimes the very ones who permit their theory to inhibit their performance. Blind allegiance to suggestion sometimes becomes a worrisome millstone, crippling artistic freedom. The danger lies in the acceptance of limitations upon one's artistic means. Advances in all arts come from persons courageous enough to do the unconventional when inspiration and reason demand. Too often, the interpreter has been unduly restricted by those too selfconscious about the alleged differences between interpretation and acting. If the literature needs lively impersonation from the reader for effective audience response, then the reader had better use it.

On the other hand, audiences do anticipate performances in oral interpretation somewhat different from those they anticipate in the theater, and it is these differences and the reasons for them that we must explore. First, by being suggestive, the interpreter encourages imaginative participation, a locus in the mind. If his behavior becomes overly literal or portraitive, the audience is stimulated to view an onstage locus. Second, the very situation is different: There is usually considerably less of what we commonly call *psychic distance* in interpretative reading situations than there is in theatrical performances. This "distance" is the psychic separation essential between a work of art and the observer in order for the observer to participate in the artistic experience. A few examples will explain this. If you wish to appreciate the beauty of a great bridge or skyscraper, you cannot do it by standing under the bridge or on the sidewalk at the base of the building. You must move away some distance in order to take in the object as an artistic whole. Likewise, in an art gallery you must stand back to appreciate a fine painting. (You may move closer to study the brush strokes, but that is a study of technique, not artistic participation.) In the theater most persons like to sit back at least a few rows from the stage. Being too close can often ruin the effect of the scene or, in the case of highly dramatic action, actually be uncomfortable.

The theater almost always provides greater psychic distance than does the interpretative reading platform, and in this difference lie some of the explanations of the usual dissimilarity between the arts of the actor and the interpretative reader. The greater psychic separation between actor and audience in the theater is provided by such elements as the greater physical distance between stage and audience, the raised level of the stage, and sometimes the presence of the proscenium arch. In addition there is the contrast between the lighted stage and the darkened auditorium, the use of properties, scenery, and the actor's make-up and costumes—in short, by the simulation of a make-believe world distinctly separate from the real world of the auditorium in which the audience sits. Actors are sufficiently removed from their audiences to lose their own identities and to be accepted as the characters they portray. Therefore, they can use whatever visible and audible manners are appropriate to their characters.

As interpretative readers, on the other hand, we usually find ourselves in intimate situations, reading to small audiences, in small rooms. (Often, we will be reading directly to the eyes of specific individuals.) We are essentially members of our own audiences. For practical purposes, we hold the book and read aloud; our attitude is one of "Since we can't all read this together, let me read it to you." Lacking most of the actor's exterior means of creating a make-believe world, we can never pretend to be other persons; the audience accepts us only as ourselves. Therefore, we can use the visible and audible techniques that seem appropriate to ourselves. Whereas the theater audience will accept the actor's scene of high emotionalism as a genuine aspect of a fictional event, our audiences, being psychologically closer to us and, psychologically therefore, more aware of our techniques, *prefer to imagine the scene for themselves,* if we will only provide the necessary stimuli.

Even though interpretative reading is a suggestive rather than a portraitive art, the reader may employ impersonation. Both acting and interpretation make use of impersonation. Acting, of course, uses it *all* the time; interpretation uses it when it is called for by the literature. The reader impersonates when some elements of characterization will assist the audience to a more complete imaginative image of the character.

The question arises, "How much impersonation does the interpreter use?" To answer this, we must ask two other questions, "How much impersonation *can* a given reader use?" and "How much impersonation *should* he use in a given situation?"

How much the reader *can* use depends on the reader's own personality. Some persons do not impersonate with ease; they just never "perform" in public. Others glory in impersonation—they have animated personalities; they can tell stories or jokes with vividness; and they are relatively uninhibited in social situations. (In extreme forms, they are exhibitionists, the life-of-the-party type.) It is obvious, is it not, that the latter type of person will tend to use more impersonation when reading orally to an audience? Remember, though, that you are not unalterably limited by your present personality; you can learn to be more dynamic in your speaking; you can learn to read more vividly than you have read before; you can develop the ability to be animated and colorful in oral reading. Read with a strong desire to communicate literary experience. Provide whatever audible and visible cues your audience needs for a lively visualization.

How much impersonation the reader *should* use is determined primarily by the type of literature. Some literary selections will permit none, as in those where the personality of the writer or persona is of little or no consequence. Humorous materials almost invariably permit more impersonation than very serious ones; in these, the reader can slice the ham a bit thicker when the audience is laughing. For example, in reading either "Song of the Queen Bee," quoted hereafter, or "Jim Bludso," quoted in Chapter 10, one could hardly expect the audience to enjoy either without some exaggerated behavior by the reader. Only a "character" would speak such lines! The character must be realized in order for the fun to occur.

It should be clear that dialogue materials from fiction or drama, will usually profit from impersonative assistance to imaginative suggestion and will suffer when readers give no personality other than their own to the characters. Imagine a reading of the following speech by Hotspur, almost losing his temper before his king, without any suggestion of Hotspur's personality!

## *from* HENRY IV, PART I

WILLIAM SHAKESPEARE

HOTSPUR. My liege, I did deny no prisoners.
  But I remember, when the fight was done,
  When I was dry with rage and extreme toil,
  Breathless and faint, leaning upon my sword,
  Came there a certain lord, neat, and trimly dress'd,
  Fresh as a bridegroom; and his chin new reap'd
  Show'd like a stubble-land at harvest-home.
  He was perfumed like a milliner;
  And 'twixt his finger and his thumb he held
  A poncet-box, which ever and anon
  He gave his nose and took 't away again;
  Who therewith angry, when it next came there,
  Took it in snuff; and still he smil'd and talk'd,
  And as the soldiers bore dead bodies by,
  He call'd them untaught knaves, unmannerly,
  To bring a slovenly unhandsome corse
  Betwixt the wind and his nobility.
  With many holiday and lady terms
  He question'd me; amongst the rest, demanded
  My prisoners in your Majesty's behalf.
  I then, all smarting with my wounds being cold,
  To be so pester'd with a popinjay,
  Out of my grief, and my impatience
  Answer'd neglectingly—I know not what,
  He should, or he should not; for he made me mad
  To see him shine so brisk and smell so sweet
  And talk so like a waiting-gentlewoman
  Of guns and drums and wounds,—God save the mark!—
  And telling me the sovereign'st thing on earth
  Was parmaceti for an inward bruise;
  And that it was great pity, so it was,
  This villanous salt-petre should be digg'd
  Out of the bowels of the harmless earth,
  Which many a good tall fellow had destroy'd
  So cowardly; and but for these vile guns,
  He would himself have been a soldier.
  This bald unjointed chat of his, my lord,
  I answered indirectly, as I said;
  And I beseech you, let not his report
  Come current for an accusation
  Betwixt my love and your high Majesty.

Equally important would it be for a reader of the opening scene of *King Lear* (where Lear divides his kingdom between his daughters as they avow their affection for him) to suggest the sincere dignity of Cordelia:

## *from* KING LEAR

WILLIAM SHAKESPEARE

CORDELIA. I love your Majesty
  According to my bond; nor more nor less.
LEAR. How, how, Cordelia! Mend your speech a little,
  Lest you may mar your fortunes.
CORDELIA.              Good my lord,
  You have begot me, bred me, lov'd me: I
  Return those duties back as are right fit;
  Obey you, love you, and most honour you.
  Why have my sisters' husbands, if they say
  They love you all? Haply, when I shall wed,
  That lord whose hand must take my plight shall carry
  Half my love with him, half my care and duty.
  Sure, I shall never marry like my sisters
  To love my father all.

In contrast to materials in which characters speak, literature that lacks characterization and is devoted to the expression primarily of ideas, such as expository prose, affords little or no opportunity for the reader to use impersonation. We need give no examples of this type of writing here, for you are at this instant reading expository prose in which there is no place for impersonation.

Of course, we have here presented the extremes: considerable impersonation and no impersonation. Between them lie innumerable degrees of character suggestion not to be overlooked by the responsive oral reader. Even the personality of a good essayist has a way of revealing itself in his discourse, and the personality of the persona in a lyric poem "speaks" in particuar rhythms, figures of speech, images, and choices of words.

How much impersonation *should* a reader use? Enough to help his listeners create their own images—not so much as to usurp their creative functions. Once you have determined the degree of impersonation appropriate to the literature, consider your own abilities, the expectations of your audience, and the psychic distance inherent in the reading situation. In other words, first adjust yourself to the demands of the literature, and then adjust your embodiment of the literature to the communicative setting.

**Animation Versus Restraint.**   Often related to matters of impersonation, but distinctly different, is the conflict between animated reading and appropriate restraint in reading. The variables we considered for determining degree of impersonation are the same ones we must refer to here for resolution of this problem: the demands of the literature, the expectations of the audience, the appropriateness of the occasion, and the personality of the reader. Sometimes a lively performance from the reader will help to communicate a particular piece of writing to a particular audience on a particular occasion, and the reader will be comfortable doing it. On the other hand, a reading may be presented with great restraint because of the opposite demands of the literature, the preferences of the audience, the reader's judgment and good taste, or the nature of the individual reader. Because of the demands of short psychic distance, oral interpretation does tend to be a restrained art but certainly not a dead one. No performing art can afford to be deadening! Within the bounds of literary demand, audience expectation, good taste, and performer capacity, one should read with all the animation necessary for effective communication while being careful to use the restraint essential to encourage listeners to participate creatively in the performance. Prohibitive rules against movement, such as abound in contest or tournament reading, have nothing to do with literature. The reader might well try to avoid explicit, portraitive, or depictive pantomime most of the time and to use the suggestive kind of action that speaks to imaginative creativity by the listeners. For this, the reader should learn to use the audible and visible means at the disposal of any speaking performer.

But the essential fact remains: Restraint indicates *control*. Control is the essence of artistry, always. The performer who controls—is restrained—has powers beyond those being employed. Restraint is not achieved by diluting energy but, rather, by condensing and refining it. Just as the genie gains strength by being confined in the bottle, the interpreter acquires strength from restraint. Cultivate the suggestive powers of animation within control.

**Spontaneity and Enjoyment.**   In Chapter 3, we shall stress that your interests and appreciation are prime requisites for the choice of materials to read aloud, for only if *you* are interested and enjoying what you read will you appeal to the interests and enjoyment of your audience. We prepare you for this advice at this point, for if you are like many conscientious students, you may become so involved in developing effective techniques that you will overplan and underenjoy. A student of music could work so hard to execute a run on the keyboard that he would play it with little personal inspiration or enthusiasm. Check on yourself to see if you are making the same mistakes. Try to retain initial experience and pleasure in your public reading. Keep your work alive and fresh, and do not be afraid to let others see that you enjoy reading. Avoid the appearance of premeditation at almost any cost.

One negative example may be enough to impress you with the importance of spontaneity. A young man once prepared to read in a statewide collegiate reading festival. He was so ambitious in his preparation that he carefully planned how to make each move from the time he left his seat until he returned to it. His preparation, unfortunately, "showed." All spontaneity was lost. His listeners could see only his technique, and consequently their pleasure was diminished. Even the young man's appreciation seemed artificial, although it had once been quite genuine. Do not let that happen to you. Always keep in mind that your technique is only the means to the ends of appreciation and enjoyment.

On the other hand, this advice should not be leaned upon as an excuse for inadequate practice. There is no such thing as too much practice; only too much *improper* practice. If you will strive to rethink the thoughts, revisualize the images, and refeel the emotions expressed by the author *each* time you read a selection aloud, you will not go stale. Your enjoyment will be greatest when you have prepared well by exploring each time you read.

Another young male student, who was not reading very well in class, shocked one of your authors after making sudden improvement on a reading: "Doc, I think I have found the answer! If you just read it aloud a few times before coming to class, you do much better!" Teachers are sometimes eloquently reminded that the "obvious" is not always really obvious!

## THE ROLE OF THE AUDIENCE

Thus far, in this chapter, we have tried to talk common sense about the conventions in public performance and of interpretation, in particular, in the hope that wise interpreters might employ good sense in performance to *better serve the literature* being communicated. Usually, our audiences are superb in their attentive receptiveness to our literary messages. Sometimes, however, they seem to be anything but! The commercial theater producer, the advertiser, and the political speaker will, at times, seemingly sacrifice all ideals in order to get favorable attention and profitable response. Fortunately, we have enough faith in the power of good literature and in the literary interest of our audiences to resist warped and hardened methods in performance. Our audiences are usually small, and our art is an intimate one.

We overheard one hard-bitten, though academic, theater man observe that oral interpreters are only persons who get together periodically to read aloud to each other! Well, it is true that at the college level, we do often get together to read in festivals, but others listen, too. The gentleman's observation was cynical; but if there is *any* truth in it (and we think there is very little), then, thank God, we not only read literature aloud but we also enjoy listening to it! The point is: We are training not only readers but also *listeners*. And, if it is true that we are training listeners, we are training audiences for literature. Therefore, we should stop at this point to observe how we can be better members of audiences, for we, too, have roles to play as audiences.

It is always amazing to us to note each semester the actions of persons who have apparently never thought of the behavior necessary for good listening. Some, arriving late, burst into the room while another person is reading aloud, move noisily to their seats, remove outdoor clothing, and stack up books; this is all done by these individuals with apparent disregard for the fact that they are distracting others who are trying to listen. (And think what the distractions do to the concentration of the *reader!*) This behavior is not only thoughtless (if such persons stopped to think, they would not act in this manner), but it is also discourteous. Yet, they do not seem aware that they are guilty of either. Then there are persons who are less noisy, yet are actually reading from a book or notebook, or are attempting to carry on a muted conversation with a neighbor. These persons are oblivious to the facts: One cannot listen and talk at the same time or listen to two persons at once. We should not have to say anything about rattling papers, drumming fingers, scraping feet, and needless coughing, but these disturbances are also present in almost any audience.

Perhaps we can blame it all on television: It *is* true that we now have a culture which turns on the television set, and then proceeds to carry on all normal home activities while the set is on, much of the time to deaf ears. The President, the newsman, the educator, and the evangelist all have to compete with disruptive behavior in millions of rooms that they cannot see. Of course, modern audiences have been spoiled by the constant and carefully studied efforts of the entertainer and the advertiser to hold (gain and re-gain) attention by entertaining devices. We *must* learn to attend without the enticement of crass gimmickry, but that takes effort. Because the television receiver is a one-way form of transmission, we are untrained in creative listening demanding feedback. The television set cannot see us or hear us. The interpretative reader can.

We have responsibilities as members of an audience. What are they? First, we must learn to listen actively and to listen with manners permitting others to listen, too. Second, we must learn to listen *creatively* so that we can participate in the literary experience. This means that we actively *respond* to images suggested by the author, that we *think* of relationships between the author's ideas and our own, that we *associate* the universals that good writers write about with our own experiences, that we give the reader honest *feedback,* and that we listen with a determined effort to *understand* and *appreciate*. To fail to listen in these ways is to waste time, for one thing, and to deprive ourselves of the opportunities to enlarge our own visions and our own sensitivities.

## EXERCISES

1. Start a personal notebook of literary selections that you may wish to read to other people sometime, perhaps to your class, perhaps to friends or public organizations.

2. Find a selection quoted in this book, possibly one from the pages that follow immediately, and prepare to read it to your class. Make a special effort to plan a good introduction, but do not plan to read the introduction. *Talk* to your audience extemporaneously and spontaneously.

3. Using a poem that is contained in this book, demonstrate two distinctly different modes of presenting it: suggestion of character and portrayal of character. Discuss with the instructor and class the relative effectiveness of the presentations.

4. What manner of audience contact would you establish and maintain in reading each of the selections quoted at the end of this chapter? Would you use eye contact or a less direct form of audience contact? Would you in any instance change the form of contact during any one of the readings? Analyze each of the selections for the degree of impersonation and animation, the requirements for introduction, and possible methods of concluding the reading effectively.

5. Make a list of ten selections quoted in this book that might permit a considerable degree of impersonation when read by some readers to some audiences.

6. Make a list of ten selections quoted in this book that do not demand impersonation by the reader.

7. In the selections that follow, which ones require that information of some sort be given listeners in advance? Which require the setting of an appropriate mood? Which are formal? Which are informal?

## SONG OF THE QUEEN BEE

### E. B. WHITE

*"The breeding of the bee," says a United States Department of Agriculture bulletin on artificial insemination, "has always been handicapped by the fact that the queen mates in the air with whatever drone she encounters."*

When the air is wine and the wind is free
And the morning sits on the lovely lea
And sunlight ripples on every tree,
Then love-in-air is the thing for me—
    I'm a bee,
    I'm a ravishing, rollicking, young queen bee.
    That's me.

I wish to state that I think it's great,
Oh, it's simply rare in the upper air,
    It's the place to pair
    With a bee.
Let old geneticists plot and plan,
They're stuffy people, to a man;
Let gossips whisper behind their fan.
    (Oh, she *does?*
    Buzz, buzz, buzz!)
My nuptial flight is sheer delight;
I'm a giddy girl who likes to swirl,
    To fly and soar
    And fly some more,
        I'm a bee.
And I wish to state that I'll *always* mate
    With whatever drone I encounter.

There's a kind of a wild and glad elation
In the natural way of insemination;
Who thinks that love is a handicap
Is a fuddydud and a common sap,
For I am a queen and I am a bee,
I'm devil-may-care and I'm fancy-free,
The test tube doesn't appeal to me,
    Not me,
    I'm a bee.
And I'm here to state that I'll *always* mate
    With whatever drone I encounter.

Let mares and cows, by calculating,
Improve themselves with loveless mating,
Let groundlings breed in the modern fashion,
I'll stick to the air and the grand old passion;
I may be small and I'm just a bee
But I *won't* have Science improving *me*,
    Not me,

I'm a bee.
On a day that's fair with a wind that's free,
Any old drone is the lad for me.

I have no flair for love *moderne*,
It's far too studied, far too stern,
I'm just a bee—I'm wild, I'm free,
    That's me.
I can't afford to be too choosy;
In every queen there's a touch of floozy,
    And it's simply rare
    In the upper air
    And I wish to state
    That I'll *always* mate
With whatever drone I encounter.

Man is a fool for the latest movement,
He broods and broods on race improvement;
What boots it to improve a bee
If it means the end of ecstasy?
    (He ought to be there
    On a day that's fair,
    Oh, it's simply rare
      For a bee.)
Man's so wise he is growing foolish,
Some of his schemes are downright ghoulish;
He owns a bomb that'll end creation
And he wants to change the sex relation,
He thinks that love is a handicap,
He's a fuddydud, he's a simple sap;
Man is a meddler, man's a boob,
He looks for love in the depths of a tube,
His restless mind is forever ranging,
He thinks he's advancing as long as he's changing.
He cracks the atom, he racks his skull,
Man is meddlesome, man is dull,
Man is busy instead of idle,
Man is alarmingly suicidal,
    Me, I'm a bee.

I am a bee and I simply love it,
I am a bee and I'm darned glad of it,
I am a bee, I know about love:
You go upstairs, you go above,

You do not pause to dine or sup,
The sky won't wait—it's a long trip up;
You rise, you soar, you take the blue,
It's you and me, kid, me and you,
It's everything, it's the nearest drone,
It's never a thing that you find alone.
   I'm a bee,
   I'm free.

If any old farmer can keep and hive me,
Then any old drone may catch and wive me;
I'm sorry for creatures who cannot pair
On a gorgeous day in the upper air,
I'm sorry for cows who have to boast
Of affairs they've had by parcel post,
I'm sorry for man with his plots and guile,
His test-tube manner, his test-tube smile;
I'll multiply and I'll increase
As I always have—by mere caprice;
For I am a queen and I am a bee,
I'm devil-may-care and I'm fancy-free,
Love-in-air is the thing for me,
   Oh, it's simply *rare*
   In the beautiful air,
     And I wish to state
     That I'll *always* mate
With whatever drone I encounter.

## SENATOR ROSEWATER'S SPEECH
### from *God Bless You, Mr. Rosewater, or Pearls Before the Swine*

KURT VONNEGUT, JR.

I should like to speak of the Emperor Octavian, of Caesar Augustus, as he came to be known. This great humanitarian, and he was a humanitarian in the profoundest sense of the word, took command of the Roman Empire in a degenerate period strikingly like our own. Harlotry, divorce, alcoholism, liberalism, homosexuality, pornography, abortion, venality, murder, labor racketeering, juvenile delinquency, cowardice, atheism, extortion, slander, and theft were the height of fashion. Rome was a paradise for gangsters, perverts, and the lazy working man, just as America is now. As in America now, forces of law and order were openly attacked by mobs, children were disobedient, had no respect for their parents or their country, and no decent woman was safe on any street, even at high noon! And cunning, sharp-trading, bribing foreigners were in the ascendency everywhere. And ground under the heels of the big city money-changers were the honest-farmers, the backbone of the Roman Army and the Roman soul.

What could be done? Well, there were soft-headed liberals then as there are bubble-headed liberals now, and they said what liberals always say after they have led a great nation to such a lawless, self-indulgent, polyglot condition: "Things have never been better! Look at all the freedom! Look at all the equality! Look how sexual hypocrisy has been driven from the scene! Oh boy! People used to get all knotted up inside when they thought about rape or fornication. Now they can do both with glee!"

And what did the terrible, black-spirited, non-fun-loving conservatives of those happy days have to say? Well, there weren't many of them left. They were dying off in ridiculed old age. And their children had been turned against them by the liberals, by the purveyors of synthetic sunshine and moonshine, by the something-for-nothing political strip-teasers, by the people who loved everybody, including the barbarians, by people who loved the barbarians so much they wanted to open all the gates, have all the soldiers lay their weapons down, and let the barbarians come in!

That was the Rome that Caesar Augustus came home to, after defeating those two sex maniacs, Antony and Cleopatra, in the great sea battle of Actium. And I don't think I have to re-create the things he thought when he surveyed the Rome he was said to rule. Let us take a moment of silence, and let each think what he will of the stews of today.

· · · ·

And what methods did Caesar Augustus use to put this disorderly house in order? He did what we are so often told we must never, ever do, what we are told will never, ever work: he wrote morals into law, and he enforced those unenforceable laws with a police force that was cruel and unsmiling. He made it illegal for a Roman to behave like a pig. Do you hear me? It became illegal! And Romans caught acting like pigs were strung up by their thumbs, thrown down wells, fed to lions, and given other experiences that might impress them with the desirability of being more decent and reliable than they were. Did it work? You bet your boots it did! Pigs miraculously disappeared! And what do we call the period that followed this now-unthinkable oppression? Nothing more nor less, friends and neighbors, than "The Golden Age of Rome."

## THE PATRIOT
### An Old Story

ROBERT BROWNING

I

It was roses, roses, all the way,
   With myrtle mixed in my path like mad:

The house-roofs seemed to heave and sway,
  The church-spires flamed, such flags they had,
A year ago on this very day!

### II

The air broke into a mist with bells,
  The old walls rocked with the crowd and cries,
Had I said, 'Good folk, mere noise repels—
  But give me your sun from yonder skies!'
They had answered, 'And afterward, what else?'

### III

Alack, it was I who leaped at the sun
  To give it my loving friends to keep!
Nought man could do, have I left undone:
  And you see my harvest, what I reap
This very day, now a year is run.

### IV

There's nobody on the house-tops now—
  Just a palsied few at the windows set;
For the best of the sight is, all allow,
  At the Shambles' Gate—or better yet,
By the very scaffold's foot, I trow.

### V

I go in the rain, and, more than needs,
  A rope cuts both my wrists behind;
And I think, by the feel, my forehead bleeds,
  For they fling, whoever has a mind,
Stones at me for my year's misdeeds.

### VI

Thus I entered, and thus I go!
  In triumphs, people have dropped down dead.
'Paid by the World, —what dost thou owe
  Me?' God might question: now instead,
'Tis God shall repay! I am safer so.

# NIGHT

### GABRIELA MISTRAL

Because you sleep, my little one,
the sunset will no longer glow;
Now nothing brighter than the dew
nor whiter than my face you know.

Because you sleep, my little one,
nothing on the highroad do we see,
nothing sighs except the river,
nothing is except me.

The plain is turning into mist,
the sky's blue breath is still.
Like a hand upon the world
silence works its will.

Not only do I rock to sleep
my baby with my singing,
but the whole world goes to sleep
to the sway of my cradle swinging.

# DOVER BEACH

### MATTHEW ARNOLD

The sea is calm to-night.
The tide is full, the moon lies fair
Upon the straits;—on the French coast the light
Gleams and is gone; the cliffs of England stand,
Glimmering and vast, out in the tranquil bay.
Come to the window, sweet is the night-air!
Only, from the long line of spray
Where the sea meets the moon-blanch'd land,
Listen! you hear the grating roar
Of pebbles which the waves draw back, and fling,
At their return, up the high strand,
Begin, and cease, and then again begin,
With tremulous cadence slow, and bring
The eternal note of sadness in.
Sophocles long ago
Heard it on the Ægean, and it brought

Into his mind the turbid ebb and flow
Of human misery; we
Find also in the sound a thought,
Hearing it by this distant northern sea.

The Sea of Faith
Was once, too, at the full, and round earth's shore
Lay like the folds of a bright girdle furl'd.
But now I only hear
Its melancholy, long, withdrawing roar,
Retreating, to the breath
Of the night-wind, down the vast edges drear
And naked shingles of the world.

Ah, love, let us be true
To one another! for the world, which seems
To lie before us like a land of dreams,
So various, so beautiful, so new,
Hath really neither joy, nor love, nor light,
Nor certitude, nor peace, nor help for pain;
And we are here as on a darkling plain
Swept with confused alarms of struggle and flight
Where ignorant armies clash by night.

# THE DOVER BITCH
## A Criticism of Life

ANTHONY HECHT

So there stood Matthew Arnold and this girl
With the cliffs of England crumbling away behind them,
And he said to her, "Try to be true to me,
And I'll do the same for you, for things are bad
All over, etc., etc."
Well now, I knew this girl. It's true she had read
Sophocles in a fairly good translation
And caught that bitter allusion to the sea,
But all the time he was talking she had in mind
The notion of what his whiskers would feel like
On the back of her neck. She told me later on
That after a while she got to looking out
At the lights across the channel, and really felt sad,
Thinking of all the wine and enormous beds

And blandishments in French and the perfumes.
And then she got really angry. To have been brought
All the way down from London, and then be addressed
As a sort of mournful cosmic last resort
Is really tough on a girl, and she was pretty.
Anyway, she watched him pace the room
And finger his watch-chain and seem to sweat a bit,
And then she said one or two unprintable things.
But you mustn't judge her by that. What I mean to say is,
She's really all right. I still see her once in a while
And she always treats me right. We have a drink
And I give her a good time, and perhaps it's a year
Before I see her again, but there she is,
Running to fat, but dependable as they come.
And sometimes I bring her a bottle of *Nuit d'Amour*.

## SNAKECHARMER

SYLVIA PLATH

As the gods began one world, and man another,
So the snakecharmer begins a snaky sphere
With moon-eye, mouth-pipe. He pipes. Pipes green. Pipes water.

Pipes water green until green waters waver
With reedy lengths and necks and undulatings.
And as his notes twine green, the green river

Shapes its image around his songs.
He pipes a place to stand on, but no rocks,
No floor: a wave of flickering grass tongues

Supports his foot. He pipes a world of snakes,
Of sways and coilings, from the snake-rooted bottom
Of his mind. And now nothing but snakes

Is visible. The snake-scales have become
Leaf, become eyelid; snake-bodies, bough, breast
Of tree and human. And he within this snakedom

Rules the writhings which make manifest
His snakehood and his might with pliant tunes
From this thin pipe. Out of this green nest

As out of Eden's navel twist the lines
Of snaky generations: let there be snakes!
And snakes there were, are, will be—till yawns

Consume this piper and he tires of music
And pipes the world back to the simple fabric
Of snake-warp, snake-weft. Pipes the cloth of snakes

To a melting of green waters, till no snake
Shows its head, and those green waters back to
Water, to green, to nothing like a snake.
Puts up his pipe, and lids his moony eye.

## *from* ROMEO AND JULIET

WILLIAM SHAKESPEARE

JULIET. Gallop apace, you fiery-footed steeds,
    Towards Phoebus' lodging: such a waggoner
    As Phaethon would whip you to the west,
    And bring in cloudy night immediately.
    Spread thy close curtain, love-performing night,
    That runaways' eyes may wink, and Romeo
    Leap to these arms, untalk'd of and unseen!
    Lovers can see to do their amorous rites
    By their own beauties; or, if love be blind,
    It best agrees with night. Come, civil night,
    Thou sober-suited matron, all in black,
    And learn me how to lose a winning match,
    Play'd for a pair of stainless maidenhoods:
    Hood my unmann'd blood, bating in my cheeks,
    With thy black mantle; till strange love, grown bold,
    Think true love acted simple modesty.
    Come, night; come, Romeo; come, thou day in night;
    For thou wilt lie upon the wings of night
    Whiter than new snow on a raven's back.
    Come, gentle night, come, loving, black-brow'd night,
    Give me my Romeo; and, when he shall die,
    Take him and cut him out in little stars,
    And he will make the face of heaven so fine
    That all the world will be in love with night
    And pay no worship to the garish sun.
    O! I have bought the mansion of a love,
    But not possess'd it, and, though I am sold,

Not yet enjoy'd: so tedious is this day
As is the night before some festival
To an impatient child that hath new robes
And may not wear them.

## TO HIS COY MISTRESS

ANDREW MARVELL

Had we but World enough, and Time,
This coyness, Lady, were no crime.
We would sit down, and think which way
To walk, and pass our long Love's Day.
Thou by the *Indian Ganges* side
Should'st Rubies find: I by the Tide
Of *Humber* would complain. I would
Love you ten years before the Flood:
And you should if you please refuse
Till the Conversion of the *Jews*.
My vegetable Love should grow
Vaster than Empires, and more slow.
An hundred years should go to praise
Thine Eyes, and on thy Forehead Gaze.
Two hundred to adore each Breast:
But thirty thousand to the rest.
An Age at least to every part,
And the last Age should show your Heart.
For Lady, you deserve this State,
Nor would I love at lower rate.
　　But at my back I always hear
Time's wingèd Chariot hurrying near:
And yonder all before us lie
Deserts of vast Eternity.
Thy Beauty shall no more be found,
Nor, in thy marble Vault, shall sound
My echoing Song. Then Worms shall try
That long preserv'd Virginity,
And your quaint Honour turn to dust,
And into ashes all my Lust.
The Grave's a fine and private place,
But none, I think, do there embrace.
　　Now therefore, while the youthful hue
Sits on thy skin like morning dew,
And while thy willing Soul transpires

At every pore with instant Fires,
Now let us sport us while we may;
And now, like am'rous birds of prey,
Rather at once our Time devour,
Than languish in his slow-chapt pow'r.
Let us roll all our Strength, and all
Our sweetness, up into one Ball,
And tear our Pleasures with rough strife
Thorough the Iron Gates of Life.
Thus, though we cannot make our Sun
Stand still, yet we will make him run.

## KUBLA KHAN

SAMUEL TAYLOR COLERIDGE

In Xanadu did Kubla Khan
A stately pleasure-dome decree:
Where Alph, the sacred river, ran
Through caverns measureless to man
   Down to a sunless sea.
So twice five miles of fertile ground
With walls and towers were girdled round:
And here were gardens bright with sinuous rills
Where blossomed many an incense-bearing tree;
And here were forests ancient as the hills,
Enfolding sunny spots of greenery.
But oh! that deep romantic chasm which slanted
Down the green hill athwart a cedarn cover!
A savage place! as holy and enchanted
As e'er beneath a waning moon was haunted
By woman wailing for her demon-lover!
And from this chasm, with ceaseless turmoil seething,
As if this earth in fast thick pants were breathing,
A mighty fountain momently was forced;
Amid whose swift half-intermitted burst
Huge fragments vaulted like rebounding hail,
Or chaffy grain beneath the thresher's flail:
And 'mid these dancing rocks at once and ever
It flung up momently the sacred river.
Five miles meandering with a mazy motion
Through wood and dale the sacred river ran,
Then reached the caverns measureless to man,
And sank in tumult to a lifeless ocean:
And 'mid this tumult Kubla heard from far

Ancestral voices prophesying war!
The shadow of the dome of pleasure
    Floated midway on the waves;
Where was heard the mingled measure
    From the fountain and the caves.
It was a miracle of rare device,
A sunny pleasure-dome with caves of ice!

  A damsel with a dulcimer
  In a vision once I saw:
  It was an Abyssinian maid,
  And on her dulcimer she play'd,
  Singing of Mount Abora.
  Could I revive within me
  Her symphony and song,
To such a deep delight 'twould win me,
That with music loud and long,
I would build that dome in air,
That sunny dome! those caves of ice!
And all who heard should see them there,
And all should cry, Beware! Beware!
His flashing eyes, his floating hair!
Weave a circle round him thrice,
And close your eyes with holy dread,
For he on honey-dew hath fed,
And drunk the milk of Paradise.

# 3

# *What Shall I Read?*

In his delightful novel *The Human Comedy*, William Saroyan tells of two little boys who wander into the public library just to look at the books. The older boy, Lionel, tells the librarian that he and little Ulysses are friends because neither one of them can read. Lionel's forthright admission that they are there to look at the books simply because they like to, astonishes the librarian, but since she can think of no law against it, she sends them into the stacks to fulfill their mission. Saroyan's description of the ensuing scene recreates in us the awe that most of us have felt when looking at the thousands of volumes on library shelves.

The two friends moved off into still greater realms of mystery and adventure. Lionel pointed out more books to Ulysses. "These," he said. "And those over there. And these. All books, Ulysses." He stopped a moment to think. "I wonder what they say in all these books." He pointed out a whole vast area of them, five shelves full of them. "All these," he said—"I wonder what they say."

A pretty book with a green cover "like fresh grass" caught Lionel's eye. He had no way of knowing what was inside the book, judging by title or the name of the author. Only the color of the cover had meaning for one so young.

A little frightened at what he was doing, Lionel lifted the book out of the shelf, held it in his hands a moment and then opened it. "There, Ulysses!" he said. "A book! There it is! See? They're saying something in here." Now he pointed to something in the print of the book. "There's an 'A'" he said. "That's an 'A' right there. There's another letter of some sort. I don't know what that one is. Every letter's different, Ulysses, and every word's different." He sighed and looked around at all the books. "I don't think I'll ever learn to read," he said, "but I sure would like to know what they're saying in there. Now here's a picture," he said. "Here's a picture of a girl. See her? Pretty, isn't she?" He turned many pages of the book and said, "See it? More letters and words, straight through to the end of the book. This is the pubalic liberry, Ulysses," he said. "Books all over the place." He looked at the print of the book with a kind of reverence, whispering to himself as if he were trying to read. Then he shook his head. "You can't know what a book says, Ulysses, unless you can read, and I can't read," he said.

No one who has observed a first-grader learning to read can fail to sense his thrill of mastering a new mode of communication. This youngster has long known that words mean something, but now, suddenly, he can *read* them and get meaning for himself. Like a toddler on his first steps, he falters often and needs assistance, but it is not long until he races through the words that are within his grasp, and he is deliriously independent in a new world where people he likes can do things he cannot do. No one who reads Saroyan's story can fail to realize that if Lionel is given the chance, he will someday soon be reading books. Most children love to learn to read. Unfortunately, somehow and at sometime, many of them lose their love for books. Reading should be an everunfolding process of achievement, pleasure, and experience.

You may be an avid silent reader. You may need no encouragement to read, and as a beginning student of interpretative reading you may have no difficulty in finding literature you wish to read in class.

On the other hand, you may be one of many students who have admittedly limited reading habits and are confused as to how to start finding reading materials. Like the student of English composition, who asks, "What shall I write about?" and the beginning student of public speaking, who asks, "What shall I talk about?" you may quite logically ask, "What shall I read?" Not only do beginning students face the problem of selecting good materials, but advanced readers also acknowledge that the choice of the *right* literature seems to be the major consideration in producing a good communicative reading. And so, whether you are planning to read to your class or to a public audience, be willing to spend time in evaluating many pieces of literature in order to select from them the few you will finally read aloud to other persons.

## CONSULT YOUR INTERESTS

You must please yourself in reading before you can hope to please a listener; therefore, your own interests should offer you clues as to what kinds of reading materials are most likely to offer you communicative success. The library nearest you has books and periodicals to fit almost every human interest and a librarian to assist you in finding what you might like to read. Nearly every drugstore has a rack of magazines and paperback books, some quite worthwhile. Before you lies the entire field of human knowledge and literary experience.

For your first experience in reading to others, you might read a selection already one of your favorites, a short article or light verse, perhaps. Then, on future assignments, read new materials. You should not limit your reading to what you already know and appreciate, but you should strive to increase the breadth of your interests. Indeed, it will be valuable to investigate forms of literature you do not customarily read.

The greater your appreciation, the greater your communicative effectiveness. Read what you really enjoy and wish to share with others, and you will conquer the most common difficulty faced by the beginner: the burdensome task of reading aloud only because the course requires it. Let's hope that you will motivate yourself to effective communicative reading by interpreting literature you really like.

## CONSULT YOUR CAPACITIES

The second requirement for the choice of good reading materials is this: Consult your capacities. Read to others only the literature that you are capable of understanding. If you lack a high degree of comprehension, do not expect your reading to make sense to your listeners. We do not suggest that you must always read simple stuff or that you should limit your choices to literary selections you presently understand or comprehend without study. After all, a major reason for studying interpretative reading is to increase your own literary understanding and appreciation. Understanding should be achieved before you read aloud. Therefore, take this opportunity to enlarge your literary horizons by reading materials that offer rewards through your repeated reading and exploring. In reading don't expect a terse " once-over " to tell you *all*, and don't discard what is not instantly comprehensible. Give a work time and familiarity to work upon you. Then, too, think of the particular skills required for your reading: dialects, for example. Some persons have astonishing dialectal abilities, whereas others just don't find it easy to reproduce British, Irish, Southern, or other unfamiliar accents. Thus, both understanding and skills are aspects of the readers' capacities to be considered in selecting material for oral interpretation. But don't give up easily! The classroom is the place to try new things, and only by trying do we truly learn.

## CONSULT YOUR AUDIENCE

We have seen that the first two requirements for choosing materials for oral interpretation lie within the *interpreter's* capacities for understanding and appreciation. The third and fourth requirements concern the same capacities in the *listeners,* for the achievement of understanding and appreciation in the audience is the fundamental goal of oral interpretation. The reader should analyze the audience as carefully as the public speaker does, and, in this analysis, should consider such characteristics of the audience as its predominant age, social and economic strata, sex, religion, nationality, race, geographical location, and the occasion for the reading. Audiences, like individuals, have their own distinctive interests. A reader who ignores the probable interests of listeners or who reads far over their probable cultural tastes is heading for unfavorable responses from them. On the other hand, it is somewhat surprising to the interpreter to discover that one can read many types of selections to many different kinds of groups, if only *he* has a great deal of personal enthusiasm for the material.

We must make one other, important, suggestion in respect to your treatment of the audience: Ask yourself whether the material will be satisfying. This point is especially significant in your choice of a portion of a longer work, in which an individual scene or segment may not have sufficient movement, development, clarity, or climax to provide a reasonably complete experience for the listener. For the present, most of your reading will be done to your class rather than to public audiences. Selections used should be of value to both you and to the class. Some of what you read will be primarily entertainment, but to choose only light or shallow material for classroom reading is to cheat both yourself and your audience. The great range of good writing available to you provides a multiplicity of literary experiences that should not be overlooked because of narrow personal tastes.

## Consult the Requirements of Oral Communication

The interpretative reader must choose literature that lends itself to being read and heard. The oral and aural mechanisms make demands not made by the pen and the eye. The speech mechanism, for example, falls easy victim to undue complications of sound. To read aloud Swinburne's extended use of alliteration in the following lines is to invite the twisted tongue:

### *from* NEPHELIDIA

ALGERNON CHARLES SWINBURNE

From the depth of the dreamy decline of the dawn
   through a notable nimbus of nebulous noonshine,
Pallid and pink as the palm of the flagflower that
   flickers with fear of the flies as they float,
Are they looks of our lovers that lustrously lean
   from a marvel of mystic miraculous moonshine,
These that we feel in the blood of our blushes that
   thicken and threaten with throbs through the throat?

Furthermore, the ear cannot relisten as the eye can reread. When the mind of a silent reader does not comprehend ideas, the eye can backtrack, reconsider relationships, and even consult a dictionary or encyclopedia in the pursuit of understanding. The ear, however, must perceive meaning the first time it hears—perhaps not the whole meaning but certainly enough to make the effort satisfying. We should consider the preferences of the ear, which are few but assertive. The ear prefers simplicity to complication, either in vocabulary or syntax. It prefers images to abstractions and prefers drama to thought. Apply these requirements to the opening lines from two essays by the famed writer of both fictional and nonfictional prose Virginia Woolf. Both are from worthy essays, but if you will but read them aloud to a friend (after studying them and even practicing them a few times in order to read intelligently), you should be able to come to some common agreement that one is not only easier to read aloud but also easier to listen to:

## *from* DEFOE[1]

The fear which attacks the recorder of centenaries lest he should find himself measuring a diminishing spectre and forced to foretell its approaching dissolution is not only absent in the case of *Robinson Crusoe* but the mere thought of it is ridiculous. It may be true that *Robinson Crusoe* is two hundred years of age upon the twenty-fifth of April 1919, but far from raising the familiar speculations as to whether people now read it and will continue to read it, the effect of the bi-centenary is to make us marvel that *Robinson Crusoe*, the perennial and immortal, should have been in existence so short a time as that. The book resembles one of the anonymous productions of the race itself rather than the effort of a single mind; as for celebrating its centenary we should as soon think of celebrating the centenaries of Stonehenge itself.

## *from* THE DUCHESS OF NEWCASTLE[2]

". . . All I desire is fame," wrote Margaret Cavendish, Duchess of Newcastle. And while she lived her wish was granted. Garish in her dress, eccentric in her habits, chaste in her conduct, coarse in her speech, she succeeded during her lifetime in drawing upon herself the ridicule of the great and the applause of the learned. But the last echoes of that clamour have now all died away; she lives only in the few splendid phrases that Lamb scattered upon her tomb; her poems, her plays, her philosophies, her orations, her discourse—all those folios and quartos in which, she protested, her real life was shrined—moulder in the gloom of public libraries, or are decanted into tiny thimbles which hold six drops of their profusion. Even the curious student, inspired by the words of Lamb, quails before the mass of her mausoleum, peers in, looks about him, and hurries out again, shutting the door.

[1] Virginia Woolf, *The Common Reader* (New York: Harcourt Brace Jovanovich, 1953), p. 89.
[2] Virginia Woolf, *The Common Reader* (New York: Harcourt Brace Jovanovich, 1953), p. 70.

We should make it clear here that the "Nephelidia" and "Defoe" selections could be read aloud successfully, but they present articulation and phrasing difficulties that would tax the abilities of the reader.

## CONSULT THE REQUIREMENTS OF LITERARY QUALITY

Most college students feel inadequate in attempting to evaluate literary worth. Part of the explanation for this difficulty probably lies in the fact that courses in literature seldom deal with a consideration of *relative* quality; everything quoted in the textbook anthology is supposed to be good writing. Students are rarely required to compare a good piece of writing with a poor one. Because their critical judgment is not exercised, students often feel at a loss in selecting material for oral reading when the evaluation is entirely their own. The successful oral interpreter is committed to performing literary works of quality. This need not restrict you to the acknowledged masterworks of the English language, but it does give you caution against selecting works that are superficial, trivial, or otherwise lacking. A concert pianist would waste everyone's time, including his own, with a child's composition; a master craftsman wastes his talents working with inferior materials.

What constitutes literary quality? The answer would, of course, be too extensive to include in this textbook, for it would fill a book of its own. However, a few basic principles can be stated here, perhaps to your advantage. First, a good piece of writing is universal; it deals with the experiences of life common to the greatest number of human beings. Shakespeare's plays, which have been enjoyed for almost four centuries, today remain unexcelled in this respect. His tragedies, of course, deal with the great (or universal) passions of life: honor, jealousy, love, and death. His comedies reveal that he employed the motives and the experiences common to all of us regardless of the century in which we live. Courtship, often treated lightly, is a perennial source of amusement, as in *The Taming of the Shrew*. Bottom in *A Midsummer Night's Dream* can be as amusing for us as he is for his companions and as he was for Elizabethan audiences. The drunken butler in *The Tempest* provokes from us the same laughs he earned in the Globe Theater. Sensing the importance of universality, Shakespeare dealt with the question of how to live and how to treat other people, and he did it in a way that interested virtually everyone.

This same factor of universality is responsible for the continuing appeal of many ancient stories, for example, the parables of Jesus. Hardly anything in the story of the Prodigal Son is out of date: arrogant youth, wasted money, parental love, the generation gap, and eventual reconciliation are still commonplace. The account of a man who was beaten and robbed but eventually rescued by a "good Samaritan" is no more foreign to human nature of the twentieth century than it was to that of the first century. Indeed, most of us have sometimes "passed by on the other side" in order to avoid a human obligation. Many modern selections also possess a high degree of universality. Peter Kane Dufault's poem "Gielgud Reading Lear," in Chapter 1, for example, is particularly strong in its universal appeal to our common sense of the grief in loss.

Second, good writing is *original*. A good writer has something new and unique to say, or he has a new way of dealing with an old concept. Compare T. S. Eliot's poem "Journey of the Magi," quoted and discussed in Chapter 5, with the following verse:

## CHRISTMAS EVERYWHERE

PHILLIPS BROOKS

Everywhere, everywhere, Christmas tonight!
Christmas in lands of the fir-tree and pine,
Christmas in lands of the palm-tree and vine,
Christmas where snow peaks stand solemn and white,
Christmas where cornfields stand sunny and bright.
Christmas where children are hopeful and gay,
Christmas where old men are patient and gray,
Christmas where peace, like a dove in his flight,
Broods o'er brave men in the thick of the fight;
Everywhere, everywhere, Christmas tonight!

For the Christ-child who comes is the Master of all;
No palace too great, no cottage too small.

Eliot added new and significant thought to the old Christmas story; Brooks had only one somewhat superficial idea: "Christmas is everywhere." Although some readers and audiences might find some charm in Brooks's delight in the overwhelming presence of Christmas, all who know literature will agree that Eliot probed much deeper and with much more originality into the meaning of Christmas.

In addition, the original writer is not content to imitate another writer, for he values his own creative spirit too highly to copy. He prefers to create his own style, characters, situations, images, figures of speech, rhythms, symbolism. In *The Caine Mutiny*, Herman Wouk wrote one of the most dramatic courtroom scenes found in modern fiction. It was so powerful that it later became a successful Broadway play. Another novel, the title of which has long been forgotten, proved to be rather interesting until the climax of the book arrived, in a scene almost identical to Wouk's trial scene, even to the mental breakdown on the stand of a major character exactly like the collapse of Captain Queeg. The second writer apparently did not have the originality to create something new for his climax. His lack of originality at the crucial point of his book is doubly sad because he had demonstrated literary skill in the earlier portions of his novel. Of course, writers cannot always be completely original; even Shakespeare borrowed his plots liberally, but he was so inventive in characterization, imagery, and language that few persons have ever objected to his use of old stories for his great plays. Originality is the unique way that the author treats the material he has chosen to write about. What is there about his writing that makes it stand out from the commonplace? What does it have that makes it more appealing than other writings on the same or a similar theme? Your ability to see freshness and originality of expression depends on the breadth of your acquaintance with literature. The factor is largely responsible for some books appealing to many generations and other books exhausting their usefulness in a fortnight. Individuality distinguishes the work of the artist from the work of the hack.

It also distinguishes one creative spirit from another. In perceiving originality and individuality, we readily distinguish novels by William Faulkner from those of Muriel Spark, plays by Arthur Miller from those of Harold Pinter, poems by T. S. Eliot from those of Marianne Moore, speeches by President Kennedy from those of President Carter, and humorous verses by Ogden Nash from those of Morris Bishop.

Third, good writing has something *significant* to say. This does not mean that it must be world-shaking in importance, or even serious; for light, humorous, or satirical writing may be significant. "Jenny Kiss'd Me," quoted in Chapter 14, is not profound—in fact, it is quite light—but it is significant, for in a few deft lines, Leigh Hunt communicates the universal delight of an aging person in a child's kiss. The concrete picture of Jenny's action and the poet's consequent thoughts about his age furnish fine contrast to Brooks's generalized shouts about Christmas. James Thurber's humor usually shows an incisive view of man's frailties. Phyllis McGinley's light verses are also the result of astute observation of life.

Fourth, good writing is a result of *accuracy* and *honesty* in the writer's perception of life. Some assembly-line writers, because they wear colored glasses of one tint or another, either deliberately or ignorantly do not make very accurate observations. For example, a newspaper versifier once philosophized about a neighbor who had a beautifully landscaped home. The "poet" came to the conclusion that a man who took such care of the outside of his home *must* unconditionally be a good man inside it. One reader took issue with this specious bit of homey reasoning, reporting that in his boyhood he had once had a neighbor whose green thumb had been responsible for a magnificent lawn and garden. The man was generous with his garden produce and was even kind to the neighborhood children. But, he was not in all ways a good man. Regularly, he beat his wife, and he was a bootlegger as well. Such a jingling paean to man's goodness as had appeared in that newspaper column is guaranteed to appear in popular publications because it pleasantly reassures unsophisticated readers by telling them what they *want* to hear about their fellow men. Just as dishonest are the writers who pander to the tastes of readers who want only a constant diet of sordidness.

We cannot choose our reading materials uncritically. We must attempt to sort the valid from the phony. When, because of our own limitations, we cannot determine literary quality, we should consult the opinions of those who should know, the literary critics. Many helpful volumes of literary explication and evaluation are to be found in every academic library.

Fifth, when good writing solicits emotional reaction by the reader, it offers *sufficient reason* for that emotion: a situation that justifies the emotion. Compare the following poems:

## THE SPIRES OF OXFORD

(As seen from the train)

WINIFRED M. LETTS

I saw the spires of Oxford
  As I was passing by,
The grey spires of Oxford
  Against a pearl-grey sky;
My heart was with the Oxford men
  Who went abroad to die.

The years go fast in Oxford,
  The golden years and gay;
The hoary colleges look down
  On careless boys at play,
But when the bugles sounded—War!
  They put their games away.

They left the peaceful river,
  The cricket field, the quad,
The shaven lawns of Oxford,
  To seek a bloody sod.
They gave their merry youth away
  For country and for God.

God rest you, happy gentlemen,
  Who laid your good lives down,
Who took the khaki and the gun
  Instead of cap and gown.
God bring you to a fairer place
  Than even Oxford town.

# THE DEATH OF THE BALL TURRET GUNNER

RANDALL JARRELL

From my mother's sleep I fell into the State,
And I hunched in its belly till my wet fur froze.
Six miles from earth, loosed from its dream of life,
I woke to black flak and the nightmare fighters.
When I died they washed me out of the turret with a hose.

In " The Spires of Oxford " the writer gives no *personal* reason for being so disturbed about the deaths of the Oxford students. Was one of them her son, or her lover? Of course, it is true that we all may think, momentarily, of the great waste of human lives in war, but we do not *feel* the loss unless we are given a concrete tragic figure. We cannot feel much for a generalized group of Oxford students; we might have felt sorry for the loss of *one* of them if the author had really brought one to life for us. In Jarrell's fine little poem, once we know that a ball turret gunner was a soldier, encased in a womblike, fiber-glass, revolving gun turret on a bomber, during World War II, we can feel the tragic loss of a young man who tells us so tersely that he did not wake up to life until the moment he was killed. We can feel the tragic irony of this boy's death. Letts merely talks about war deaths; Jarrell creates the tragedy.

Sixth, good writing comes to us in a *form* that is *appropriate* to its message. Consider the last two selections again. The rhythm of the former is inappropriate for a message of tragedy: an unrelieved ta-tah, ta-tah, ta-tah that jangles along rather jauntily. The regular rhyme scheme also contributes to a merry kind of atmosphere. The verses are filled with trite expressions that sound very familiar to us: " As I was passing by," " pearl-grey sky," " My heart was with," " The years go fast," " The golden years and gay," " the bugles sounded," " For country and for God," " God rest you, happy gentlemen," " laid your good lives down," and others. Surely, some of these seem overfamiliar to you. Jarrell, on the other hand, has used no monotonous meter, only one rhyme—for a concluding unity—and no clichés. In a title and five lines, he has said all that needs to be said.

Seventh, good writing has tremendous powers of suggestion. We have already spoken of the art of oral interpretation as an art of suggestion to the imagination, properly so, because literature itself has that power, and the best literature is the most suggestive. The mark of a good book or poem is often not so much what it says as what it leaves unsaid and prompts you to think, feel, and imagine for yourself. Imagery is a part of suggestion, but images are often only means to the stimulation of larger concepts not literally expressed. Look for the between-the-lines ideas and feelings. In them an author wins your participation in his book or poem. What images does he prompt you to recall? What connotations does he stimulate you to make? Why has he not wrapped up every thought in denotative meanings and extensive elaboration? Why may he even have been deliberately obscure? The answer to these questions is that the most enjoyable and most meaningful writing is that which provokes in the reader his own creative responses. The writer leaves much unsaid so that you must fill in details, draw inferences, and probe the depths. The more you "think about it," which is to say the more you respond to the literature, the more meaningful it becomes through its compelling complexities.

The power of the following poem, for example, lies not at all in the words themselves (there are only twenty-four words including the title) but, rather, in the glittering vividness of a human experience not spelled out in crude detail.

## BETWEEN WALLS

WILLIAM CARLOS WILLIAMS

the back wings
of the

hospital where
nothing

will grow lie
cinders

in which shine
the broken

pieces of a green
bottle

This is as far as we shall pursue this subject now; however, you should seek out literary quality. By reading good materials, make interpretative reading a profitable experience for both the audience and yourself. You will find that many other parts of this book will furnish insights into literary quality. Chapter 5 should be especially helpful.

## CONSULT THE AUTHORITIES

"But how do I find suitable reading materials?" you may ask. The answer is simple: "Look for them." One systematic way to start would be for you to consult a list of recommended books. Many different authors and agencies have prepared such lists. Some are available in paperback books designed to help a person improve his reading. It is likely that your bookstore has such books in stock. You will also find several very helpful books on specialized types of literature, such as drama, the short story, the novel, and poetry. In addition, we recommend book reviews in periodicals as helpful leads to good books.

Librarians are very helpful in steering interested readers to useful guides. On your own, you might find anthologies of great help. In these collections, gathered by experts, you will find selections by many authors. We have included a long list of modern anthologies in the Appendix. We are confident that the titles will offer something of interest to almost every student.

## CONSULT THE RANGE OF LITERATURE

Your major concern may be what *kind* of literature to read to audiences. Your authors think that virtually all literature of good quality is potentially suitable for oral interpretation. Some respected authorities apparently feel that only a few types are suitable. For example, some, recognizing that interpretation is ideally suited to the communication of poetry, actually limit their consideration almost exclusively to poetry. We cannot question the fact that poetry does reach its fruition in oral interpretation, but we feel that other forms of writing also deserve oral communication. Some authorities tend to exclude play reading from the activity of the oral reader, and yet it seems to us that plays constitute a great body of effective literature for oral interpretation. Still others are prone to ignore fine literary materials from nonfictional literature: essays, articles, description, adventure, and biography, among others. And, finally, there are some who even neglect the field of prose fiction, the novel and the short story, because of the work involved in finding just the right selections and in adapting them for reading to specific audiences in limited time periods. Our point should be restated: All good writing is potentially good material for oral interpretation.

## CONSULT THE LIBRARY

The most satisfactory method of looking for something to read is to browse in the books themselves. By so doing, you not only catch Lionel's enthusiasm for the presence of books, but you also have freedom of movement, a chance to look the book over before drawing it from the library, and a delightful degree of solitude away from the bustling circulation desk. If your library permits your entrance to the stacks, locate the shelves holding the type of book you think you want. Pick one out; leaf through it; read a line here, a paragraph there. If it appeals to you, check it out for home use and give it a real chance to interest you. If it does not, keep looking.

In fiction, you will find many shelves of novels, old and new, good and bad, dull and exciting. You will also find many collections of short stories, classified by authors, by types, and by subject matter. If you do not know any authors well, take out an anthology that appeals to you. In it you will probably find some stories you will enjoy. Then go back to the library and search for more stories by the same author. At this point, that alphabetical card catalogue comes in very handy. You can follow exactly the same procedure concerning poetry and drama. The library contains volumes of the works of individual poets and dramatists, but the beginning student will usually prefer to make his first selection from an anthology, which also often assists him with helpful information about a writer and his writings. Anthologies have been published to please readers with almost every conceivable interest, on subjects as diverse as humor and love songs; religion and satire; the familiar and the bizarre; the scientific and the fantastic; personal letters and public speeches; the poetry of the then and now, the here and there.

Spend some time pursuing your individual interests in literature, and you will probably find materials that you will enjoy communicating to audiences.

## CONSULT LITERATURE IN ORAL INTERPRETATION TEXTS

Last, we recommend that you read the literature quoted in this book, for we have tried to include a wide selection of literature for your study, and, we hope, appreciation. It represents a wide range of literary types, subject matter, and—yes!—even quality. We hope that some of it will be very meaningful to you. Other oral interpretation texts also have fine collections of literature. We have listed several of the leading texts in the Appendix to this book.

# Two

## Finding the Meaning

# 4 *The Nature of Meaning*

On the level of everyday experience, no one doubts that communicators must understand ideas if they are to make them clear to others. You would not try to direct a tourist to spots of interest in your town unless you knew where the places were. The teacher of geometry must comprehend theories and postulates in order to teach them. Perhaps you have tried to answer a little child's question. "How does the grass grow?" or "Who made God?" and found you simply could not do so because you did not understand the matter yourself. As a student of speech you may already know how hopeless it is to try to make a point clear to an audience if you do not grasp it yourself. All the techniques for effective public speaking are doomed to failure unless you know your subject.

Just as certainly, communicative oral interpretation requires that you be highly responsive to the literature you are interpreting. Quite often the poor reader knows only the relatively simple mechanical process of translating black marks on a page to sound waves. Good oral interpretation is never the process of transferring mere symbols to the listeners' ears without involving the minds of both reader and listeners. Your success in getting your listeners to respond to a selection is not likely to exceed your own response to that selection.

Since the days of Samuel Silas Curry, a great teacher of oral interpretation about seventy years ago, no authority in the field has taken significant exception to the idea that effective oral communication of literature can be expected only from a reader who has achieved a thoroughgoing "impression" of the material himself. The modern study of oral interpretation first took its cue from Curry's formula: "IMPRESSION must precede and determine all EXPRESSION."[1] Subsequently, modern psychology has established a strong relationship between the processes and contends that expression may constitute or be concurrent with impression. Sometimes, we do not know exactly what we want to say until we say it: Voicing and acting do develop understandings! Curry was right in saying that interpreters must gain impressions in order to express, but the process is not so simple. Impression to the point of understanding may come before the reading performance, but we should expect *other* impressions, insights, nuances, images, relationships, and moods to develop *while* we read.

[1] Samuel Silas Curry, *Foundations of Expression* (Boston: The Expression Company, 1907), p. 11.

The process of uncovering meaning in literature begins when you first read a selection, and it should continue throughout your analysis, rehearsals, and performance. As you prepare for a reading, your exploration of meaning should entail a combination of silent as well as oral study. Your attempts at expressing the literature will confirm certain ideas; will lead to the rejection of others; and will open up entirely new possibilities. The expressions of rehearsal, then, are important parts of the process of gaining impressions. Finally, when you communicate the literature to an audience, you should still be open to new impressions. The facial expressions, laughter, tension or relaxation, and other responses offered by an audience become a part of the literature at the moment of its performance. Naturally, you will not forsake the impressions you have gained from prior study and rehearsal, but you should remain open to the new insights that can only occur when an audience is dynamically present and responding.

As an oral reader, you are first, most importantly, and continually concerned with your own perception of the intellectual, emotional, and artistic elements of meaning. In this text we will explore the nature of meaning; sources of meaning; and techniques for its discovery. Together, these considerations should help you to arrive at the *total response* to literature that is necessary for effective oral interpretation.

## WHAT IS MEANING?

The psychologist will tell you that the essence of meaning is response. In a laboratory experiment a fish may be subjected to a tiny electric shock. In response it feels pain and withdraws from the stimulus. Its pain and withdrawal constitute the meaning of the shock. If food is placed on the surface of the water and the stimulus of that food reaches its senses, its response may be to approach the food; perhaps it may even begin to secrete the appropriate digestive juices. These responses, then, are the meanings it attaches to these elements injected into its environment. Further experimentation can result in conditioning its reactions. Conceivably it may so often be shocked and then immediately given food that its responses may be associated. Eventually the fish may respond to the shock as if it were food. The shock treatment may become a call to lunch. In the same way, a dog can be conditioned to respond to his master's voice or to the sight of his feeding pan.

So it is on any level of life that meaning is the response an organism makes to a stimulus. To a baby the meaning of a hot stove may be pain and the meaning of a spoon, unpleasant medicine. The child who is only beginning to use language illustrates this principle on an elementary level. Already the youngster has learned that the presence of his mother is accompanied by the satisfaction of his needs: She gives him food or soothes his troubled spirit.

Always she says, "Mamma feed baby," or "Mamma help." Soon the words alone are enough to soothe. Then, perhaps suddenly, the child begins to say "Mamma," for the word means hunger pangs alleviated or cares dissolved. He can as easily learn to respond with fear to the word "Mamma" or any other. Meaning at the word level too is responsive, whether it be physical, mental, or emotional.

In the course of our learning a language, this process is repeated over and over again until we have mastered a long and involved set of word symbols with which we have come to associate certain responses. The baby hears "No" and desists from what he is doing. "Hot" or "Hurt" may produce the same general response. "Come" is followed by outstretched arms, "Pretty" by a smile, "Bye-Bye" by waving, and "Kiss" by an obediently offered cheek. Soon the responses have become fixed so that they are combined into intelligent reactions to phrases, sentences, and even extended patterns of speech. The eighteen-month-old baby may react quite accurately to "Love Daddy," "Go to Mamma," "Build a house," "Get your shoes," "Put it in the waste basket," "Watch the TV," and even more complicated sentences. Eventually he learns to utter the same symbols himself in order to express the responses within him or to elicit responses from someone else. Pleased and proud of the way he has arranged his blocks and wanting you to admire his creation, he says, "See." When he wants the door opened, he says, "In." If a toy is damaged, he runs to tell Mother, "Broke," and perhaps to add, "Mamma fix." Soon he is saying "Read book," "Rock baby," and, before long, "Mom, come here!"

Then we are exposed to written language, and we learn a new step in the stimulus-response pattern. We now learn to respond to the printed word by making the sounds of the word, which in turn evoke the response already learned for it. For a long time we are able to complete only the first step in reading, which is to say, the word when we see it written. (Pity the reader who never gets beyond this stage!) Slowly then the pattern is completed, and we learn to respond to the printed symbol with a whole set of reactions dictated and limited by the experiences we have had.

The point of this discussion is that for the reader, and the listener too, meaning is simply *response*. It may include purely logical designations (if such there be!) and the most involved emotional reactions. It is almost never solely one or the other, but nearly always both. Meaning is as complicated as the experiences of the reader and may often include a multitude of them. It must remain forever the great uncertain, unmeasurable quantity in communication. There is so much of reality for which language tries to stand that, while writers and dictionary makers alike may try to refine meanings, responses to words will remain always personalized and varied. They will include all of the experiences of all the minds involved in communication. For this reason "finding the meaning" is the single most significant and difficult part of oral interpretation.

We proceed now to a more detailed analysis of what is meant by *meaning* as it is involved in the study of oral interpretation. Incidentally, we would not have you believe that the nature of meaning is something that can be fully explained and understood in the abstract: Meaning is something that must be experienced. We can, however, elaborate upon the theory and then illustrate.

Remembering that our nutshell definition of meaning is "response," we turn to the first step in the evolution, transmission, and reception of literary meaning. Suppose there is a poet who, like all other good poets, possesses more sensitivity than the average human being. The poet comes upon something: perhaps an object, a person, or an experience, perhaps a multiplicity of experiences. For Tennyson, that "something" was a "flower in the crannied wall"; for Edwin Arlington Robinson, it was the man "Miniver Cheevy"; for Frost, it was an experience of "Stopping by Woods on a Snowy Evening"; for T. S. Eliot, it was years of experience with "hollow men." That stimulus, or many of them, is the beginning of literature. To the stimulus, the poet responds with ideas, emotions, and something less easily defined that we shall call *appreciations*. The response may be relatively simple and isolated, or it may be (and usually is) highly involved and not truly separable from a multitude of responses to other stimuli. At any rate, meaning is born, and with it perhaps an impulse to create a poem.

Stung by that impulse the poet utilizes skills, and what may be a long or a short gestation period follows. It is said that Thomas Gray spent seven years creating "An Elegy Written in a Country Churchyard." William Saroyan says he wrote *The Time of Your Life* in just a few days. Coleridge spent an hour or so on "Kubla Khan."

The making of a poem is a responsive act, and the poem itself is a responsive product. Using the sound symbols of language, the poet creates a work of art, and using marks on a page he represents there the poem itself.

Eventually then, someone, perhaps you, encounters that page. You scan the marks silently. Even better, you read them aloud. With ideas, emotions, and appreciations, you respond to the poem. Theoretically, your responses may be consistent with the ideas, emotions, and appreciations originally experienced by the poet, but in actuality they can never be exactly the same. The poem may not hit you at all; it may seem dull; it may turn you off rather than on; it may recall a multitude of your own intellectual and emotional experiences; or it may jolt you into thoughts, feelings, and a sense of literary appreciation you have never experienced before. You may "get it" easily and quickly, or you may be prompted to think that surely more profound responses can be achieved with further study. In short, meaning for you, as it was for the poet, is a responsive act. As such, it is in you rather than in the poem. As such, it may continue and change with rereading, study, and reflection.

Indeed, a poem you choose to read to others will normally require much extensive analysis. In order to achieve appropriate and adequate responses in yourself, you will examine the poem intellectually, emotionally, and in terms of the artistic skills embodied in it. In the next chapter you will find a series of steps for such literary analysis. You will not, however, always find such a routine approach to the meaning of a selection adequate for your purposes as an oral interpreter. You should seek to embody the literature in your total mental-emotional-physical responses to it: the poem becomes part of you. As this happens, your responses to it will, of course, grow and change.

When you interpret the poem for others, you will strive for maximum awareness of all it can mean to you. You will respond in terms of ideas, emotions, and appreciation, and your responses will become communicative as they are effectively expressed audibly and visibly. Your act of reading aloud will be an embodiment simultaneously of both impression and expression. True, you will have tried to achieve your intellectual-emotional-esthetic meaning before attempting to communicate it to others, but meaning is more than simple understanding and more than preliminary impression. It is implicit in the act of expression, too. It is *your response*. It is *total response*.

As you read and after you finish, the members of your audience hopefully find "meaning" or "meanings" prompted by the poem as you saw it, as you expressed your understanding of it in audible and visible signals, as they received those signals, and as they in turn respond to them. Here too, the perception of meaning is a responsive act with dimensions in ideas, emotions, and appreciations. To each person, meaning is distinctly individual. For the audience, as well as for the writer and the reader, meaning is *response*.

Now, let us examine the sequence of responsive acts that makes up a specific literary experience. William Stafford's poem "Traveling Through the Dark" recounts an actual incident in the poet's life. At the time of the experience, he had no realization that a poem was imbedded in what seemed to him merely a "routine event":

Wednesday nights, late, I drive 75 miles home over the Coast Range, after teaching an evening class in Tillamook. Thursday mornings at breakfast my children—Bret, Kim, Kit, Barbara—ask, "What did you see last night, Daddy?" And one Thursday morning I found myself telling them an incident, just a routine event on that narrow mountain road. Amidst the story, while they listened wide-eyes to Daddy's far, late adventure, I realized that the world had offered to me again an event which could not be held small; a quick wash of feeling signaled for the children and for me that a poem or story had happened, regardless of whether we wrote it down or called it so.

As you read the poem, you should respond to the details of the incident as well as to the "wash of feeling" that make up the poem.

# TRAVELING THROUGH THE DARK

WILLIAM STAFFORD

Traveling through the dark I found a deer
dead on the edge of the Wilson River road.
It is usually best to roll them into the canyon:
that road is narrow; to swerve might make more dead.

By glow of the tail light I stumbled back of the car
and stood by the heap, a doe, a recent killing;
she had stiffened already, almost cold.
I dragged her off; she was large in the belly.

My fingers touching her side brought me the reason—
her side was warm; her fawn lay there waiting,
alive, still, never to be born.
Beside that mountain road I hesitated.

The car aimed ahead its lowered parking lights;
under the hood purred the steady engine.
I stood in the glare of the warm exhaust turning red;
around our group I could hear the wilderness listen.

I thought hard for us all—my only swerving—,
then pushed her over the edge into the river.

What ideas, emotions, and esthetic appreciations entered into your response to "Traveling Through the Dark"? Did you recall similar experiences you have had? Could you visualize the narrow road, the canyon, and the deer? Did you respond emotionally to the situation? Whatever the details of your responses, they constitute for you the meanings of the poem.

Perhaps you will have explicit responses to the following selection because you will draw upon your years of experience in school. You, too, have known high school study halls, assignments in math, the stories by Poe, and perhaps have worked on the high school paper. You have known busy janitors, weary teachers, and "emptyheaded" pupils. If you engaged in the activity program that kept you around after the less involved members of the student body had gone, you have known the noises and silences of a nearly deserted school building. As you read, you will use your experiences, and they will help to determine the meanings you find.

## *from* A SENSE OF SHELTER

JOHN UPDIKE

The study hall was a huge low room in the basement of the building; its coziness crept into Tartarus. On the other side of the fudge-colored wall the circular saw in the woodworking shop whined and gasped and then whined again; it bit off pieces of wood with a rising, somehow terrorized inflection—*bzzzzzp!* He solved ten problems in trigonometry. His mind cut nearly through their knots and separated them, neat stiff squares of answer, one by one from the long but finite plank of problems that connected Plane Geometry with Solid. Lastly, as the snow on a ragged slant drifted down into the cement pits outside the steel-mullioned windows, he read a short story by Edgar Allan Poe. He closed the book softly on the pleasing sonority of its final note of horror, gazed at the red, wet, menthol-scented inner membrane of Judy Whipple's yawn, rimmed with flaking pink lipstick, and yielded his conscience to the snug sense of his work done, of the snow falling, of the warm minutes that walked through their shelter so slowly. The perforated acoustic tiling above his head seemed the lining of a long tube that would go all the way: high school merging into college, college into graduate school, graduate school into teaching at a college—section man, assistant, associate, *full* professor, possessor of a dozen languages and a thousand books, a man brilliant in his forties, wise in his fifties, renowned in his sixties, revered in his seventies, and then retired, sitting in the study lined with acoustical books until the time came for the last transition from silence to silence, and he would die, like Tennyson, with a copy of *Cymbeline* beside him on the moon-drenched bed.

After school he had to go to Room 101 and cut a sports cartoon into a stencil for the school paper. He liked the building best when it was nearly empty, when the casual residents—the real commuters, the do-nothings, the trash—had cleared out. Then the janitors went down the halls sowing seeds of red wax and making an immaculate harvest with broad brooms, gathering all the fluff and hairpins and wrappers and powder that the animals had dropped that day. The basketball team thumped in the hollow gymnasium; the cheerleaders rehearsed behind drawn curtains on the stage. In Room 101 two empty-headed typists with stripes bleached into their hair banged away between giggles and mistakes. At her desk Mrs. Gregory, the faculty sponsor, wearily passed her pencil through misspelled news copy on tablet paper. William took the shadow box from the top of the filing cabinet and the styluses and little square plastic shading screens from their drawer and the stencil from the closet where the typed stencils hung, like fragile scarves, on hooks. B-BALLERS BOW, 57–42, was the headline. He drew a tall b-baller bowing to a stumpy pagan idol, labelled "W" for victorious Weiserton High, and traced it in the soft blue wax with the fine loop stylus. His careful breath grazed his knuckles. His eyebrows frowned while his heart bobbed happily on the giddy prattle of the typists. The shadow box was simply a black frame holding a pane of glass and lifted at one end by two legs so the light bulb, fitted in a tiny tray, could slide under; it was like a primitive lean-to sheltering a fire. As he worked, his eyes smarting, he mixed himself up with the light bulb, felt himself burning under a slanting roof upon which a huge hand scratched. The glass grew hot; the danger in the job was pulling the softened wax with your damp hand, distorting or tearing the typed letters. Sometimes the center of an o stuck to your skin like a bit of blue confetti. But he was expert and cautious. He returned the things to their places feeling airily tall, heightened by Mrs Gregory's appreciation, which she expressed by keeping her back turned, in effect stating that other staff members were undependable but William did not need to be watched.

In the hall outside Room 101 only the shouts of a basketball scrimmage reverberated; the chant of the cheerleaders had been silenced. Though he had done everything, he felt reluctant to leave.

## CAN LANGUAGE POSSESS "ABSOLUTE" MEANING?

If you will compare your responses to the Stafford and Updike selections just quoted with the responses others had, you will surely find that the same language evoked a considerable range of meanings. From all the possible intellectual, emotional, and esthetic responses that might be made to these or other works of literature, how can we select those combinations of meaning that fulfill the author's intent?

If it were possible to find a set of language symbols with clear, specific, unquestionable meanings, our task would be much easier. In the Stafford and Updike selections is there any segment that has such absolute meaning? We can simplify this profound question by applying it to a short sentence:

I am going to Chicago.

Does it not have a clear, definite, unquestionable meaning? Is it not an example of the expression of an absolute meaning? Apparently so, for the words are in normal order and among the simplest and most easily recognized in English. A readily understood definition of each may be easily found. Surely it therefore follows that we know positively the meaning of that sentence. Suppose, however, that you read it aloud just to make sure: " I am going to Chicago. "

If you understood the meaning to be simply that you are going to Chicago and not anywhere else, you emphasized the single word "Chicago" by raising the pitch, increasing the loudness, and extending the duration on that word alone. If you have great enthusiasm because you are going to that particular city, your vocal emphasis was probably greater and your face probably revealed pleasure. If you understood the meaning to be that you, and no one else, are going, you undoubtedly emphasized the word " I " vocally and perhaps also visibly. A strong sense that you are going to Chicago and no one is going to stop you, would result in emphasis on " am." A special sense of being on your way, as opposed merely to an expression of intent, might be communicated by emphasizing the word " going." The idea that you are going to Chicago rather than coming away from there would call for an emphasis on the preposition " to ".

The meaning that might at first have appeared to be absolute and quite simple has become five different possibilities. As a matter of fact, there are many more possible meanings in that sentence. For example, any two or more of those mentioned above can be combined: "I *am* going to *Chicago.*" Try others yourself.

Thus far we have spoken of different meanings that ca. be expressed by means of three speech variables: pitch, loudness, and duration. Other variables, rate and quality, enable us to communicate additional meanings. If you lack enthusiasm for going to Chicago, you will probably utter the sentence quite slowly. On the other hand, a great deal of enthusiasm for going will perhaps prompt you to employ a distinctive vocal quality.

We can imagine that if your enthusiasm for going were just about as great as it could possibly be, your vocal utterance would be accompanied by visible signals as well: a broad grin, clapping hands, raised eyebrows—your whole being would express your pleasure. The meaning might even include the direction to Chicago, and so you might point.

Theoretically, we could go on indefinitely demonstrating the different meanings and the ways in which they could be expressed. Furthermore, we could do the same with any word, sentence, paragraph, story, or poem. " Yes " can mean almost anything from a positive affirmation to an inquiry. It can even mean " No." Experiment a bit to see how many different meanings you can find and then communicate with " Yes ".

Is there, then, no definite, clear, absolute meaning? Cannot words on a page say this and only this, no more and no less? To put it a little more academically, can words or phrases ever be completely *denotative* or literal rather than *connotative* in their meanings? What does the word *rose* mean to you? The dictionary defines the noun form alone in six different ways, from a sixty-four-word definition of the flower to a much shorter one of the nautical compass card called a rose. It defines a rose as " a perforated nozzle for delivering water in fine jets." A rose is also " a form in which diamonds and other gems are cut." Even the words of these definitions are only symbols. Words that define words are symbols and must in turn be defined with word symbols. The process goes on interminably. Thus there is really so much chance for misinterpretation that it is a wonder that we ever understand anything that anyone ever says! Any definition can only approximate that concept of a rose that you have in your mind and that you have acquired and retained in terms of your *senses* as they have been involved in experiences. To you the word symbol " rose " may mean the red roses on Grandmother's casket or the yellow ones that Dad loves. To someone else " rose " may call to mind the rose thorns he got in his hands as a youngster. Others may be reminded of the pink roses in a special corsage. The ex-service man may think of the compass card he used in the Navy. To more than a few people "rose" means rose-fever sniffles and sneezes. You cannot say that "a rose is a rose," for to each person it means something different.

In a military or industrial order for material or in a legal document, great effort is made to employ language symbols that cannot be misinterpreted. Qualifying phrases and detailed definitions mount into long paragraphs in the interest of accuracy of meaning, as the following paragraph demonstrates.

If any premium or installment of premium be not paid as herein provided, and if there be at the expiration of the time herein provided for such payment accumulated cash dividends credited on account of this Policy at least equal to the payment required, then said payment shall be made by the application of an equal amount of such credit, or if such credit be less than the required payment then out of such credit, if sufficient, shall be paid a semiannual or quarterly installment of the annual premium. If such credit shall not be sufficient to pay a quarterly installment of the annual premium, this paragraph shall not apply.

The fact that misinterpretations still occur with disturbing frequency, even when such paragraphs are written, is evidence enough that most words abound with meanings. Insurance companies employ banks of lawyers to protect their *own interpretations* of their policies. Many a lawsuit is concerned with that very matter.

Perhaps words are never purely literal or objective designations of demonstrable realities. Certainly this is true when words attempt to represent " what goes on inside the skin "[2] of the speaker or writer, for he alone can be directly acquainted with the so-called " territory " of reality to which his words refer. From the cry and gurgle of the infant, whose vocalization surely represents some state of reality inside himself, to the sophisticated utterances of poets and philosophers, whose words again stand for attitudes and convictions inside themselves, there are obviously communicative efforts that can never be said to have denotative meanings. In much the same sense, all meanings are connotative. Any given term is not so much a symbol for an objective reality as it is a symbol for that reality *as the speaker or writer perceives it.* We must, therefore, conclude that seldom, if ever, may an absolute meaning be ascribed to any word.

[2] Irving J. Lee, *Language Habits in Human Affairs* (New York: Harper & Row, Publishers, 1941), p. 144.

## RELATIONSHIP OF EXPERIENCE TO MEANING

Experience plays a vital role in the choice of meaning. Here is a portion of a letter:

Dad is better every day. He has been helping Helen elevate corn and is so happy that he can do it. Helen brings the corn in from the field. Her foot still bothers, especially at night, but nothing serious.

I went to a tea yesterday afternoon at Anna Hessler's church in Galesburg. Six of us neighbors went, and we rode with Marie Swanson. It was a Swedish affair—"a little bit of Sweden." I'd rather have stayed home but couldn't let Anna down.

Frost again last night and 25 this morning. Have you had snow yet?

In all probability it means very little to you. Perhaps there are terms in the letter for which you have no personal- or vicarious-experience references at all. If, however, you had known " Dad "—his character, his appearance, his age, the sound of his voice—and the pathetic story of his many illnesses, you could read the letter more intelligently. If you had painted and used that corn elevator or a similar one, or even if you had only seen one used, you would know what the story is about. Apparently, Helen's foot has been injured. How? What is the story? Knowing it would make you a more appreciative reader. If you had ever been a part of that rural community, you could better appreciate its neighborly relations. If you knew Mother, who wrote the letter, you would understand why she says, " I'd rather have stayed home." Is she bored with her neighbors or does she simply love her home and want to participate in its every activity? Finally, suppose that you knew the thermometer on the front porch and remembered the biting chill of twenty-five degrees on a fall day in northern Illinois. Surely if you had had all these experiences, you could draw at will upon your experiences as you read the letter, making its words literally come alive, and you could approach an understanding of what the word symbols meant as Mother wrote them.

We suggest that you press this point further. Read the lyric poem " Barter " by Sara Teasdale in Chapter 5. It will be most meaningful to you if you can draw upon a well-stocked memory of lovely impressions: leaping, sizzling flames of a campfire in the night, blue waves churned white against a cliff, the gentle wonder of a little child's face, and the firm grip of loving arms. " Old Women " by Babette Deutsch may be most truly poignant if you have seen your own sick mother's hands fumble helplessly at the sheets where once she knew romance with her husband and expectant joy at the birth of her child. You will find the reality only in terms of sensations, thoughts, and emotions you have previously known. Read Martin Luther King's classic address entitled " I Have a Dream " and discover that the depth of your response is directly proportional to your relevant experiences. If you are black or if you have identified yourself with the black dream of freedom, you will certainly find the speech profoundly inspiring.

But, you say, "Barter," "Old Women," and "I Have a Dream" are charged with emotions. Surely the more prosaic forms of composition make no such requirements of the reader. Might not I pick up a piece of writing that you would not call "literature" at all and read it with understanding without all of this reference to previous experience? Suppose we find out. The following is an exact quotation from a booklet on the operation of a household refrigerator. Notice the words we have italicized and ask yourself whether this paragraph would be meaningful to you without the experiences they inevitably call to mind.

*Wash* the *exterior* with a *clean cloth* and *water*. *Soap* will *discolor* and *scouring powders* eventually *cut* the *gloss*. *Polish* with a good *wax base polish*. Wash the *interior, ice trays, shelves,* and *freezing unit* with a *lukewarm baking soda solution*. Never use *hot water* on any part of the *refrigerator*. *Ice trays* have a treated surface (to aid in *removing cubes*) which will be destroyed by hot water, soap, or *scouring powders*.

If each of these italicized words calls to mind a clear memory of an experience, even these instructions become far more understandable. Does not the reference to removing ice cubes call up the sensations of an experience? Actually the simplest word is definable only in terms of some kind of experience. The words themselves are only symbols for experience. Without experiences, full appreciation—yes, even simple understanding—is impossible. Understanding of all meaning centers in the experiences that have created the personality of the reader. The psychologist would say that such understanding is *egocentric*.

## THE KEY TO UNDERSTANDING

The one great key to the understanding and appreciation of literature is this: We respond in terms of our personal and our secondhand experiences. Rarely, if ever, do we respond (think or feel) outside these experiences.

Our comprehension of the thought and the emotion of a piece of literature exists in terms of our direct experience: what we have actually done, felt, and thought. Or in terms of our indirect experience: what we have participated in vicariously through the medium of listening to and watching others, reading what others have written, listening to the radio and recordings, watching television, movies, and plays. Understanding that all meaning is egocentric is the key to the appreciation of literature and to that of all the other arts as well.

Our fullest thinking is what employs most intensely the most experience. If you and several other students have recently endured the rigors of registration in a college or university, you will certainly be able to sit down together and decide on improvements you would like to see made in this traditional headache of higher education. Your registrar and the registration officers could also think about their job—perhaps more fully than you, because they have had even more experiences with it. The most adequate thinking about the problems of living in a dormitory or fraternity house is likely to occur in those who have had and can vividly recall such experiences.

Some persons, however, can employ vicarious experiences more vividly than others can employ personal ones. Often, we who have had many vicarious experiences and have learned to marshal them at will, can find more pleasure in a piece of literature than can another person who has had direct personal experience with the people, places, events, and ideas involved. Your appreciation of *A Gift of Joy* by Helen Hayes may be greater than that of most readers if your knowledge of theater is greater than theirs. Your responses to *A Canticle for Leibowitz* by Walter M. Miller, Jr., may be more vivid and disturbing if in preparation for reading that novel you take time to meditate upon the horrifying possibilities of nuclear war.

All of us can and do combine our personal experiences with the second-hand ones. Unconsciously we weave a fabric of the two, so that the glowing colors of the genuine are interwoven with the more elusive and subtle hues of the vicarious. Suppose you have occasion to read the following lines from " The Man with the Hoe " by Edwin Markham:

Bowed by the weight of centuries he leans
Upon his hoe and gazes on the ground,
The emptiness of ages is in his face,
And on his back the burden of the world.

The meaning of the lines will involve your own image of the poor and repressed you may have known, your thoughts and feelings when you saw Millet's famous painting of the same name, and also your vicarious knowledge of the poverty, hunger, ignorance, and hopelessness that still exist in the world. Suppose you read " Owners and Tenants " from Steinbeck's *The Grapes of Wrath* at the end of the next chapter. Your response to that selection will be implemented, colored, and enhanced by knowledge of some other such things you have read, including Goldsmith's " The Deserted Village," particularly such lines as these:

Ill fares the land, to hastening ills a prey,
Where wealth accumulates, and men decay;

Your imagination will combine images from eighteenth-century literature, knowledge of depression and dust-bowl days in America, and whatever additional meaningful experiences you may have accumulated, be they personal or vicarious. Or, again let us suppose, that perhaps you are reading a biography of Albert Schweitzer. If you had previously read " The Deserted Village," you would have had vicarious experience with the " village preacher ":

A man he was to all the country dear,
And passing rich with forty pounds a year;

.    .    .

More skill'd to raise the wretched than to rise.

.    .    .

. . . to relieve the wretched was his pride
And even his failings lean'd to Virtue's side;
But in his duty prompt at every call,
He watched and wept, he prayed and felt for all.

Henceforth you will take with you this preacher and your own personal acquaintance with gentle, unassuming, charitable people as you read. Then, someday when you read of St. Francis of Assisi, these experiences will enhance your responses to the stories of him. All of them will go with you again. We weave together the personal and the vicarious, the literal and the imaginative.

## IMPLICATIONS

The egocentric nature of meaning also provides an effective clue to the quality of literature. That literature is best that most effectively suggests the significant details to the reader. It challenges him to interpret egocentrically. The role of good literature is the achievement of vital experiences for the reader. Literature even provides so-called new experiences: You are invited to climb Mt. Everest with Hillary or stop with Frost by a wood on a snowy evening. You are enabled to share in the thoughts and emotions of countless writers who have spoken to us throughout history from all the world's cultures. These literary excursions into different worlds are made possible, however, only as you draw on the personal and vicarious experiences you have already had. Just as a child learns that a mountain (which he has never seen) is a high hill (which he *has* seen), so we all have new experiences in terms of the old. The challenge of good literature is the challenge to respond to it.

# READER'S FREEDOM

Are you as the oral interpreter entitled to pick *any* of your responses to the literature as they are made possible by your personal and vicarious experiences and then try to convey those meanings to your audience? Theoretically, yes. You are free to choose, and your integrated response *is* the meaning. You should strive to fuse all that you are with all that the literature can be. The exercise of this freedom; the integration of intellectual, emotional, and esthetic responses; the energetic and unrestricted pursuit of meanings: these are the challenges of oral interpretation.

Naturally, all of us are capable of choosing and expressing meanings only in terms of our own abilities and experiences, personal and vicarious. In a single reading, we cannot hope to capture all the possible meanings in a work of literature. But, as we energetically seek out meanings that are available to us, we can expect to discover and communicate meanings that will be new to our audience.

# READER'S RESPONSIBILITIES

Having observed that there is no absolute meaning inherent in language, that response to language symbols is egocentric, and that the reader is free to choose and express meanings in terms of his abilities and experiences, we now examine the responsibilities of the reader. The definition of interpretative reading that we derived in Chapter 1 suggests the broad range of such responsibility:

| *Interpretation is* | *The interpreter is expected to* |
|---|---|
| the communication | —be communicative |
| of the reader's experience | —achieve personal understanding |
| of the author's | —preserve authorial intent |
| ideas and feelings | —integrate intellectual and emotional responses |
| to the eyes and ears | —respond vocally and physically |
| of an audience, | —involve the listeners |
| so that both the reader and the audience experience | —elicit empathic involvement |
| and appreciate | —elicit total understanding |
| the author's literary creation | —preserve and cultivate literary art |

These responsibilities should in no way curtail the extent of the interpreter's freedom, but they do define the boundaries in which the search for meaning must be conducted.

Anyone who practices the speech skills is responsible for their honest use. Any public speaker ought to be responsible for the validity of the response he elicits from his hearers. Any good training in public speaking emphasizes the necessity for reliability in the speaker. In like manner, you the interpreter must also be a responsible moral agent. You must respond to language symbols with integrity.

The complexities of creativity and imagination render it impossible for us to select any one set of meanings as " right " and all others as " wrong." We can, however, discern relative degrees of accuracy, precision, consistency, and fullness. Assessment of an author's probable intentions and recollection of personal experiences provide important foundations for developing justifiable interpretations, but these are not blueprints for success. Interpreters must rigorously analyze literature, and sensitively involve themselves in the experiences it presents, in order to achieve performances that satisfactorily fulfill its potential for expressing meaning.

An author may sometimes write lines in which he has apparently implied several different meanings. Much of this multiplicity of meaning results from the conscious intentions of the author, but writers may also say more than they intend—more, indeed, than they are aware of. Authorial intent, then, is not a wholly reliable or complete guide to meaning in literature. It is, for writer and interpreter alike, a starting point: it points the way toward meaning in literature, but it does not insure arrival at the destination.

Just as your assessment of an author's intent is important to your discovery of meaning, your own actual and vicarious experiences are vital inroads to literature. The experience in a work, however, will never be identical to your own. All too often, interpreters force the literature to fit within their personal backgrounds, attitudes, and beliefs. In so doing, they deny themselves the opportunity to explore new ways of thinking and feeling. The literature, then, offers a convenient mirror to their previous experiences, but it cannot become a lamp that lights the way to new realms of understanding.

Like the artist, you create truth as you see it. To discover the " truth " of a literary work, you begin by considering your own experiences and the probable intentions of the author. As you move closer to performance, then, you must be prepared to exclude yourself and your knowledge of the author, so that the meanings in the literature come through. Use your background and personality to understand and communicate the literature, but never use the literature to display your background and personality. Consider the author's intentions, but do not allow yourself to be limited by these assumptions.

## EXERCISES

1. Practice reading aloud the following sentences to see how many different meanings you can convey with each.

Do you hate me?
I love you.
Look at the beautiful girl.
I shall speak when I am ready.
Professor Thompson's examinations are easier to understand than his lectures.
No, I don't think so.

2. Bring to class all or part of a personal letter with which you can demonstrate how your own experiences enhance appreciation of meaning.

3. Do the same with a poem.

4. Using a musical composition or a painting, demonstrate that here, too, appreciation of meaning is egocentric. This is a rewarding experience.

5. Have a friend respond to the following words and describe what each calls to mind.

| | | | | |
|---|---|---|---|---|
| puke | crimson | candidate | drink | belly |
| doctor | tobacco | oratory | vault | guts |
| brotherhood | prayer | flower | graft | cute |
| chalice | war | bomb | work | bitch |

Now find dictionary definitions of the words and prepare to illustrate for the class the differences between denotation and connotation. You will need to make a note of each response and each definition.

6. Make a serious attempt to find or write a paragraph in which the meaning or meanings will be absolute. You can achieve only very limited success in the attempt, but do your best. Be prepared to measure your success by asking the members of the class to interpret the paragraph for you.

7. Both of the following two passages describe features of landscapes familiar to their authors. The first might be set in virtually any town in the United States, and the second is set in Russia, perhaps a century ago. Can you respond fully to both by drawing on your personal experiences? Probably, you will have to look up the meaning of "eschatological." And, we presume that a name like "Mironositzkoe" could not be pronounced easily. Does the appearance of unfamiliar words and places restrict your response?

## *from* PACKED DIRT, CHURCHGOING, A DYING CAT, A TRADED CAR

JOHN UPDIKE

Different things move us. I, David Kern, am always affected—reassured, nostalgically pleased, even, as a member of my animal species, made proud—by the sight of bare earth that has been smoothed and packed firm by the passage of human feet. Such spots abound in small towns: the furtive break in the playground fence dignified into a thoroughfare, the trough of dust underneath each swing, the blurred path worn across a wedge of grass, the anonymous little mound or embankment polished by play and strewn with pebbles like the confetti aftermath of a wedding. Such unconsciously humanized intervals of clay, too humble and common even to have a name, remind me of my childhood, when one communes with dirt down among the legs, as it were, of presiding fatherly presences. The earth is our playmate then, and the call to supper has a piercingly sweet eschatological ring.

## *from* GOOSEBERRIES

ANTON CHEKHOV

The sky had been overcast since early morning; it was a still day, not hot, but tedious, as it usually is when the weather is gray and dull, when clouds have been hanging over the fields for a long time, and you wait for the rain that does not come. Ivan Ivanych, a veterinary, and Burkin, a high school teacher, were already tired with walking, and the plain seemed endless to them. Far ahead were the scarcely visible windmills of the village of Mironositzkoe; to the right lay a range of hills that disappeared in the distance beyond the village, and both of them knew that over there were the river, and fields, green willows, homesteads, and if you stood on one of the hills, you could see from there another vast plain, telegraph poles, and a train that from afar looked like a caterpillar crawling, and in clear weather you could even see the town. Now, when it was still and when nature seemed mild and pensive, Ivan Ivanych and Burkin were filled with love for this plain, and both of them thought what a beautiful land it was.

8. Can you recall a moment in your childhood that made so lasting and stark an impression as the incident recounted in the following poem?

## INCIDENT

COUNTEE CULLEN

Once riding in old Baltimore,
  Heart-filled, head-filled with glee,

I saw a Baltimorean
  Keep looking straight at me.

Now I was eight and very small,
  And he was no whit bigger,
And so I smiled, but he poked out
  His tongue, and called me "Nigger."

I saw the whole of Baltimore
  From May until December;
Of all the things that happened there
  That's all that I remember.

9. What is the attitude in the following poem? Fond reminiscence? Recollection of terror? How might the feelings you have toward your own father influence your response?

## MY PAPA'S WALTZ

### THEODORE ROETHKE

The whiskey on your breath
Could make a small boy dizzy;
But I hung on like death:
Such waltzing was not easy.

We romped until the pans
Slid from the kitchen shelf;
My mother's countenance
Could not unfrown itself.

The hand that held my wrist
Was battered on one knuckle;
At every step you missed
My right ear scraped a buckle.

You beat time on my head
With a palm caked hard by dirt,
Then waltzed me off to bed
Still clinging to your shirt.

10. What experiences would you have to have had in order to respond intensely to the following selection?

## *from* THE BABY PARTY

F. SCOTT FITZGERALD

He was in a good humor today—all the things in his life were going better than they had ever gone before. When he got off the train at his station he shook his head at an importunate taxi man, and began to walk up the long hill toward his house through the crisp December twilight. It was only six o'clock but the moon was out, shining with proud brilliance on the thin sugary snow that lay over the lawns.

As he walked along drawing his lungs full of cold air his happiness increased, and the idea of a baby party appealed to him more and more. He began to wonder how Ede compared to other children of her own age, and if the pink dress she was to wear was something radical and mature. Increasing his gait he came in sight of his own house, where the lights of a defunct Christmas tree still blossomed in the window, but he continued on past the walk. The party was at the Markeys' next door.

As he mounted the brick step and rang the bell he became aware of voices inside, and he was glad he was not too late. Then he raised his head and listened—the voices were not children's voices, but they were loud and pitched high with anger; there were at least three of them and one, which rose as he listened to a hysterical sob, he recognized immediately as his wife's.

"There's been some trouble," he thought quickly.

Trying the door, he found it unlocked and pushed it open.

The baby party began at half past four, but Edith Andros, calculating shrewdly that the new dress would stand out more sensationally against vestments already rumpled, planned the arrival of herself and little Ede for five. When they appeared it was already a flourishing affair. Four baby girls and nine baby boys, each one curled and washed and dressed with all the care of a proud and jealous heart, were dancing to the music of a phonograph. Never more than two or three were dancing at once, but as all were continually in motion running to and from their mothers for encouragement, the general effect was the same.

As Edith and her daughter entered, the music was temporarily drowned out by a sustained chorus, consisting largely of the word *cute* and directed toward little Ede, who stood looking timidly about and fingering the edges of her pink dress. She was not kissed—this is the sanitary age—but she was passed along a row of mamas each one of whom said "cu-u-ute" to her and held her pink little hand before passing her on to the next. After some encouragement and a few mild pushes she was absorbed into the dance, and became an active member of the party.

Edith stood near the door talking to Mrs. Markey, and keeping one eye on the tiny figure in the pink dress. She did not care for Mrs. Markey; she considered her both snippy and common, but John and Joe Markey were congenial and went in together on the commuting train every morning, so the two women kept up an elaborate pretense of warm amity. They were always reproaching each other for "not coming to see me," and they were always planning the kind of parties that began with "You'll have to come to dinner with us soon, and we'll go in to the theatre," but never matured further.

"Little Ede looks perfectly darling," said Mrs. Markey, smiling and moistening her lips in a way that Edith found particularly repulsive. "So *grown-up*—I can't *believe* it!"

Edith wondered if "little Ede" referred to the fact that Billy Markey, though several months younger, weighed almost five pounds more. Accepting a cup of tea she took a seat with two other ladies on a divan and launched into the real business of the afternoon, which of course lay in relating the recent accomplishments and insouciances of her child.

# 5　Developing Our Responses to Literature

Armed with the sum of your past experiences and willing to respond fully to intellectual and emotional stimuli, you are ready to begin the analytical process of gaining impressions from the literature you plan to perform. These critical efforts should lead you, ultimately, to a "vivid-realization-of-idea-at-the-moment-of-utterance."[1] In subsequent chapters, we shall explore in depth the physical and vocal means at your disposal to express your responses to ideas and emotions in the literature. For the present, though, we are concerned primarily with the formulation of those responses.

Developing our responses to literature is a highly involved and abstract process. To reduce literary analysis to a formula is to be crudely simplistic, but the need for clarity and the necessity for specific suggestions require us to outline a few possibly helpful procedures. In a hopelessly limited number of pages, we shall try to lead you in the right direction. Our suggestions will not constitute a complete guide to finding meaning in a piece of literature. Nor will they be a one-and-only guide.

This chapter is divided into three areas, each of which, in turn, is subdivided. The areas of literary analysis are expressed as questions. What are the ideas presented in the literature? What are the emotional responses that may be stimulated by the literature? Who are the speakers behind the ideas and emotions in the literature?

Your knowledge of our answers to these questions or even your skill in applying the principles to an examination of a specific selection will *not* guarantee a sensitive response. Nor will you find that every suggestion we make is always necessary in achieving a maximum understanding of what you read. We hope we can be useful in helping you develop your responses to literature, but do not think that finding literary meaning is like following a recipe.

## WHAT ARE THE IDEAS PRESENTED IN THE LITERATURE?

**One.**　When you have chosen material to read aloud, you have probably already completed the first step of analysis, which is a complete reading for

---

[1] Donald C. Bryant and Karl R. Wallace, *Fundamentals of Public Speaking* (4th ed.; New York: Appleton-Century-Crofts, 1969), p. 233.

overall enjoyment, understanding, and appreciation. (If your selection is part of a longer whole, you will almost always find it essential to read the entire piece.)

Let us suppose you have chosen to read the following poem.

## THE GREAT LOVER

RUPERT BROOKE

I have been so great a lover: filled my days
So proudly with the splendor of Love's praise,
The pain, the calm, the astonishment,
Desire illimitable, and still content,
And all dear names men use, to cheat despair,
For the perplexed and viewless stream that bears
Our hearts at random down the dark of life.
Now, ere the unthinking silence on that strife
Steals down, I would cheat drowsy Death so far,
My night shall be remembered for a star
That outshone all the suns of all men's days.
Shall I not crown them with immortal praise
Whom I have loved, who have given me, dared with me
High secrets, and in darkness knelt to see
The inenarrable godhead of delight?
Love is a flame—we have beaconed the world's night;
A city—and we have built it, these and I;
An emperor—we have taught the world to die.
So, for their sakes I loved, ere I go hence,
And the high cause of Love's magnificence,
And to keep loyalties young, I'll write those names
Golden forever, eagles, crying flames,
And set them as a banner, that men may know,
To dare the generations, burn, and blow
Out on the wind of Time, shining and streaming.
These I have loved:
                White plates and cups, clean-gleaming,
Ringed with blue lines; and feathery, faery dust;
Wet roofs, beneath the lamplight; the strong crust
Of friendly bread; and many-tasting food;
Rainbows; and the blue bitter smoke of wood;
And radiant raindrops couching in cool flowers;
And flowers themselves, that sway through sunny hours,
Dreaming of moths that drink them under the moon;
Then, the cool kindliness of sheets, that soon

Smooth away trouble; and the rough male kiss
Of blankets; grainy wood; live hair that is
Shining and free; blue-massing clouds; the keen
Unpassioned beauty of a great machine;
The benison of hot water; furs to touch;
The good smell of old clothes; and other such—
The comfortable smell of friendly fingers,
Hair's fragrance, and the musty reek that lingers
About dead leaves and last year's ferns—
                Dear names,
And thousand others throng to me! Royal flames;
Sweet water's dimpling laugh from tap or spring;
Holes in the ground; and voices that do sing—
Voices in laughter, too; and body's pain,
Soon turned to peace; and the deep-panting train;
Firm sands; the little dulling edge of foam
That browns and dwindles as the wave goes home;
And washen stones, gay for an hour; the cold
Graveness of iron; moist black earthen mold;
Sleep; and high places; footprints in the dew;
And oaks; and brown horse chestnuts, glossy-new;
And new-peeled sticks; and shining pools on grass—
All these have been my loves. And these shall pass.
Whatever passes not, in the great hour,
Not all my passion, all my prayers, have power
To hold them with me through the gate of Death.
They'll play deserter, turn with the traitor breath,
Break the high bond we made, and sell Love's trust
And sacramental covenant to the dust.
—Oh, never a doubt but, somewhere, I shall wake,
And give what's left of love again, and make
New friends, now strangers—
                But the best I've known,
Stays here, and changes, breaks, grows old, is blown
About the winds of the world, and fades from brains
Of living men, and dies.
                Nothing remains.

O dear my loves, O faithless, once again
This one last gift I give: that after men
Shall know, and later lovers, far-removed,
Praise you, "All these were lovely"; say, "He loved."

As a part of your reading for overall enjoyment, understanding. and
appreciation, you ought to discover whatever theme or dominant ideas

you find. That is probably easy to do upon reading " The Great Lover." In the poem the author seems to be expressing his exultation in the thousand details of life, familiar and dear through memory—a zest for living. He wants us to remember him as one who loved the experiences of his senses.

Finding a theme or thesis is, however, not always this easy. Indeed, some poems and many short stories, novels, and plays cannot in fairness be treated this way. In those instances, we suggest you simply try to make sure you grasp an overall impression. Upon doing so, you are ready to proceed to further analysis. If your responses prove sound, you will be able to discover how every aspect of the poem contributes to the whole. Perhaps, the theme or that overall impression you think you have found may be modified as you probe deeper into the selection. The remaining steps will enhance both your understanding and your enjoyment of the selection.

**Two.** The second step is to make sure that you understand the meaning of words as they are used in the selection. Doing this is not usually as simple as it sounds. We find only one really unusual word in " The Great Lover ": *inenarrable* in the fifteenth line means " indescribable." Words need not be long or unfamiliar, however, to be inadequately understood. The very title could be easily misunderstood, for it does not refer as might first be imagined to a famous romantic lover but to one who has an intense affection for the experience of the senses.

Go on through the whole selection to get an accurate and full under- standing of every word employed. Be sure to understand *desire illimitable* (unrestricted wants and curiosity), *perplexed and viewless, random, immortal, godhead* (the dictionary will tell you this means " essence "), *beaconed* (notice how this means more than just " illuminated " and suggests the searching ray of a lighthouse), *many-tasting food* (the meaning here is as broad as your eating experience!), *unpassioned, benison* (here we have not only a synonym for " blessing " but also a suggestion of dignity), *reek, dimpling laugh, deep-panting train* (do you see the comparison with a great dog gasping for its breath?), *browns, dwindles, washen* (do not let a passive present participle floor you!), *deserter,* and *sacramental covenant.* Every word, like the brick in the wall, is a part of the whole.

Did you notice the capitalized words? In this case *Death, Love,* and *Time* were all personifications of those realities. Each was referred to as a personality. Sometimes capitalized words are references and allusions, as in the following quotations:

What was Lincoln's mysterious power, and whence? . . . Inspired, he was truly, as Shakespeare was inspired; as Mozart was inspired; as Burns was inspired; each, like him, sprang directly from the people.

—HENRY WATTERSON, *The Secret of Lincoln's Power*

And yet, in the El Dorado of which I have told you, but fifteen per cent of lands are cultivated.

—HENRY GRADY, *The Race Problem in the South*

We see all around us a terrible alienation of the best and bravest of our young: the very shape of a generation seems turned on its head overnight. Bob Moses Parris is gone, Stokely Carmichael and Rap Brown stand in his place—and beyond them are others more militant, offering dark visions of an apocalyptic future.

—ROBERT F. KENNEDY, *To Seek a Newer World*

## THE WORLD IS TOO MUCH WITH US

WILLIAM WORDSWORTH

The world is too much with us; late and soon,
Getting and spending, we lay waste our powers:
Little we see in Nature that is ours;
We have given our hearts away, a sordid boon!
This Sea that bares her bosom to the moon,
The winds that will be howling at all hours
And are up-gather'd now like sleeping flowers,
For this, for everything, we are out of tune;
It moves us not.—Great God! I'd rather be
A Pagan suckled in a creed outworn,
So might I, standing on this pleasant lea,
Have glimpses that would make me less forlorn;
Have sight of Proteus rising from the sea;
Or hear old Triton blow his wreathed horn.

*Lincoln, Shakespeare, Mozart, Burns, El Dorado, Bob Moses Parris, Stokely Carmichael, Rap Brown, Pagan, Proteus,* and *Triton* are not words to skip; find the background of each, for it is essential. If you have tried to read John Milton's poems such as "L'Allegro," "Il Penseroso," or *Paradise Lost*, you know that you are helpless to understand them until you have studied classic mythology. References and allusions are probably more important in reading Milton than in reading any other English writer, but they must be understood in all reading whether they are emphasized with capital letters or not.

Surely you have noticed by now that in many instances words are not clear if you use only a literal, dictionary definition. These matter-of-fact definitions, which are so often inadequate, we call "denotative meanings." As we learned in Chapter 4, "The Nature of Meaning," the clearest and most important meanings are those that refer to experience. These we call

" connotative meanings." This kind of meaning is demonstrated in Brooke's line from " The Great Lover "—*radiant raindrops couching in cool flowers*— if you have ever seen a great crimson rose with the jewels of a recent rain nestling among its petals. Other brilliant connotations might be found for *grainy wood, live hair, blue-massing clouds,* and *body's pain,* to mention only a few. Eventually all meaning partakes of this connotative quality and is most poignant only when it does. The best words in literature are usually those that tell whole stories in themselves—and personal stories at that.

The meaning of a word in isolation becomes more sharply defined and more potently expressive as that word is placed within the context of a literary work. As an effective interpreter, you must certainly understand and appreciate the interrelationships between words that create rich connotations. But, as you do so, be careful that you do not erroneously assume the meaning of a word solely from its context. What is the meaning of the word *lea* in Wordsworth's sonnet that you just read? Did you assume that it refers to some vantage point overlooking the sea? If so, you missed the full impact of the closing portion of the poem. A lea is a meadow: Wordsworth desires the Pagan imagination to stand on an inland meadow and imagine it to be a sea where he can visualize the Pagan gods rising from the " waves." To appreciate literature fully, you must understand the meanings each word brings to the writing (denotations and possible connotations), as well as the significance each word derives from the context of the surrounding language.

**Three.** Expanding the scope of our analysis from individual words to word groups and thought centers, we examine the cooperative interaction of words to form connected speech. The process involves an understanding of English usage and idiom. It is pursuit of the literal sense.

In responding to the printed page, we cannot be concerned directly and exclusively with individual words. To restrict ourselves to such a word-by-word response is to be like a child first learning to read aloud. He treats each word separately and in exactly the same way: " SEE—THE—CAT.— SEE—THE—CAT—RUN." No one will contend that such reading reveals to the child or his listener an adequate grasp of the sense. The pianist who hits every note with the same force and without attention to timing, or the painter who executes every line with the same width, intensity, and direction will not communicate effectively. When each word stands alone, nothing stands out; nothing seems to be more important than anything else. It takes time for the child reader to learn to group words into thoughts and to master emphasis. Even many adults have not yet learned to do so. For effective oral interpretation, a sense of word groups and thought centers is essential.

A word group, thought unit, or phrase is a segment of language expressing an idea that may be held in the human consciousness indefinitely. The single word *dog* carries a very hazy meaning to most of us. To make the meaning more concrete, other words must actually be used with the word. For example, consider how much more each successive word group means to you.

dog

little dog

little cocker spaniel

the little brown cocker spaniel from across the street

The little brown cocker spaniel from across the street ran up to me.

Each successive word group means more to you than the preceding one because in each case the idea becomes more complete, concrete, and specific. In each successive group you are able to picture the situation more fully. "Dog" cannot be held in mind very long, but "little dog" will remain there a bit longer. "The little brown cocker spaniel from across the street" is quite clear as a descriptive phrase. When you add "ran up to me," you have a complete word group, a complete thought unit.

Single words—out of context—seldom can say enough to constitute thought units. The following poem represents a very unusual instance where every word elicits an independent, vivid response:

## THREE BILLION YEARS PLUS A FEW MINUTES

WILLIAM T. BARRY

ooze
cohesion, opulence
twinges, space, undulations
slithering, boring, hatching, germination
increase, complexity, blooming, coordination, cooperation
predation, parasitism, migration, competition, adaptation, selection
crowding, starvation, disease, populations, diversity, camouflage, mimicry

specialization, reduction, exclusion, conversion, blight, drouth
pressure, defeat, decline, smoke, decimation
explosion, abuse, ignorance, teeming
contamination, residual, choking
silence, stillness
ooze

More often, however, complete and concrete responses are stimulated not by individual words, but by carefully fitted series of words. As an intelligent reader you are usually more concerned with word groups than with separate words. Words, as words, lie inert upon the page. Word groups whine for interpretation.

Apply our definition of a word group—a segment of language expressing an idea that may be held in the human consciousness indefinitely—to the following sentence:

One hot day in December I had been standing perfectly still for a few minutes among the dry weeds when a slight rustling sound came from near my feet, and glancing down I saw the head and neck of a large black serpent moving slowly past me.

—W. H. HUDSON, *Far Away and Long Ago*

The sentence has thirteen possible word groups, some more specific and image-provoking than others: (1) "One hot day" creates an image that we may think about for some time. (2) "In December" is a clear-cut concept. It is not hard to visualize (3) "I had been standing," (4) "perfectly still," (5) "for a few minutes," and (6) "among the dry weeds," as they follow in a logical progression, gradually building a more complete image. The phrase (7) "when a slight rustling sound" adds a new element to the total picture, but it is an element that may be held in the consciousness alone, nevertheless. The same is true of the next phrase, (8) "came from near my feet," as it adds a new idea to the preceding one. (9) "And glancing down" describes a specific act that is easily visualized. The subject and verb (10) "I saw" of the second main clause describe another act that might conceivably stand alone in the consciousness. The longest word group in the sentence is (11) "the head and neck of a large black serpent." When thinking of the serpent, one can easily see in his mind's eye the image of the last two word groups: (12) "moving slowly" and (13) "past me."

Do not assume that an intelligent person would read the sentence as it is divided here. We have merely exhausted all possibilities in this example. Short word groups are often linked together into longer, more meaningful ones, and different readers often link them in different ways.

With slants (/) we have indicated below the word grouping we might actually use in showing the sense of the Hudson quotation as we see it.

One hot day in December / I had been standing perfectly still for a few minutes among the dry weeds / when a slight rustling sound came from near my feet, / and glancing down / I saw the head and neck of a large black serpent / moving slowly past me.

When you have made a careful analysis of the word grouping in any selection, you will have recognized that some groups of words and some single words are more important than others. These we call the *thought centers.* They carry the burden of the sense and they stand out from the rest. Identification of the thought centers allows you to focus on the key ingredients of the author's message. The words of each thought unit cluster about the center to form a unified, completed idea. Thus, the thought center exists as the nucleus of the word group.

In the following selection we have separated word groups with slants (/), and we have italicized the thought centers. You will probably sometimes disagree with our choice of groups and centers. If this proves to be the case, do not be disturbed, for grouping and centering are, within limits, individual matters, permitting much variety of response among different readers.

## THE UNKNOWN CITIZEN
### (To JS/07/M/378 This Marble Monument Is Erected by the State)

W. H. AUDEN

He was found by the *Bureau of Statistics* to be
One *against* whom there was no *official complaint*, /
And all the reports on his *conduct* agree
That, in the *modern* sense of an *old-fashioned* word, / he was a *saint*, /
For in *everything* he did / he *served* the *Greater Community*./
Except for the *War* / till the day he *retired* /
He worked in a *factory* and never got *fired*, /
But *satisfied* his *employers*, / *Fudge Motors Inc.* /
Yet he wasn't a *scab* / or *odd* in his *views*, /
For his *Union* reports that he paid his *dues*, /
(Our report on his *Union* shows it was *sound*) /
And our *Social Psychology* workers found
That he was *popular* with his *mates* / and liked a *drink*. /
The *Press* are convinced that he *bought* a paper *every* day /
And that his *reactions* to *advertisements* were *normal* in every way. /
*Policies* taken out in his *name* prove that he was *fully insured*, /
And his *Health-card* shows he was *once* in hospital / but left it *cured*. /
Both *Producers Research* and *High-Grade Living* declare
He was *fully* sensible to the *advantages* of the *Installment Plan* /
And had *everything necessary* to the *Modern* Man, /
A *phonograph*, / a *radio*, / a *car* / and a *frigidaire*. /
Our researchers into *Public Opinion* are content
That he held the *proper opinions* for the *time* of *year*; /
When there was *peace*, / he was *for* peace; / when there was *war*, /
    he *went*. /
He was *married* / and added *five children* to the population, /
Which our *Eugenist* says was the *right* number for a parent of his *generation*, /
And our *teachers* report that he never *interfered* with *their* education. /
Was he *free*? / Was he *happy*? / The question is *absurd*: /
Had anything been *wrong*, / we should *certainly* have *heard*.

Recognizing word grouping and discovering thought centers are extremely important in finding the meaning of any writing, especially more involved selections. If you master the process now, you will be ready for succeeding chapters in which you will employ the elements of voice to communicate the grouping and the centering to your listeners.

**Four.** Related to and going beyond the analysis of thought groups and centers is the study of emphasis and subordination. Within thought groups are words of varying significance. Some are essential to the meaning; others are only connective tissue.

In conversation, awareness of these factors is no problem at all. Seldom, if ever, do you think consciously of which words to emphasize or de-emphasize. Emphasis is a physical expression of mental activity. When the mind centers on or subordinates the idea expressd by a word, the physical result—audible and visible—is emphasis or de-emphasis. In the words of Tin Pan Alley, we all "do what comes naturally" when we speak our own minds. But in the world of the arts, to do what comes naturally is often highly difficult. Actors soon learn that it is hard to seem natural on the stage. To seem natural in oral interpretation is for most of us no less difficult. We shall be quite elementary. What follows is a simple but thorough analysis of emphasis and subordination.

Let us consider a simple declarative sentence:

I am sending Christmas cards and gifts.

We can recognize immediately that the sentence is a single thought group. At no place would the speaker try to divide it into more than one thought.

Which words are important? Which are unimportant? The answers to these questions depend on what the speaker has in mind. But if we assume that the intention is quite simple, we will probably say these words are of greatest importance:

*I am sending Christmas cards and gifts.*

Although "I" is the subject of the sentence and states who is sending the items mentioned, it is surely not intended to be stressed. "Sending" is the important verb, which states the action of the subject. Additional emphasis on this word would be intended if the speaker were indicating that he was "sending" rather than "receiving" gifts. "Christmas" is, of course, a very important adjective, stating the kind of cards and gifts. "Cards" and "gifts" carry the whole point of the sentence.

An adequate response to the sentence requires emphasis on all these words, but surely if the meaning is particularized, one or more of the words is intended to stand out over the rest. It may be any one of them, even the unlikely "I."

Next let us consider the same sentence in regard to the remaining un-important words. " Am " is an auxiliary verb, probably of little importance, unless the speaker were strongly asserting that he *is* sending out the articles, in which case the sense would involve an emphasis on " am ": " I *am* sending. . . ." When the basic verb carries the meaning, as " sending " does here, the role of the auxiliary is minimal: It is contracted with the subject, and so the sense in this instance is " I'm *sending*. . . ." The same principle is illustrated in " and "; the sense is revealed as the phrase is read, *cards 'n' gifts*. When words are emphasized, they retain their distinctive identities; when de-emphasized, their forms differ—often radically—in pronunciation.

Those who habitually read all words with undiscerning stress or those who unstress the important and emphasize the unimportant reveal a basic inadequacy in their own personal response to literature, for the degree of emphasis is inherent in the meaning. Effective audible and visible communi-cation is completely dependent on adequate comprehension of the material read at the moment of utterance. It is thus unrealistic for us to divide our book into processes for getting meaning and processes for expressing meaning. They obviously occur simultaneously! But, we do separate them in some instances and we do so with admitted arbitrariness, for purposes of clarified explanation. In this instance, we refer you to Chapter 8 in which we give additional consideration of the processes of emphasis and sub-ordination as aspects of audible communication.

**Five.**    The next stage of discovering the ideas presented in the literature is to study the organization of the selection. Just as words fit together, with varying degrees of emphasis and subordination, to form word groups, so the individual units of thought combine to compose the organization of the whole. Whether a piece was carefully blueprinted by its author before com-position, as so clearly seems the case with the novels of Thomas Hardy, or whether it was born spontaneously, as Coleridge said happened with " Kubla Khan," all literature worthy of the name does have structure. For example, many poems are as carefully organized as a good speech. The speaker first sets up his purpose and central idea, like the runway of a great bridge, and then he makes sure that every major point in his organization directly supports that idea, like the piling under a bridge.

The following lines from " Create Great Peace," which are part of a longer poem, adhere to a readily recognizable plan: an initial question and answer stating the theme, the need for a " great peace;" then an elaboration of that idea; then a challenge; and finally a look at the prospects if man refuses to devote himself to peace.

## *from* CREATE GREAT PEACE

JAMES OPPENHEIM

Would you end war?
Create great Peace . . .
The Peace that demands all of a man,
His love, his life, his veriest self;
Plunge him in the smelting fires of a work that becomes his child. . . .

Give him a hard Peace: a Peace of discipline and justice. . . .
Kindle him with vision, invite him to joy and adventure:
Set him at work, not to create *things*
But to create *men:*
Yea, himself.

Go search your heart, America. . . .
Turn from the machine to man,
Build, while there is yet time, a creative Peace . . .
While there is yet time! . . .
For if you reject great Peace,
As surely vile living brings disease,
So surely shall your selfishness bring war.

Each successive idea or incident in a literary work builds on what has come before. Events in a story may be related chronologically, or the author may reveal incidents through a series of flashbacks. Sometimes an author will hold back key information from his readers or from a character and then offer a surprise at the end. O. Henry, for instance, was famous for his surprise endings. Look for cause-effect relationships; for important contrasts of idea; for moments of discovery; for conflicts and resolution. In short, uncover the development and explanation of ideas the author has used to make his work known to us, for the structure of the literature determines the structure of the performance.

**Six.** As the final stage of determining what ideas are in the literature, we suggest you write a paraphrase. Doing so is a means of testing your grasp of meaning; of confirming or rejecting your impressions; and insuring your precise comprehension of the sense of the total work. To *paraphrase* is to translate the literature into your own thought processes: You adapt it to your own idiom. Consequently, the good paraphrase avoids the original author's words, although it is written as if he were writing it. Do not use such expressions as "the author says" but try to employ your own clear and original phrasing of *what* he says. In your verbs, use the same person he

uses. Keep as close as possible to the form and tone of the original as you
understand it. Proceed sentence by sentence.

While paraphrasing destroys a work of art with all that form, style, and
sound can offer, the act of trying to put a selection into your own terms
forces precise responses to the printed page. Paraphrasing is somewhat
analogous to the original process of composition in which the author himself
engaged. In that process he was probably concerned simultaneously with
both what he meant and how to say it. We do not contend that if you understand a selection well, you will always be able to express that understanding
in your own words, but we do say that by paraphrasing, you can promote
your own responses to the literature.

While asking you to paraphrase, we must also provide a word of warning.
The best literature is often the hardest to paraphrase. Meaning and form
are not separate entities. Selections of fine poetic quality cannot be adequately
transformed into different words. To paraphrase the Gettysburg Address
by saying, "Eighty-seven years ago our ancestors established in North
America a country that had not existed before," would be to destroy the
dignity, simplicity, and ringing clarity of the original. Paraphrasing is just
as difficult as translating from one language to another, a process in which
exact equivalence is impossible.

If, however, you will regard making a paraphrase as one of several steps
to be pursued in finding ideas in the literature, and if you will always remember that determining fully what a selection means is really an endless
process, the time spent in paraphrasing will be worthwhile. It will promote
your understanding.

You will find that different kinds of literature require different types of
paraphrase. You may wish to use the *condensative* paraphrase, often called
the précis. In most prose materials, such as exposition or narration, you
can boil down the author's language to considerably fewer words. Or, on the
other hand, some works, such as most good verse or terse prose writings, are
already so concise that they cannot be condensed further. In these, the author
has already distilled experience into a very few carefully chosen words. For
such literature you will find that you must write an *expansive* paraphrase
that uses more words than were required by the original author. For example,
it is unlikely that you could rewrite "The World Is Too Much with US" in
fewer than the 118 words that Wordsworth used. In this instance a paraphrase
will undoubtedly be an expansive one, such as the following 189 words:

The activities of every day are excessively important in our lives; constantly
acquiring and expending, we exhaust our resources. Our appreciation of nature
is minimal; we have devoted ourselves to that which is not worthwhile. Our lives
are ugly and wasted! The great sweep of the ocean in the moonlight, the mighty
winds that can break into a roar but are calm and peaceful now like endless
fields of quiet and drowsing flowers, for these and for all the magnificence of

nature we are not receptive; they are not meaningful to us.

Almighty God! I'd rather I were a believer in falsehoods, nurtured from the cradle in archaic conceptions, if by being so, I could from this lovely spot see things that would give me joy and direction—if I could have here a vision of mythical Proteus, the ancient sea-god who could assume different forms, coming up out of the sea; or if I could hear Triton, a classical sea-god too, with the head and trunk of a man and the tail of a fish, blowing his conch-shell trumpet to raise or calm the waves.

Paraphrasing is a self-disciplinary effort to probe for and to conceive meanings, but it is also an appropriate, though limited, test of our own comprehension. By trying to make a paraphrase you test, at least partially, whether you understand the so-called intellectual content, and perhaps you test your comprehension of the emotional content too, although probably to a lesser degree.

Sometimes, of course, the meaning is so clear that to write a paraphrase would be a waste of time. As our experiences with literature increase, this is more often the case. But as literature becomes more obscure, paraphrasing is likely to be an aid to understanding. Remember, though, that the paraphrase always destroys the literary *work*, even as it helps to reveal some of its meanings. The paraphrase diminishes the impact of the literature by denying the contribution of language sound and shape to the total meaning of the piece.

## WHAT ARE THE EMOTIONAL RESPONSES THAT MAY BE STIMULATED BY THE LITERATURE?

Man is inherently and inescapably emotional. Joy and sadness, love and hate, excitement and boredom, pleasure and pain, tranquility and agitation, comedy and tragedy, praise and derision, hope and despair, courage and fear, boldness and caution—these and all the other emotions provide the essential character of living. They pervade the whole of our existence, and they are central to our embodiment of literature.

If we are to make adequate responses to any piece of writing, we must look not only to its logical designations, but also to the emotional responses which it may stimulate. The emotion that resides within ideas and events is equally important to the meaning of literature as is the intellectual sense. In a tense dramatic scene the emotion may seem to virtually jump off the page, while emotion in a philosophical essay may be more subtly hidden between the lines. But, as we discovered in Chapter 4, *some* emotion is always present. Our task is to discover the emotion so that we may emphatically respond to it and stimulate our listeners accordingly. Therefore, we turn to several techniques for enhancing our emotional responses to literature.

**Seven.** Your overall emotional responses to a literary selection are based on its mood or moods. All of us have read stories that made us laugh. We have been excited by a good mystery thriller. Have you ever found yourself sitting nervously on the edge of your seat, perspiring, anxiously reading ahead to find out what fate awaits the hero? Or maybe you have felt like crying while reading about lovers who are forced to separate, or about the death of a character you have come to know and like. The point is that each of us has found himself responsive to some author's effort to communicate mood. It is this responsiveness that we ask you to cultivate and enhance.

An author's effort to create a mood or moods is inseparable from the other aspects of literary skill. Mood is the emotional setting that derives from the ideas and incidents as well as from the language in which they are cast. Poe's familiar poem "The Raven" offers a convenient example of careful language choice and selective content detail that combine to elicit a vivid and consistent mood. The speaker is alone at midnight in a ghostly room with a lamp and dying fire that only partially illuminate the enveloping blackness; in strange and ancient books he has vainly sought relief from bereavement; and then he hears a tapping at the window and is overwhelmed with fear; opening the shutter, he allows a great black and solemn bird to enter; and that unwelcome guest keeps saying just one word, "Nevermore." In describing carefully chosen detail, the author uses terms that provoke vivid imagery, of which more will be said later. Furthermore, he employs words that are rich in inherent color. In the instance of "The Raven," that color is black—black both to the eye and to the spirit. In addition, he chooses his words for their sound values. The accents are long and heavy, the inflections are generally downward, and the sounds themselves are somber. Finally, the author may structure his sentences in patterns appropriate to the mood or moods he wants the reader to feel. In "The Raven" the typical sentence is six long lines, a whole stanza. Furthermore, the sentences make repetitious patterns, and every stanza ends with "more," either in "nothing more" or "nevermore." Thus, Poe carefully chose his content detail, used terms that provoke vivid imagery, employed words rich in inherent color, gave careful attention to sound values, and built his sentences in patterns appropriate to the mood. Although many good writers are less effective than Poe in creating mood, they make use in varying degrees of the same means for doing so.

In "The Raven" there is obviously a single overriding mood. Brooke's "The Great Lover," with its unflinching joy in life, is another instance where one dominant mood prevails. Often, however, the predominant mood may prove elusive. There may be an underlying mood that upon first reading does not seem dominant. You may, for example, miss the underlying mood of "When in Disgrace with Fortune and Men's Eyes" at the end of this chapter because only the last lines express the exultant happiness that is basic to the poem. Upon first reading "Dover Beach" you may have the same experience. The beautiful and romantic setting suggests that the mood is one of basic faith and security, but again the last lines show this conclusion to be incorrect. The effective oral interpreter will always seek to sense the overriding mood of the total selection he is reading, elusive though that mood may be.

Underlying the overall mood of a work, and contributing to it, there will generally be a number of more subtle fluctuations in the emotional climate. Seldom will you find a single mood (for example, humour or seriousness) that pervades the whole selection. The most intense tragedies of Shakespeare have their elements of comic relief, and the funniest modern comedies contain serious or tender moments. You simply have not said enough when you have said that happiness is the mood of "When in Disgrace with Fortune and Men's Eyes." "Dover Beach" cannot be reduced to one continuous mood that persists throughout. Each successive word and idea in a selection advances the establishment of mood, sometimes offering further reinforcement and elaboration; at other times subtly shifting the emotion: and at others, reversing the mood entirely.

Consider the progression of moods in the following selection, where the speaker identifies " seven ages " of life. To perform this selection you would need to read the entire play and, thereby, acquaint yourself with the setting in the forest of Arden; with Jaques, the cynical, melancholy, yet humorous lord who utters this perspective on life; and with the other characters whose views contrast with his. But, reading this segment in isolation, you can still discern a sequence of moods that changes through each of the ages in a person's life.

## *from* AS YOU LIKE IT Act II, Scene VII

### WILLIAM SHAKESPEARE

All the world's a stage,
And all the men and women merely players;
They have their exits and their entrances;
And one man in his time plays many parts,
His acts being seven ages. At first the infant,
Mewling and puking in the nurse's arms;
Then the whining school-boy, with his satchel
And shining morning face, creeping like snail
Unwillingly to school. And then the lover,
Sighing like a furnace, with a woeful ballad
Made to his mistress' eyebrow. Then a soldier,
Full of strange oaths, and bearded like the pard,
Jealous in honour, sudden and quick in quarrel,
Seeking the bubble reputation

Even in the cannon's mouth. And then the justice,
In fair round belly with good capon lin'd,
With eyes severe and beard of formal cut,
Full of wise saws and modern instances;
And so he plays his part. The sixth age shifts
Into the lean and slipper'd pantaloon,
With spectacles on nose and pouch on side;
His youthful hose, well sav'd, a world too wide
For his shrunk shank; and his big manly voice,
Turning again toward childish treble, pipes
And whistles in his sound. Last scene of all,
That ends this strange eventful history,
Is second childishness and mere oblivion;
Sans teeth, sans eyes, sans taste, sans everything.

Barry's poem " Three Billion Years plus a Few Minutes " reflects a similar evolution of mood, as it traces the full cycle of the earth's formation, development, and demise. For any literature you present, you should look not only for the predominant mood but for the minor ones as well. Even the mood of sorrow at a funeral may encompass such a contrasting mood as humor, when persons recall amusing events or quotations of the deceased. A reader's response to complexities of mood often distinguishes vivid and intense interpretation from what is colorless and dull.

Perhaps we can emphasize the importance of mood by giving you a warning. Never assume that there is no mood to communicate. A human being is not thoroughly neutral about anything; if he were, he would be a machine. The most misleading and uninteresting of all oral reading is that in which the reader seems to feel no mood at all and so will let the listener supply his own.

**Eight.** The contemporary poet-critic John Ciardi has written: "It is almost safe to say that a poem is never about what it seems to be about."[2] Poems, however, are not the only writings that employ symbolism. As a matter of fact, all words are symbols, and any employment of words is employment of symbolism. To the literary critic, symbolism is the use of a word, phrase, passage, or entire selection that signifies a reality that in itself also has significance. The thing referred to has meaning beyond itself. Thus, the cross and the outline of a fish may be said to be symbols of Christianity, and weighing scales are a symbol of justice. These are widely known conventional symbols, but writers also use their own private symbols. The complexity of meanings that an expert in language can evoke with rich symbolism is almost miraculous; but even more remarkable than the com-

[2] John Ciardi. " Robert Frost: The Way to the Poem," *The Saturday Review of Literature*, April 12, 1958. p. 13.

plexity is the clarity and precision of communication through symbols. In a symbol there is at once concealment and yet revelation, revelation more vivid than the literal. The challenge to the reader is to penetrate the symbols, to feel and think his way into them, and thus to go beyond the obvious, making as sure as he can that he does not obscure the author's intention. This careful exploration of symbolism is another step in developing your response to the emotional values in literature. The mood that evolves from the literal objects and events in a selection is enhanced and sometimes modified by the added significance of symbolic meanings.

Surely the story of Jonah and the whale has more significance than the mere events of the story. There must be a "moral." Its exact meaning is, of course, subject to the interpretation placed upon it by the individual reader, but one writer has analyzed it this way:

The story is told as if these events had actually happened. However, it is written in symbolic language and all the realistic events described are symbols for the inner experiences of the hero. We find a sequence of symbols which follow one another: going into the ship, going into the ship's belly, falling asleep, being in the ocean, and being in the fish's belly. All these symbols stand for the same inner experience: for a condition of being protected and isolated, of safe withdrawal from communication with other human beings. They represent what could be represented in another symbol, the fetus in the mother's womb. Different as the ship's belly, deep sleep, the ocean, and fish's belly are realistically, they are expressive of the same inner experience, of the blending between protection and isolation.

In the manifest story events happen in space and time: *first*, going into the ship's belly; *then*, falling asleep; *then* being thrown into the ocean; *then*, being swallowed by the fish. One thing happens after the other, and although some events are obviously unrealistic, the story has its own logical consistency in terms of time and space. But if we understand that the writer did not intend to tell us the story of external events, but of the inner experience of a man torn between his conscience and his wish to escape from his inner voice, it becomes clear that his various actions following one after the other express the same mood in him; and that *sequence in time* is expressive of *growing intensity* of the same feeling. In his attempt to escape from his obligation to his fellow men Jonah isolates himself more and more until in the belly of the fish, the protective element has so given way to the imprisoning element that he can stand it no longer and is forced to pray to God to be released from where he had put himself.

—ERICH FROMM, *The Forgotten Language*

Employment of symbolic meanings may range from the extremely simple use of a simile to language structures so abstruse that only the most erudite critics bother to argue their exact meanings. Let us look at four uses of the rose (each in a different poem) as a symbol of woman's beauty. The first use is a simile, a comparison that no one can miss:

## MY LOVE IS LIKE A RED RED ROSE

ROBERT BURNS

My love is like a red red rose
    That's newly sprung in June:
My love is like the melodie
    That's sweetly played in tune.

So fair art thou, my bonnie lass,
    So deep in love am I:
And I will love thee still, my dear,
    Till a' the seas gang dry.

Till a' the seas gang dry, my dear,
    And the rocks melt wi' the sun:
And I will love thee still, my dear,
    While the sands o' life shall run.

And fare thee weel, my only love,
    And fare thee weel awhile!
And I will come again my love,
    Tho' it were ten thousand mile.

A more subtle use of the same symbol is provided in the following poem:

## GO, LOVELY ROSE!

EDMUND WALLER

Go, lovely Rose!
Tell her, that wastes her time and me,
    That now she knows,
When I resemble her to thee,
How sweet and fair she seems to be.

Tell her that's young
And shuns to have her graces spied,
    That hadst thou sprung
In deserts, where no men abide,
Thou must have uncommended died.

Small is the worth
Of beauty from the light retired:
    Bid her come forth,
Suffer herself to be desired,
And not blush so to be admired.

    Then die! that she
The common fate of all things rare
    May read in thee:
How small a part of time they share
That are so wondrous sweet and fair!

Another poet has more briefly made a similar use of the rose:

## PIAZZA PIECE

JOHN CROWE RANSOM

—I am a gentleman in a dustcoat trying
To make you hear. Your ears are soft and small
And listen to an old man not at all;
They want the young men's whispering and sighing.
But see the roses on your trellis dying
And hear the spectral singing of the moon;
For I must have my lovely lady soon.
I am a gentleman in a dustcoat trying.

—I am a lady young in beauty waiting
Until my true love comes, and then we kiss.
But what grey man among the vines is this
Whose words are dry and faint as in a dream?
Back from my trellis, Sir, before I scream!
I am a lady young in beauty waiting.

Here, the rose is not something the lady is "like" but a mirror in which the lady is supposed to see her own beauty. The rose's dying is a symbol of the lady's imminent death. Death (amid other clues of her identity: "dustcoat," "old," "spectral," "grey," "dry," "faint," "dream") awaits her, somewhat impatiently.

Incidentally, you might like to wonder if the old man in the poem is a symbol of death. Perhaps, on the other hand, he could be just what he seems to be: an evil old man trying to seduce the young lady. To interpret the poem, you would have to decide which is the case.

Even more subtle is another poet's use of the worm-eaten rose to symbolize the corruption of physical love:

# THE SICK ROSE

WILLIAM BLAKE

O Rose, thou art sick!
The invisible worm
That flies in the night,
In the howling storm.
Has found out thy bed
Of crimson joy,
And his dark secret love
Does thy life destroy.

Great writers often become much involved with expressing their meanings symbolically, however, and students of literature have to dig deep to perceive their meanings. In the following poem, the writer has given new significance to an old story, which is only partially evident from a first or second reading:

# JOURNEY OF THE MAGI

T. S. ELIOT

"A cold coming we had of it,
Just the worst time of the year
For a journey, and such a long journey:
The ways deep and weather sharp,
The very dead of winter."
And the camels galled, sore-footed, refractory,
Lying down in the melting snow.
There were times we regretted
The summer palaces on slopes, the terraces,
And the silken girls bringing sherbet.
Then the camel men cursing and grumbling
And running away, and wanting their liquor and women,
And the night-fires going out, and the lack of shelters,
And the cities hostile and the towns unfriendly
And the villages dirty and charging high prices:
A hard time we had of it.
At the end we preferred to travel all night,
Sleeping in snatches,
With the voices singing in our ears, saying
That this was all folly.

Then at dawn we came down to a temperate valley,
Wet, below the snow line, smelling vegetation;

With a running stream and a water-mill beating the darkness,
And three trees on the low sky,
And an old white horse galloped away in the meadow.
Then we came to a tavern with vine-leaves over the lintel,
Six hands at an open door dicing for pieces of silver.
And feet kicking the empty wine-skins.
But there was no information, and so we continued
And arrived at evening, not a moment too soon
Finding the place; it was (you may say) satisfactory.

All this was a long time ago, I remember,
And I would do it again, but set down
This set down
This: were we led all that way for
Birth or Death? There was a Birth, certainly,
We had evidence and no doubt. I had seen birth and death,
But had thought they were different; this Birth was
Hard and bitter agony for us, like Death, our death.
We returned to our places, these Kingdoms,
But no longer at ease here, in the old dispensation,
With an alien people clutching their gods.
I should be glad of another death.

Even on the first reading, the perceptive reader will recognize the "three trees on the low sky" as the three crosses on Golgotha and the "pieces of silver" as the currency for which Christ was sold; this should convince the reader that many other items in the poem must also be symbolic. A student of interpretative reading analyzed the second part of this poem as follows:[3]

Then at dawn we came down to a temperate valley,
Wet, below the snow line, smelling vegetation;

Valleys, caves, and other depressions are ancient symbols for woman. This valley has vegetation in it, in other words, life resulting from the woman.

With a running stream—

Water is also an old symbol for woman and also for spiritual rebirth; hence, life. A *running stream* would symbolize the eternal life. This stream would represent Christ, issued from Mary.

[3] The authors extend their appreciation to Mr. Lynn Hagman for permission to use his analysis here.

. . .and a water-mill beating the darkness,

This mill is powered by Christ's promise of everlasting life and is beating at ignorance and evil indicated by *darkness*.

And three trees on the low sky,

This is a grim prophecy of Christ's death. The crosses, themselves, were ancient symbols for trees, which are, in turn, religious symbols, looking upward toward God. The *three trees* might also stand for the Tree of Life, the Tree of Knowledge, and the Tree of Heaven.

An old white horse galloped away in the meadow.

A white horse has long been a symbol associated with a Saviour God. Among many others, Christ has been pictured as riding a white horse. The white horse in this poem is old and is running *away*, probably another prophecy of Christ's death, amidst the symbols of his birth. The end of the poem makes much of the relationship of this Birth and Death, of Death *being* Birth, etc.

Then we came to a tavern with vine-leaves over the lintel,

Ivy also symbolizes eternal life.

Six hands at an open door dicing for pieces of silver,

*Six hands* means that there were three beings. They could be either the Fates or the Christian Trinity. Three is an ancient sacred number. These beings are at an open door, an opening to knowledge, another symbol for Christ. They are gambling for pieces of silver, the currency for which Christ was sold. Perhaps the outcome of this game will decide the fate of Christ.

And feet kicking the empty wine skins.

From Mark 2:22: "And no man putteth new wine into old skins: else the new wine doth burst the skins, and the wine is spilled, and the skins will be marred; but new wine must be put into new skins." Perhaps the empty wine-skins stand for the archaic, rigid customs and laws of ancient Judaism, which were cracked and made useless when the new wine of Christianity was poured into them. After Christ's death, Christianity had apparently died out but it had ruined the old system and left it marred beyond repair. The feet are kicking the old skins, thus demonstrating further contempt for the old dispensation.

Whether the poet would agree with the student's interpretation of his poem, we do not know, but we can see that the student's research in ancient symbols does reveal many interesting insights to this aspect of the poem, and they are seemingly consistent with the Christian theme and apparently with the rest of the poem.

There are many interesting writings in which the pursuit of symbolism is especially rewarding: "The Rime of the Ancient Mariner" by Coleridge, "Stopping by Woods on a Snowy Evening" by Frost, "The Hollow Men" by Eliot, *Mosses from an Old Manse* by Hawthorne, *Moby Dick* by Melville, *The Red Badge of Courage* by Crane, "The Bear" by Faulkner, *Lord of the Flies* by Golding, *Ulysses* by Joyce, *The Grapes of Wrath* by Steinbeck, and *The Cave* by Warren, to mention only a few.

The study of symbolism in literature can be an interesting and highly rewarding pursuit. Although it may become so fascinating that the student attempts to ascribe meanings to "symbols" that do not really exist, to ignore the possibilities for symbolic meanings in literature is folly.

**Nine.** A final aspect of our response to emotion in literature is experiencing images that stimulate our imaginative senses. It is primarily the images in language that vivify and personalize. If it were not for images, we would react to language symbols like a calculating machine in response to figures or like a photoelectric cell in response to a beam of light. Instead, we are forever different from the mechanical device, which retains nothing from experience, for we respond out of the experience of our senses. Images are appeals to the senses which involve us fully in the vibrant "flesh" of the literature. Some of the possibilities of imagery include:

| | | |
|---|---|---|
| sight | touch | balance |
| hearing | thirst | movement |
| smell | pain | hunger |
| taste | temperature | |

Images flash upon our "inward eye" and stimulate our imaginative senses. Can you recall the taste of an onion? Can you re-experience the touch of a dog's silky ear, the odor of rotten eggs, the feeling of oppressive heat on a humid day, or the movement involved in a dance step you know? Can you sense what it is to be smacked in the face with a handful of snow, or run until you gasp for breath, or to lie on your back staring up at the summer sky? If you are like many people, the recollection of chalk squeaking on a blackboard brings on an uncomfortable shudder. All of these sensory combinations are images.

The possible types of imagery expand further as we include the inward senses of our emotions. Can you recall how you felt when humiliated in public, embarrassed by a terrible faux pas, enthralled by a beautiful person, inspired spiritually, musically transported, hopelessly infatuated, bitterly jealous, or meanly envious of another's success? Your re-experience of a specific incident might involve a tightening in the stomach, a dryness in the throat, or a shiver that goes up the spine. Even though the actual stimulus is no longer present, you are able to respond to the feeling it evoked.

We know a successful college student who is blind. He tells us that he can sense the presence of an obstruction before him. He is also able to recreate an image of that sensation, to produce it in his mind when the reality is not present. This is imagery too. Still more possibilities occur as we combine images and translate one into another in a process called *synesthesia*. For example, sight and taste may go together, and one who has smoked excessively says he has a "dark brown taste" in his mouth; or we may say that something "smells hot" when our senses of temperature and smell coalesce. Your experiences with imagery need not be confined to any list.

Literature invites us to participate physically in its imagery, to respond with our senses as well as our minds. For some illustrations of imagery in literature we need look no farther than the classic examples to be found in "The Great Lover." In the middle section of the poem there are about fifty distinct images. The words in parentheses identify them for you. Some of these pictures depend on eye recollections, and so we shall call them sight images. Others are images of hearing, smell, taste, and touch. As you read these lines, concentrate on seeing, smelling, touching, and tasting. Try to recall similar details from your own experience that will help you to sense the imagery of the poem. If you can share the poet's love for life, you will not only understand the poem, but you will be a part of its meanings.

These I have loved:
     White plates and cups, clean-gleaming,
          (sight)
Ringed with blue line; and feathery, faery dust;
  (sight)        (sight and touch)
Wet roofs, beneath the lamp-light; the strong crust
 (sight and touch)   (sight)    (touch)
Of friendly bread; and many tasting food;
         (taste)
Rainbows: and the blue bitter smoke of wood;
 (sight)    (sight)  (smell)
And radiant raindrops couching in cool flowers;
  (sight)      (movement)  (temperature and sight)
And flowers themselves, that sway through sunny hours,
    (sight)        (movement)  (sight and temperature)
Dreaming of moths that drink them under the moon;
     (sight)   (movement)    (sight)

Then, the cool kindliness of sheets, that soon
    (temperature)         (touch)
Smooth away trouble; and the rough male kiss
   (movement)           (touch)
Of blankets; grainy wood; live hair that is
        (touch and sight)    (touch)
Shining and free; blue massing clouds; the keen
  (sight)            (sight)
Unpassioned beauty of a great machine;
        (sight)
The benison of hot water; furs to touch;
    (touch and temperature)   (touch)
The good smell of old clothes; and other such—
    (smell)
The comfortable smell of friendly fingers,
       (smell)
Hair's fragrance, and the musty reek that lingers
    (smell)          (smell)
About dead leaves and last year's ferns—

                Dear names,

And thousand others throng to me! Royal flames;
           (movement)      (sight)
Sweet water's dimpling laugh from tap or spring;
   (taste)     (sight) (hearing)   (sight) (sight)
Holes in the ground; and voices that do sing—
  (sight)             (hearing)
Voices in laughter, too; and body's pain,
   (hearing)          (pain)
Soon turned to peace; and the deep-panting train;
                (hearing)
Firm sands; the little dulling edge of foam
  (touch)          (touch)
That browns and dwindles as the wave goes home.
  (sight)        (sight)       (movement)

  The following lines from " Journey of the Magi " are similarly dense with imagery. A full response to these images incorporates your senses of sight, hearing, smell, touch, temperature, and movement:

Then at dawn we came down to a temperate valley
                   (temperature)
Wet, below the snow line, smelling vegetation:
(touch)              (smell, sight)

With a running stream and a water-mill beating the darkness,
    (sight, movement, hearing)
And three trees on the low sky,
    (sight)
And an old white horse galloped away in the meadow.
      (sight, movement, hearing)

Different selections of literature vary greatly in the amount and vividness of imagery they employ. In " The Unknown Citizen," for instance, the sparse imagery remains rather distant and detached. "Three Billion Years plus a Few Minutes " offers a continuous succession of images, but they are too fleeting and abstract to elicit more than a generalized sensory response. While these authors do not present concrete, vivid images that entice us to linger with our senses, their use of imagery is still vitally important. The coldly removed images of "the Bureau of Statistics," "reports on his conduct," and "the Greater Community " serve well to connote an impersonal, dehumanized state whose citizens are "unknown." And, for a poem where "Three Billion Years plus a Few Minutes" pass by in perhaps a minute or two, a flash of unrelenting, blurred images seems most appropriate.

Imagery is part of meaning, for it is part of your response to language symbols. The difficulty in ascertaining the meaning of language comes from the diversity of images aroused in us according to our various experiences. The image exists only as the reader or listener is able to recall some experience or combination of experiences, either personal or secondhand. Therefore, the images that come to mind will be different from those of someone else. In fact, the image in your mind may or may not be the same as that intended by the author. As we have already observed in talking about your personal role in reading, you should try to reproduce as nearly as possible the author's intention, but the images will always be *your personal* possessions. They will be appealing and vital in proportion to your experience and ability to recall.

## WHO ARE THE SPEAKERS BEHIND THE IDEAS AND EMOTIONS IN THE LITERATURE?

The preceding nine steps of analysis have led us through a study of ideas and emotions in literature. The remaining steps seek to uncover the human personalities that give voice to the intellectual sense and the feelings that are evoked. In any selection, we will be concerned with three speakers: the author (voice *of* the literature), a persona (voice *in* the literature), and an interpreter (performing voice that assimilates characteristics of the persona in order to satisfy the probable intentions of the author).

Before we examine author, persona, and interpreter individually, it may be helpful to clarify the fundamental relationship between the three. Consider who is speaking in the following lines that are taken from a longer poem:

## *from* "SOLILOQUY OF THE SPANISH CLOISTER"

ROBERT BROWNING

Gr-r-r—there go, my heart's abhorrence!
  Water your damned flower-pots, do!
If hate killed men, Brother Lawrence,
  God's blood, would not mine kill you!
What? your myrtle-bush wants trimming?
  Oh, that rose has prior claims—
Needs its leaden vase filled brimming?
  Hell dry you up with its flames!

The author of these lines was Robert Browning, a nineteenth-century poet. He was the speaker *of* the work, the creator of the language. Our allegiance must be toward Browning's intentions, if they are discernible. To do so, however, we must recognize that the persona (the personality actually uttering the imaginative language) is not Browning at all. The persona in this instance is a Spanish friar who is expressing his hatred for Brother Lawrence. To understand what Browning attempted to communicate, we must assimilate the characteristics of the persona he chose for the poem, the fictional voice through which he is speaking.

Next, then, we need to consider the performing voice of the interpreter. As performer of "Soliloquy of the Spanish Cloister," you would need to study the attitudes and feelings of the friar as he vindictively assails his "heart's abhorrence," and you would need also to consider Browning's reasons for presenting this character to us. The best performances occur when the interpreter achieves the author's intent through the persona's voice.

In our example, author and persona are clearly different. This is not always the case, however; authors will frequently appear to speak directly to us in their own voices. Nevertheless, it is useful to make the distinction between the speaker *of* the work and the speaker *in* the work so that we will be receptive to all possibilities that may occur.

**Ten.**  Because literature represents, in some way, an author's response to his environment, information we can gather pertinent to the author's life, his philosophies, his other writings, and the location where he lived may possibly be useful for our understanding of his work. No utterance exists apart from him who made it. There is, you might say, something auto-biographical in even the shortest quotation. Hirsch says we must "posit the author's typical outlook, the typical associations and expectations which form in part the context of his utterance."[4]

Any literary work utilizes personal experience. It may be a literal relation of experience, or it may be a modification. It may involve actual or vicarious experience. It may be a projection from experience. In all cases, it has its roots in the experiences of the author.

Any good encyclopedia or perhaps the introductory commentary in the anthology where the selection is found should be of help. You will find that Rupert Brooke was one of the more promising young English poets in the early part of this century. In college he was known as a brilliant and attractive young man enthralled with the experience of living and dedicated to a career of writing. His teachers expected great things of him; and in 1913 with the publication of his first volume of verse, they proudly saw their hopes being realized. Rupert Brooke would go far. But when Britain declared war, he enlisted at once. He died in 1915 aboard a hospital ship in the Mediterranean Sea. A man, who delighted in life as few men have, gave it up at twenty-eight. His love of this world was never withered by age. In his poetry, he remains an exuberant youth. Now look at " The Great Lover " again in the light of what you know about the man.

Efforts we make to study biographical matters take us outside the literature. We must guard against becoming so fascinated by the incidents of an author's life or philosophy that our primary attention strays from the literature. Aware of this danger, some critics argue that nothing outside the literature itself need be considered. Wordsworth said that if books are good, " they contain within themselves all that is necessary to their being comprehended and relished." Don Geiger writes that " one needs to know nothing of the poet's life to understand the meaning of his poem."[5]

For most works it is entirely possible for you to appreciate the literature while knowing nothing of its creator. Thus far in this text, we have introduced you to a variety of literature without offering any commentary about authorship. We assume you were able to respond to the selections, although knowledge about the authors may, in some cases, have enhanced your appreciation and understanding. Look back to William Stafford's poem "Traveling Through the Dark " and the accompanying biographical insight in Chapter 4. The author's explanation of the background for the poem is helpful, but it cannot replace answers we must receive within the experience of the poem itself.

To some degree, literature will almost always reflect who the author was (or wished to be, or imagined being). The notion we gain of an author from an examination of the literature has been termed the " implied author " by

---

[4] E. D. Hirsch, "Objective Interpretation," in John Oliver Perry (ed.), *Approaches to the Poem* (San Francisco; Chandler Publishing Company, 1965), pp. 100, 101.

[5] Don Geiger, *The Dramatic Impulse in Modern Poetics* (Baton Rouge, La.: Louisiana State University Press, 1967), p. 119.

Wayne C. Booth: "The 'implied author' chooses, consciously or un-consciously, what we read; we infer him as an ideal, literary, created version of the real man; he is the sum of his own choices."[6] Writers reveal quite a lot about themselves by the sort of tale they choose to tell; by the ideas they present; and by the attitudes they adopt. By combining what you are able to discover about an author's life with the image projected through the literature, you should have ample basis for understanding the speaker *of* the work, the controlling voice of the literature.

**Eleven.** The second speaker we are concerned with is the persona, the speaker *in* the literature who imaginatively utters its language. The term *persona* means mask: it is the guise adopted by an author when he chooses to speak in a voice other than his own. As we noted, Browning adopted the persona of a Spanish friar in "Soliloquy of the Spanish Cloister." Other selections we have examined in this chapter also utilize personae that are clearly not the direct speech of the author. In "Piazza Piece," Ransom speaks as an old "gentleman in a dustcoat" in the first stanza, and as "a lady young in beauty" in the second. Eliot assumes the persona of one of the three magi in "Journey of the Magi." In these instances, the speaker *in* the literature differs obviously from the author. Close analysis of other writings, combined with an investigation of their authors' lives, may reveal more subtle shades of difference between the author and the mask he wears.

Failing to notice distinctions between the author and the persona can result in complete misinterpretations of meaning. The persona in Auden's "The Unknown Citizen," for instance, bears little in common with the poet. As a representative of "the State," the persona eulogizes a man known as "JS/07/M378." He notes that the man did the right things, held the right views, and thereby "served the Greater Community." The persona, here, is greatly pleased at a life which exhibited no individuality, no departure from statistical expectations, no resistance to a planned, mundane, friction-less existence. Man becomes a number, and human feeling is old-fashioned. Auden, of course, is in complete disagreement with this mechanized existence. He is manipulating the persona to make him appear absurd and to make an ironic comment about the intrusion of technological advancement in our lives. If you were to confuse the views of the persona with the intentions of the author, you would miss the point of the poem entirely.

In many selections an author will employ multiple personae. A play, for instance, may contain many different characters. A short story or novel usually has a narrator (perhaps the voice of the author, but possibly an adopted persona) and characters that speak to one another as part of the story's unfolding events. Each of these speakers has individual physical

[6] Wayne C. Booth, *The Rhetoric of Fiction* (Chicago: The University of Chicago Press, 1961), pp. 74–75.

characteristics; a separate personality; and a distinct function in the literature. Each will speak through your performance.

Whereas our study of the author embraces material drawn both within and outside the specific selection, the analysis of a persona is confined to information the author chooses to present in the literature itself. The speaker in the work resides in the fictional world that is created in the literature and has no life outside that environment. Consequently, we may know a great deal about some personae, while others remain more vague. In the following passage, three people speak: an unnamed narrator (the " I " of the story), Mr. Shawnessy, and General Jacob J. Jackson. As you read the selection, consider how much the author reveals about each of the three.

## *from* RAINTREE COUNTY

ROSS LOCKRIDGE, JR.

Fighting for Freedom from Shiloh to Savannah

is the name of the goddam thing, the General said. I happen to have a few hundred pages of it stuffed into my coatpocket here, Shawnessy, and if you have a little time, I'd like to have you glance it over and tell me frankly what you think of it. There you are.

—Thanks, General. Be glad to look at it.

—By the way, you were in the War, weren't you? the General said.

—Yes, Mr. Shawnessy said.

He and some fifty other members of the Raintree County Post of the Grand Army of the Republic were standing in a shapeless mass at the middle of the intersection, waiting to form ranks and march down to the Schoolhouse for the outdoor banquet. General Jacob J. Jackson, Raintree County's outstanding military figure, a hero of two wars, had arrived in Waycross only a few minutes before to lead the march.

The General, a hearty man in his middle sixties, was a little shorter than Mr. Shawnessy. Broadshouldered, deepchested, he was built like an athlete except for the hard bulge of his belly. Freeflowing gray hair fell thickly from his thinning dome to lie upon his shoulders and blend over his ears into the great ball of a beard. Out of this beard his voice blew like a horn of cracked brass, having no variations in pitch or volume between a hard bray and a hoarse whisper. The General was now standing in one of his characteristic postures, arms folded over chest, head thrust back, left foot forward. One could see the bulge of his right calfmuscle in the army trousers. His small blue eyes glared. The muscles around his cheekbones twitched as if under his beard the General were gritting his jaw teeth. A dress sword and two Colt revolvers hung from his belt. He held a broad Western hat adorned with military cord.

The General made everyone else look like a supernumerary. Most of the other veterans were in uniform too, but only the General seemed clothed in heroic dignity.

—I'm a practical man, the General was saying, a man of action, and I hate like hell to write.

—For a man who hates to write, General, you've ground out a lot of copy in your time, Mr. Shawnessy said. Let's see, how many books is it now?

The General's chest swelled, and there burst from his throat a series of distinct hahs, of exactly the same timbre as his speaking voice.

—Well, let's see, he said. I began with *Fighting for the Flag*, and followed it up with *Memoirs of a Fighting General*. Then there was *Four Years at the Front or Fighting for the Cause* and of course *A Fighting Man's History of the War in the West*. I've also done that series called *Fights I have Fought from Chapultepec to Chickamauga or Tales of Two Wars*. Then, there's that goddam thing my publishers have had me doing called *Fifteen Historic Fights from Marathon to Manassas*.

—I hadn't seen that one, General, Mr. Shawnessy said. I didn't know you went in for European battles.

—Once you understand war, the General said, one goddam battle is like another. By the way, it's time to march, isn't it?

—Just about, Mr. Shawnessy said. I think the band's about ready.

—Fall in, boys! the General barked.

The narrator of this passage is not a participant in the scene he describes. As teller of the story, he is vitally important, of course, since it is through his eyes that we learn all we are to discover. But nothing in the passage suggests that the narrator is any other than the author relating his story to us. Since we are given no clues to the contrary, we can presume that he does not represent a distinct fictional persona.

Mr. Shawnessy is introduced as one of fifty veterans who are to participate in the festivities. We are given no physical description of him, except that he is a little taller than the General. His function in the selection is to direct our attention toward the General, about whom we learn a great deal. We know his reputation, are told of his physical characteristics in some detail, and even receive descriptions of his vocal features. Clearly, Lockridge wants us to devote the bulk of our attention to General Jackson as the dominant figure in the passage. While a reading of the whole book reveals that Mr. Shawnessy is the central figure, he is nevertheless relatively unimportant to this passage.

All of the steps of analysis help us to discern who the personae are in literature. They are identified by the communication of ideas, by the evocation of mood, and by the creation of images—by narrative description as well as by their own words and actions. Always, we must remember that personae are the puppets of the author, who continually manipulates the strings that give them life.

**Twelve.** The final step in analysis, we suggest, is that you consider how your understanding of the separate elements can be combined into a reading that accurately and effectively gives voice to the literature. As the interpretative speaker of literature, you should strive for a voice that fulfills the challenge of personae, and achieves the purposes of the author, as you perceive them through empathic response and through study. Your grasp of ideas and emotions should coalesce to reveal the total identity of the work. It is necessary to consider how all aspects of the literature work together to create its meanings.

See if you can discern a dominant feature of the literature to which other elements contribute. In "The Great Lover," the author concentrates primarily on pleasurable *imagery*. "Create Great Peace" focuses on the *idea* of peace. "My Love Is Like a Red Red Rose" revolves about the *emotion* of undying love. "Raintree County" focuses on the *character* of General Jackson. You can not expect that one element will always emerge as dominant, but you should discover a satisfying unity in all good literature, a harmonious interaction of style and content. As interpreter of the literature, it is your job to see how all the pieces fit together to form the whole. Once you have done so, you will have the necessary impressions on which to base your communicative expression of the literature.

## SUMMARY

While developing our responses to literature is a highly involved and abstract process not reducible to a formula, we have for the sake of clarity spoken of three areas of literary analysis and made twelve suggestions:

A. What ideas are presented in the literature:
   1. Read it all and try to state the theme or dominant idea.
   2. Make sure you understand the various kinds of meanings of all significant words.
   3. Determine word grouping and centering.
   4. Study emphasis and subordination.
   5. Study organizational structure.
   6. Try to write a good paraphrase.
B. What emotional responses it may stimulate:
   7. Cultivate your response to the mood or moods of the writing.
   8. Strive to perceive symbolism.
   9. Experience the imagery.
C. Who the speakers are:
   10. See if information about the author may help.
   11. Identify the characteristics of personae.
   12. Consider how all elements work together to direct a performance of the literature.

These steps cannot be rigidly followed as a formula, but they do explain at least some of the means to promote our responses to literature. In short, *they tell us what to look for.* While following this sequence of steps, you should continually remain open to any insights that may occur. Perhaps you will become strikingly aware of imagery when examining word meanings. Or, maybe you will respond to a musical flow of language while working to uncover mood. As you embark on your study of a specific selection, you are treading on uncharted ground. No map of critical procedures can unerringly guide your exploration of these imaginative territories. At best, the steps we suggest may offer a few compass points for direction. You will have to make the journey yourself every time you encounter a new selection of literature. Although the way is not always easy, the rewards of experiencing literature fully make the trip well worth the effort.

## EXERCISES

1. Find the thought centers in the following sentences. Be sure you know which word groups belong together and what relation they have to other words or groups of words.

a. Ability involves responsibility; power, to its last particle, is duty.

—A. MACLAREN

b. What I admire in Columbus is not his having discovered a world, but his having gone to search for it on the faith of an opinion.

—A. R. J. TURGOT

c. Falsehoods not only disagree with truths, but usually quarrel among themselves. —DANIEL WEBSTER

d. As love increases, prudence diminishes.

—FRANCOIS, DUC DE LA ROCHEFOUCAULD

e. O Wild West Wind, thou breath of Autumn's being,
Thou, from whose unseen presence the leaves dead
Are driven, like ghosts from an enchanter fleeing.

Yellow, and black, and pale, and hectic red,
Pestilence–stricken multitudes: O thou,
Who chariotest to their dark wintry bed

The wingéd seeds, where they lie cold and low,
Each like a corpse within its grave, until
Thine azure sister of the spring shall blow

Her clarion o'er the dreaming earth, and fill
(Driving sweet buds like flocks to feed in air)

With living hues and odours plain and hill:
Wild Spirit, which art moving everywhere;
Destroyer and preserver; hear, Oh, hear!
　　　　　　　—PERCY BYSSHE SHELLEY, " Ode to the West Wind "

f.　A good name is to be chosen rather than great riches, and favor is
　　better than silver or gold.　　　　　　　　　　　*—Proverbs*

g.　The wicked flee when no one pursues, but the righteous are bold as a
　　lion.　　　　　　　　　　　　　　　　　　　*—Proverbs*

h.　The way of a fool is right in his own eyes, but a wise man listens to
　　advice.　　　　　　　　　　　　　　　　　　*—Proverbs*

i.　If a man has a talent and cannot use it, he has failed. If he has a talent
　　and uses only half of it, he has partly failed. If he has a talent and learns
　　somehow to use the whole of it, he has gloriously succeeded, and won a
　　satisfaction and a triumph few men ever know.　　—THOMAS WOLFE

j.　A powerful agent is the right word. Whenever we come upon one of
　　those intensely right words in a book or a newspaper the resulting
　　effect is physical as well as spiritual, and electrically prompt.
　　　　　　　　　　　　　　　　　　　　　　—MARK TWAIN.

k.　My method is to take the utmost trouble to find the right thing to say,
　　and then to say it with utmost levity.　　—GEORGE BERNARD SHAW

l.　Good name in man and woman, dear my lord,
　　Is the immediate jewel of their souls:
　　Who steals my purse steals trash; 'tis something, nothing,
　　'Twas mine, 'tis his, and has been slave to thousands;
　　But he that filches from me my good name
　　Robs me of that which not enriches him,
　　And makes me poor indeed.　　　　　—SHAKESPEARE, *Othello*

m.　The marvelous new militancy which has engulfed the Negro com-
　　munity must not lead us to a distrust of all white people, for many of
　　our white brothers, as evidenced by their presence here today, have
　　come to realize that their destiny is tied up with our destiny.
　　　　　　　　　　　　　　　　　　—MARTIN LUTHER KING, JR.

n.　Not since the founding of the Republic—when Thomas Jefferson
　　wrote the Declaration of Independence at 32, Henry Knox built an
　　artillery corps at 26, Alexander Hamilton joined the independence
　　fight at 19, and Rutledge and Lynch signed the Declaration for South
　　Carolina at 27—has there been a younger generation of Americans
　　brighter, better educated, more highly motivated than this one.
　　　　　　　　　　　　　　　　　　　　—ROBERT F. KENNEDY

o. A teacher who can arouse a feeling for one single good action, for one single good poem, accomplishes more than he who fills our memory with rows on rows of natural objects, classified with name and form.

—GOETHE

p. Since I do not foresee that atomic energy is to be a great boon for a long time, I have to say that for the present it is a menace. Perhaps it is well that it should be. It may intimidate the human race into bringing order into its international affairs, which, without the pressure of fear, it would not do. —ALBERT EINSTEIN

2. Read the following two poems for overall understanding. The first takes a powerful slap at the horrible, impersonal nature of war. The second offers a more subtle comparison between "sweet disorder" and art that is "too precise." Try to state the theme or dominant idea of both.

## BUTTONS

CARL SANDBURG

I have been watching the war map slammed up for advertising in front of the newspaper office.
Buttons—red and yellow buttons—blue and black buttons—are shoved back and forth across the map.

At laughing young man, sunny with freckles,
Climbs a ladder, yells a joke to somebody in the crowd
And then fixes a yellow button one inch west
And follows the yellow button with a black button one inch west.
(Ten thousand men and boys twist on their bodies in a red soak along a river edge,
Gasping of wounds, calling for water, some rattling death in their throats.)
Who would guess what it cost to move two buttons one inch on the war map here in front of the newspaper office where the freckle–faced young man is laughing to us?

## DELIGHT IN DISORDER

ROBERT HERRICK

A sweet disorder in the dress
Kindles in clothes a wantonness:
A lawn about the shoulders thrown
Into a fine distraction:
An erring lace, which here and there

Enthralls the crimson stomacher:
A cuff neglectful, and thereby

Ribands to flow confusedly:
A winning wave (deserving note)
In the tempestuous petticoat:
A careless shoestring in whose tie
I see wild civility:
Do more bewitch me, than when art
Is too precise in every part.

3.  To appreciate these next poems, it will be necessary for you to understand the significance of the names Ted Williams, Randall Jarrell, and Jim Crow.

## DREAM OF A BASEBALL STAR

GREGORY CORSO

I dreamed of Ted Williams
leaning at night
against the Eiffel Tower, weeping.

He was in uniform
and his bat lay at his feet
—knotted and twiggy.

'Randall Jarrell says you're a poet!' I cried.
'So do I! I say you're a poet!'

He picked up his bat with blown hands;
stood there astraddle as he would in the batter's box,
and laughed! flinging his schoolboy wrath
toward some invisible pitcher's mound
—waiting the pitch all the way from heaven.

It came; hundreds came! all afire!
He swung and swung and swung and connected not one
sinker curve hook or right-down-the-middle.
A hundred strikes!
The umpire dressed in strange attire
thundered his judgment: YOU'RE OUT!
And the phantom crowd's horrific boo
dispersed the gargoyles from Notre Dame.

And I screamed in my dream:
God! throw thy merciful pitch!
Herald the crack of bats!
Hooray the sharp liner to left!
Yea the double, the triple!
Hosannah the home run!

## JIM CROW CAR

LANGSTON HUGHES

Get out the lunch-box of your dreams
And bite into the sandwich of your heart,
And ride the Jim Crow car until it screams
And, like an atom bomb, bursts apart.

4. After you have identified the predominant mood in the following two selections, try to discover the internal changes in mood that contribute to the overall feeling.

## AN ELEMENTARY SCHOOL CLASS ROOM IN A SLUM

STEPHEN SPENDER

Far far from gusty waves, these children's faces.
Like rootless weeds the torn hair round their paleness.
The tall girl with her weighed-down head. The paper-seeming boy with
    rat's eyes. The stunted unlucky heir
Of twisted bones, reciting a father's gnarled disease,
His lesson from his desk. At back of the dim class,
One unnoted, sweet and young: his eyes live in a dream
Of squirrels' game, in tree room, other than this.

On sour cream walls, donations. Shakespeare's head
Cloudless at dawn, civilized dome riding all cities.
Belled, flowery, Tyrolese valley. Open-handed map
Awarding the world its world. And yet, for these
Children, these windows, not this world, are world,
Where all their future's painted with a fog,
A narrow street sealed in with a lead sky,
Far far from rivers, capes, and stars of words.

Surely Shakespeare is wicked, the map a bad example
With ships and sun and love tempting them to steal—

For lives that slyly turn in their cramped holes
From fog to endless night? On their slag heap, these children
Wear skins peeped through by bones and spectacles of steel
With mended glass, like bottle bits on stones.
All of their time and space are foggy slum
So blot their maps with slums as big as doom.

Unless, governor, teacher, inspector, visitor,
This map becomes their window and these windows
That open on their lives like crouching tombs
Break, O break open, till they break the town
And show the children to the fields and all their world
Azure on their sands, to let their tongues
Run naked into books, the white and green leaves open
The history theirs whose language is the sun.

## WHEN IN DISGRACE WITH FORTUNE

WILLIAM SHAKESPEARE

When, in disgrace with fortune and men's eyes,
I all alone beweep my outcast state,
And trouble deaf heaven with my bootless cries,
And look upon myself, and curse my fate;
Wishing me like to one more rich in hope,
Featured like him, like him with friends possess'd,
Desiring this man's art, and that man's scope,
With what I most enjoy contented least;
Yet in these thoughts myself almost despising,
Haply I think on thee—and then my state,
Like to the lark at break of day arising
From sullen earth, sings hymns at heaven's gate;
For thy sweet love remember'd such wealth brings
That then I scorn to change my state with kings.

5. Two out of three of the following selections are rich in imagery. Which piece has the least amount of imagery, and how does that affect your reading of it?

## *from* THE EVE OF ST. AGNES

JOHN KEATS

St. Agnes' Eve—Ah, bitter chill it was!
The owl, for all his feathers, was a-cold;

The hare limped trembling through the frozen grass,
And silent was the flock in woolly fold:
Numb were the Beadsman's fingers, while he told
His rosary, and while his frosted breath,
Like 'pious incense from a censer old,
Seemed taking flight for heaven, without a death,
Past the sweet Virgin's picture, while his prayer he saith.

# THE PARABLE OF THE GOOD SAMARITAN

LUKE 10:30–36, REVISED STANDARD VERSION

A man was going down from Jerusalem to Jericho, and he fell among robbers, who stripped him and beat him, and departed, leaving him half-dead. Now by chance a priest was going down that road; and when he saw him he passed by on the other side. So likewise a Levite, when he came to the place and saw him, passed by on the other side. But a Samaritan, as he journeyed, came to where he was; and when he saw him, he had compassion, and went to him and bound up his wounds, pouring on oil and wine; then he set him on his own beast and brought him to an inn, and took care of him. And the next day he took out two denarii and gave them to the innkeeper, saying, "Take care of him; and whatever more you spend, I will repay you when I come back." Which of these three, do you think, proved neighbor to the man who fell among the robbers?

# BARTER

SARA TEASDALE

Life has loveliness to sell—
    All beautiful and splendid things,
Blue waves whitened on a cliff,
    Climbing fire that sways and sings,
And children's faces looking up
Holding wonder like a cup.

Life has loveliness to sell—
    Music like a curve of gold,
Scent of pine trees in the rain,
    Eyes that love you, arms that hold,
And for your spirit's still delight,
Holy thoughts that star the night.

Spend all you have for loveliness,
    Buy it and never count the cost,

For one white singing hour of peace
  Count many a year of strife well lost,
And for a breath of ecstasy
Give all you have been or could be.

6. Both of the following poems offer a glimpse of an individual. The first talks about the person, while the second is in the words of the person. How would our insight into the individuals change if "Mamie beat her head" was altered to "I beat my head" and "i go alone" was altered to "he goes alone"?

## MAMIE

CARL SANDBURG

Mamie beat her head against the bars of a little Indiana town and dreamed of romance and big things off somewhere the way the railroad trains all ran.

She could see the smoke of the engines get lost down where the streaks of steel flashed in the sun, and when the newspapers came in on the morning mail she knew there was a big Chicago far off, where all the trains ran.

She got tired of the barber-shop boys and the post-office chatter and the church gossip and the old pieces the band played on the Fourth of July and Decoration Day,

And sobbed at her fate and beat her head against the bars and was going to kill herself

When the thought came to her that if she was going to die she might as well die struggling for a clutch of romance among the streets of Chicago.

She has a job now at six dollars a week in the basement of the Boston Store

And even now she beats her head against the bars in the same old way and wonders if there is a bigger place the railroads run to from Chicago where maybe there is
    romance
    and big things
    and real dreams
    that never go smash.

## INDIAN SCHOOL

NORMAN H. RUSSELL

in the darkness
of the house of the white brother
i go alone and am frightened
strange things touch me
i cannot breathe his air
or eat his tasteless food

on his walls
are pictures of the world
that his walls shut out
in his hands are leaves of words
from dead mens mouths

he speaks to me with only
the sounds of his mouth
for he is dumb and blind
as the staggering old bear
filled with many arrows
as the rocks that lie on the mountain

and in his odd robes
uglier
than any other creature i have ever seen

i am not wise enough to know
gods purpose in him.

7. These poems are from Edgar Lee Masters' *Spoon River Anthology*.
They are supposed inscriptions on tombstones, spoken by deceased residents
of the area surrounding the Spoon River in central Illinois. Concentrate on the
distinctive persona in each.

## DEACON TAYLOR

I belonged to the church,
And to the party of prohibition;
And the villagers thought I died of eating watermelon.
In truth I had cirrhosis of the liver,
For every noon for thirty years,
I slipped behind the prescription partition
In Trainor's drug store
And poured a generous drink
From the bottle marked
"Spiritus frumenti."

## LUCINDA MATLOCK

I went to the dances at Chandlerville,
And played snap-out at Winchester.
One time we changed partners,

Driving home in the moonlight of middle June,
And then I found Davis.
We were married and lived together for seventy years,
Enjoying, working, raising the twelve children,
Eight of whom we lost
Ere I had reached the age of sixty.
I spun, I wove, I kept the house, I nursed the sick,
I made the garden, and for holiday
Rambled over the fields where sang the larks,
And by Spoon River gathering many a shell,
And many a flower and medicinal weed—
Shouting to the wooded hills, singing to the green valleys.
At ninety-six I had lived enough, that is all,
And passed to a sweet repose.
What is this I hear of sorrow and weariness,
Anger, discontent and drooping hopes?
Degenerate sons and daughters,
Life is too strong for you—
It takes life to love Life.


## CARL HAMBLIN

The press of the Spoon River Clarion was wrecked,
And I was tarred and feathered,
For publishing this on the day the Anarchists were
   Hanged in Chicago:
"I saw a beautiful woman with bandaged eyes
Standing on the steps of a marble temple.
Great multitudes passed in front of her,
Lifting their faces to her imploringly.
In her left hand she held a sword.
She was brandishing the sword,
Sometimes striking a child, again a laborer,
Again a slinking woman, again a lunatic.
In her right hand she held a scale;
Into the scale pieces of gold were tossed
By those who dodged the strokes of the sword.
A man in a black gown read from a manuscript:
'She is no respecter of persons.'
Then a youth wearing a red cap
Leaped to her side and snatched away the bandage.
And lo, the lashes had been eaten away
From the oozy eye-lids;

The eye-balls were seared with a milky mucus;
The madness of a dying soul
Was written on her face—
But the multitude saw why she wore the bandage."

## SILAS DEMENT

It was moonlight, and the earth sparkled
With new-fallen frost.
It was midnight and not a soul was abroad.
Out of the chimney of the court-house
A grey-hound of smoke leapt and chased
The northwest wind.
I carried a ladder to the landing of the stairs
And leaned it against the frame of the trap-door
In the ceiling of the portico,
And I crawled under the roof and amid the rafters
And flung among the seasoned timbers
A lighted handful of oil-soaked waste.
Then I came down and slunk away.
In a little while the fire-bell rang—
Clang! Clang! Clang!
And the Spoon River ladder company
Came with a dozen buckets and began to pour water
On the glorious bon-fire, growing hotter,
Higher and brighter, till the walls fell in,
And the limestone columns where Lincoln stood
Crashed like trees when the woodman fells them . . .
When I came back from Joliet
There was a new court-house with a dome.
For I was punished like all who destroy
The past for the sake of the future.

## SCHROEDER THE FISHERMAN

I sat on the bank above Bernadotte
And dropped crumbs in the water,
Just to see the minnows bump each other,
Until the strongest got the prize,
Or I went to my little pasture,
Where the peaceful swine were asleep in the wallow,
Or nosing each other lovingly,
And emptied a basket of yellow corn,

And watched them push and squeal and bite,
And trample each other to get the corn.
And I saw how Christian Dallman's farm,
Of more than three thousand acres,
Swallowed the patch of Felix Schmidt,
As a bass will swallow a minnow.
And I say if there's anything in man—
Spirit, or conscience, or breath of God
That makes him different from fishes or hogs,
I'd like to see it work!

## CATHERINE OGG

"Tombstone" Johnson, head of the school board,
Ashamed that he sprang from an egg,
And a wriggling sperm,
But proud that man was created from dust,
Though dust is dirtier than eggs,
Ousted me from my place in the school
For showing a picture to the pupils
Of a child emerging from an egg shell,
And telling them all the beauty and wonder
Of evolution that makes a mind
Out of an egg and sperm.
So I retired and struggled along,
And starved a little, and brooded much
To the end of the farce!

## FIDDLER JONES

The earth keeps some vibration going
There in your heart, and that is you.
And if the people find you can fiddle,
Why, fiddle you must, for all your life.
What do you see, a harvest of clover?
Or a meadow to walk through to the river?
The wind's in the corn; you rub your hands
For beeves hereafter ready for market;
Or else you hear the rustle of skirts
Like the girls when dancing at Little Grove.
To Cooney Potter a pillar of dust
Or whirling leaves meant ruinous drouth;
They looked to me like Red-Head Sammy

Stepping it off, to "Toor-a-Loor."
How could I till my forty acres
Not to speak of getting more,
With a medley of horns, bassoons and piccolos
Stirred in my brain by crows and robins
And the creak of a wind-mill—only these?
And I never started to plow in my life
That some one did not stop in the road
And take me away to a dance or picnic.
I ended up with forty acres;
I ended up with a broken fiddle—
And a broken laugh, and a thousand memories,
And not a single regret.


## HARRY WILMANS

I was just turned twenty-one,
And Henry Phipps, the Sunday-school superintendent,
Made a speech in Bindle's Opera House.
"The honor of the flag must be upheld," he said,
"Whether it be assailed by a barbarous tribe of Tagalogs
Or the greatest power in Europe."
And we cheered and cheered the speech and the flag he waved
As he spoke.
And I went to the war in spite of my father,
And followed the flag till I saw it raised
By our camp in a rice field near Manila,
And all of us cheered and cheered it.
But there were flies and poisonous things;
And there was the deadly water,
And the cruel heat,
And the sickening, putrid food;
And the smell of the trench just back of the tents
Where the soldiers went to empty themselves;
And there were the whores who followed us, full of syphilis;
And beastly acts between ourselves or alone,
With bullying, hatred, degradation among us,
And days of loathing and nights of fear
To the hour of the charge through the steaming swamp,
Following the flag,
Till I fell with a scream, shot through the guts.
Now there's a flag over me in Spoon River!
A Flag! A flag!

8.   Examine these selections by employing all the critical procedures we
have discussed in this chapter.

## FLOOD

IRVING FELDMAN

The first day it rained we were glad.
How could we know? The heavy air
Had lain about us like a scarf, though work
Got done. Everything seemed easier.
In the streets a little mud.

With the first faint drops, a tiny breeze
Trembled the cornsilk, and the frailest leaves
Turned on their stems this way and that.
Coming from the fields for lunch
I thought it my sweat.

On the second day streamlets ran
In the furrows; the plow stuck,
The oxen balked. On the third day
The rain ran from the roof like a sea.
I thought I would visit town.

Farmers from their farms, merchants from stores,
Laborers, we filled the town. I
Stayed with a cousin. We were told
The granary was full, we could live
A thousand days should the river rise impetuously.

The fifth day the clouds seemed hung
From the tops of the tallest trees. The sun
We did not see at all. And the rain
Beat down as if to crush the roof.
I did not shave or write my wife.

On the sixth day, we moved the women
And children to the town church, built
On the highest ground hard by the granary.
We finished work on the levee.
The river was thick with silt.

A dark drizzle started in my head.
Next day it trickled on the walls of my skull

Like black earth drifting down a grave.
We resolved to stay in the church come what will.
That day I did not leave my bed.

From where the rain? and why on us?
Not even the wisest knows or dares guess.
Did we not plan, care, save, toil,
Did we lay idle or lust, did we waste or spoil?
Therefore, why on us?

The husbandman from his flock,
Husband from wife, the miser from his heap,
The wise man from his wit, from her urn
The widow—are tumbled all, as a man might knock
The ashes from his pipe.

And the days descended in a stream,
So fast they could not be told apart.
In the church all went black.
Once I lay with Lenah as in a dream.
Another time I found myself at Adah's back.

If no one gets up at dawn to wind
The clock, shall not the state run down?
If no one gets up to go to the fields
To feed the cows, to sow the wheat,
To reap, how shall the state grow fat?

One comes telling us Noah has built a boat
That through the flood he may ride about,
And filled it all with animals.
Just like the drunken fool, that slut-
Chaser, to think of no one else.

I feed my friends and kin; twenty-nine thrived
In my home. But mad Noah harangues the air
Or goes muttering in his cuff
As though a god were up his sleeve.
Who is Noah to get saved?

I am a farmer, I love my wife,
My sons are many and strong, my land is green.
This is my cousin, he lives in town,
An honest man, he rises at dawn.
We were children together.

Shall not the world run down?
Why on us? Did we not plan?
Does not black blood flow before my eyes
And blackness brim inside my skull?
Did we lie idle? Did we spoil?

Out of its harness the mind wild as a horse
Roams the rooms and streets. There are some that say
Noah sits amid the rude beasts in his ark
And they feed one upon the other in the dark
And in the dark they mate. And some say worse:

That a griffin was born, and centaur
And sphinx hammer at the door.
Groans and moans are heard, by some the roar
Of giant Hippogriff. Still others cry
That all about the earth is dry!

Dry as if no rain had fallen,
As if we were not awaiting the swollen
River, as if the clouds did not sit
On our chimneys, or the waters
Tumble past our windows in spate.

And some here say a dove has come,
Sure, they think, the sign of a god.
And others say that Noah walks the street
Puffed with news. But bid him wait!
We are busy with our flood.

# OWNERS AND TENANTS

JOHN STEINBECK

The owners of the land came onto the land, or more often a spokesman for the owners came. They came in closed cars, and they felt the dry earth with their fingers, and sometimes they drove big earth augers into the ground for soil tests. The tenants, from their sun-beaten dooryards, watched uneasily when the closed cars drove along the fields. And at last the owner men drove into the dooryards and sat in their cars to talk out of the windows. The tenant men stood beside the cars for a while, and then squatted on their hams and found sticks with which to mark the dust.

In the open doors the women stood looking out, and behind them the children—corn-headed children, with wide eyes, one bare foot on top of the other bare foot, and the toes working. The women and the children watched their men talking to the owner men. They were silent.

Some of the owner men were kind because they hated what they had to do, and some of them were angry because they hated to be cruel, and some of them were cold because they had long ago found that one could not be an owner unless one were cold. And all of them were caught in something larger than themselves. Some of them hated the mathematics that drove them, and some were afraid, and some worshiped the mathematics because it provided a refuge from thought and from feeling. If a bank or a finance company owned the land, the owner man said, The Bank—or the Company—needs—wants—insists —must have—as though the Bank or the Company were a monster, with thought and feeling, which had ensnared them. These last would take no responsibility for the banks or the companies because they were men and slaves, while the banks were machines and masters all at the same time. Some of the owner men were a little proud to be slaves to such cold and powerful masters. The owner men sat in the cars and explained. You know the land is poor. You've scrabbled at it long enough. God knows.

The squatting tenant men nodded and wondered and drew figures in the dust, and yes, they knew, God knows. If the dust only wouldn't fly. If the top would only stay on the soil, it might not be so bad.

The owner men went on leading to their point: You know the land's getting poorer. You know what cotton does to the land; robs it, sucks all the blood out of it.

The squatters nodded—they knew. God knew. If they could only rotate the crops they might pump blood back into the land.

Well, it's too late. And the owner men explained the workings and thinkings of the monster that was stronger than they were. A man can hold land if he can just eat and pay taxes; he can do that.

Yes, he can do that until his crops fail one day and he has to borrow money from the bank.

But—you see, a bank or a company can't do that, because those creatures don't breathe air, don't eat side-meat. They breathe profits; they eat the interest on money. If they don't get it, they die the way you die without air, without side-meat. It is a sad thing, but it is so. It is just so.

The squatting men raised their eyes to understand. Can't we just hang on? Maybe the next year will be a good year. God knows how much cotton next year. And with all the wars—God knows what price cotton will bring. Don't they make explosives out of cotton? And uniforms? Get enough wars and cotton'll hit the ceiling. Next year, maybe. They looked up questioningly.

We can't depend on it. The bank—the monster has to have profits all the time. It can't wait. It'll die. No, taxes go on. When the monster stops growing, it dies. It can't stay one size.

Soft fingers began to tap the sill of the car window, and hard fingers tightened on the restless drawing sticks. In the doorways of the sun-beaten tenant houses, women sighed and shifted feet so that the one that had been down was now on top, and the toes working. Dogs came sniffing near the owner cars and wetted on all four tires one after another. And the chickens lay in the sunny dust and fluffed their feathers to get the cleansing dust down to the skin. In the little sties the pigs grunted inquiringly over the muddy remnants of the slops.

The squatting men looked down again. What do you want us to do? We can't take less share of the crop—we're half starved now. The kids are hungry all the time. We got no clothes, torn an' ragged. If all the neighbors weren't the same, we'd be ashamed to go to meeting.

And at last the owner men came to the point. The tenant system won't work any more. One man on a tractor can take the place of twelve or fourteen families. Pay him a wage and take all the crop. We have to do it. We don't like to do it. But the monster's sick. Something's happened to the monster.

But you'll kill the land with cotton.

We know. We've got to take cotton quick before the land dies. Then we'll sell the land. Lots of families in the East would like to own a piece of land.

The tenant men looked up alarmed. But what'll happen to us? How'll we eat?

You'll have to get off the land. The plows'll go through the dooryard.

And now the squatting men stood up angrily. Grampa took up the land, and he had to kill the Indians and drive them away. And Pa was born here, and he killed weeds and snakes. Then a bad year came and he had to borrow a little money. An' we was born here. There in the door—our children born here. And Pa had to borrow money. The bank owned the land then, but we stayed and we got a little bit of what we raised.

We know that—all that. It's not us, it's the bank. A bank isn't like a man. Or an owner with fifty thousand acres, he isn't like a man either. That's the monster.

Sure, cried the tenant men, but it's our land. We measured it and broke it up. We were born on it and we got killed on it, died on it. Even if it's no good, it's still ours. That's what makes it ours—being born on it, working it, dying on it. That makes ownership, not a paper with numbers on it.

We're sorry. It's not us. It's the monster. The bank isn't like a man.

Yes, but the bank is only made of men.

No, you're wrong there—quite wrong there. The bank is something else than men. It happens that every man in a bank hates what the bank does, and yet the bank does it. The bank is something more than men, I tell you. It's the monster. Men made it, but they can't control it.

The tenants cried: Grampa killed Indians, Pa killed snakes for the land. Maybe we can kill banks—they're worse than Indians and snakes. Maybe we got to fight to keep our land, like Pa and Grampa did.

And now the owner men grew angry. You'll have to go.

But it's ours, the tenant men cried. We—

No. The bank, the monster owns it. You'll have to go.

We'll get our guns, like Grampa when the Indians came. What then?

Well—first the sheriff, and then the troops. You'll be stealing if you try to stay, you'll be murderers if you kill to stay. The monster isn't men, but it can make men do what it wants.

But if we go, where'll we go? How'll we go? We got no money.

We're sorry, said the owner men. The bank, the fifty-thousand-acre owner can't be responsible. You're on land that isn't yours. Once over the line maybe you can pick cotton in the fall. Maybe you can go on relief. Why don't you go on west to California? There's work there, and it never gets cold. Why, you can reach out anywhere and pick an orange. Why, there's always some kind of crop to work in. Why don't you go there? And the owner men started their cars and rolled away.

The tenant men squatted down on their hams again to mark the dust with a stick, to figure, to wonder. Their sun-burned faces were dark, and their sun-whipped eyes were light. The women moved cautiously out of the doorways toward their men, and the children crept behind the women, cautiously, ready to run. The bigger boys squatted beside their fathers, because that made them men. After a time the women asked, What did he want?

And the men looked up for a second, and the smolder of pain was in their eyes. We got to get off. A tractor and a superintendent. Like factories.

Where'll we go? the women asked.

We don't know. We don't know.

And the women went quickly, quietly back into the houses and herded the children ahead of them. They knew that a man so hurt and so perplexed may turn in anger, even on people he loves. They left the men alone to figure and to wonder in the dust.

After a time perhaps the tenant man looked about—at the pump put in ten years ago, with a goose-neck handle and iron flowers on the spout, at the chopping block where a thousand chickens had been killed, at the hand plow lying in the shed, and the patent crib hanging in the rafters over it.

The children crowded around the women in the houses. What we going to do, Ma? Where we going to go?

The women said; We don't know, yet. Go out and play. But don't go near your father. He might whale you if you go near him. And the women went on with the work, but all the time they watched the men squatting in the dust—perplexed and figuring.

# Three

## Expressing Responses to Meaning

# 6

# *Communication: Expression of Responses*

In the preceding two chapters, we stressed the importance of impression, of the interpreter having a thorough and appropriate response to literature. We must hasten to reiterate that impression and expression are not really separable processes. The act of giving expression to literature is our response to the literature, and we have contended that response is meaning. Our responses consist of visible and audible behavior, which, if appropriate and controlled, enable us as readers to communicate the literary experience to others. How we perform when reading arises from our experience in the literature—our empathic responses to images and tensions suggested in the literature—at the very moment we read it aloud.

If the simultaneity of impression and expression seems strange at first, we must report that many writers have admitted to writing for the purpose of discovering what they wish to say! In addition, we know of a fine college teacher who requires her students of writing to read copiously so that they will be *impressed* with *something,* and she requires her students of reading to write regularly so that they will be forced to *express* their *responses!*

It is only for "academic" reasons that we consider expression and impression separately. Having focused on impression, we now focus on expression, realizing that in each case, we are involved with concurrent elements in an interrelated process of impressing in order to express, and expressing in order to be impressed.

In the chapters that follow, we shall discuss separately five major aspects of oral communication. The first is devoted to the means of visible response and communication, and the other four, to the means of audible response and communication. Of course, such a book division is purely arbitrary and unnatural, for when we communicate, we simultaneously use all the means at our disposal, visible and audible, to project our meanings. Not only do we couple sound with activity, but in the sounds we make, we also combine several vocal techniques at the same time. For the time being, let us look at their roles in the interpretative reader's responses to literature.

First, read this story:

# ONE FOR YES

J. P. DONLEAVY

In a rented pair of blue tinted eyeglasses, crossing by the fish market and moving down Owl Street past the wide steps of the treasury building. The middle of the month of August. Reaching out across the weeks to sink clutching fingers into this harmless Wednesday.

On the early morning streets messengers trotting in and out of doors. Just this instant I feel good. Ships moving out to sea on the high tides. Barges carrying western trains headed north across the narrow waters. Bridges and highways humming with tires. Smell of coffee across this downtown.

I stop. Look up. Obstructing me in my forward motion, a face coming out of prepsterhood. Quickly steering a detour into the gutter, and nearly getting cut down with machines, I had to leap back from the honking horns. Too late, too weak and vulnerable to turn and run this crazy time in my personal history. A smooth jawed figure. Grey natty topcoat, cream shirt and fat striped tie. And eyes that turned on their glow.

"I know you, hey aren't you George Smith. Not so fast like you were at the building site, that time."

"Beep."

"Ha you're George Smith all right."

"Beep."

"What do you mean, beep for an old friend. We were prepsters together."

"Beep."

"Ha ha George. It is you. Greetings. No kidding. Well how are you. I read that nifty write up in the papers. I mean you're a somebody. I mean I'm not doing badly. I'm doing all right. Got myself a little old partnership. But I mean how are you, all right."

"Beep beep."

"Now wait a minute. George ha ha. I know this is a funny situation."

"Beep."

"But a jokes a joke. O.K."

"Beep beep."

"Now hold it. Let's not make a meeting like this in the middle of Owl Street with all the congestion, holding things up. I mean you're located here. What do you say."

"Beep."

"Gee George is there something wrong. Are they crowding you. This has kind of gone on too long to be comic. I can take a hint, if that's it. What are you saying this beep to me for. If you don't want to recognise me say so."

"Beep beep."

"What is it. Is this a method, something happened and you use this method. I mean they said in the papers you were building a mausoleum, that costs, I know,

I mean are you nervous."

"Beep."

"It's a method."

"Beep."

"I see that's one beep. O now I remember. The rude noise you made to the reporters. O I'm catching on, a voice lapse. It's one beep, maybe, for yes."

"Beep."

"And two for no."

"Beep."

"I'm sorry, I didn't know anything about this George. Is it permanent."

"Beep."

"Gee that's tough, on your wife and kids. I heard you got married. Only guessing you got kids. To Shirl. What a girl. She'd never even give me a tumble. Remember the tea dances. Those white linen suits Shirl used to wear. She was beautiful."

"Beep."

"But I just didn't know you had this problem. I guess you're under specialists."

"Beep."

"New method like this must tax the mind. You must want to really say something once in awhile. Like an opinion."

"Beep beep."

"Is that right. If there's anything you need. I know you have money. But if you're bothered by a problem, spiritual, you know. Why you holding your hand to your ear. You're not deaf too."

"Beep."

"O, gee, that's tough. You lip read."

"Beep."

"You remember Alice. You know I married her."

"Beep beep."

"She only mentioned you the other day. How Shirl followed you right across the ocean. The ocean. I'm saying the ocean. My Alice, yes, mentioned you. She mentioned you. This is a really rotten world. Real rotten. It's rotten. Guy's speech and hearing cut off in his prime. I said in your prime. It's a shame. But you can still see. I said see, you can still see. To lip read. From behind the blue glasses."

"Beep."

"Thank God for that. Can they do something for you. I said, help you. Can they help you."

"Beep beep."

"It makes you sick, doesn't it. A disgrace. I said it was a disgrace."

"Beep."

"Believe me I'm really sorry for what's happened to you. I mean that sincerely. I said, I'm sorry. Sincerely."

"Beep beep beep."

"That's three. I got it. For thanks."

"Beep."

"Only George, I'm sort of in a hurry. Like to hang on, talk over old times. Sure would like to hear. I mean, get together won't we. I mean sometime, old sport, when you're all right again. You'll be all right. Thing is not to worry. I said, don't worry. Looking at my watch. Got to be dead on time, somewhere. An appointment. I wish you all of God's luck that someday you may be well again. Hope your health comes back. I mean that."

"Beep beep beep."

"Sorry I got to rush. But if you can read my lips I'm saying the cure may be in prayer George. Pray. So long."

"Beep beep beep beep."

"Ha ha, goodbye."

"Beep."

"See you."

"Beep beep beep beep."

We trust that you have just had a unique literary experience and that increased acquaintance with the story will provoke even more significant responses to it. If you are familiar with J. P. Donleavy's writing, you have probably already reached certain conclusions about the author's meanings in this story. Donleavy is known as a writer of *black humor*, which is an irreverent view of the human condition that moves us to laugh at matter we normally consider serious.

The events of "One for Yes" are not difficult to grasp. The narrator is walking along a busy city street on a pleasant August morning when he suddenly sees a displeasing sight: an old school chum he would like to avoid. He tries to escape but fails and is trapped into an unwanted conversation. Eventually, after an unusual dialogue, the other fellow hastily departs.

Beyond the surface events just described, the story stirs up at least two quite divergent interpretations. (The author may have intentionally been ambiguous—a desirable quality, not a fault, in good literature.) In the first interpretation, the narrator is thought to be pretending an inability to speak normally and is playing a rude game with his adversary in answering all questions with either one "beep" for "yes," or two for "no," eventually adding a third "beep" for "thanks," and a fourth for meanings not made obvious by the context. In a second interpretation, the narrator is thought to have suffered an actual illness or accident that really prevents him from conversing in any other way than by beeping. The first interpretation calls for simple, cold-blooded mischief on the narrator's part, a behavior most of us would secretly and malevolently like to vent on bores rather than submit to fatuous conversation with them. We focus on George Smith as our "hero," and our pleasure in reading the story with this interpretation arises from having launched a "perfect squelch" vicariously and harmlessly and in an absurdly comic way. The second interpretation contends that there is evidence that Smith has actual physical or mental problems, which are made more tragic by his friend's appalling embarrassment and empty sympathy. These are uncomfortably universal, for who of us has not felt incapable of saying the right things to others about their personal misfortunes? We now focus on the old chum and are pained because we recognize our own inadequacies for genuine compassion.

We cannot accept either interpretation as the sole meaning of the story; the presence of ambiguity credits the author with stimulating the reader to more complex responses than a simple story would provide. Accepting both basic meanings *concurrently* give us the pleasure-pain experience so characteristic of black humor. We suspect that Donleavy has deliberately avoided making his intent unmistakably clear. Did you notice that he has provided no explanatory narration after the first three paragraphs? As it is, the story is worthy of several readings, not just one; we are intrigued sufficiently to want to read it more than once for the detection of subtleties.

Of course, one's interpretation of the story will affect his oral reading of it. If meaning is response, then our oral reading should be our analysis; our analysis, our reading. Is it any wonder that leading theorists in oral interpretation staunchly maintain that the art, being a personal embodiment, is potentially the ultimate form of literary analysis? Our embodiment of " One for Yes " is the way we read it aloud. It is our physical behavior: our posture and bearing, our bodily tones and tensions, our actions, and our facial expressions. It is also the quality of our voices as we experience the events of the fiction, the speed at which we utter various thoughts, our basic speech rhythms (and those suggested for various characters), our pauses, the extent of time we spend on individual sounds, the highness or lowness of our voice pitch, the extent of pitch range we utilize, our intonational patterns, the loudness, the softness, and so on. Let's examine some possibilities for various " readings " of this story deriving from different responses to it.

One matter that we must clear up immediately is the point of view of the entire story. If we were to delete the first three paragraphs, we should have only a dialogue—a virtual playlet—with no obviously expressed point of view. In such an instance, the reader would be free to alternate his focus—as in the reading of drama—from one character to the other, adopting, in turn, the full bodily tones and vocal suggestions of each character. Donleavy, however, did provide us with those three opening paragraphs of narration, which establish the identity of the speaker through whom we receive the story. The narrator is clearly the one trying to escape: It is not he but the other man—the aggressive one—who speaks first. Because the scene is introduced by one character, it is presented primarily from his point of view. However, he does step aside and let the scene occur before our imaginations without further narrative commentary; therefore, the other character, as well, is given a good deal of opportunity to develop on his own in our interpretations—that is, as long as we recognize that the point of view or context is clearly colored at the beginning. (To what extent Smith is a mouthpiece for the author we cannot say precisely, although we are bound to make some assumptions.)

The basic physical attitude used by the reader throughout the story will be that of his conception of George Smith. The physical behavior implicit in the lines of the old schoolmate will be distorted by Smith's impression of him, not as we might see them enacted by a second character upon a stage or screen. This is true in everyday life: In describing a conversation we have had with a person, we reveal to others our own perception of that person by the way in which we quote him. Thus, in quoting someone as saying, " I will not join such a movement! " we may register pride in his action or register disgust, disappointment, dismay, or any other attitude we may have at the moment we utter the words. What our listeners hear and see is our subjective reaction. So it is with the narrator in literature, be he the author or a fictive persona. He may even distort his own previous behavior in the telling, just as we often do.

## PHYSICAL RESPONSE

What will be the reader's physical response to the story? The first two paragraphs indicate a buoyancy in the narrator that should certainly have an effect on any reader's physical behavior while reading. This buoyancy may be somewhat restrained in the reader who believes that Smith is really physically or mentally ill. On the other hand, if Smith is considered to be a well man putting on an impudent, insulting act, the reader will probably have normal or even exaggerated physical energy.

Cues for physical tone or action will be found in the literature. It is easy to see that a sensitive reader of " One for Yes " will have an empathic response to Smith's desire to avoid the other man. Surely you can recall the over-powering presence of an unpleasant person who pressed too closely on you in conversation. George Smith feels this aversion. How would a reader's posture or bearing reveal the basic attitudes of each character? One character would probably lean forward; the other, backward. Do the bodily attitudes or predominant facial expressions of either or both of the characters change at any point in the reading? Look for a turning point in the story, after which the apparent aggressive-regressive traits of the two characters are reversed and become increasingly opposite until the end of the story. It is difficult to tell whether George's illness is real or feigned; bodily response may make this clear or may deliberately preserve the ambiguity. (Actually, a faked illness might cause George's body to sag more than a real one!)

Are Smith's bodily actions and facial expressions different when he says " Beep " and " Beep beep "? How about " Beep beep beep "? And " Beep beep beep beep "? (Yes, what *is* he saying in four beeps?)

Even though we read from George Smith's point of view, we may characterize the other fellow in suggestive action or expression. When he learns that George is "deaf," he might well begin to speak louder, exaggerate articulatory activity, and resort to suggestive gesture in an increased effort to communicate with him. Examine such lines of his as "I'm looking at my watch," "An appointment," and "Pray" for statements probably aided by action, even specific pantomime.

The more we study (respond to) this little story, the more we see how important a role visible expression and action will play in its effective communication. (*Note:* We *could* as accurately have said: ". . . how important a role visible expression and action will play in *experiencing* this piece of literature.")

We are tempted to go through the story, line by line, and write a complete analysis of the physical tones and actions suggested by the words, but this would constitute a description of only one performance by one person at one time. Many nineteenth-century elocutionists illustrated their textbooks with photographs of ladies in long white dresses posing melodramatically for such emotions and attitudes as *hate, adoration, jealousy, fear, bashfulness,* and literally dozens (and dozens!) of others. These became mandatory prescriptions to the performer for the representation of specific attitudes or emotions. We should constantly keep in mind that physical behavior is highly individualized and subject to variance even within *one* individual's response to the *same* literature on *different* occasions. Recognizing this, modern speech has thrown off the prescribed poses of the elocutionist, but has perhaps gone to the other extreme, and has too long ignored the importance of visible expressiveness in human communication. Professor Ray L. Birdwhistell is the dynamic proponent of a relatively infant science called *kinesics,* the study of body-motion behavior in communication. Of course, kinesics does not yet offer an instructional panacea, but it does provide insight into the complex nature of human visible activity. We shall have more to say about this aspect of communication in the next chapter.

## ORAL RESPONSE

What will be the reader's oral response to "One for Yes"? Obviously, George Smith's speech will be affected by the reader's conception of Smith's health. One must make a decision whether an ill George Smith is able to make anything more than a flat, electronic "beep," which would certainly make George sound robot-like. Even if "beep" is the only sound he can make, the reader must still decide how it sounds: Is it high or low pitched? Short or long? Loud or soft? Automatic or subject to some variation? Accompanied by pauses? On the other hand, is it capable of inflection? If one beep means "yes," will it be spoken with a *yes* intonation, and two beeps with a *no* intonation? If Smith is putting on an act, he may speak the beeps with feeling. (On the other hand, his "act" might reach a mechanical near perfection, with perhaps an occasional slip to pique the listeners' curiosity.)

If the reader goes to the narrative paragraphs for hints of the nature of Smith's speech, he finds terse notations rather than flowing sentences. He might ask if this is a further indication of a difficulty on Smith's part in expressing himself, but an examination of Donleavy's other stories in the same volume *(Meet My Maker the Mad Molecule)* reveals that this mode is characteristic of the author's style of writing rather than a suggestion of the character's thinking, speaking, or writing. Also characteristic of the author is his lack of punctuation other than periods and commas. Thus, the omission of question marks and exclamation points, contrary to what one might have surmised at first glance, offers no suggestion of the intonations, if any, used by the characters.

We said earlier in this chapter that the audience will "see" the other fellow only through Smith's impression of him, resulting in whatever physical suggestion the responsive oral reader provides. The same is true in audible matters: We shall "hear" the old school chum only through Smith's reactions to him. The reader will have to fathom Smith's interpretation of what happened that August morning. Paragraph 3 furnishes some indication of the adversary's appearance. It also shows how he affects Smith. One can feel that whereas the pace in he first two paragraphs was probably smooth and unhurried, suggesting mild exhilaration, the third paragraph begins with a jolt, followed by a quickening pace, and then by resignation and possibly malevolence. Smith's pleasure in his adversary's pain could be indicated by a pace that picks up near the end as the poor fellow tries to escape. In light of the context, what is Smith's attitude? In the third paragraph, the reader's voice needs to be responsive to the distaste apparent in "And eyes that turned on their glow." The chum reveals himself through his language. In paragraph 4 he tactlessly reminds Smith that he got away once before. In later paragraphs he says "Ha" and "Ha ha," indicative of a boisterous fellow whose laugh is perhaps too hearty or perhaps unduly embarrassed. His sudden shifts from one subject to another in paragraph 10 suggest that he is a loud and fast talker who does not wait for an answer but impolitely goes on to other subjects. His repetitions of the meaningless phrase "I mean" tell us something else about his personality. One can imagine how his speech is affected during this scene, changing from an overwhelming cockiness to a diminishing self-assurance and then to a virtual panic at the end of the story. One can also "hear" his boisterous entrance, his deflation, and his flight, in his degrees of loudness, his variations in rate, his pauses during his mounting confusion, and his increased vocal tension as he escapes.

Audible communication has been subject to considerably more study than has visible communication. Linguists have been trying to systematize the investigation, but some aspects of their work have been known for centuries. Certainly, the sensitive reader studies the language used in any piece of literature. He pays close attention to grammar and syntax in order to determine the bare ideas expressed, and he goes beyond this to study the connotative values in language that, we have already suggested, help us to determine the author's attitude toward what he is saying. The author's distinct style, his degree of objectivity-subjectivity, his ability to characterize —all these are to be found in the language.

But implicit in human speech are other factors that go along with language. These are what the linguists call " paralanguage," the vocal accompaniment of language, which includes:

1. Such variables of speech as:
   a. Time (rate, pause, duration, rhythm).
   b. Loudness (softness, as well, and forms of attack-touch).
   c. Pitch (normal highness or lowness of voice, range of pitch; also including changes of pitch in steps and slides, constituting intonation).
   d. Quality (timbre or essential nature of the voice).
2. Such vocal activities as:
   a. Laughing or crying, yelling or whispering, moaning or groaning, and belching or yawning.
   b. Uh, uh-uh, and uh-huh.
3. Such prelinguistic considerations—that is, the effect upon speech—of matters as physiology of the speaker, sex, age, health, build, rhythm, position in social group, and mood.

We shall devote four chapters to a consideration of the voice variables and the part they play in audible communication. Our discussion of " One for Yes " should already have been a sufficient indication that vocal activities and prelinguistic considerations are vital in responses to literature.

Before ending this discussion of the expression of responses, we should distinguish between two kinds of interpreters' performing attitudes. One seems to say to the audience: "Watch (and hear) me responding to the literature I'm reading." This is clearly putting the reader before the literature, exactly what the old-time elocutionist often did. The audience is encouraged to respond to vocal and physical technique and not to the literature itself. Of course, a second sort of performing attitude is desirable. Here, the interpreter acts in behalf of the literature with a subliminal message that is something like: "Respond with me to the literature." The effective reader's disciplined responses focus on the *literature*. The reader wants listeners to have *their* own unique, but still, appropriate, responses.

# A POSTSCRIPT TO "ONE FOR YES"

Because Mr. Donleavy published "One for Yes" as a separate short story, or sketch, we have analyzed it as such, without reference to the fact that the episode appears also in his novel *A Singular Man*, actually published a year before *Meet My Maker the Mad Molecule*. Neither the copyright date for "One for Yes" nor the time it was written is ascertainable; therefore, we do not know whether the author wrote it as a sketch and then included it in his novel or extracted it from his novel to publish it separately. However, the fact that it was published as an independent unit justifies our interpreting it as an individual piece of literature intended to stand on its own feet.

Reading the novel, however, does give one insights into the character of George Smith that the sketch alone does not. There are only a few differences in the actual scripts: minor changes in form, for the most part. Three changes appear in the novel: the addition of a second paragraph further describing activity on the streets that morning and containing references to Smith's apartment, his maid, and one of his two secretaries; the addition of four short sentences by the prepster mentioning that Smith had been a colonel in a foreign army; and, a slightly different ending containing some interesting lines:

Smith ducking into the inhuman stream. Entering Dynamo House. So many have wives and little ones. Like the lonely have themselves. I've just the strength to climb these stairs. Ugliness brings taunts and jeers from passers-by. Elegance invites assault from strangers. Old friendships promote beeps.

This ending obviously clears up the fact that George Smith can speak and has beeped on purpose to his former friend. One must read the rest of the novel, of course, to fully understand the character of George Smith. On the second page of the novel, the reader finds Smith saying to himself, "show people you're in command of the situation by not saying much, don't let them get in close, keep everyone at arm's length, stop smiling kindly," The picture of a wealthy man, estranged from his wife and four children, living behind a thick steel door in a lavish apartment house, riding in a bulletproof limousine, unable to relate—other than sexually—with any human being, carrying a fortune around in a paper sack and then drunkenly dumping it out the window of a high building to watch human animals scrounge for it below, madcappedly trying to escape from old friends and then trying as desperately to find them, carrying on an absurd correspondence with mysterious business adversaries who constantly threaten to ruin him, conducting his own financial empire from a dark, nondescript office with only one or two secretaries, and finding satisfaction in only one thing: building a huge, air-conditioned mausoleum for himself—all these make us laugh at and yet feel sorry for the emptiness of George Smith (and perhaps ourselves) in an affluent, often valueless, society. One reviewer has written that Smith's world is a " threnody of indefinable sorrows and terrors " and that he lives in a "lonely, surrealistic opulence, warding off a thousand unnamable threats."[1] Perhaps many can find something of themselves in George Smith and his world, even in his paranoia! (Some readers will see no connection or relevance.) Perhaps some of the total message of *A Singular Man* is suggested in the burlesque sketch called " One for Yes."

# EXERCISES

Following are a wide range of literary types. Read them and make some initial conscious observations of the nature of your visible and audible responses to them. Then, choose one selection for a detailed written analysis, such as we have made in this chapter. (We trust that your study will lead to an act of communication.)

In the first selection, we have interjected some comments to illustrate a kind of verbalization you might employ in some instances.

## *from* THE CAINE MUTINY

HERMAN WOUK

In Herman Wouk's excellent, best-selling novel, *The Caine Mutiny*, is a scene in which three young men, striving to make good in a naval cadet school during World War II, are learning to disassemble and reassemble Springfield rifles. The men are in their room on the tenth floor of a building in New York City.

Willie wrestled vainly with the bolt for a while and panted, "They should have bilged me on lordosis. It would have been more dignified. I'll be out of this Navy tomorrow—Get in there, lousy damn spring—" He had never touched a gun before. The potential deadliness of it meant nothing to him. It was simply a troublesome assignment: a knotty page of Beethoven, an overdue book report on *Clarissa Harlowe*.

"Jam the butt of that bolt in your stomach, see?" said Keefer. "Then press the spring down with both hands."

Anyone who has had a similar experience in the army can immediately sympathize with Willie's plight. But if the reader has had no direct experience with a rifle, he can recall any personal frustrating experience in which

[1] *Newsweek*, November 11, 1963, p. 110.

he has been forced to learn something entirely foreign to his past experience and to learn it under pressure of time. Wouk has already drawn such a comparison in Willie's life. Willie must learn to strip the rifle by the next morning or suffer unpleasant consequences: discharge from the Navy. College students face the same crisis when they must learn a very difficult principle the night before a final examination.

As we read this passage, we therefore sense Willie's almost panic-stricken frustration. We are relieved, though, when we read these words:

Willie obeyed. The spring yielded slowly. The end of it sank at last into the rim. "It works! Thanks, Rollo—"

We are disturbed again when:

At that moment the spring, still unsecured, escaped between his fingers and leaped from the bolt. It soared across the room. The window was conveniently open. The spring sailed out into the night.

His roommates stared at him in horror. "That's bad, isn't it?" quavered Willie.

"Anything happens to your rifle, boy—that does it," said the Southerner, walking to the window.

We feel despair for Willie as we recall the almost inhuman lack of sympathy for human error in the armed services. We are excited by the hero's problem, and we rush on to find out what he is going to do.

"I'll run downstairs," Willie said.

Here is a glimmer of hope—that Willie can recover the lost piece.

"What, during study hour? Twelve demerits!" Keggs said.

Despair again. Demerits are serious.

"Come here, fella." Keefer pointed out through the window. The spring lay in a rain gutter at the edge of a steeply slanting copper-covered roof projection beneath the window. The tenth floor was set slightly back from the rest of the building.

The words force us to visualize the picture. We again have hope!

"I can't get that," said Willie.

Frustrating despair, again.

"You better, fella."

The forces of duty and necessity are speaking, forcing Willie to attempt the impossible.

> Keggs peered out. "You'd never make it. You'd fall off."
> "That's what I think," said Willie. He was not at all a daredevil. His mountain climbing had been done in plenty of stout company, and with much gulping horror. He hated high places and poor footing.

Willie's fears and tensions inhabit us.

> "Look fella, you want to stay in the Navy? Climb out there. Or d'you want me to do it?"

No one wishes to be a coward. Shame drives us to do what we are mortally afraid to do.

> Willie climbed out, clinging to the window frame. The wind moaned in the darkness. Broadway twinkled far, far below. The ledge seemed to drop away beneath his trembling legs. He stretched a hand vainly toward the spring, and gasped, "Need another couple of feet—"

If you are afraid of high places, Willie's plight catches you in the pit of the stomach. Painful muscular tensions grip you there. Listen to a movie audience gasp whenever a film camera peeks over the top ledge of a tall city building. By the process of empathy the audience is actually on that ledge! We are now projecting ourselves into the fictional person of Willie Keith.

> "If only we had a rope," said Keefer. "Look man. One of us gets out with you, see, and hangs onto the window. And you hang onto him. That does it."

Because of our own nature, we judge that Willie would gladly have climbed back into the room and given up, but Keefer's determined and daring efforts to help Willie force him into greater efforts to retrieve the lost spring.

> "Let's get it over with," said Keggs anxiously. "If he gets caught out there we all bilge." He sprang through the window, stood beside Willie, and gripped his hand. "Now get it." Willie let go of the window, and inched downward, clinging to Kegg's powerful grip. He teetered at the edge of the roof, the wind whipping his clothes. The spring was in easy reach. He grasped it and thrust it into a pocket.

Without waiting for the finish of the episode, we experience some relief, but the author has not finished with us!

Ensign Acres might have picked a less awkward moment to make his study-hour round of the tenth floor, but he chose this one. He walked past the room, peeped in, stopped short, and roared, "Attention on deck! What the hell is going on here?"

Keggs neighed in terror and let go of Willie's hand. Willie lunged and clutched him around the knees. The two midshipmen swayed back and forth on the ledge, not far from death. But Keggs' urge to live was slightly stronger than his fear of ensigns. He reared backward and fell into the room on his head, hauling Willie through the window on top of him.

Terror and relief! A parade of images, ideas, and strong emotions are released, each of which must register in the mind and body of the oral interpreter while in action.

"Birches" and "The Campus on the Hill" are both philosophical poems, but they are radically different. Even though there may be a fundamental idea to glean in each poem, there is also in each, an indication of attitude, feeling, and mood. The one is quite personal; the other, more coldly objective and removed.

## BIRCHES

ROBERT FROST

When I see birches bend to left and right
Across the lines of straighter darker trees,
I like to think some boy's been swinging them.
But swinging doesn't bend them down to stay.
Ice-storms do that. Often you must have seen them
Loaded with ice a sunny winter morning
After a rain. They click upon themselves
As the breeze rises, and turn many-colored
As the stir cracks and crazes their enamel.
Soon the sun's warmth makes them shed crystal shells
Shattering and avalanching on the snow-crust—
Such heaps of broken glass to sweep away
You'd think the inner dome of heaven had fallen.
They are dragged to the withered bracken by the load,
And they seem not to break; though once they are bowed
So low for long, they never right themselves:
You may see their trunks arching in the woods
Years afterwards, trailing their leaves on the ground
Like girls on hands and knees that throw their hair
Before them over their heads to dry in the sun.
But I was going to say when Truth broke in
With all her matter-of-fact about the ice-storm

I should prefer to have some boy bend them
As he went out and in to fetch the cows—
Some boy too far from town to learn baseball,
Whose only play was what he found himself,
Summer or winter, and could play alone.
One by one he subdued his father's trees
By riding them down over and over again
Until he took the stiffness out of them,
And not one but hung limp, not one was left
For him to conquer. He learned all there was
To learn about not launching out too soon
And so not carrying the tree away
Clear to the ground. He always kept his poise
To the top branches, climbing carefully
With the same pains you use to fill a cup
Up to the brim, and even above the brim.
Then he flung outward, feet first, with a swish,
Kicking his way down through the air to the ground.
So was I once myself a swinger of birches.
And so I dream of going back to be.
It's when I'm weary of considerations,
And life is too much like a pathless wood
Where your face burns and tickles with the cobwebs
Broken across it, and one eye is weeping
From a twig's having lashed across it open.
I'd like to get away from earth awhile
And then come back to it and begin over.
May no fate willfully misunderstand me
And half grant what I wish and snatch me away
Not to return. Earth's the right place for love:
I don't know where it's likely to go better.
I'd like to go by climbing a birch tree,
And climb black branches up a snow-white trunk
*Toward* heaven, till the tree could bear no more,
But dipped its top and set me down again.
That would be good both going and coming back.
One could do worse than be a swinger of birches.

## THE CAMPUS ON THE HILL

### W. D. SNODGRASS

Up the reputable walks of old established trees
They stalk, children of the *nouveaux riches;* chimes
Of the tall Clock Tower drench their heads in blessing:

"I don't wanna play at your house;
I don't like you any more."
My house stands opposite, on the other hill,
Among meadows, with the orchard fences down and falling;
Deer come almost to the door.
You cannot see it, even in this clearest morning.
White birds hang in the air between
Over the garbage landfill and those homes thereto adjacent,
Hovering slowly, turning settling down
Like the flakes sifting imperceptibly onto the little town
In a waterball of glass.
And yet, this morning, beyond this quiet scene,
The floating birds, the backyards of the poor,
Beyond the shopping plaza, the dead canal, the hillside lying tilted in the air,
Tomorrow has broken out today:
Riot in Algeria, in Cyprus, in Alabama;
Aged in wrong, the empires are declining,
And China gathers, soundlessly, like evidence.
What shall I say to the young on such a morning?—
Mind is the one salvation?—also grammar?—
No; my little ones lean not toward revolt. They
Are the Whites, the vaguely furiously driven, who resist
Their souls with such passivity
As would make Quakers swear. All day, dear Lord, all day
They wear their godhead lightly.
They look out from their hill and say,
To themselves, "We have nowhere to go but down;
The great destination is to stay."
Surely the nations will be reasonable;
They look at the world—don't they?—the world's way?
The clock just now has nothing more to say.

" Mother " is about as personal a subject as one can find. Following are two excellent poems about two mothers. Although neither may be at all like your own, try to respond as the poets appear to. There are many poems about " mother," some good, some terrible. Bring others to class for comparison and evaluation in order to see how some stimulate much response, and some, very little.

## TO MY MOTHER

GEORGE BARKER

Most near, most dear, most loved and most far,
Under the window where I often found her

Sitting as huge as Asia, seismic with laughter,
Gin and chicken helpless in her Irish hand,
Irresistible as Rabelais, but most tender for
The lame dogs and hurt birds that surround her,—
She is a procession no one can follow after
But be like a little dog following a brass band.

She will not glance up at the bomber, or condescend
To drop her gin and scuttle to a cellar,
But lean on the mahogany table like a mountain
Whom only faith can move, and so I send
O all my faith, and all my love to tell her
That she will move from mourning into morning.

## MOTHERS

NIKKI GIOVANNI

the last time i was home
to see my mother we kissed
exchanged pleasantries
and unpleasantries pulled a warm
comforting silence around
us and read separate books

i remember the first time
i consciously saw her
we were living in a three room
apartment on burns avenue

mommy always sat in the dark
i don't know how i knew that but she did

that night i stumbled into the kitchen
maybe because i've always been
a night person or perhaps because i had wet
the bed
she was sitting on a chair
the room was bathed in moonlight diffused through
those thousands of panes landlords who rented
to people with children were prone to put in windows

she may have been smoking but maybe not
her hair was three-quarters her height

which made me a strong believer in the samson myth
and very black

i'm sure i just hung there by the door
i remember thinking: what a beautiful lady

she was very deliberately waiting
perhaps for my father to come home
from his night job .or maybe for a dream
that had promised to come by
"come here" she said "i'll teach you
a poem: *i see the moon*
>*the moon sees me*
>*god bless the moon*
>*and god bless me"*
i taught it to my son
who recited it for her
just to say we must learn
to bear the pleasures
as we have borne the pains

[10 mar 72]

A "malaprop" (stemming from "mal apropos") is a gross misuse of a word. Coming from ignorance, it is often rippingly funny. Sheridan, in Mrs. Malaprop, gave us one of the great comic characters in English drama. Her innocent misuse of words still has to be pointed enough to reach the audience. This calls for considerable vocal and physical characterization.

## *from* THE RIVALS

RICHARD BRINSLEY SHERIDAN

MRS. MALAPROP. There, Sir Anthony, there sits the deliberate simpleton who wants to disgrace her family, and lavish herself on a fellow not worth a shilling.

LYDIA LANGUISH. Madam, I thought you once—

MRS. MAL. You thought, miss! I don't know any business you have to think at all—thought does not become a young woman. But the point we would request of you is, that you will promise to forget this fellow—to illiterate him, I say, quite from your memory.

LYD. Ah, madam! our memories are independent of our wills. It is not so easy to forget.

MRS. MAL. But I say it is, miss; there is nothing on earth so easy as to forget, if a person chooses to set about it. I'm sure I have as much forgot your poor dear uncle as if he had never existed—and I thought it my duty so to do; and let me tell you, Lydia, these violent memories don't become a young woman.

SIR ANTHONY ABSOLUTE. Why sure she won't pretend to remember what she's ordered not!—ay, this comes of her reading!

LYD. What crime, madam, have I committed, to be treated thus?

MRS. MAL. Now don't attempt to extirpate yourself from the matter; you know I have proof controvertible of it.—But tell me, will you promise to do as you're bid? Will you take a husband of your friends' choosing?

LYD. Madam, I must tell you plainly, that had I no preference for any one else, the choice you have made would be my aversion.

MRS. MAL. What business have you, miss, with preference and aversion? They don't become a young woman; and you ought to know, that as both always wear off, 'tis safest in matrimony to begin with a little aversion. I am sure I hated your poor dear uncle before marriage as if he'd been a blackamoor—and yet, miss, you are sensible what a wife I made!—and when it pleased Heaven to release me from him, 'tis unknown what tears I shed! But suppose we were going to give you another choice, will you promise us to give up this Beverley?

LYD. Could I belie my thoughts so far as to give that promise, my actions would certainly as far belie my words.

MRS. MAL. Take yourself to your room. You are fit company for nothing but your own ill-humours.

LYD. Willingly, ma'am—I cannot change for the worse. (*Exit.*)

MRS. MAL. There's a little intricate hussy for you!

SIR ANTH. It is not to be wondered at, ma'am,—all this is the natural consequence of teaching girls to read. Had I a thousand daughters, by Heaven! I'd as soon have them taught the black art as their alphabet!

MRS. MAL. Nay, nay, Sir Anthony, you are an absolute misanthropy.

SIR ANTH. In my way hither, Mrs. Malaprop, I observed your niece's maid coming forth from a circulating library!—She had a book in each hand—they were half-bound volumes, with marble covers!—From that moment I guessed how full of duty I should see her mistress!

MRS. MAL. Those are vile places, indeed!

SIR ANTH. Madam, a circulating library in a town is as an evergreen tree of diabolical knowledge! It blossoms through the year!—and depend on it, Mrs. Malaprop, that they who are so fond of handling the leaves, will long for the fruit at last.

MRS. MAL. Fy, fy, Sir Anthony, you surely speak laconically.

SIR ANTH. Why, Mrs. Malaprop, in moderation now, what would you have a woman know?

MRS. MAL. Observe me, Sir Anthony. I would by no means wish a daughter of mine to be a progeny of learning; I don't think so much learning becomes a young woman; for instance, I would never let her meddle with Greek, or

Hebrew, or algebra, or simony, or fluxions, or paradoxes, or such inflammatory branches of learning—neither would it be necessary for her to handle any of your mathematical, astronomical, diabolical instruments.—But, Sir Anthony, I would send her, at nine years old, to a boarding-school, in order to let her learn a little ingenuity and artifice. Then, sir, she should have a supercilious knowledge in accounts;—and as she grew up, I would have her instructed in geometry that she might know something of the contagious countries;—but above all, Sir Antony, she should be mistress of orthodoxy, that she might not mis-spell, and mis-pronounce words so shamefully as girls usually do; and likewise that she might reprehend the true meaning of what she is saying. This, Sir Anthony, is what I would have a woman know;—and I don't think there is a superstitious article in it.

SIR ANTH. Well, well, Mrs. Malaprop, I will dispute the point no further with you; though I must confess that you are a truly moderate and polite arguer, for almost every third word you say is on my side of the question.

Following are five modern poems of a considerable range of form and syntax. In addition to responding to imagery in them, take into consideration the effect of the structure of the poem upon your responses. Look at the shape of the piece upon the page, line lengths, stanzaic structure, directness of statement, vocabulary, rhyme, and so on.

## THE DESERT MOTORCYCLIST

DIANE WAKOSKI

Road as wide open
as my shoulders when I am loving
the tides
the dry sand that blows against you like rain—
I am riding away from you:
away from your voice that troubles me,
like a leak in the basement,
away from your timidities
about frogs and salamanders,
away down this desert road,
purple and bloody with dusk.

Pools of the afternoon spray me,
distorting your image.
You caged me in water,
imprisoned me in tide pools/remembering I am the spiny starfish,
softer inside than evolution should allow.

Now I run away
to my dry desert,
the place where there is enough space
for my imagination
and nothing to drown it.

Desert motorcyclist:
that is me.
And it is always the man,
never the machine
who betrays me.

## I KNOW I'M NOT SUFFICIENTLY OBSCURE

RAY DUREM (1915–63)

I know I'm not sufficiently obscure
to please the critics—nor devious enough.
Imagery escapes me.
I cannot find those mild and gracious words
to clothe the carnage.
Blood is blood and murder's murder.
What's a lavender word for lynch?
Come, you pale poets, wan, refined and dreamy:
here is a black woman working out her guts
in a white man's kitchen
for little money and no glory.
How should I tell that story?
There is a black boy, blacker still from death,
face down in the cold Korean mud.
Come on with your effervescent jive
explain to him why he ain't alive.
Reword our specific discontent
into some plaintive melody,
a little whine, a little whimper,
not too much—and no rebellion!
God, no! Rebellion's much too corny.
You deal with finer feelings,
very subtle—an autumn leaf
hanging from a tree—I see a body!

# LET ME LIVE OUT MY YEARS

JOHN G. NEIHARDT

Let me live out my years in heat of blood!
Let me die drunken with the dreamer's wine!
Let me not see this soul-house built of mud
Go toppling to the dust—a vacant shrine.
Let me go quickly, like a candle light
Snuffed out just at the heyday of its glow.
Give me high noon—and let it then be night!
Thus would I go.
And grant that when I face the grisly Thing,
My song may trumpet down the grey Perhaps.
O let me be a tune-swept fiddle string
That feels the Master-Melody—and snaps!

# CRISIS IN THE ZOO

DON GEIGER

Flamingo, peacock, lizard, and white bear:
among exotic forms of nature's birth,
smiling, hand in hand, we stroll on slowly,
forgetting burdens hardly worth our care
in a place that has so many ways to show
how little man is needed by the earth.

Someone cries, there's something funny here!
A chimp is dead; we hurry to the news,
and find flies noising in a heap of wool,
occasionally riffled by the air.
His mate beside him cracks a peanut shell
and, mistress of her passions, slowly chews.

We are dismayed—not by creatures freed
from obligatory building of their souls
(she does not wonder whom she'll turn to now,
and keepers, rushing up, assure her needs)—
but by the monstrous weight of pressing vows
our simian hands have uttered while we strolled.

# MY FATHER MOVED THROUGH DOOMS OF LOVE

E E CUMMINGS

my father moved through dooms of love
through sames of am through haves of give,
singing each morning out of each night
my father moved through depths of height

this motionless forgetful where
turned at his glance to shining here;
that *if* (so timid air is firm)
under his eyes would stir and squirm

newly as from unburied which
floats the first who, his april touch
drove sleeping selves to swarm their fates
woke dreamers to their ghostly roots

and should some why completely weep
my father's fingers brought her sleep:
vainly no smallest voice might cry
for he could feel the mountains grow.

Lifting the valleys of the sea
my father moved through griefs of joy;
praising a forehead called the moon
singing desire into begin

joy was his song and joy so pure
a heart of star by him could steer
and pure so now and now so yes
the wrists of twilight would rejoice

keen as midsummer's keen beyond
conceiving mind of sun will stand,
so strictly (over utmost him
so hugely) stood my father's dream

his flesh was flesh his blood was blood:
no hungry man but wished him food;
no cripple wouldn't creep one mile
uphill to only see him smile.

Scorning the pomp of must and shall
my father moved through dooms of feel;
his anger was as right as rain
his pity was as green as grain

septembering arms of year extend
less humbly wealth to foe and friend
than he to foolish and to wise
offered immeasurable is

proudly and (by octobering flame
beckoned) as earth will downward climb,
so naked for immortal work
his shoulders marched against the dark

his sorrow was as true as bread:
no liar looked him in the head;
if every friend became his foe
he'd laugh and build a world with snow.

My father moved through theys of we,
singing each new leaf out of each tree
(and every child was sure that spring
danced when she heard my father sing)

then let men kill which cannot share,
let blood and flesh be mud and mire,
scheming imagine, passion willed,
freedom a drug that's bought and sold

giving to steal and cruel kind,
a heart to fear to doubt a mind,
to differ a disease of same,
conform the pinnacle of am

though dull were all we taste as bright,
bitter all utterly things sweet,
maggoty minus and dumb death
all we inherit, all bequeath

and nothing quite so least as truth
—i say though hate were why men breathe—
because my father lived his soul
love is the whole and more than all

# 7

*Visible*
*Communication*

## Its Primacy

The communication of the earliest primitive man was probably almost entirely visible rather than oral. Although he grunted, whimpered, roared, and chuckled, he must have signaled most of his intentions and desires with movements of his body. In the nineteenth century, Wilhelm Wundt, a German psychologist, theorized that the language of primitives was gesture. In the twentieth century, Sir Richard Paget has further theorized that when manlike creatures began to use tools, which, of course, they had to hold in their hands, their communication turned more to facial movement and that eventually oral sounds and facial movements joined to make words. It is unlikely that these ideas can ever be fully established, but they do imply that visible communication is more basic than the oral.

We can imagine dawn man communicating with his fellows, and perhaps with some other forms of life as well, by a threatening fist or widespread claws, a pointing finger, movements of either retreat or aggression, or perhaps more subtle behavioral patterns. Other men *saw* what he meant.

We need not look to vague conjecture for evidence that audible speech is a fairly recent acquisition. The various parts of the so-called speech mechanism —the tongue, teeth, lips, mandible, maxilla, soft palate, hard palate, lungs, and even the larynx itself—have far more fundamental functions than the formation of speech sounds. The tongue is used in tasting, in manipulating food, and in sucking. The teeth, mandible, and maxilla seem designed primarily for the mastication of food. The hard palate is employed in sucking and as a wall between the mouth and the nasal cavity. The soft palate is contractible and permits normal breathing through the nose or enforced respiration through the mouth when more oxygen is required. The lungs are organs of respiration. Finally, the fundamental function of the larynx is a valvular one. It is employed to close the tracheal passageway from the lungs in order that pressure may be created for such basic acts as lifting, defecation, and giving birth. This function may be readily understood if you will grasp the edges of the chair seat on which you sit and try to lift yourself, chair and all. In making the exertion you involuntarily close the vocal folds and shut off the exit of air from the lungs. When the muscular tension is eased, the breath is expelled in a grunt.

*169*

These basic processes of tasting, sucking, chewing, breathing, and exertion are ones of survival and appear to be the functions for which the organs we have discussed were originally evolved. Some authorities tell us that the speech production in which these parts of the body are now employed is an overlaid function, that we have found an additional role for the organs beyond the more basic ones. They point out that no animal has a true organ of voice except certain birds.

Why discuss all these factors now? The reason is to demonstrate clearly and forcefully that speech was first of all visible and that to this day visible speech is most "natural."

An analysis of typical human behavior shows that visible speech was not only primary in man's evolution but remains primary to this day. A careful timing of effective gestures in speaking reveals that they precede momentarily the utterance of the idea with which they are associated. It seems right to point with the hand a fraction of a second before shouting, "Look there!" but observe how foolish you appear if first you shout and then point. As any student of theater will tell you, the action must precede the word. To reverse the process is to create the style of acting we associate with old-time melodrama. What better evidence could there be of the primacy of visible speech?

Not only is visible or nonverbal speech a fundamentally natural mode of communication, but we all depend heavily on it. When you are communicating orally to others, they are watching you: they are interpreting your actions as well as your sounds. If actions speak louder than words, the two together must speak louder than either alone. Nonverbal communication can both say a great deal by itself and supplement what comes out of the mouth. Furthermore, what your audience sees can serve to hold attention or, conversely, can detract from attention. Behavior that either calls attention to itself or communicates meaning inconsistent with the speaker's intention is a liability. Finally, the use of the whole body in speaking or reading actually promotes poise.

# KINESICS

The kinesiologist, who was mentioned in the previous chapter, observes that language experts have generally assumed verbal behavior to be *the* channel of social interaction. He reflects that communication scholars have been preoccupied with the written word and have assumed that literacy represents the communicative process at its best. Attempts to perfect communication have concentrated upon its verbal aspects. Although there is today a growing recognition that communication is far more complex than previously thought, lexicographers, grammarians, philosophers, and even semanticists continue to focus attention almost exclusively on verbal behavior and to regard the nonverbal only as a modifier of the verbal.

Kinesics is a science of analyzing visible body behavior. It regards the entire visible body as potentially communicative and seeks to identify units of communicative body motions and to determine their meanings. It discovers that some units are employed in some cultures but not in others, and that meanings communicated by some units differ in different cultures. It predicts that the " kinemic catalogue " of the American culture will probably contain between fifty and sixty items, observes that some communicative behavior to which specific meanings are attached is employed either with or without vocalic accompaniment, and concludes that Americans " move as well as speak " their language.[1]

We make here this brief reference to kinesics in order to call your attention to the fact that some modern scholarship is being applied to the visible aspects of communication. Nineteenth-century speech teachers such as François Delsarte placed great importance upon gesture, facial expression, stance, and body movement, but they lacked the scientific methods now being employed, and they sought to impose visible techniques on the speaker and reader. The results were often disastrous and contributed in large part to the disrepute into which elocution fell. Current research in kinesics is descriptive and avoids the sort of prescriptive assistance attempted by the elocutionists. Its value lies not in telling us what to do while performing but, rather, in emphasizing again the importance of communicating meaningfully with the eyes of your audience.

## EMPATHY

Many people saw and heard the distinguished actor Charles Laughton in his celebrated reading tours. Perhaps most who saw him did not notice his platform behavior. After all, he was an accomplished artist and did not call attention to himself as much as to what he was reading, but it was especially interesting to notice how he achieved his amazing audience response. Informality seemed to be his motto, for he came to the platform laden with a huge and awkward assortment of books tucked high under his chin. Smiling broadly, he flung them onto the waiting table, leaned on the improvised speaker's stand, and said, " Hello." He seemed to engage us in conversation for a few moments before beginning his " speech." We hardly knew when his program began and his visiting ended. Smiling with us, he read Thurber. When he had finished a humorous piece, he laughed with us, shifted his position as if to relax, scratched himself comfortably, and searched with us for another. His face mirrored his thoughts and feelings, and our faces mirrored his face. We saw during Mr. Laughton's entire program an excellent example of the role of *empathy* in public speaking and reading.

[1] Ray L. Birdwhistell, "Communication Without Words," unpublished manuscript dated August 1964, *passim*. (Copy in possession of authors.)

By means of empathy he promoted our relaxation, prompted our anticipation, enhanced our pleasure, made us laugh, promoted our involvement in literary experiences, and helped us to love books.

Although we have spoken rather glibly of empathy, it is most difficult to define. The Greeks combined *en* (meaning " in " or " into ") with *pathos* (meaning " feeling ") to make *empatheia*, which in English has become *empathy*. The etymological meaning is thus an " in-feeling " or a " feeling into." The term has been employed in the arts for many years and in modern times has also been utilized in psychology and psychiatry. Indeed, the word has become so popular that it is variously used, but the central focus of its meaning continues to be a " feeling into." It is this " feeling into," this involvement, that Mr. Laughton achieved.

Perhaps the simplest illustration of empathic response occurs when you smile at someone who has smiled at you. It is the way a baby learns to smile and the reason that most adults smile at babies. It accounts for epidemics of yawns when people are together. Sometimes coughing, clearing the throat, and sniffing come in epidemics too. If you watch such a phenomenon sometime, and can be at all objective about the matter, you will see that it takes place in response to the initial behavior of some one or a few people present. One coughs and others follow suit.

Several years ago in a high school speech class there was a good looking, intelligent young man who prepared his speech with great care and then spoke clearly and emphatically. There was just one difficulty, however. This young man's audience could never relax to listen. Always they squirmed in their seats and gave the speaker a most unsatisfactory response. The difficulty was that this speaker scratched. Every time he faced the class he systematically but unobtrusively scratched. No wonder his listeners could not sit still and listen. They scratched too. Empathy is sometimes a negative matter for the speaker.

One more illustration may serve to underline the startling power of empathy. One time a college class in interpretation decided to employ the principle of empathy in a number of stunts about the campus. One good actor pulled an old trick. He stood on the campus during the rush to the noon meal and gazed intently at the tower on one of the buildings. More than fifty people collected about him to examine the same tower and the sky beyond. Of course, imaginations went to work, tongues began to wag, and many were late to lunch—all because people stopped to do what they saw others doing. That handful of interpretation students was responsible for other peculiar happenings on the campus that day. Unexplained fits of coughing swept classes. Several groups of students were seen actually running to classes. Some ordinarily serious philosophy sessions gave way to fits of giggling.

Empathy is part of our daily lives in many small ways. Have you sat in a movie as the heroine smiled into the face of her beloved, and smiled too? Have you watched a football game and strained every muscle as Number

Nineteen dodged, twisted, dashed, stumbled, and careened down the field to a touchdown? Have you seen a boxing match in person or on television, and felt your own fists drawn tight and your breaths quick and short? Have you watched a television comic and observed another observer with the same silly expression on his face? In each of these instances, enjoyment of these experiences is probably directly proportional to one's empathic participation in them.

We have seen that empathy is a phenomenon of human nature wherein one person " feels into " the experiences of another. In our examples, that " feeling into " was obvious to an observer because it involved overt, externalized responses. We could see or hear it happening. Empathic responses may also be covert or internalized but nonetheless real. Empathy goes much deeper than mere muscular responses and may be one of the most important factors for success in the communicative arts.

Empathy functions in oral interpretation in at least four ways. First, it operates to guide the reader's response to the literature. Participation in the attitudes and behavior of a story shows on the face, the hands, the posture, in fact, in the interpreter's total body response. To this degree the reader is not simply revealing appreciation for the selection, but is fully engaged in the activity of the story at the moment of its utterance. Every thought and action is *vital now* as an integral part of the bodily tensions implied by the literature. Such full empathic participation in the literary event is essential to effective oral interpretation.

Second, empathy functions in the audience response to the reader. As we have already seen, an audience tends to duplicate the tensions, responses, attitudes, and feelings of the speaker. If, therefore, the speaker wants his listeners to be relaxed, he must appear relaxed. If he wants them to experience tensions, he must show those tensions himself. By participating fully and expressively in the literary experience, the performer elicits appropriate physical responses from the audience.

Third, if genuine communication is taking place, the interpreter will experience an empathic response to the audience. Once drawn empathically into the communicative act, audience members become integral participants in the performance of literature. As the listener duplicates tensions of the reader, so the reader is influenced by the physical behavior of the audience. Their empathy is, then, reciprocal, and the degree of bodily involvement is intensified for all. When reader and listeners share this empathic exchange, the experience is magnified considerably beyond the capabilities of any individual's private reading.

The fourth instance of empathy occurs as the product ,of the preceding three: the audience responds empathically to the literature. Listeners' interactions with the performer offer the stimulus to their " feeling into " the literature, the consummation of the communicative act.

We should recognize also that the reader experiences a response to himself, and that the audience member responds to himself and to other listeners. Who has not heard the axiom "To look like is to feel like?" To smile is to feel like smiling more. To laugh is to laugh more. To express anger is to feel angry. To show concern is to be concerned. Certainly the principle is subject to its limitations. We cannot work mood miracles just be pretending, but the communicator's response to self offers basic help to better communication. You may add to calmness by acting calm. You may enhance feelings by physically expressing those feelings. You may be startled to discover that you not only shake because you are afraid but *are afraid* because you *shake*. There is something in the old advice to whistle as you pass a cemetery; for if you run, you will become more and more afraid the faster you run. Indeed, the individual seems to experience a response to himself.

## CRITERIA FOR EFFECTIVENESS

The success of any aspect of expressive behavior can be measured in terms of whether it promotes desirable audience responses. If a feature of voice helps to achieve an audience reaction consistent with the literature, it is good to have that feature. If it does not help or if it detracts, it is bad to have it. So it is with the visible aspects of speech too. Any appearance or behavior that helps the audience respond to the literature is desirable. Any facial expression, gesture, body position, step, or even item of dress that works to the contrary is undesirable and may be referred to as "negative visible action." This term includes mannerisms of face, hands, and body that draw attention away from the thought and feeling expressed. Any violation of the indefinite but, nevertheless, important criterion of good taste may seriously interfere with communication. Effective speakers and readers are careful not to offend their audiences with behavior that seems unsuitable or that calls special attention to itself. However, even the best speakers often have habitual, negative, visible actions such as slouching, always keeping their hands in their pockets, removing their glasses, overusing a single gesture, or contorting their faces. Such speakers may succeed in their speaking, but they do so *in spite of* these liabilities of visible action. They should strive to eliminate from their speech any habitual behavior that detracts or distracts.

The moment the audience becomes conscious of your attempts to employ empathy, then the facial expression or the behavior involved in that attempt becomes a distraction from your purpose and constitutes negative visible action. Techniques of speech must never call attention to themselves. When they do, the techniques have become liabilities, not assets. Just as the expert skier seems to glide effortlessly down the slope, and the ballerina appears to suspend herself weightlessly in air, the effective interpreter learns to control physical techniques so that (even though considerable practice has preceded the performance) all movements seem to be thoroughly natural and spontaneous. It is the novice skier who must visibly struggle to remain in an upright position, the novice dancer who has noticeable difficulty maintaining balance during a pirouette, and the novice interpreter whose yet-to-be-developed techniques of physical expression call attention to themselves.

To achieve appropriate physical responses in performance, you should seek behavior that is comfortable for you; that elicits the active participation of your audience; and that reflects accurately the nature of the literature you perform. There can be no "one size fits all" formula for visible communication. Appropriateness must be redefined for every individual reader and for every selection of literature. We suggest that you begin by considering the conventions of interpretative reading that we discussed in Chapter 2. By adhering to conventions regarding the manuscript, familiarization, focus, and suggestion, you will satisfy the normative expectations of your audience. In most instances, such practice, without blind adherence, will facilitate communication of the literature. Always, you should consider the demands of the specific selection, however, as unconventional works may call for unconventional performing responses. Every piece of literature you encounter will possess unique characteristics that should find expression in your physical embodiment of that work.

How do we accomplish all this? How can we develop empathic responses to literature that promote similar responses from an audience? Easy answers are simply not available, but there are two general means by which you can achieve appropriate physical communication. The first, which we might refer to as a "natural" mode, is to read the literature and follow your natural inclinations. Certainly, this occurs in life. If something angers you, your body automatically acts angry, looks angry, IS ANGRY. No effect is required for you to convey anger. It is automatic. To some degree, this should occur in your response to literature. If you concentrate on the ideas and feel the emotions as you read aloud, your body will naturally respond in kind. Read the following poem, and see what bodily responses naturally occur.

## HOW ANNANDALE WENT OUT

E. A. ROBINSON

They called it Annandale—and I was there
To flourish, to find words, and to attend:
Liar, physician, hypocrite, and friend,
I watched him; and the sight was not so fair
As one or two that I had seen elsewhere:
An apparatus not for me to mend—
A wreck, with hell between him and the end,
Remained of Annandale; and I was there.
I knew the ruin as I knew the man;
So put the two together, if you can,

Remembering the worst you know of me.
Now view yourself as I was, on the spot—
With a slight kind of engine. Do you see?
Like this . . . . You wouldn't hang me? I thought not.

On a first reading, you probably had little or no physical response. This poem presents a puzzle which must be worked out for its understanding. Consequently, your initial responses were probably more intellectual than they were emotional. Once you, realize, however, that the person in the poem is a physician who is defending his mercy killing of a person named Annandale, your empathic involvement should increase. When you further realize that Annandale (reduced from a human being to an apparatus, an "it") was the speaker's friend, the situation becomes more poignant, more tense, and most likely evokes an even stronger reaction from you. Reread the poem, aloud this time, imagining yourself as that doctor on trial for his life. If you can empathize with the speaker's complex mixture of emotions—his grief for the loss of a friend, his feeling of guilt, perhaps, for not being able to save his life, his conviction that the body could not have been saved by anyone, and his uncertainty regarding how he will be judged for his actions—your reading will reflect this empathy and will supply you with a solid foundation for effective visible communication. Such natural responsiveness to the literature is at the core of every effective oral reading.

The second means by which to derive appropriate physical responses, which we may refer to as the "technical" mode, is to consider individual techniques of communicative performance that refine and focus your responses into clear and vivid expressions. You can never be sure that what *feels* natural to you will *appear* natural to your audience. Some of your natural gestures or facial expressions might be confusing or distracting and should be avoided; others may need to be heightened and projected. Sometimes, the literature will contain implied actions that are not immediately clear and require special consideration. In "Annandale," for example, the speaker evidently does something as he says "Like this . . . ." Like what? What does he do at this point? Is he trying to coax his audience into visualizing Annandale as he appeared? Is he attempting to assume a position that mirrors the "slight kind of engine?" To read the poem effectively, you would need to decide what the speaker is doing at this point and to apply a combination of nonverbal cues to suggest that action to your audience.

We cannot offer you more specific advice for achieving natural, empathic physical responses, because these occur from within you. If you apply your energies openly and actively, physical responses should occur in the vicarious experiences of literature just as they do in the actual experiences of life. We can, however, explore the techniques of physical expression more fully and will do so within five categories: personal appearance, posture, movement, gesture, and facial expression.

## PERSONAL APPEARANCE

By the term *personal appearance* we mean the reader's attitude, manner, grooming, and dress. From the very moment the audience becomes aware of his physical presence, these features communicate meaning. The psychologist would say that by this means he establishes a "set" or a readiness for the message he is to convey. Indeed, the kinesiologist says that the oral communicator may actually communicate specific ideas and attitudes before he opens his mouth. Common sense tells us that the reader's appearance and behavior at the outset is at the very least communicating his own personality and that, if he can achieve a degree of audience acceptance before speaking, subsequent success is all the more likely. The salesman who first faces a prospective client is wise to try for an affirmative response, even before mentioning the product. In the terms of the trade, he should "sell himself first." It is no less incumbent on the speaker or reader to achieve acceptance. When you come before an audience to read, you can help your audience to accept you by behaving and dressing in such a way as to satisfy whatever standards are maintained in the group.

On days when you are to perform, you should make certain that items of your appearance will not be distractions. Uncomfortable clothing, hair that must be repeatedly swept out of the eyes, glasses that slip down on the nose, or apparel that is noticeably inappropriate to the literature are bothersome not only to the reader but to the audience as well. Application of a little common sense will keep such seemingly trivial, superficial matters from disrupting your communication.

Your attitude, too, is a part of personal appearance. By the expression on your face and the set of your body you can make observers consider you unpleasantly cocky or disconcertingly unsure. Certainly you will want your audience to feel that you have something worth saying, that you want to say it, that you are fully prepared, and that you regard this audience as fully capable of appreciating what you are about to say. If your behavior reflects uncertainty on any of these points, the audience will sense that uncertainty. Let your manner bespeak appropriate confidence but not arrogance. In the moments before you speak, you can incline an audience in your favor or you can create obstacles later to be surmounted.

## POSTURE

The second aspect of visible action is posture. Simply expressed, *posture* is the arrangement of the bones and muscles of the body. How are you standing? Your posture is good if it promotes the most effective use of your body. Can you breathe freely and deeply? Can you speak calmly and forcefully? Can you use your hands, arms, shoulders, trunk, and head readily and with ease? Can you step quickly and gracefully? If the answer to each of these questions is "yes," your posture is probably satisfactory for reading and speaking. Good posture is that arrangement of the parts of your body that enables you to employ them with maximum effectiveness. Good posture is good physical readiness.

If, however, you have formed poor posture habits, the best posture may not seem natural to you. One of the worst kinds of posture is the stoop. If you stand with your shoulders hunched and your head forward, you restrict your breathing by confining the chest cavity and pushing the rib cage down against the abdomen. The result may be inadequate loudness of voice and inability to sustain voice as long as you may need to. You may even cause a tension in the region of your larynx that will result in a tight, inflexible voice, unpleasant both to you and to your listeners. The swayback posture is probably just as poor for health as for speech. If you allow your spine to sway forward at the middle of the back, your pelvis will be tipped out of its normal alignment; your abdomen will protrude unduly; your neck will thrust forward; and speech will be as difficult as in the stooped position. Another kind of poor posture often results from the teaching of well-meaning parents and teachers. We call this the ramrod or military posture. Perhaps you have been told to stand up straight, throw your shoulders back, and pull your abdomen in. Of course, this position is uncomfortable to maintain, for throwing the shoulders back upsets the normal balance of the body, and pulling the abdomen in may confine the muscles of the diaphragm. In any event, the position produces such tensions as to make speech difficult. If you have bad habits of posture, it is desirable to correct them.

Stand erect and easily before an audience. Let your shoulders fall into a natural position. Allow your whole body to relax without slouching. Lift your chin until your eyes look out on a horizontal plane. Strive for muscular readiness so that every demand that oral communication places on you can easily be met. See that you can breathe, gesture, bend, or step without hesitation.

Using the position of physical readiness we have described as a normative posture, you can make subtle adjustments to accommodate demands of specific selections of literature. Appropriate postures for various selections will range from tense to relaxed, from stiffly formal to casual, from confident to tentative. Often, your posture might change during the reading of a selection. In "Dover Beach," quoted in Chapter 2, Matthew Arnold begins by saying "The sea is calm to-night." Probably, you would wish to utter the opening lines of this poem from a relaxed, calm position, receptive to the sights and sounds of the tranquil night. As the poem continues, however, the mood shifts to the realization that we are "Swept with confused alarms of struggle and flight." The interpreter who is empathically involved in the performance might subconsciously assume a somewhat more tense position in response to the altered focus of the poem. An overt shift in posture during a performance of " Dover Beach " would destroy the unity of the literature, but subtle postural responses to its progression of idea and emotion seem necessary. For the reading of all literature, make certain that your posture is responsive to the language while, at the same time, communicatively open to your audience.

## MOVEMENT

For purposes of discussion, we distinguish movement (motions of the whole body) from gesture (motions of arm, head, or other part of the body). The distinction is arbitrary for, in practice, the communicator's movement and gesture cohere into a unified body response to the literature and to the audience.

Whereas an actor might move extensively about the stage during a performance, the oral reader usually remains mostly in one spot. Typically, the oral interpreter stands before the audience taking, at most, a step or two during the course of a reading. There is no rule that prohibits movement, but other aspects of the interpretative setting combine to restrict the reader from extended movement. Walking around during an interpretative reading does nothing to further the oral reader's *suggestive* communication of literature, and it serves as a distraction to the audience's concentration.

Once you remove the manuscript and perform from memory, possibilities for effective movement are increased. Still, however, the suggestive nature of interpretation makes limited movement the normally advisable course. *Economy* of movement (maximum effect with minimal observable effort) is desirable for any art. For the interpreter, economy of movement is particularly important in order to establish the locus imaginatively instead of literally on the stage. If the interpreter were to move a great deal, these motions would entice the audience into viewing the performer *as the character*, and not as a reader sharing the experience with them. The locus would shift from the minds of the audience to the stage, and the essential quality of the reading setting would be lost.

When is movement effective in an interpretative reading? As with all aspects of expression, movement is desirable when it is in response to qualities in the literature and to the requirements of communication. When movement seems random—when it is not motivated by necessities of communicating the literature—it poses a distraction. The most likely points where movement will be motivated are at significant transitions in idea or mood, and at places where particular emphasis is needed.

If, after introducing your selection, you step a bit closer to your audience to read, you can help "move" yourself and them into the literary experience. In addition to assisting the transition from speaking an introduction to reading the literature, movement can effectively reinforce important transitions within the work. You might appropriately take a step or two between the stanzas of Ransom's " Piazza Piece " (quoted in Chapter 5), for instance, to assist the move from " I am a gentleman in a dustcoat trying " to " —I am a lady young in beauty waiting." Kingsley's " Young and Old " (quoted in Chapter 9) contains a similar transition from the first stanza's description of " When all the world is young " to the second's " When all the world is old." In both cases, the attitude of the poem changes between stanzas, the interpreter's posture would appropriately be altered, and movement would be *one way* of assisting the transition.

Movement for emphasis offers a physical reinforcement that may aid the literature's intent to " move " an audience. Let us consider a few lines from Browning's " My Last Duchess " quoted in Chapter 9. Because this poem is a dramatic monologue, the reader is almost bound to use some impersonation. The likelihood that movement *might* be productively employed is thereby increased. The speaker is the Duke of Ferrara who is telling the envoy of his prospective bride about his late wife:

> Oh, Sir, she smiled, no doubt,
> Whene'er I passed her; but who passed without
> Much the same smile? This grew; I gave commands;
> Then all smiles stopped together. There she stands
> As if alive.

When he says " all smiles stopped together," the Duke probably is implying that he had his last Duchess put to death. This is certainly important to the envoy, for it warns of a fate that may befall the new Duchess if she is not careful; and it is important to us, for it confirms the ominous character of the Duke. Certainly a competent reader could convey the necessary emphasis of this line while standing still, but movement could be used. Let us imagine, for example, that during the preceding lines the Duke has been pacing, frustrated by the recollection of his wife's flirtations. The reader might take a few steps, stopping on the word " commands." Then, as all the performer's movement stops, " all smiles " come to a stop. Another way of emphasizing the same line would be to utter the words " all smiles stopped together," pause for a moment, then take a step or two. This movement would allow further time to contemplate the significance of the statement, and it would help to shift the focus from the living Duchess of the past to the present picture of her " as if alive."

We suggest that you experiment with possibilities for movement, but we advise caution. Be careful that your movement does not destroy the illusion of reading, that it does not compete with other suggestive aspects of your performance, and that it does not rob your audience of an imaginative experience by placing the locus of action on stage. Above all, take care that your movements do not seem preplanned. If the audience senses premeditated movement, their attention is drawn to the techniques of performance and away from the literary experience.

## GESTURE

Since classical times, students of oral communication have recognized three kinds of gesture: descriptive, suggestive, and emphatic. Descriptive gestures point out physical placement, proportion, or detail. We use our body to indicate where something is. Perhaps we use our eyes, head, shoulder, or all three. We use our hands and arms to indicate relative sizes. We gesture to show shape; we gesture to show movement. Such visible action may have been the earliest form of speech and is certainly one of the most common forms today. The second kind of gesture is suggestive. It is much like descriptive gesture but is used for less concrete subject matter. We may shrug our shoulders to indicate indifference or may throw up our arm to show that someone has departed. We may cast our eyes upward as we speak of God. The third kind of gesture, emphatic, is employed to underline what our words say and may be typified by a clenched fist, nodding head, or even stamping foot. These three kinds of gesture are as appropriate in oral interpretation as in any other kind of speech.

From another point of view, we can speak of two categories of gesture: the nearly instinctive and the learned. The nearly instinctive includes the nonverbal behavior that seems to be physiologically determined and involuntarily produced by the individual without being culturally conditioned. This category encompasses such actions as opening wide the eyes when trying to see better, holding the head when it aches, engaging in extraneous movement when restless, catching your breath when frightened, and perhaps even holding your nose when offensive odors assail you. Learned gesture includes the movements that are culture linked and conventional. They derive their shape and meaning from the culture, although the individual uses them as involuntarily as he does the nearly instinctive type. The same action may have different meanings in different cultures. An Arab may stroke his beard to signal the presence of an attractive woman, but for a Jew to do the same thing may mean that he is thinking deeply. The same meaning may be communicated with different actions in different cultures. When the Arab strokes his beard, the Italian may pull at the lobe of his ear, and the American may purse his lips for a whistle, but all are saying the same thing. It appears that most communicative nonverbal behavior is of this second sort, culture linked and learned. The individual acquires a nonverbal vocabulary as certainly as he acquires a verbal one.

Many years ago elocutionists taught a long and involved catalogue of gestures in much the same manner as primary teachers taught the alphabet. A certain movement meant repulsion. Another meant challenge. There were gestures for fear, pleading, dismay, and a multitude of other moods and assertions. The student practiced long hours to learn specific movements. In order to execute the hand movements gracefully, he was enjoined to lead with the wrist, from an ellipse, curve the fingers, and in general to pose. There were similar standards for the use of the trunk, the shoulders, the face, the legs, and the feet. The result of such instruction was often gesture, not of the whole body, but of isolated members of the body. All too frequently gesture was obviously a "thing apart." Of course, such practices became stylized and were expected by audiences. Consequently, speech behavior that would seem absurd to us could often pass unnoticed or be highly admired for its own sake. Popular taste, however, was eventually pushed to the breaking point by the excesses of the elocutionist, and a revulsion set in.

Today it is recognized that gesture should be a matter of the whole body, that it should be a part of and spring from the thought. The whole organism of man is involved in thinking. The mind is not an isolated part of the body. It is an activity, a function. Thought does not involve the brain alone, or even the nervous system alone. The brain, nerves, glands, and muscles work together as a whole. Full experience of the thought involves, theoretically at least, full employment of the body. Because experience of the thought is the goal of the oral interpreter, he must involve his whole body in that thought.

Total bodily activity is necessary for thinking. Total activity is also necessary for communicating thought from one person to another. It is inherent in the act of speech. Watch a small child as he quivers with excitement, jumps up and down, smiles broadly, and uses his hands, arms, torso, and legs to voice a simple idea. His parents and teachers will expend much effort in the frustrating task of calming down the expert communicator, but as an adult engaged in conversation, he will still make extensive use of his whole body in the process of communicating. Notice how people go about ordinary conversation. If you have never really paid attention to conversational behavior, you may be surprised. When people converse, they shake their heads and lift their eyebrows, and changes of feeling play across their faces. They shrug their shoulders; their hands are almost never still. They are not trying to make speeches but are merely trying to make others understand what they have in mind. Unconscious of using action, they are talking the way people have always talked—actively.

The kinesiologist points out, however, that while we speak of a gesture as if it were a distinct entity, it is really not. A specific action is performed with almost imperceptible variations, so that the sincerity of a smile may be left open to question, the turn of a hand may range from emphatic to casual, or the nod of the head may communicate anything from agreement to simple recognition of what has just been said. Furthermore, a specific action is always accompanied by a variety of other acts that modify the message. The smile may be accompanied by either negative or affirmative head movements. A salute may be performed with a sneer and a twist of the body. A simple turn of the hand may be done with simultaneous communication by the shoulders, the face, and even the stance.

In brief, thought is an " all-of-the-body " process, and so, too, is speaking. Within limits imposed by the presence of a manuscript, oral reading also involves total bodily activity.

The presence of the manuscript and the understanding that gesture must be a part of thought and spring from thought, together with the fact that movement must never call attention to itself, prompt many oral interpreters to perfer *covert* gesture rather than *overt*. That is, they think that the most communicative movement is change in the general body tonicity, in the diffused and the overall degree of tension and relaxation. Anger is expressed, not with a clenched fist alone, but with a general heightening of body tension. Such covert action may actually be far more effective than wide, sweeping movements. The body speaks as a whole. Ideas and feelings are cause, and total body response is effect. Gesture derives from the urge to communicate.

To gain freedom in the use of the body, the reader may want to use large and full movements in his practice. On the actual occasion of reading to an audience, he will probably exercise some restraint. Restraint is meaningful, however, only when there is something to be restrained. For most of us, there is little or no danger of employing too much visible action in oral reading. Indeed, we need to enlarge or " project " our normal visible action. Practicing in the way suggested may help us to use more bodily action before the audience, despite stage fright that may tend to subdue us.

It should be recognized that two factors usually determine what constitutes effective gesture. The first is the speaker's personality. If you are an active, aggressive individual, you probably employ far more gesture than the average person. On the other hand, if you are more quiet in your behavior, it is right and proper for you to use less gesture. No one can tell you that you must gesture just as someone else does, for we are all different. Nothing is so characteristic of individual personality as the use of one's body. The second factor to determine what constitutes effective gesture is the material being read. For example, broad humor ordinarily requires far larger action than most other forms of reading material. By contrast, covert body action is often more suitable for abstract and serious content. The frequency, size, and degree of explicitness of your gestures must reflect the imaginative action of the literature you read. Your sense of propriety is your guide.

## FACIAL EXPRESSION

Of all the expressive parts of the body, the face is usually the most reliable single indicator of mood and attitude. To carefully observe somebody, we generally fix our gaze primarily on the eyes, attending most directly to their facial expressions. A person's words may bespeak calm, while his face betrays his actual feelings. Imagine, for example, somebody who is bravely trying to face the loss of a loved one. Even though the voice might be under control, a quivering lip, tension in the brow, or repeated blinking of the eyes gives away his agony. Conversely, a person might feign interest or concern, while a blank face indicates that he or she is insincere. When confronted with such disparity between word and countenance, we most likely will rely on the face to determine the individual's true feelings. It is, therefore, highly important for the facial expressions of oral readers to be consistent with the moods of the literature they communicate. Great vocal involvement can be severely undermined by an obviously uninvolved, passive face.

The guiding principle must be to suit the expressions of the face to the emotional state of the speaker in the literature. If you are empathically involved in the ideas and feelings, then this alignment should be natural. Sometimes, however, special consideration of the facial expressions may be necessary. Suppose, for example, that you are to read the following words spoken by Macbeth, who has just heard of his wife's death:

## *from* MACBETH

### WILLIAM SHAKESPEARE

To-morrow, and to-morrow, and to-morrow,
Creeps in this petty pace from day to day,
To the last syllable of recorded time;
And all our yesterdays have lighted fools
The way to dusty death. Out, out, brief candle!
Life's but a walking shadow; a poor player,
That struts and frets his hour upon the stage,
And then is heard no more: it is a tale
Told by an idiot, full of sound and fury,
Signifying nothing.

The words are philosophical: Macbeth is pondering the very significance of life. But, he is also responding to his wife's death. The face of the reader would, appropriately, convey the controlled reflectiveness of the language as well as the personal response to the death. When you add to these considerations the complexities of the whole play—Lady Macbeth's loss of reason, Macbeth's murderous quest for power, and Macbeth's own impending death —the demands on the reader's expressive capabilities are increased immensely.

Let us turn to another selection. In Chapter 5, we noted that the intent of a persona might differ from the intent of the author. In Auden's "The Unknown Citizen," the persona speaks in favor of a conformist "State" that the poet opposes. A reader might effectively convey the irony of this poem by energetically uttering the words while remaining facially passive. This planned inconsistency of expression could help to illustrate the emptiness and superficiality of the sentiments mouthed by the speaker, thereby fulfilling the author's intentions.

A third instance where an interpreter might wish to pay special attention to facial expression occurs in Barker's poem "To My Mother," quoted in Chapter 6. In the last line, the speaker says his mother "will move from mourning into morning." The meaning is clear enough on the printed page, but when read aloud the words "mourning" and "morning" sound alike. Facially, the interpreter can help to resolve this ambiguity by opening the eyes broadly and relaxing the facial muscles in a physical awakening into the hoped for "morning."

Throughout the performance of any literary selection, the expressions of your face will communicate a great deal to your audience and will affect your own feelings as you read. Facial expressions are the reader's most fundamental gestures, the focal point of the total bodily response necessary for effective communication.

## STAGE FRIGHT

Perhaps you call it tension, but if you are like most of us you do have an experience that many people refer to as stage fright. You might be surprised at the tensions suffered by experienced teachers when facing new classes. Most of our great speakers and actors have confessed they have known the same feeling. Do not think that your own fear before an audience is unique or even that it is greater than many others feel. Actually, you would be a peculiar, vegetable-like creature indeed if you were a stranger to stage fright.

What can you do about stage fright? *First*, you must realize that elimination of all tension is not desirable. You need only to *utilize* your nervous energy to increase instead of to hinder your effectiveness. *Second*, do not forget that the way you feel is nothing new or different but is common to all speakers. *Third*, prepare—prepare—prepare. Give yourself reason for confidence. Without much preparation you may, it is true, be able to "fool part of the people part of the time," but if you want to be confident you must be satisfied with no less than a thoroughgoing study of the content and, then, much conscientious practice in actually reading your selection aloud. It is only the rank novice who feels that he can interpret confidently and effectively without several hours of preparation for every quarter hour of reading. *Fourth*, act as if you were confident. Remember that, as observed earlier, you respond to yourself. Instill courage in yourself by employing positive movements. Do not hesitate or shrink from your audience. *Fifth*, consciously focus your attention on the meaning of the words you are reading at the moment you are reading. If your mind is filled with the feelings and ideas in your selection, there will be no room for thoughts about yourself. *Sixth*, try to replace fear with another emotion. Your psychology professor will tell you that if the thalamus, which is the seat of your emotions, is filled with hate, for example, there is no room for fear. Witness the angry fighter! Apply this principle to yourself as you speak. Replace stage fright with strong emotional feelings associated with the ideas you are expressing. *Seventh*, deliberately set out to communicate visibly. Respond to an idea or feeling with all of yourself. Doing so may seem awkward at first, but force yourself to be an active communicator. *Eighth*, and last, remember at all times that oral reading is communication and that you must focus all your energy on responding meaningfully to the literature. There can be little time or strength to waste in self-consciousness and fear.

## EXERCISES

1. Observe several speakers or readers in person or on television and analyze their visible action. Look for examples of negative visible action.

2. Attend a movie or observe a speaker and watch the empathic responses of the audience. Notice the responses that the speaker or actor must have wanted. Does he receive any empathic responses he would consider undesirable?

3. For a striking demonstration of empathy, go to some athletic event and watch the faces and bodies of the observers. What relation does empathy seem to have to their enjoyment?

4. Observe a speaker before he goes into action and analyze the response you make before he says a word. Look for personal appearance and attitude.

5. For freedom of communicative bodily activity, plan and tell a complete story without words. Perhaps you will want to explain the setting before you begin.

6. Speak the following sentences with visible action. Remember that your purpose is simply to communicate effectively. Within the limits of good taste, use your whole body.

   a. On one side sat all the men, and on the other the women.

   b. Mankind must make its choice: either peace with freedom or war with the gradual destruction of all rights.

   c. Why you rat! I could knock your teeth out!

   d. "When he came up out of the water, immediately he saw the heavens opened and the Spirit descending upon him like a dove; and a voice came from heaven, 'Thou art my beloved Son; with thee I am well pleased.'"

e. "Give me thy hand, Kate: I will unto Venice, To buy apparel 'gainst the wedding day."

f. "I swear I'll cuff you, if you strike again."

g. "Go get some water,
And wash this filthy witness [blood] from your hand."

h. He swept down the field, shouldering his way through the opposition.

i. Be he wise or foolish, the law's the law.

j. Me? Why, I wouldn't hurt a baby!

k. Stop, thief!

l. You're a liar!

m. "I went to the woods because I wished to live deliberately, to front only the essential facts of life, and see if I could not learn what it had to teach, and not, when I came to die, discover that I had not lived."

n. "'You must not—you shall not behold this!' said I, shudderingly, to Usher, as I led him, with a gentle violence, from the window to a seat."

o. "'Who comes?' demanded the scout, throwing his rifle carelessly across his left arm, and keeping the forefinger of his right hand on the trigger, though he avoided all appearance of menace in the act."

7. Both of the following poems are by the same poet, and both describe an action. The first is very quiet and slow, while the second is a blaring, whirling rush of motion. To practice reading the poems, try acting out the movements of the cat and of the dancers, and then experiment with postures and gestures that will communicate the kinesthetic imagery to an audience.

## POEM

WILLIAM CARLOS WILLIAMS

As the cat
climbed over
the top of

the jamcloset
first the right
forefoot

carefully
then the hind
stepped down

into the pit of
the empty
flowerpot


## THE DANCE

WILLIAM CARLOS WILLIAMS

In Breughel's great picture, The Kermess,
the dancers go round, they go round and
around, the squeal and the blare and the
tweedle of bagpipes, a bugle and fiddles
tipping their bellies (round as the thick-
sided glasses whose wash they impound)
their hips and their bellies off balance
to turn them. Kicking and rolling about
the Fair Grounds, swinging their butts, those
shanks must be sound to bear up under such
rollicking measures, prance as they dance
in Breughel's great picture, The Kermess.

8.   Consider the importance of facial expression in the performance of the
following poem. As you read the selection, try to visualize the girl, imagine
her "sleepy pirouette," and consider the implications of this unforgettable
moment. Do these responses naturally lead to facial expressions?


## PIAZZA DI SPAGNA, EARLY MORNING

RICHARD WILBUR

         I can't forget
   How she stood at the top of that long marble stair
   Amazed, and then with a sleepy pirouette
Went dancing slowly down to the fountain-quieted square;

      Nothing upon her face
   But some impersonal loneliness,—not then a girl,
      But as it were a reverie of the place,
         A called-for falling glide and whirl;

> As when a leaf, petal, or thin chip
> Is drawn to the falls of a pool and, circling a moment above it,
>     Rides on over the lip—
> Perfectly beautiful, perfectly ignorant of it.

9.   The following poem describes familiar animal movements that have grown to perfection in a heaven that is without pain, or fear, or blood. There exists only the joy of wholly fulfilling instincts in a perpetual enactment of natural roles. How might the oral interpreter utilize physical responses that will help to communicate the subtle and unique images of the poem?

## THE HEAVEN OF ANIMALS

JAMES DICKEY

Here they are. The soft eyes open.
If they have lived in a wood
It is a wood.
If they have lived on plains
It is grass rolling
Under their feet forever.

Having no souls, they have come,
Anyway, beyond their knowing.
Their instincts wholly bloom
And they rise.
The soft eyes open.

To match them, the landscape flowers,
Outdoing, desperately
Outdoing what is required:
The richest wood,
The deepest field.

For some of these,
It could not be the place
It is, without blood.
These hunt, as they have done,
But with claws and teeth grown perfect,

More deadly than they can believe.
They stalk more silently,
And crouch on the limbs of trees,
And their descent
Upon the bright backs of their prey

May take years
In a sovereign floating of joy.
And those that are hunted
Know this as their life,
Their reward: to walk

Under such trees in full knowledge
Of what is in glory above them,
And to feel no fear,
But acceptance, compliance.
Fulfilling themselves without pain

At the cycle's center,
They tremble, they walk
Under the tree,
They fall, they are torn,
They rise, they walk again.

10. Why would it be necessary for an oral reader to draw on a total bodily response to communicate the following passage?

## *from* THE CIRCUS OF DR. LAO

### CHARLES G. FINNEY

Sonorously the great bronze gong banged and rang; and from all over the circus ground the people, red and black and white, left the little sideshow tents and shuffled through the dust. The midway was thick with them for a minute or two as they crowded toward the big tent. Then the midway was desolate, save for its wreath of dust, as the people all disappeared beneath the canvas. And the ringing of the bronze gong diminuendoed and died.

The big tent was a dull creamy lacquer within. Black swastikas were painted on it and winged serpents and fish eyes. There were no circus rings. In the center of the floor was a big triangle instead, a pedestal adorning each angle. Doctor Lao, in full showman's dress of tails and high hat and cracking whip, attained the top of one of the pedestals and blew on a whistle. At a far entrance a seething and a rustling was heard. Chinese music, monotonous as bagpiping, teetled through the tent. Figures could be seen massing at the far entrance. The grand march was starting. The main performance had begun.

Snorting and damping, the unicorn came leading the grand march. Its hoofs had been gilded and its mane combed.

"Notice it!" screamed Doctor Lao. "Notice the unicorn. The giraffe is the only antlered animal that does not shed its antlers. The pronghorn antelope is the only horned animal that sheds its horns. Unique they are among the deciduous beasts. But what of the unicorn? Is it not unique? A horn is hair; and antler is bone; but that thing on the unicorn's head is metal. Think that over, will you?"

Then came the sphinx, ponderous and stately, shaking its curls.

"Say something to them!" hissed Majordomo Lao.

"What walks on four legs, two legs, three legs?" simpered the androgyne.

Mumbo Jumbo and his retinue came. The satyr syrinxed. The nymphs danced. The sea serpent coiled and glided. Fluttering its wings, the chimera filled the tent with smoke. Two shepherdesses drove their sheep. A thing that looked like a bear carried the kiss-blowing mermaid in its arms. The hound of the hedges barked and played. Apollonius cast rose petals. Her eyes blindfolded, her snakes awrithe, the medusa was led by the faun. Cheeping, the roc chick gamboled. On the golden ass an old woman rode. A two-headed turtle, unable to make up either of its minds, wandered vaguely. It was the damnedest collection Abalone, Arizone, had ever seen.

Mr. Etaoin, sitting behind Larry Kamper, said to Miss Agnes Birdson: "Well, that's the whole outfit, I guess, except for the werewolf. I wonder where it is?"

Larry turned around. "See that old woman on the donkey's back? There's yer goddam werewolf."

Round and round the great triangle the animals walked, danced, pranced, fluttered, and crawled, Master of Ceremonies Lao directing them from his pedestal. They roared and screamed and coughed; rising from strings and reeds the Chinese music teetled monotonously and waveringly whined. Too close upon the fastidious unicorn, the sphinx accidently nuzzled its rump; and the unicorn exploded with a tremendous kick, crashing its heels into the sphinx's side. The hermaphrodite shrieked. With its great paws it struck and roweled the unicorn's neck and back. The unicorn leaped like a mad stallion, whirled and centered its horn in the sphinx's lungs. Nervous, the chimera dodged about, its flapping wings fanning up dust clouds. The sea serpent reared into a giant S, launched a fifty-foot strike, caught the chimera by a forefoot, and flung seven loops about its wings and shoulders. The hound of the hedges curled in a tight ball, looking like a stray grass hummock. The Russian passionately kissed the mermaid. Lowering his horns, taking a short run for it, the satyr spiked Mumbo Jumbo in the rump when the black god's back was turned. The old woman changed back into a wolf and ravened at the roc chick. The little faun threw stones at Dr. Lao. The nymphs and shepherdesses and lambs hid and whimpered. From the face of the medusa the blindfold fell; eleven people turned to stone.

"Oh, misery!" screamed the doctor. "Why do they have to fight so when there is nothing to fight about? They are as stupid as humans. Stop them, Apollonius, quickly, before someone gets hurt!"

The thaumaturge hurled spell after spell among the hysterical beasts. Spells of peace, mediation, rationality, arbitration, and calmness flashed through the feverish air and fell like soft webs about the battlers. The din lessened. Withdrawing his horn from the sphinx's lungs, the unicorn trotted away and cropped at sparse grass. The sphinx licked at its lacerated side. The sea serpent loosed the chimera, yawned his jaws back into place. Shaking itself, the hound of the hedges arose and whined. The mermaid patted the bear. Mumbo Jumbo forgave the satyr. The werewolf remetamorphosed. The faun stopped throwing rocks. Back came the nymphs and shepherdesses and lambs. Once again the medusa assumed her blindfold.

After the storm, tranquillity. Peace after battle. Forgiveness after hate.

# 8 Principles Fundamental to Audible Communication

Audible communication is a more sophisticated method of communication than is visible communication. We have seen that visibly we communicate attitudes, actions or tensions, emphasis, and even subliminal messages. With the voice, however, the human being is able to express specific significance, even when it may be subtle or abstract. With the voice, man communicates messages ranging from the most intellectual to the most emotional, although we know that most messages are really delicate and indefinable concoctions of both the mind and heart, so to speak. In short, it is the voice on which we depend to communicate most of our contexts and our attitudes, although we are, at the same time, expressing ourselves visibly.

The essence of vocal communication is change, or variability, in actions of the voice. Time, loudness, pitch, and quality are the four voice variables. It is these which we shall examine in the following chapters. In these four basic variables, and in the subforms of them, the voice reacts to our mental and emotional impulses in expressing idea and feeling. As to idea, the voice phrases and emphasizes in response to the mind's grouping and centering, as we have seen in Chapter 5. While the mind perceives ideas in terms of word relationships, the voice phrases the words. While the mind centers on interesting, significant concepts, the voice emphasizes the words which express them. Phrasing is accomplished primarily by means of pause and intonation; emphasis, primarily by intricate combinations of duration, loudness, and pitch. Attitudes are expressed by all the voice variables.

## COMMUNICATION OF IDEAS

We need to say little in this chapter about phrasing, except to reiterate that it is the result of mental grouping. Primarily, the voice separates thought groups by pauses between each. Additionally, intonations suggest continuing thought through rising inflection, or completed thought through downward inflection. Most people who can recognize the division of language into distinct thought groups are able to convert their understanding into meaningful phrases. In Chapters 9 and 11, we will explore the ways pauses and intonations achieve the phrasing of speech. We need to speak extensively of emphasis and subordination, for they are accomplished through complex simultaneous relationships of several of the vocal techniques.

Within thought groups are words of varying significance. Some are the thought centers; some only tie essential words together. Emphasis falls on thought centers, the physical result of mental activity. The reader must communicate by emphasizing the important and subordinating the unimportant. Just as a painter casts into shadows the least significant aspects of his subject and highlights what he wishes to attract attention, so the speaker finds that it is just as important to subordinate the unimportant words as it is to emphasize the important centers. A good rule to remember is this: Conserve emphasis, for the more you try to emphasize, the less you actually emphasize. Find reason to subordinate as much as possible. One spotlighted area on a darkened stage focuses attention readily; general lighting on all areas diffuses attention.

What follows is an explanation of several syntactical and mental principles operative as we *think*, automatically resulting in emphasis and subordination.

**Types of Words.** Any word may be important; any word may be unimportant. The meaning determines relative importance. *Generally speaking*, however, we can make these observations about probable importance of words according to their grammatical function:

*Nouns* are usually important words. They are primary to us most of the time because they are the names of the things we are thinking about. Eliminate the nouns, and you "don't know *what* you're talking about!" Read the following passage without the nouns and you will quickly realize how important nouns are:

| | |
|---|---|
| To him who in the _____ of _____ holds | (Love, Nature) |
| _____ with her visible _____, she speaks | (Communion, forms) |
| A various _____; for his gayer _____ | (language, hours) |
| She has a _____ of _____, and a _____ | (voice, gladness, smile) |
| And _____ of _____, and she glides | (eloquence, beauty) |
| Into his darker _____, with a mild | (musings) |
| And healing _____, that steals away | (sympathy) |
| Their _____, ere he is aware. | (sharpness) |

—WILLIAM CULLEN BRYANT, *"Thanatopsis"*

*Verbs* are also primary, for they communicate action, occurrence, and mode of being. Without the verbs, nothing *happens*, and nothing *is*. We have italicized the main verbs (except forms of "to be") in the first 20 lines of the following poem. Note how important they are to the movement, color, and spirit of the poem. If you have any trouble with this exercise, you may learn more by marking the verbs in the rest of the selection. Again, read a passage aloud, leaving out the verbs, then read it with the verbs included. *Feel* the difference!

# ULYSSES

ALFRED, LORD TENNYSON

It little *profits* that an idle king,
By this still hearth, among these barren crags,
*Match'd* with an aged wife, I *mete* and *dole*
Unequal laws unto a savage race,
That *hoard*, and *sleep*, and *feed*, and *know* not me.
I cannot *rest* from travel: I will *drink*
Life to the lees: all times I have *enjoy'd*
Greatly, have *suffer'd* greatly, both with those
That *loved* me, and alone; on shore, and when
Thro' scudding drifts the rainy Hyades                    10
*Vext* the dim sea: I am *become* a name;
For always roaming with a hungry heart
Much have I *seen* and *known*; cities of men
And manners, climates, councils, governments,
Myself not least, but *honour'd* of them all;             15
And *drunk* delight of battle with my peers,
Far on the ringing plains of windy Troy.
I am a part of all that I have *met*;
Yet all experience is an arch wherethro'
*Gleams* that untravell'd world, whose margin *fades*      20
For ever and for ever when I move.
How dull it is to pause, to make an end,
To rust unburnish'd, not to shine in use!
As tho' to breathe were life. Life piled on life
Were all too little, and of one to me                     25
Little remains: but every hour is saved
From that eternal silence, something more,
A bringer of new things; and vile it were
For some three suns to store and hoard myself,
And this gray spirit yearning in desire                   30
To follow knowledge like a sinking star,
Beyond the utmost bound of human thought.
    This is my son, mine own Telemachus,
To whom I leave the sceptre and the isle—
Well-loved of me, discerning to fulfill                   35
This labour, by slow prudence to make mild
A rugged people, and thro' soft degrees
Subdue them to the useful and the good.
Most blameless is he, centred in the sphere
Of common duties, decent not to fail                      40
In offices of tenderness, and pay

Meet adoration to my household gods,
When I am gone. He works his work, I mine.
   There lies the port; the vessel puffs her sail:
There gloom the dark broad seas. My mariners,                         45
Souls that have toil'd, and wrought, and thought with me—
That ever with a frolic welcome took
The thunder and the sunshine, and opposed
Free hearts, free foreheads—you and I are old;
Old age hath yet his honour and his toil;                             50
Death closes all: but something ere the end,
Some work of noble note, may yet be done,
Not unbecoming men that strove with Gods.
The lights begin to twinkle from the rocks:
The long day wanes: the slow moon climbs: the deep                    55
Moans round with many voices. Come, my friends,
'Tis not too late to seek a newer world.
Push off, and sitting well in order smite
The sounding furrows; for my purpose holds
To sail beyond the sunset, and the baths                             60
Of all the western stars, until I die.
It may be that the gulfs will wash us down:
It may be we shall touch the Happy Isles,
And see the great Achilles, whom we knew.
Tho' much is taken, much abides; and tho'                            65
We are not now that strength which in old days
Moved earth and heaven; that which we are, we are;
One equal temper of heroic hearts,
Made weak by time and fate, but strong in will
To strive, to seek, to find, and not to yield.                       70

   *Adjectives* and *adverbs* are accorded secondary rank because they modify
nouns and verbs; however, when they provide unique descriptions of kind
or manner, then the mind may find their concepts of *primary* interest, with
the vocal result, emphasis. EXAMPLES: The *handsome* man walked *confidently* toward the *open* door. The *hideous* man walked *awkwardly* toward
the *closed* door.
   In "Ulysses," examine the following adjectives and adverbs in the first
20 lines. Which seem to reveal concepts most interesting to you?
   *Adjectives:* Line 1, *idle*; 2, *still, barren*; 3, *aged*; 4, *unequal, savage*; 7, *all*;
10, *scudding, rainy*; 11, *dim*; 12, *hungry*; 17, *ringing, windy*; 20, *untravell'd*.
Don't you find *idle, barren, savage, scudding*, and *untravell'd* more interesting
than the others? Why? Be sure to study their functions in context however.
   *Adverbs:* Line 1, *little*; 5, *not*; 8, *Greatly, greatly*; 12, *always*; 15, *not, all*;
19, *wherethro'*.

Identify adjectives and adverbs in remaining portions of the poem.

The rest of the word classes are considered auxiliary because they usually serve only to tie the primary and secondary words together. They usually carry no significance in themselves; consequently, the mind does not find them interesting enough to center upon. Of course, the physical result is subordination rather than emphasis.

*Articles* are usually so unimportant that they are almost always subordinated. The habit of many beginning readers of giving the articles *a, an*, and *the* the same stress as nouns and verbs does more to obscure meaning and to make the reading seem childish and unnatural than any other mistake one could make. We rarely pronounce the article *a* in its long form $\bar{a}$ [e], except in the rare instance of pointing out a single item such as " There is *a* [meaning only " one "] table in the room." In all other cases, we would quite naturally pronounce *a* as an unaccented *uh*[ə]. (The article *a* precedes only words beginning with a consonant; before words beginning with a vowel, it is spelled *an*.) Our treatment of the article *the* is similar. We pronounce *the* as *thē* [ði] only in pointing out a single item, such as in " He is *the* authority on the subject." In all other instances, we use one of two other pronunciations of the word. When *the* precedes a word beginning with a vowel, we pronounce it as if its own vowel were a short *i* [ɪ] as in this sentence: " I saw a bird flying in the air." When *the* precedes a word beginning with a consonant, however, we normally pronounce it as an unaccented *thuh* [ðə] as in this sentence: " I saw a bird flying in the sky." These uses are normal, natural, and correct. Unfortunately, the distinctions are not commonly understood and many persons when reading pronounce all *a*'s as $\bar{a}$ [e] and all *the*'s as *thē* [ði]. Except when the meaning consists of pointing out a single item as important, slide over the articles, push them into the background, just as you normally do in conversational speech.

*Prepositions* should also usually be unstressed, except when the sense of the passage makes them important. Lincoln's " of the *people, by* the people, and *for* the people " is the most famous example of the sense being carried by important prepositions, but this is a noted exception.

*Pronouns*, which are words used in place of nouns, and which refer to a person, an idea, or an object already mentioned, are almost always subordinated. Only when some other principle—such as contrast, to be discussed shortly—throws the weight on a pronoun, should it be emphasized.

*Connectives* should usually be unstressed, especially when they are monosyllables such as *and, but, for, as*, and *or*. Multisyllabic connectives such as *nevertheless, therefore*, and *consequently* will naturally have accented syllables, for it is impossible to speak them without accenting at least one of the syllables, but that is not emphasis. Connectives may require emphasis in some instances, but they are often given too much importance by the unthinking neophyte.

*Auxiliary verbs* and forms of the verb *to be* are usually of low interest value and, therefore, are seldom emphasized because they usually serve words of higher interest. A local radio station staff seems addicted to reading news items as: "The President *will* play golf this weekend." (As if anyone said he wouldn't!) Forms of *to be* are only emphasized when a strong assertion of "being" is suggested by the context.

Examine such auxiliary words in "Ulysses": Line 1, *It, an*; 2, *By, among*; 3, *with, an, I, and*; 4, *unto, a*; 5, *That, and, and, and, me*; 6, *I, from, I, will*; 7, *to, the, I, have*; 8, *have, with, those*; 9, *That, me, and, on, and*; 10, *Thro',  the*. Because there are no forms of *to be* among those examples, look at them in these lines: 11, 18, 19, 22, 25, 26, 28.

Before leaving this subject, we should note that we have cited examples in a metrical poem, where the pull of metrical stress may *seem* to make some unimportant words emphatic. Such stress, which does not take place in prose, should not be confused with the emphasis of centering, however. We shall deal with this matter again in Chapter 14 on the reading of verse.

Although the principles just explained and illustrated are usually true, let us repeat our first statement of this section: "Any word may be important; any word may be unimportant. The meaning determines relative importance." A few samples from conversational speech will demonstrate that words that are usually insignificant may occasionally be *vitally important*:

*Bill:*   You caught some fish?

*Joe:*   (Sadly) I caught *a* fish.

*Father:*   Now, Son, this is *the* way to putt.

*Mother:*   Can't you, for once, throw waste *into* the basket instead of *at* it?

*Mary:*   The new neighbor kids are named John, James, and Joan. *She* seems nice.

*Father:*   Before I give you the key to the car, you will cut the grass, spade the garden, clean your room, *and* [*pause for thought and impressiveness*] anything else I think of!

*He:*   Let's stay home tonight.

*She:*   I'd like to go to a movie.

*He:*   But I don't want to go to a movie.

*She:*   We *will* go to a movie, if you know what's good for you!

*Son* (or *Daughter*):   I've tried every way I know and this problem just won't work out.

*Father* (or *Mother*):   Well, don't give up. There *is* a way to solve it, or it wouldn't have been assigned to you.

**New Ideas—Old Ideas.**   The distinction between new ideas and old ideas is very important! In intelligent writing, the train of thought is to be found in the flow from one new idea to another new idea. Mixed in with the succession of new ideas, however, are to be found repetitions or "echoes" of the old ideas. The new ideas are to be emphasized because the mind finds them interesting; the echoes will be subordinated because they are not of primary interest to the mind. Echoes are always unimportant.

*Example:* Consider the use of the word *islands* in this paragraph:

> All of us, without exception, live on *islands*. But *some* of these islands   1
> on our planet are so much larger than the *others* that we have decided to   2
> let them belong to a class of their own and have called them *"continents."*   3
> A *continent* therefore is an *island* which "contains" or "holds together" more   4
> territory than just an *ordinary* island like England or Madagascar or Man-   5
> hattan.                                                                                                        6
>
> —HENDRIK WILLEM VAN LOON, *Van Loon's Geography*

This is the first paragraph of a chapter. In the first line " islands " are mentioned for the first time. It is the word that focuses attention on the main point of the paragraph. It must be emphasized. In line 2, however, " islands " is used again, and here it is an echo of the preceding idea; " islands " is repeated only for coherence or clearness. The new idea in this sentence is to be found expressed in the word " some," which should receive the emphasis. In line 2, " others " should be emphasized because it is the new idea in contrast to " some." In line 4, " continents " becomes the new idea, but in the following sentence, both " continent " and " island " should be emphasized, for they are the important nouns in a highly significant definition, the author's main point. The author has repeated both to emphasize the relationship. In line 6, however, the word " island " is again an echo, to be unstressed, whereas the emphasis should be placed on the new idea in the word " ordinary."

Consider another example of new and old ideas in this piece of light verse:

## TRAFFIC

ANONYMOUS

He was *right, dead* right                      1
   As he *hurried* along.                   2
But he's *just* as dead                              3
   As though he were *wrong*.             4

In *death* as in *life*                                    5
   He fell for a *cause;*                         6
At *last* has a *country*                             7
   *Not* of *men* but of *laws.*              8

(By the way, did you notice the pronouns in this verse? The first pronoun is unimportant because it is generalized or universal. It refers to anyone or everyone. After that, "he" is always an echo referring back. This is the principle of the unimportant pronoun: It is usually an echo. Notice also "her" and "she" referring to "moon" in the poem "Silver" below.)

**Assertion—Implication.** The principle of "assertion—implication" is similar to the principle of "new ideas—old ideas." The train of thought to be communicated is what is asserted. Therefore, the mind centers on it. On the other hand, the concepts that are obvious in a given context, therefore, taken for granted, are implied. Implied material should not be centered on because it is not of great interest. For example, in Van Loon's paragraph on islands just discussed, "planet," in line 2, is pure implication, for it is obvious to all that the author is speaking of our world. "Territory," in line 5, is also implication because an island obviously contains, or holds together, territory. In De la Mare's little poem, which follows, "night," "sees," "trees," "beams," "dog," "water," and "stream" are all implied and will be subordinated.

## SILVER

WALTER DE LA MARE

Slowly, silently, now the moon
Walks the night in her silver shoon;
This way, and that, she peers, and sees
Silver fruit upon silver trees;
One by one the casements catch
Her beams beneath the silvery thatch;
Couched in his kennel, like a log,
With paws of silver sleeps the dog;
From their shadowy cote the white breasts peep
Of doves in a silver–feathered sleep;
A harvest mouse goes scampering by,
With silver claws and silver eye;
And moveless fish in the water gleam,
By silver reeds in a silver stream.

**Repetitions for Emphasis.** Authors will often repeat a word or phrase in order to emphasize it or to create a desired psychological effect. (The wise public speaker also knows the persuasive value of well-planned and well-executed repetition.) De la Mare's frequent repetition—ten times in fourteen lines—of *silver* is certainly one of design. The word *silver* should receive careful consideration in each case. Not only is the idea "silver" predominant, but, also, the sound value of the word is important to the poem.

**Contrasts, Comparisons, Parallels, and Words in Balance.** Whenever ideas are contrasted (differences), compared (likenesses), paralleled (several items in identical syntactical arrangement), or in balance (not different or alike, but together or opposed), they will be found interesting to the mind and therefore will be emphasized. Ben Franklin's proverbs are full of contrasts, and parallels. Read them aloud, emphasizing the thought centers:

Fools need advice most, but Wise Men only are the better for it.
You may delay, but Time will not.
Virtue may not always make a Face handsome, but Vice will certainly make it ugly.
The honest man takes pains, and then enjoys pleasures; the knave takes pleasures, and then suffers pains.
Where there's marriage without love, there will be love without marriage.

Shakespeare made frequent use of comparisons:

We are such stuff
As dreams are made on . . .
. . .
But man, proud man,
Drest in a little brief authority
Most ignorant of what he's most assured,
His glassy essence, like an angry ape,
Plays such fantastic tricks before high heaven
As make the angels weep.
. . .
He hath a heart as sound as a bell.
. . .

(He also wrote [in *Much Ado about Nothing*]: "Comparisons are odorous.")

Perhaps a further look at parallel structure is in order. It is a prime form of good writing, particularly in expository uses. We find it interesting to focus on the *new elements* in a repetitious syntax. We show you two examples from the great anthropologist, naturalist, and writer, Loren Eiseley:

It was an uncanny business if there had been anyone there to see. It was a journey best not observed in daylight, it was something that needed swamps and shadows and the touch of the night dew. It was a monstrous penetration of a forbidden element, and the Snout kept his face from the light. It was just as well, though the face should not be mocked. In three hundred million years it would be our own. —from *The Immense Journey*

Note that Eiseley here builds a climactic interest through three sentences beginning "It was an . . . ." and then varies his structure just slightly by stating the fourth time "It was just . . . ." surprising the reader who expects the exact parallelism to continue.

Look at another Eiseley example of parallel structure:

If you cannot bear the silence and the darkness, do not go there; if you dislike black night and yawning chasms, never make them your profession. If you fear the sound of water hurrying through crevices toward unknown and mysterous destinations, do not consider it. Seek out the sunshine. It is a simple prescription. Avoid the darkness.

It is a simple prescription, but you will not follow it. You will turn immediately to the darkness. You will be drawn to it by cords of fear and longing. You will imagine that you are tired of the sunlight; the waters that unnerve you will tug in the ancient recesses of your mind; the midnight will seem restful—you will end by going down.

I am a case of this sort.                              —from *The Night Country*

Words in balance are just like parallel structure except that they are more often only two in number and they are neither contrasted nor compared.

She is sweet and sincere.
The house is old and roomy.

For more literary examples of words in balance, look in the first Eiseley quotation, where "swamps" and "shadows" are both objects of the verb "needed." In the last quotation, "silence" and "darkness" are objects of "bear," as are "night" and "chasms" objects of "dislike." They are in balance, the one against the other. "Unknown" and "mysterious" are adjectives modifying "destinations" and are neither identical nor opposites. One more example is found in the second paragraph: "cords of *fear* and of *longing*."

**Causal and Conditional Relationships.**    As a thinking being, the human sees logical relationships in his society, his science, his philosophy, and his religion. Among these are the causal and the conditional. One action or state may cause another to occur: This relationship we call the causal, or cause-and-effect, relationship. One action or state may be necessary to the occurrence of another: This relationship we call the conditional. In the interpretative reading of literature, we must never fail to see such logical relationships and emphasize the key words, for they are invariably important.

*Examples:*

Causal:

If you prick us, do we not bleed? if you tickle us, do we not laugh? if you poison us, do we not die? and if you wrong us, shall we not revenge?
> —SHAKESPEARE, *The Merchant of Venice*

Conditional:

To give a satisfactory answer to this mighty question, it is indispensable to have an accurate and thorough knowledge of the nature and the character of the cause by which the Union is endangered.
> —JOHN C. CALHOUN

Conditional:

"Had he and I but met
By some old ancient inn,
We should have sat us down to wet
Right many a nipperkin!

Causal:

"But ranged as infantry,
And staring face to face,
I shot at him as he at me,
And killed him in his place."
> —THOMAS HARDY, "The Man He Killed"

**Climax.** Climactic structure always demands careful emphasis by the reader. A climax is a turning point, or a point of highest interest, or a point of greatest tension. Authors build words, phrases, clauses, sentences, paragraphs, or even chapters into suspenseful and emphatic climaxes. Climaxes are integral parts of essays, speeches, stories, novels, poems, and plays. The poor reader who fails to see the point of greatest importance, to feel the point of greatest tension, or to realize the crucial moment, reads without real overall impact. Climaxes do not just happen in literature; they are constructed by good writers to create desired effects in readers and listeners. Never read with a uniformity of intensity. Locate all climaxes and study their relative degrees of importance. Build the appropriate degree of tension for each as if you were climbing mountains, through the foothills and small peaks, until you reach the highest peak: the main climax of the selection.

The pattern of most climactic interest is a rising interest that reaches the peak either at the end of a literary unit or very near the end:

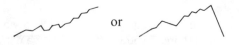

or

If the peak of interest occurs too soon, what follows can only be anticlimactic, therefore, less interesting:

In reading tense scenes, readers sometimes begin at too high a degree of vocal tension and have no place to go when the climax occurs; therefore, the climax lacks power through lack of contrast:

The tension, or interest value, of good writing is never this monotonous line:

---

*Examples:* Study climaxes in the following examples:

For, lo, the winter is past; the rain is over and gone; the flowers appear on the earth; the time of the singing of birds is come, and the voice of the turtle is heard in our land.

*—The Song of Solomon*

There is no right to strike against public safety by anybody, anywhere, anytime.

—CALVIN COOLIDGE

Dancing is the loftiest, the most moving, the most beautiful of the arts, because it is no mere translation or abstraction from life; it is life itself.

—HAVELOCK ELLIS

Hath not a Jew eyes? hath not a Jew hands, organs, dimensions, senses, affections, passions? fed with the same food, hurt with the same weapons, subject to the same diseases, healed by the same means, warmed and cooled by the same winter and summer, as a Christian is? If you prick us, do we not bleed? if you tickle us, do we not laugh? if you poison us, do we not die? and if you wrong us, shall we not revenge?

—SHAKESPEARE, *The Merchant of Venice*

**Structural Emphasis.** Writers use structural methods to emphasize important ideas. The expert uses words in designed structure, to do as the architect does with materials; to emphasize important meanings and to de-emphasize, or subordinate, features of lesser significance. In sentences, paragraphs, and whole compositions you will find the most important ideas expressed in the first and last positions, which are usually most emphatic. Consider the differing shades of meaning in the following sentence and the variations we have given it:

When you have eliminated the impossible, whatever remains, however improbable, must be the truth.

—ARTHUR CONAN DOYLE

However improbable, the truth is whatever remains after you have eliminated the impossible.

The truth is whatever remains after you have eliminated the impossible, no matter how improbable it is.

Within a sentence in its normal word order, the most important thought group is likely to be in the *main clause* rather than in a subordinate one: "I see all the new plays when I visit New York City." Changing the order of the clauses adds significance to the subordinate clause: "When I visit New York City, I see all the new plays." In the structure of English sentences, the usual word order is "subject, verb, object." When a good writer changes this order, he usually does so for the purpose of emphasizing those *words out of order:*

Mine be a cot beside the hill;
A beehive's hum shall soothe my ear;
A willowy brook that turns a mill,
With many a fall shall linger near.

—SAMUEL ROGERS, " A Wish "

To-morrow, and to-morrow, and to-morrow,
Creeps in this petty pace from day to day
To the last syllable of recorded time,

—SHAKESPEARE, *Macbeth*

How sharper than a serpent's tooth it is
To have a thankless child!

—SHAKESPEARE, *King Lear*

You will also find that thoughts *most fully developed* by the author are usually his most important ideas, and you must find means for emphasizing them. You already know that authors use *repetition* as a means for emphasizing their most important points.

Last, you should be aware that writers use *word choice* to emphasize their meanings. It is obvious to us at all times that superlatives, such as *most, best,* and *worst* are emphatic, but it is not so immediately apparent that synonyms are not equal to each other, rather, the selection of the precise word is a type of structural emphasis. Consider the various impacts of the following synonyms for two words:

> *Friend:* acquaintance, associate, colleague, companion, confidant(e), intimate, comrade, chum, pal, buddy, sidekick
>
> *Hatred:* aversion, detestation, abhorrence, loathing, repugnance, antipathy, execration, abomination, ill will, malevolence, malignity, animosity, rancor, enmity, malice, disfavor, disaffection

This chapter has been primarily concerned with the grammatical-syntactical-structural factors in language that result from the logical thought processes of the writer and that, in turn, direct the logical thought processes of the silent and oral reader. Normally, we speak in accordance with these principles without conscious attention to what needs emphasizing or de-emphasizing, but the person who is faced with the translation of printed symbols into speech, often finds it essential to analyze writing in these terms in order to read intelligently.

Yet, in looking forward at this time to the actions of the voice in expressing meaning, we must recognize that not only logic governs the voice, but also the speaker's attitudes and emotions. Even the fictional mood of the literature or the mood of the reading occasion will color speech by altering phrasing, emphasis, and subordination from what is seemingly most apparent in the mere words. And so, while logical syntax is vital, it is not the entire basis for a consideration of the vocal action of any speaker. We shall give more attention to these matters as we see how the voice acts in terms of time, loudness, pitch, and quality.

As we have already said, the voice, in tandem with the visible personality, reveals our attitudes and emotions. We can look at an angry person and usually be fully aware of his emotional state. We can hear another speak, even in a language that is foreign, and discern whether he is happy or sad, calm or agitated. All the vocal variables contribute to the "tone of voice." To demonstrate quickly that attitudes are expressed by various actions of the voice, let's try a few quite different "readings" of a single brief dialogue. We ask you what we have asked students for some years: "What would you have seen and heard had you been there?"

## DIALOGUE

A:  Do you want any dessert?

B:  By the tone of your voice, I think I'll be lucky to get anything.

A:  What would you want, if I'll get it?

B:  How about some ice cream?

A:  What kind?

B:  What flavors do you have?

A:  Name one. You like vanilla?

B:  Give me one small dip.

A:  We serve two.

B:  I just want one small dip.

A:  You'll pay for two.

B:  I want just one.

A:  OK, I'll bring you one.

. . .

A:  Here's one small dip.

B:  Why didn't you put something on it?

A:  I did—my finger. It slipped.

B:  Put some pineapple on it.

. . .

A:  Well, here it is.

B:  Why did you put your finger in it?

A:  It'll taste good when I get home.

When faced with "interpreting" this scene out-of-context and with no narrative assistance from an author, students have come up with a multitude of notions as to what happened in it and between whom. You obviously have your own picture of place, time, and characters. Three of the many interpretations that have been expressed have been approximately like the following descriptions. There are, of course, many others possible. The point is: Each interpretation will demand distinct vocal and bodily behavior. Try reading or acting each scene, noting that vocal interpretation becomes radically different for each character in each scene.

*Scene 1:* A truck stop. The waitress, somewhere between youth and middle age, is as inelegant as the place she works in. It is late at night, and she is tired. So is her customer, a hardened driver, tired.

Read her first question in a tired manner. Your feet hurt. It's nearly time to go home. Everyone has given you a rough time today. This guy gets difficult. Now, read his answer. He's tired; he's been fighting the road and the "bears" all day. He just wants one dip. He's reasonable at first, but he eventually does get a bit nasty. Rather late in the game he asks her why she didn't put something on it. He knows he should have asked for that pineapple earlier. Then he becomes angry when he sees she has been so careless as to stick her dirty finger into his ice cream!

*Scene 2:* A greasy-spoon diner. Early evening. A society matron has decided to " try " a diner for dinner. She gets " playful " in ordering from a character-cook-waiter somewhat like the one who serves Dagwood in the comicstrip occasionally. He, of course, resents her superiority and finally puts her down with his last line.

Play the scene, imaginatively, and feel how the muscular nature of each character helps establish what the voice of each does, in terms of rate, pause, duration, loudness, inflections, and basic voice qualities.

*Scene 3:* A young pair of lovers soon after the honeymoon. Make it as playful and as suggestive as you wish. Complex intonations are called for.

It may be of value for pairs of readers to enact these scenes in class, along with other different interpretations of the scene. Actually, not one of these is what your author saw and heard happen, but he's not telling because he does not want to close your " ear " to the numerous possibilities.

We hope this dialogue has demonstrated through *your* speaking mechanism that human attitudes show up very concretely in the voice. Could we make a list of emotions, attitudes, moods, affective states? Hardly. Start at the " A's " of a small dictionary, making a list of just the adjectives and adverbs delineating attitudinal behavior, such as: *abrasive, accusingly, acidly, acrimonious, affable, amused, angrily, arrogantly,* and so on. They will appear by the thousands, our possible manners of feeling. Literature is as life is, full of attitudes as well as ideas. As a speech artist, your voice will be sensitive to them.

## EXERCISES

In the quotations below find examples of: echoes, implications, repetitions for emphasis, contrasts, comparisons, parallels, causal and conditional relationships, climaxes, and instances of structural emphasis. Be ready to read them aloud in class.

  a. All religion, all life, all art, all expression come down to this: to the effort of the human soul to break through its barrier of loneliness, of intolerable loneliness, and make some contact with another seeking soul, or with what all souls seek, which is (by any name) God.

—DON MARQUIS

  b. Strange, when you come to think of it, that of all the countless folk who have lived before our time on this planet not one is known in history or in legend as having died of laughter.   —SIR MAX BEERBOHM

  c. The chess-board is the world, the pieces are the phenomena of the universe, the rules of the game are what we call the laws of Nature.

The player on the other side is hidden from us. We know that his play is always fair, just, and patient. But also we know, to our cost, that he never overlooks a mistake, or makes the smallest allowance for ignorance. —THOMAS HENRY HUXLEY

d. Pride is an established conviction of one's own paramount worth in some particular respect; while vanity is the desire of rousing such a conviction in others. Pride works from within; it is the direct appreciation of oneself. Vanity is the desire to arrive at this appreciation indirectly, from without. —ARTHUR SCHOPENHAUER

e. Young men think old men are fools; but old men know young men are fools. —GEORGE CHAPMAN

f. To live content with small means; to seek elegance rather than luxury, and refinement rather than fashion; to be worthy, not respectable, and wealthy, not rich; to study hard, think quietly, talk gently, act frankly; to listen to stars and birds, to babes and sages, with open heart; to bear all cheerfully, do all bravely, await occasions, hurry never. In a word, to let the spiritual, unbidden and unconscious, grow up through the common. This is to be my symphony. —WILLIAM HENRY CHANNING

g. Be not angry that you cannot make others as you wish them to be, since you cannot make yourself as you wish to be. —THOMAS À KEMPIS

h. No house should ever be *on* any hill or on anything. It should be *of* the hill, belonging to it, so hill and house could live together each the happier for the other. —FRANK LLOYD WRIGHT

i. Romantic plays with happy endings are almost of necessity inferior in artistic value to true tragedies. Not, one would hope, simply because they end happily; happiness in itself is certainly not less beautiful than grief; but because a tragedy in its great moments can generally afford to be sincere, while romantic plays live in an atmosphere of ingenuity and make-believe. —GILBERT MURRAY

j. It is not only what we have inherited from our fathers that exists again in us, but all sorts of old dead ideas and all kinds of old dead beliefs . . . . They are not actually alive in us; but there they are dormant, all the same, and we can never be rid of them. Whenever I take up a newspaper and read it, I fancy I see ghosts creeping between the lines. There must be ghosts all over the world. —HENRIK IBSEN

k. But the artist appeals to that part of our being which is not dependent on wisdom; to that in us which is a gift and not an acquisition—and, therefore, more permanently enduring. He speaks to our capacity for delight and wonder, to the sense of mystery surrounding our lives: to our sense of pity, and beauty, and pain. —JOSEPH CONRAD

After speaking so much about the types of words, their functions, and relative importance, we cannot resist the impulse to quote for you this delightful love poem:

## PERMANENTLY

KENNETH KOCH

One day the Nouns were clustered in the street.
An Adjective walked by, with her dark beauty.
The Nouns were struck, moved, changed.
The next day a Verb drove up, and created the Sentence.

Each Sentence says one thing—for example, "Although it was a dark rainy day when the Adjective walked by, I shall remember the pure and sweet expression on her face until the day I perish from the green, effective earth."
Or, "Will you please close the window, Andrew?"
Or, for example, "Thank you, the pink pot of flowers on the window sill has changed color recently to a light yellow, due to the heat from the boiler factory which exists nearby."

In the springtime the Sentences and the Nouns lay silently on the grass.
A lonely Conjunction here and there would call, "And! But!"
But the Adjective did not emerge.

As the Adjective is lost in the sentence,
So I am lost in your eyes, ears, nose, and throat—
You have enchanted me with a single kiss
Which can never be undone
Until the destruction of language.

How many contextual principles can you find in operation in the writing of this uniquely structured poem? What attitudes are apparent in vocabulary and structure? After looking at its form analytically, read it aloud, with probably an increased awareness of how the poet has achieved her purpose.

## WHEN YOU HAVE FORGOTTEN SUNDAY: THE LOVE STORY

GWENDOLYN BROOKS

—And when you have forgotten the bright bedclothes on a Wednesday and a Saturday,

And most especially when you have forgotten Sunday—
When you have forgotten Sunday halves in bed,
Or me sitting on the front-room radiator in the limping afternoon
Looking off down the long street
To nowhere,
Hugged by my plain old wrapper of no-expectation
And nothing-I-have-to-do and I'm-happy-why?
And if-Monday-never-had-to-come—
When you have forgotten that, I say,
And how you swore, if somebody beeped the bell,
And how my heart played hopscotch if the telephone rang;
And how we finally went in to Sunday dinner,
That is to say, went across the front room floor to the ink-spotted
   table in the southwest corner
To Sunday dinner, which was always chicken and noodles
Or chicken and rice
And salad and rye bread and tea
And chocolate chip cookies—
I say, when you have forgotten that,
When you have forgotten my little presentiment
That the war would be over before they got to you;
And how we finally undressed and whipped out the light and
   flowed into bed,
And lay loose-limbed for a moment in the week-end
Bright bedclothes,
Then gently folded into each other—
When you have, I say, forgotten all that
Then you may tell,
Then I may believe
You have forgotten me well.

# 9 Audible Communication Through Time

Both sound and silence are chiefly characterized by time. Within a framework of silence, the organist paints a musical picture with sound. As long as he keeps his finger upon a key, the organ produces a tone. However, one continuous tone does not communicate. Other sounds and silences must be incorporated to produce music. So it is with the interpretative reader. A sound in itself does not produce meaning or feeling; sounds and silences, properly arranged, do. Since the lives of sounds and silences are measured in time, time becomes one of the major considerations of the reader.

When speaking of time, we refer to four aspects: the rate of speaking, the length of sound, the use of silence, and patterns of sound.

These we call *rate, duration, pause,* and *rhythm.*

## RATE

The most obvious element of time is rate, or rapidity of utterance, measurable in terms of the number of words per minute.

**Factors Controlling Rate.** Rate is, to some extent, dependent on the personality of the individual reader. We all have our normal, or habitual, rates of speaking. Some of us customarily talk slowly, deliberately; others talk rapidly most of the time. We are accustomed to such individual differences. Television and radio audiences have had both deliberate and rapid speakers among their favorite announcers, commentators, comedians, and even politicians.

A major element determining rate of utterance in oral interpretation is the emotional content of the material. An exciting story, or one with considerable action, is likely to be read at a comparatively rapid rate, while a somber, serious selection will need to be read at a slow rate. Light verse with little seriousness of purpose, such as limericks, will be read rather rapidly:

There was an old man from Peru,
Who dreamed he was eating his shoe.
   He woke in a fright
   In the middle of the night
And found it was perfectly true.        —ANONYMOUS

On the other hand, literature as seriously contemplative as this poem by Walt Whitman deserves more time for contemplation:

## A NOISELESS PATIENT SPIDER

WALT WHITMAN

A noiseless patient spider,
I mark'd where on a little promontory it stood isolated,
Mark'd how to explore the vacant vast surrounding,
It launched forth filament, filament, filament, out of itself,
Ever unreeling them, ever tirelessly speeding them.
And you O my soul where you stand,
Surrounded, detached, in measureless oceans of space,
Ceaselessly musing, venturing, throwing, seeking the spheres to connect
    them,
Till the bridge you will need be form'd, till the ductile anchor hold,
Till the gossamer thread you fling catch somewhere, O my soul.

The belief that rate is closely related to the nature of the emotion expressed has been substantiated by experimental research efforts revealing that the emotions of anger, fear, and indifference are expressed in rapid rates (along with short duration of phonations and short pauses), whereas such emotions as contempt and grief cause the rate of speech to be slow.[1]

Of course, we should recognize that a slow rate may be caused either by making pauses longer and more frequent (as was found to be characteristic of the slow rate of grief) or by prolonging both phonations and pauses (as was the case in contempt).

Certain practical considerations inherent in the reading situation also determine rate: the mood of the speaker (hopefully, but unfortunately not always, suggested by the literature), and the nature of the audience and the occasion. We know that when we are nervous or excited, we tend to speak faster. Many a television or radio speaker has carefully timed his talk, only to find—to his amazement—that under pressure of producing the program, he has finished ahead of time. He simply talked faster than he planned because he was excited. Beginning readers do the same: They tend to read much too rapidly. They race through thought groups, sentences, and paragraphs, unaware that they have lost their audience. The solution to this type of reading is not to try to "slow down" but to increase one's concentration

[1] Grant Fairbanks and LeMar W. Hoaglin, "An Experimental Study of the Durational Characteristics of the Voice During the Expression of Emotion," *Speech Monographs*, VIII (1941), 85–90.

on ideas or images in the literature. Spend more time thinking, visualizing, and experiencing while uttering words and while pausing, and you will be less likely to read with excessive speed. We shall see later in this chapter how the relationships between the complexity of the material, the nature of the audience and the occasion, and the acoustical situation, determine the length of thought groups and the number and length of pauses; they also determine how fast a reader can effectively utter sound and yet communicate.

The reader, therefore, needs to be able to adjust normal rate to a variety of possible circumstances related to the occasion, audience, and intellectual and emotional requirements of the material. Furthermore, one must be sensitive to the changes of rate demanded *within* a particular selection, as we shall see presently.

**Examples of Rate Usage.**   By listening analytically to recordings of professional readers, we can study the uses of rate by those who should be able to utilize them best. We listened to fifty-five recordings of poetry by nineteen different readers, timed them, counted the words in the selections, and computed the rates in words per minute. A table listing these readings appears at the end of this chapter. Each rate is calculated from the reading of an entire poem and, thus, is affected by the time spent in pausing, even between stanzas. While this rather simple approach to the study of rate may not be scientifically sophisticated, it suffices to indicate that good readers do use variation of rate as a technique.

The rates of reading varied from very slow, 91 words per minute for Carl Sandburg reading his own poem "Grass," to very fast, 210 words per minute for Edith Evans reading Carroll's nonsensical "Father William." Thus, the extremes represent a difference of 119 words per minute, quite a range, indeed!

An individual reader uses a wide range of rates in reading a variety of materials. Edith Evans read "Father William" at an extremely fast rate, as we have just noted, but she read "She Walks in Beauty" quite slowly, at a rate of only 106. John Gielgud read "That Time of Year" at only 118, but "So We'll Go No More A-Roving" at a fast 171. Basil Rathbone, normally a fast reader, varied from 123 for "How Do I Love Thee," to 193 for "Invictus." Claire Bloom, like Gielgud, chose a slow rate—116—for "That Time of Year" but read "It Was a Lover and His Lass," a light-hearted lyric, at 147. John Neville did not limit himself to his slow rate of 100, which he used for the Milton poem, but read more rapidly—145—for "The Passionate Shepherd to His Mistress." Accomplished readers, therefore, recognize—at least subconsciously—that different pieces of literature, because of their emotional contents or intellectual "weights," require different time treatments in interpretation. We recommend that you examine the selections just mentioned to appreciate how their emotional contents dictate the appropriate reading rates.

No one can establish ironclad rules as to specific rates for specific selections or specific moods, however. We see on the table that "She Walks in Beauty" received four different rates on these recordings: Evans, 106; Power, 109; Portman, 138; and Corwin, 150. A study of the poem should lead us to believe that it should be read at a predominantly slow rate. A study of these recordings might reveal that some are more effective than others, but, of course, we must acknowledge that factors other than rate may also make one reading better than another. Corwin's rate of 150 would seem to indicate that he did not make much use of rate to communicate the quiet beauty of the poem, although he *may* have used other techniques effectively. On the other hand, anyone who listens to the two recordings of Dylan Thomas' "Do Not Go Gentle into That Good Night" will adjudge the poet's own recording to be considerably superior to the one by Norman Rose, with the use of rate playing a significant role in this superiority. Thomas took the time to think, feel, and experience; Rose only skimmed the surface—the words. One might also contend, with some justification, that Rathbone's rapid 161 tends to keep his reading of "Ode to the West Wind" from being as effective as Gielgud's, which is read at only 122 words per minute. One might feel that Neville's 108 for "When, in Disgrace with Fortune" is irritatingly slow and Rathbone's 152, superficially rapid.

Some interesting agreements in rate appear on the table: the almost identically slow rates for Bloom and Gielgud in reading a Shakespearean sonnet; the similar middle-range rates for Portman and Scourby in reading Wordsworth's "Upon Westminster Bridge;" and the fast rates of Johnson and Evans in reading "Father William."

The average rate for the fifty readings was 140 words per minute. For ten sonnets, the average was 125; for eighteen serious, contemplative poems (other than the sonnets), the average was 134; for nineteen light, cheerful verses, the average was 154. One might draw some general conclusions from these averages if one also recognizes that the readers used a *range* of rates for each type of literature.

Study the table to learn about the uses of rate. If you are fortunate enough to be able to listen to some of the recordings, you can study the actual readings and perhaps compare them with other recordings, professional or amateur, of the same materials. Rate is worth studying; the ability to vary the rate to suit the material is worth cultivating.

**Examples of Rate Variety.**   Not only do accomplished interpreters vary their rates from selection to selection, but they also vary their rates to communicate the changing emotional tensions *within* a selection. John Gielgud read the first stanza of Kingsley's "Young and Old" at a rate of 184, but he slowed to 128 for the second stanza. Read the poem to determine why:

# YOUNG AND OLD

CHARLES KINGSLEY

When all the world is young, lad,
    And all the trees are green;
And every goose a swan, lad,
    And every lass a queen;
Then hey for boot and horse, lad,
    And round the world away;
Young blood must have its course, lad,
    And every dog his day.

When all the world is old, lad,
    And all the trees are brown;
And all the sport is stale, lad,
    And all the wheels run down;
Creep home, and take your place there,
    The spent and maimed among:
God grant you find one face there,
    You loved when all was young.

The following example should further demonstrate that good readers are sensitive to the emotional content of literature and consequently vary their rate—automatically—to communicate the changing emotional tensions within a selection.

Alexander Scourby and Frank Silvera have each recorded readings of "My Last Duchess." We have computed their rates for the entire poem and for various portions, and have indicated them in the text that follows. A few minutes spent in considering these uses of rate will demonstrate to you that proficient readers are sensitive to the psychological and dramatic motivations in literature. Scourby reads faster than Silvera; Scourby's overall rate is 150 words per minute as compared with Silvera's 124. In spite of this difference in basic rate, probably caused both by the readers' personalities and their interpretations, Scourby and Silvera vary their rates for this poem in similar fashion.

# MY LAST DUCHESS
## Ferrara

ROBERT BROWNING

That's my last Duchess painted on the wall,
Looking as if she were alive; I call

That piece a wonder, now: Frà Pandolf's hands
Worked busily a day, and there she stands.
ˋWill't please you sit and look at her?

*Rates:* SCOURBY, 168; SILVERA, 120. (Silvera's opening is very slow and
    thoughtful.)

                       I said
'Frà Pandolf' by design, for never read
Strangers like you that pictured countenance,
The depth and passion of its earnest glance,
But to myself they turned (since none puts by
The curtain I have drawn for you, but I)
And seemed as they would ask me, if they durst,
How such a glance came there; so, not the first
Are you to turn and ask thus. Sir, 'twas not
Her husband's presence only, called that spot
Of joy into the Duchess' cheek: perhaps
Frà Pandolf chanced to say

*Rates:* SCOURBY, 164; SILVERA, 139. (Scourby has almost maintained
    his fairly matter-of-fact pace; Silvera has quickened his pace slightly.)

                'Her mantle laps
Over my Lady's wrist too much,' or 'Paint
Must never hope to reproduce the faint
Half-flush that dies along her throat;'

*Rates:* SCOURBY, 136; SILVERA, 136. (Scourby has slowed considerably
    and Silvera has slowed imperceptibly until they use the identical rate.)

              such stuff
Was courtesy, she thought, and cause enough
For calling up that spot of joy. She had
A heart . . . how shall I say? . . . too soon made glad,
Too easily impressed; she liked whate'er
She looked on, and her looks went everywhere.
Sir, 'twas all one! My favour at her breast,
The dropping of the daylight in the West,
The bough of cherries some officious fool
Broke in the orchard for her, the white mule
She rode with round the terrace—all and each
Would draw from her alike the approving speech,
Or blush, at least.

*Rates:* SCOURBY, 154; SILVERA, 127. (Scourby's faster rate through this portion would seem to emphasize the poetic aspect of the work, whereas Silvera's detailed squeezing for impersonative factors emphasizes the dramatic.)

> She thanked men,—good; but thanked
> Somehow . . . I know not how . . . as if she ranked
> My gift of a nine-hundred-years-old name
> With anybody's gift. Who'd stoop to blame
> This sort of trifling?

*Rates:* SCOURBY, 116; SILVERA, 110. (It is interesting that both readers see fit to read this portion at a slow rate.)

> Even had you skill
> In speech—(which I have not)—to make your will
> Quite clear to such an one, and say 'Just this
> Or that in you disgusts me; here you miss,
> Or there exceed the mark'—and if she let
> Herself be lessoned so, nor plainly set
> Her wits to yours, forsooth, and made excuse,
> —E'en then would be some stooping, and I choose
> Never to stoop. Oh, Sir, she smiled, no doubt,
> Whene'er I passed her; but who passed without
> Much the same smile?

*Rates:* SCOURBY, 168; SILVERA, 134. (They agree on speeding up for this portion, but Scourby does so much more drastically.)

> This grew; I gave commands;
> Then all smiles stopped together. There she stands
> As if alive.

*Rates:* SCOURBY, 80; SILVERA, 87. (Such extremely slow rates are accompanied by long pauses, filled with much thought.)

> Will't please you rise? We'll meet
> The company below, then. I repeat,
> The Count your Master's known munificence
> Is ample warrant that no just pretence
> Of mine for dowry will be disallowed;
> Though his fair daughter's self, as I avowed
> At starting, is my object. Nay, we'll go
> Together down, Sir! Notice Neptune, though,

Taming a sea-horse, thought a rarity,
Which Claus of Innsbruck cast in bronze for me.

*Rates:* SCOURBY, 162; SILVERA, 127. (Each reader has returned to his
basic area of rate. These differ widely and contribute to the considerable
difference in the two interpretations of the poem.)

Determining the exact rate for a reading is important only to *illustrate*
how good readers use rate. We should note here that although good readers
differ in the rates they employ for reading the same selection, they *vary their
rates to suit the type of material.* They use rate to help communicate the
content of the literature.

Rate is a fundamental and interesting aspect of oral reading. You should
learn to do the following:

1. Control your rate of reading so that you do not, under pressure, read
   too rapidly for your listeners to comprehend your reading.
2. Develop the ability to read at a variety of speeds so that you may be
   able to respond to literary demands for various rates.
3. Study the material you choose to read, and read it at a rate that is
   appropriate to the intellectual and emotional content. This principle
   means that you will alter your rate within a selection as the ideas and
   emotions change.

## DURATION

The second aspect of time is duration, or length of sound. Some of our
speech sounds are normally short; some, normally long. Although little
research has established precise psychological effects of sound lengths in
American speech, we can recognize that duration of sound has significance.
The consonants p [p], b [b], t [t], and d [d], for example, are relatively short
sounds. They are called *plosives,* and their lives end with their explosion
from our lips and tongue; they cannot be prolonged. The consonants m [m],
n [n], ng [ŋ], and l [l] are relatively long sounds. They are called *continuants,*
for they can be prolonged indefinitely by the speaker. Thus, we can conclude
that in our speech, normally some sounds are long, some short. It is also
true that in our speaking, we deliberately make the same sounds sometimes long, sometimes short. (In some foreign languages the length given
a vowel in a word may actually determine the meaning of the word. Such
is not the case in English, where the vowel length rarely affects specific
denotation.)

We should, however, learn to determine the effect that sound length has
on meaning and feeling. We almost always use duration as a means for

emphasizing. When we stress a syllable or word—in addition to using vocal techniques yet to be considered—we usually extend the length of the sound. In fact, extended duration is probably the most important technique for determining emphasis. Thus, duration is a means of communicating intellectual significance; it is a result of centering. As the mind centers on the important thoughts, the voice lingers on the significant words to convey their importance.

In addition, duration is a valuable tool for achieving emotional communication because it is a natural aspect of emotional expression. Because difference in word-length is inherent in the sounds from which words are made, duration is inherent in the attitudinal or gestural nature of many words. Whereas the sensitive speaker naturally has an empathy to language sounds, the would-be effective speaker must learn the *use* of a tool which really is a natural sensitivity to sound values. Consider the following list of words. None of them is long in terms of number of letters. But if you will look at them intently, speaking them while letting your mind focus upon the feeling that is likely to go along with each, you will discover that subjectively, at least, some of them are long and some of them are short in terms of sound: *short, long, fast, slow, walk, stroll, hop, crawl, sit, lounge, peppy, lazy, flip, rumble.*

Duration is significant to the oral interpreter also because sounds are often allied with sense. For example, we know that words containing the short i [ɪ] often suggest smallness, e.g., *bib, bit, chip, dim, fib, fig, fin, nit, pin, pip, sip, skip, slim, snip, tip,* and *tit.* We know also that words beginning with fl [fl] sometimes suggest moving light, as in *flame, flare, flash,* and *flicker;* sometimes, flatness, as in *flake, flat, float, flock, flotilla, flood, floor, flounder,* and *flow;* sometimes, quick movement, as in *flag, flail, flap, flaunt, flay, flee, fleet, flick, fling, flip, flit, flog, flop, flounce, flourish, fluent, flurry,* and *flutter.* We know that words beginning with gl [gl] often suggest light, e.g., *glamor, glance, glare, glass, glaucous, glaze, gleam, glimmer, glimpse, glint, glisten, glister, gloaming,* and *gloss.* We know that words ending in er [ɚ] often suggest repetition, e.g., *bicker, chatter, flicker, flutter, glimmer,* and *sputter.* We know that words, by their sounds, often suggest a state of mind or behavior or appearance, e.g., *droopy, gloomy, grisly, grumble, happy, lovely, merry, morbid,* and *sluttish.* Duration is especially important in the case of onomatopoetic words, in which the sound of the word is a direct imitation of the sense of the word, such as: *bang, crash, cuckoo, hiss, hush, moan, murmur, pingpong, roar, rustle,* and *sock.*[2]

Sensitivity to duration of sounds is vital in reading both of the following poems. One is relaxed; one, tense. Yet both seem to call for short duration. Note the effect created in the Whitman poem of clipping short words of potentially long duration, such as *hall, wall,* and *ball.*

---

[2] See Chapter 14 for further consideration of onomatopoeia in poetry and verse.

## GIRL'S-EYE VIEW OF RELATIVES
### First Lesson

PHYLLIS MCGINLEY

The thing to remember about fathers is, they're men.
A girl has to keep it in mind.
They are dragon-seekers, bent on improbable rescues.
Scratch any father, you find
Someone chock-full of qualms and romantic terrors,
Believing change is a threat—
Like your first shoes with heels on, like your first bicycle
It took such months to get.

Walk in strange woods, they warn you about the snakes there.
Climb, and they fear you'll fall.
Books, angular boys, or swimming in deep water—
Fathers mistrust them all.
Men are the worriers. It is difficult for them
To learn what they must learn:
How you have a journey to take and very likely,
For a while, will not return.

## LISTENING TO GROWNUPS QUARRELLING

RUTH WHITMAN

standing in the hall against the
wall with my little brother, blown
like leaves against the wall by their
voices, my head like a pingpong ball
between the paddles of their anger:
I knew what it meant
to tremble like a leaf.

Cold with their wrath, I heard
the claws of the rain
pounce. Floods
poured through the city,
skies clapped over me,
and I was shaken, shaken
like a mouse
between their jaws.

In "Dover Beach," quoted in Chapter 2, Matthew Arnold has used a preponderance of long sounds in the first part of the poem and jarringly short ones in the conclusion that suggest the chaos that underlies the apparent serenity of the night.

The expressive interpreter is aware of sound lengths and reads them with sensitivity, for proper use of duration is one of the most effective techniques at the disposal of the reader for communicating emotion and sensory imagery.

Command of duration is usually a late accomplishment in the training of the oral interpreter, but you should begin to acquire skill in using it as soon as possible. Practice holding onto long vowels and continuant consonants, and clipping off short sounds, just to learn how it feels to do so. Learn to appreciate the taste, or flavor, of words. Enjoy words for their sound as well as for the images they suggest. We know that superior speakers use more voiced time than do inferior ones.

## PAUSE

The third element of time is pause. A pause is, of course, the absence of sound but do not confuse a pause and a hesitation. A hesitation is accidental, "dead" silence that communicates only negatively, because it is filled with the embarrassment of the moment rather than with literary meaning. A pause is a purposeful, "living" silence that is charged with appropriate meaning. A good pause anticipates, reinforces, emphasizes, and thrusts home meaning. During the pause, both the reader and the listener think, feel, experience, and appreciate.

**Pauses Assist Communication.**   To demonstrate for your own satisfaction that judicious use of the pause is essential to effective communication, read the following passage aloud to a friend. Read it rapidly, with no pauses. Ask your friend what ideas he has received. It is probable that neither of you will get much meaning.

The true rule in determining to embrace or reject anything is not whether it have any evil in it but whether it have more of evil than of good there are few things wholly evil or wholly good almost everything especially of govern-ment policy is an inseparable compound of the two so that our best judgment of the preponderance between them is continually demanded.

—ABRAHAM LINCOLN

Now read the same paragraph, pausing as indicated below. Then see how many of the ideas your listener has absorbed. Notice, also, how much more you, yourself, have gained from this reading.

The true rule / in determining to embrace or reject anything, / is not whether it have any evil in it, / but whether it have more of evil than of good. / There are few things wholly evil / or wholly good. / Almost everything, / especially of government policy, / is an inseparable compound of the two, / so that our best judgment of the preponderance between them / is continually demanded.

Pauses do help to communicate meaning. They must, however, be used in the right places; one does not pause just anywhere. You have probably already reached the conclusion that pauses most commonly fall *between* thought groups, and you are correct. When the reader pauses elsewhere, he does so purposely to anticipate, emphasize, experience, or appreciate a particular detail, but if he merely hesitates within a thought group, he will destroy meaning. Consider the effect on meaning if we break up thoughts by placing pauses in the wrong places:

The little brown cocker / spaniel from across / the street ran / up to me wiggled / all over licked / his chops and whined for / affection.

Now contrast that effect with the one obtained by placing the pauses between thought groups.

**Punctuating with Pauses.**  We have seen that pauses assist in communicating. Pauses represent mental activity and as such, they are the major devices available to the speaker for punctuating. (Other methods are intonations and visible cues.) The writer may have his commas and periods, his interrogation and exclamation points, his colons and semicolons, his hyphens and dashes, but he wishes that he had pauses in place of all of them! The pause, used by one who has mastered it, is far superior in indicating relationships of phrases, in emphasizing, and in building suspense than any punctuation marks at the disposal of the writer.

**Written Punctuation Versus Oral Punctuation.**  Do not make the mistake of assuming that written punctuation determines the interpreter's oral punctuation. Victor Borge's comedy routine in which he attempts to reproduce written punctuation vocally by means of a different comic sound for each mark of punctuation is funny simply because it is preposterous. But it also indicates the independence of oral punctuation from written forms. It is true that you often pause where a writer has placed a period or a comma, but you will not always do so. What then, is the purpose of written punctuation? *Only* to aid you—or any silent reader—in getting the meaning.

Just as the writer uses punctuation to communicate meaning to the eye, so all speakers use pauses to indicate significance to listeners' ears. From the meanings obtained, the reader then constructs his own oral punctuation to help relay those meanings to a listener. Most beginners have the mistaken notion that a comma, for instance, always demands a pause, but only the uninitiated would pause at all these commas:

Three cheers for the Red, White, and Blue!

They know, and will, therefore, say, that kings are servants, not proprietors of the people.

—BENJAMIN FRANKLIN

Who, then, art thou, vain dust and ashes!

—THOMAS PAINE

Sometimes, the emotional state of the speaker will cause him to "telescope" thoughts with no pauses between them. He might even have to gasp for breath in the middle of a thought group. For example, consider a scene in a play where a boy rushes into a farm kitchen, yelling:

Maw, come quick! The barn's on fire! Where's Paw? We've got to get the tractor, cows, and horses out! Somebody call the fire department!

Is he going to take time to pause?

Although written punctuation and oral punctuation are not identical, we can generally say that periods, question marks, exclamation points, colons, semicolons, and dashes are used where the sense demands that we pause, for these marks are usually placed at the end of complete ideas. We do not *have* to pause at any of them, however!

We usually pause many more times than there are marks of written punctuation. The reason for this is that pausing and phrasing (or grouping) are intricately related. Chapters 5 and 8 have explained the important mental processes of centering and grouping. These materialize in terms of emphasis and phrasing, the latter by means of intonations and pauses that give individual groups identity or reveal relationships between thought groups.

**Pausing Is Individual.** We have already seen that the following single sentence contains thirteen possible thought groups.

One hot day / in December / I had been standing / perfectly still / for a few minutes / among the dry weeds / when a slight rustling sound / came from near my feet / and glancing down / I saw / the head and neck of a large black serpent / moving slowly / past me.

Where would you pause in reading that sentence? Certainly not at the end of every thought group! Although the author's basic meaning may be

quite simple, different readers may pause (or phrase by intonation) intelligently in many different places, depending on the particular shades of
meaning they wish to convey. Let's play the numbers game for a moment.
How many different ways are there possible for persons to phrase that
sentence with different combinations of pauses? Few realize the mathematical
potentiality for variation in interpretation, for not many will guess that there
are 4,096 different combinations of pauses in reading that sentence. There are
twelve possible places to pause. You figure it out. Of course, there are considerably far fewer good, appropriate, natural ways to do it, but the terrific
possibility for individuality in interpretation is ever present. Naturally,
phrasing bears a direct relationship to focusing attention on (emphasizing)
the thought centers. Read the sentence with several different subtleties in
mind and note variations in centering and phrasing. Your pauses will undoubtedly vary from one reading to another.

Let us compare transcriptions of three professional readings of the same
literary selection and note the places in which they paused. Norman Corwin,
best known as a writer, John Gielgud, the British actor, and Alexander
Scourby, the American actor, have recorded their readings of Shelley's
poem "Ozymandias." We have indicated short pauses with one virgule (/)
and long ones with two (//). (Our classification of "short" and "long" is
arbitrary and inaccurate—how short is "short?"; how long is "long?"—
but necessary for this demonstration.) Try reading the passages aloud as they
are marked. Listen to the recordings if you have access to them.

*Norman Corwin's Pauses:*

I met a traveller / from an antique land
Who said: // Two vast and trunkless legs of stone
Stand in the desert. // Near them, / on the sand, /
Half sunk, / a shattered visage lies, / whose frown, /
And wrinkled lip, / and sneer of cold command,
Tell / that its sculptor well those passions read
Which yet survive, stamped on these lifeless things,
The hand that mocked them, / and the heart that fed: /
And on the pedestal / these words appear: //
"My name is Ozymandias, king of kings: /
Look on my works, ye Mighty, / and despair!" //
Nothing / beside / remains. // Round the decay
Of that colossal wreck, boundless and bare, /
The lone and level sands / stretch / far away.

*John Gielgud's Pauses:*

I met a traveller from an antique land
Who said: // Two vast and trunkless legs of stone

Stand in the desert. // Near them, on the sand, /
Half sunk, / a shattered visage lies, / whose frown,
And wrinkled lip, and sneer of cold command, /
Tell that its sculptor / well those passions read /
Which yet survive, / stamped on these lifeless things, /
The hand that mocked them, / and the heart that fed: //
And on the pedestal / these words appear: //
"My name is Ozymandias, / king of kings: //
Look on my works, ye Mighty, / and despair!" //
Nothing beside remains. // Round the decay
Of that colossal wreck, / boundless and bare, /
The lone and level sands / stretch / far away.

*Alexander Scourby's Pauses:*

I met a traveller from an antique land
Who said: Two vast and trunkless legs of stone
Stand in the desert. // Near them, on the sand, /
Half sunk, / a shattered visage lies, whose frown,
And wrinkled lip, and sneer of cold command, /
Tell that its sculptor well those passions read
Which yet survive, / stamped on these lifeless things, /
The hand that mocked them / and the heart that fed: //
And on the pedestal / these words appear: //
"My name is Ozymandias, / king of kings: /
Look on my works, ye Mighty, and despair!" //
Nothing beside remains. // Round the decay
Of that colossal wreck, / boundless and bare, /
The lone and level sands stretch far away.

By studying the marks, we can detect certain interesting similarities and differences in the readers' placement of the pause. What conclusions can you reach for the following questions?

1. Can you see any value in pausing, as Corwin did, in the first line?
2. Would you agree with Scourby that there is no need for a pause until the middle of the third line?
3. Why do all three readers have long pauses after the following words: "desert," "appear," "despair," and "remains"?
4. The differences in the placement of pauses in the long sentence in lines 3 to 11 are striking. Read the sentence aloud each of the three ways. In which places would *you* use pauses to fit your interpretation? Evaluate the logic of the phrasing of each of the professionals in reading this sentence.

5. Do you agree with Corwin's method of breaking up the short sentence "Nothing beside remains" with short pauses?
6. Do you approve of Gielgud's method of setting off "stretch" with short pauses? Does it aid in communicating the feeling of desolation?
7. What conclusions can you draw on the relative effectiveness of long or short pauses in specific places?
8. After listening to the recordings, which reader would you say used pauses best to contribute to poetic rhythm?

**Factors Governing Phrasing and Pausing.** Various factors determine length of phrasing and the number and length of pauses (consequently, also the rate of reading): (1) the complexity, abstractness, and mood of the literary meanings, (2) the capabilities of the audience, (3) the acoustical situation, and (4) the nature of the occasion for the act of communication.

When the literature is concrete or light in vein, the reader will think in relatively long thought units and need relatively little time for pausal thinking. The audience can absorb this kind of content somewhat easily. (The consequent rate will be comparatively rapid.) Such would be the case with the following conversational satire:

## MICKEY SAVES THE WORLD

ARTHUR HOPPE

Herewith is another unpublished chapter in that unpublished textbook *A History of the World, 1950–1999.* The title of this chapter is "Today Disneyland, Tomorrow Disney World."

It was late in 1965 that Mr. Walt Disney, who created Mickey Mouse out of an old bottle of ink, announced plans to build a $100 million Disney World in the State of Florida. This revelation filled the hearts of all Floridians with joy. And they swore to call a special session of their Legislature, build a network of new highways and otherwise prepare for Mr. Disney's coming. The instant success of Disney World naturally led to the proposal that he take over West Virginia. His triumph in creating a neat, clean Povertyland out of the abandoned coal mines and slag heaps is well known. Tourists came by the thousands to ride the little mine cars and throw pork chops and grits in hygienic, Saran-wrapped packages to the well-scrubbed poor. Following that success, the conversion of Washington, D.C., into Historyland caused little notice.

And in 1973, when an electronically operated Congressman rose before a crowd of applauding tourists in the galleries to propose changing the name of the nation to "The United States of Disney Country," the measure passed unanimously. Actually, the Disneyans, as citizens were now called, lived much the same lives as before. They spent their days riding around in cars and their evenings being entertained by various machines, such as one that simulated live people moving about on a screen and another that simulated live music on a magnetic tape. The Disneyans still thrilled to the exploration of space. But they did so in simulated rockets. And they still plunged into the exotic watery depths, but in simulated submarines in artificial concrete pools. All of which was much safer.

The Nation was open from 10 a.m. to 10 p.m. every day of the year, and the annual festivals to Mickey and Minnie Mouse and the Great Dog Pluto attracted pilgrims from all over the world. The war in Vietnam ended in its fifty-third year with the conversion of that country to Jungleland. (The ride through the Mekong Delta with stuffed Vietcong firing blanks from the riverbanks proved the greatest attraction.) And with the establishment of Disneygrad the following year, it was only a matter of time before the entire world became a wholly owned subsidiary of Disney Enterprises, Inc. And what a utopia it was—neat, clean, orderly, with enough simulated thrills and artificial adventure for one and all.

Well, almost all. There was one old man (no one else ever grew old) who missed the past. "I miss tears," he said, "and automobile horns and the smell of manure and the common cold and dandelions and getting drunk and how you feel when someone dies."

Naturally, he was declared insane and locked up in a windowless dungeon. But it was a neat, clean, well-lighted dungeon with a big television screen and twenty-four-hour Muzak. All Disneyans were surprised when he killed himself.

"After all," they said, "he had everything a man could want."

In reading the following sentences expressing abstract thought you will have to use frequent pauses and longer phrases in order to assimilate the thought groups yourself and in order to communicate them successfully. (The resulting rate will be slow.)

So art, whether it be painting or sculpture, poetry or music, has no other object than to brush aside the utilitarian symbols, the conventional and socially accepted generalities, in short, everything that veils reality from us, in order to bring us face to face with reality itself. It is from a misunderstanding on this point that the dispute between realism and idealism in art has arisen. Art is certainly only a more direct vision of reality.

—HENRI BERGSON

The capabilities of the audience also determine the frequency of phrasing and pausing done by the interpreter. If the listeners are well equipped to comprehend the ideas expressed by the writer, the reader will not have to phrase or pause so often or pause so long as he will when the listeners do not have the educational or cultural background, or the maturity necessary to enable them to understand the ideas readily. Because we are usually very familiar with the material that we read aloud, we tend to think too little while reading; therefore, we read too rapidly for our listeners, who must have time to think the ideas through for the first time. *Take your time.* If you fill pauses with thought, you will seldom read too rapidly for your listeners.

The nature of the occasion will affect your phrasing. You are well aware that formal or solemn occasions require greater dignity and usually a slower rate than do light or frivolous occasions. Let your own common sense direct your phrasing.

**Emphasizing with Pauses.**   The pause is a vital technique for emphasizing important ideas. You can emphasize by pausing *before, after,* or *both before* and *after* an important word or phrase. You will recall that in reading " Ozymandias," Gielgud " stretched " the word " stretch " with two pauses. In W. H. Hudson's sentence about the serpent, several possibilities for emphasizing by pausing present themselves. What would be the effect of pausing in each of the following instances? (The marks represent *possible pauses* for *emphasis*; pauses for phrasal breaks are *not* indicated.)

One hot day in / December / I had been standing perfectly still / for a few minutes among the dry weeds when a slight / rustling sound came from near my feet, and glancing down I saw / the head and neck / of a large / black / serpent / moving / slowly / past me.

Of course, no one would pause for emphasis in all the places indicated, but each might well be used to emphasize a particular thought or shade of thought.

The pause *before* is often called the *pause for suspense, effect,* or *anticipation.* It says to the listener " This next word in particularly important," or " This is going to be the main point of this story," or " Here's the joke! " It is a prime element of the actor's art of timing, and, deprived of the pause for suspense, our favorite comedians would be without one of their most effective comic techniques. The chief element of comedy is surprise or incongruity; the pause of anticipation before the point of a story, joke, or " punch line " makes it even more surprising, and, therefore, funny. It need not be a long pause; it is often very short.

Consider how you might pause in the last line of each of the following anonymous verses to heighten comic reaction:

Ah, love Devon ...
Where it rains eight days out of every seven!

What could be viler
Than the verse of Malcolm Bryler?
God knows,
Unless it's his prose!

A promise made
Is a debt unpaid.

I won't print and you won't see
The verse written on World War III.

On the other hand, such anticipatory pauses for comic effect may be quite long. Hal Holbrook's recordings of his Mark Twain lectures provide literally dozens of *long* pauses.

**Breathing During Pauses.**  By this time, you are probably persuaded that the uses of the pause are worth the interpretative reader's efforts to learn them. One more point needs to be made in behalf of the pause. It seems obvious to everyone that the reader inhales air during pauses, but the beginning reader often wonders " Which pauses? " You do not have to wait for the end of a sentence in order to take in air, as you might think. If you are able to inhale quickly and silently—usually through the mouth—you may breathe during even a short pause, provided you do not interfere with the meaning.

# RHYTHM

The fourth element of time is rhythm.[3] Rhythm in literature is an anticipated pattern created by a more or less regular recurrence of some element: a word, a phrase, an idea, a vocal accent, a pause, a sound, or a grammatical construction. We are aware of the metrical beats in verse as we are of the beats established by percussionists in both simple and complex forms of music. We forget, however, that there are " prose " rhythms in our lives, such as the rhythm of going to work in the city and the rhythm of a leisurely walk in the country, the rhythms of play and the rhythms of meditation. There are the rhythms in the speech of different languages and even in the dialects of a single tongue. Good literature reveals these rhythms of life and speech.

Our love for rhythm seems to be innate: Witness the responses of a toddling youngster to the music of a brass band! Children love to beat on toy drums, tin cans, or even the side of a house. They stamp their feet, chant nursery rhymes or nonsense syllables, not unlike the cultural dances of primitive peoples. As we grow more civilized, we learn to restrain our responses to rhythm, to some extent, but our love for rhythm—nay, our dependence upon rhythm—is still present. We live in rhythms; yes, we are governed by rhythm; and we would not be without rhythm!

Physiologically, we are rhythmical. We eat regularly, eliminate regularly, breathe regularly, sleep regularly, play regularly—if we value our health. Emotionally, we are rhythmical, too, for psychologists say that all of us feel

---

[3] See Chapters 13 and 14 for further treatments of rhythm in prose and verse.

alternate periods of relative depression and exhilaration. Intellectually, we are rhythmical as well. Following periods of concentration, we must have periods of relaxation.

Persons in different walks of life live in different rhythms. You might find it interesting to consider the rhythms in your daily, weekly, seasonal, and yearly activities. You are quite likely to be surprised at how regular you are in your living. You will notice, of course, certain irregularities, such as an occasional weekend or holiday trip, but if you were to plot your activities during your residence in college, you would discover, even more to your amazement, that there is a great regularity to even the irregularities. You might conclude from this study of your rhythms that regular rhythm is the sustenance of your life, but that it is the regular *irregularities* that add spice to life. Keep these principles in mind as we now consider rhythm in literature.

Literary rhythm can be extremely regular, as in:

/ ∪ / ∪ / ∪ /
Mary had a little lamb.

∪ / ∪ / ∪ /
Its fleece was white as snow.

∪ / ∪ / ∪ / ∪ /
And everywhere that Mary went

∪ / ∪ / ∪ /
That lamb was sure to go.

In this nursery rhyme, we find a regular alternation of heavy and light beats, which is called *meter*. Meter may be somewhat more varied and complex than that, however:

## LA BELLE DAME SANS MERCI

JOHN KEATS

∪ / ∪ / ∪ / ∪ /
'O what can ail thee, knight-at-arms,

∪ / ∪ / ∪ / ∪ ∪
Alone and palely loitering?

∪ / ∪ / ∪ ∪ ∪ /
The sedge has wither'd from the Lake,

∪ / / /
And no birds sing.

∪ / ∪ / ∪ / ∪ /
'O what can ail thee, knight-at-arms!

∪ / ∪ ∪ ∪ / ∪ /
So haggard and so woe-begone?

˘   /  ˘  /  ˘˘˘  /
The squirrel's granary is full,

·˘  ˘  /   ˘   /
And the harvest's done.

"La Belle Dame Sans Merci" is a very rhythmical poem, and yet the variations in it are pleasing to the ear. Although, by comparison with much of the best verse, it is still highly regular in its metrical pattern. Some poetry, called *vers libre*, or free verse, has such an irregular rhythm that it is said to have no meter:

## DEATH SNIPS PROUD MEN

CARL SANDBURG

Death is stronger than all the governments because the governments are men and men die and then death laughs: Now you see 'em, now you don't.

Death is stronger than all proud men and so death snips proud men on the nose, throws a pair of dice and says: Read 'em and weep.

Death sends a radiogram every day: When I want you I'll drop in—and then one day he comes with a master-key and lets himself in and says: We'll go now.

Death is a nurse mother with big arms: 'Twon't hurt you at all; it's your time now; you just need a long sleep, child; what have you had anyhow better than sleep?

Because there is no meter in Sandburg's poem, look for the recurring elements (words, ideas, structure) that do provide rhythm, nevertheless. Rhythm is not limited to verse, it is also found in prose. We find it in the parallel structure, alliteration, and other recurrences in this oration by one of America's great orators:

## AT THE TOMB OF NAPOLEON

ROBERT INGERSOLL

A little while ago, I stood by the grave of the old Napoleon—a magnificent tomb of gilt and gold, fit almost for a dead deity—and gazed upon the sarcophagus of rare and nameless marble, where rest at last the ashes of that restless man. I leaned over the balustrade and thought about the career of the greatest soldier of the modern world.

I saw him walking upon the banks of the Seine, contemplating suicide. I saw him at Toulon—I saw him putting down the mob in the streets of Paris—I saw him at the head of the army of Italy—I saw him crossing the bridge of Lodi with the tri-color in his hand—I saw him in Egypt in the shadows of the Pyramids—I saw him conquer the Alps and mingle the eagles of France with the eagles of the crags. I saw him at Marengo—at Ulm and Austerlitz. I saw him in Russia, where the infantry of the snow and the cavalry of the wild blasts scattered his legions like winter's withered leaves. I saw him at Leipsic in defeat and disaster—driven by a million bayonets back upon Paris—clutched like a wild beast—banished to Elba. I saw him escape and retake an empire by the force of his genius. I saw him upon the frightful field of Waterloo, where Chance and Fate combined to wreck the fortunes of their former king. And I saw him at St. Helena, with his hands crossed behind him, gazing out upon the sad and solemn sea. I thought of the orphans and widows he had made—of the tears that had been shed for his glory, and of the only woman who ever loved him, pushed from his heart by the cold hand of ambition. And I said I would rather have been a French peasant and worn wooden shoes. I would rather have lived in a hut with a vine growing over the door, and the grapes growing purple in the kisses of the autumn sun. I would rather have been that poor peasant with my loving wife by my side, knitting as the day died out of the sky—with my children upon my knees and their arms about me—I would rather have been that man and gone down to the tongueless silence of the dreamless dust, than to have been that imperial impersonation of force and murder, known as "Napoleon the Great."

These examples should indicate to you that rhythm exists in literature in very regular form, called *meter*, and also in looser, more flowing phrases, in both verse and prose. As interpreters, we should be sensitive to the presence of rhythms wherever and in whatever form they *exist*.

Rhythm, in literature, reflects the human experience with rhythm in life. Since we delight in rhythms in life, and like them to have varieties, we also appreciate the same virtues in literature. Rhythm is a structuring factor that contributes to the emotional impact of the literature as it makes its effect upon the ear. As one reads aloud, one should, like a dancer, be susceptible to the pulsations.

## EXERCISES

1. With the aid of the table that follows, listen to some of the recordings that are listed, and write a short paper presenting your observations concerning the effective or ineffective use of rate by the readers involved. (Those marked with an asterisk are quoted in this textbook.)

| Reader | Poet | Poem | Rate (words per minute) |
|---|---|---|---|
| Carl Sandburg | Sandburg | Grass | 91 |
| John Neville | Milton | On His Blindness | 100 |
| Geraldine Brooks | E. B. White | Disturbers of the Peace | 104 |
| Dorothy Parker | Parker | One Perfect Rose | 104 |
| Edith Evans | Byron | She Walks in Beauty | 106 |
| John Neville | Shakespeare | *When, in Disgrace | 108 |
| Tyrone Power | Byron | She Walks in Beauty | 109 |
| Norman Corwin | Milton | On His Blindness | 109 |
| Dylan Thomas | Thomas | *Do Not Go Gentle | 110 |
| Dylan Thomas | Thomas | *In My Craft or Sullen Art | 116 |
| Claire Bloom | Shakespeare | That Time of Year | 116 |
| John Gielgud | Shakespeare | That Time of Year | 118 |
| Carl Sandburg | Sandburg | Prayers of Steel | 120 |
| John Gielgud | Shelley | Ode to the West Wind | 122 |
| Basil Rathbone | E. B. Browning | How Do I Love Thee? | 123 |
| Dylan Thomas | Thomas | Poem in October | 124 |
| John Gielgud | Eliot | *Journey of the Magi | 127 |
| Geraldine Brooks | E. B. White | Springtime Crosstown Episode | 132 |
| John Neville | Wordsworth | *The World Is Too Much with Us | 136 |
| Eric Portman | Byron | She Walks in Beauty | 138 |
| Alexander Scourby | Yeats | The Lake Isle of Innisfree | 138 |
| Alexander Scourby | Milton | On His Blindness | 138 |
| Alexander Scourby | Gilbert | To the Terrestrial Globe | 139 |
| Dorothy Parker | Parker | Parable for a Certain Virgin | 139 |
| Eric Portman | Wordsworth | Upon Westminster Bridge | 139 |
| Geraldine Brooks | Parker | Love Song | 140 |
| Robert Frost | Frost | *Stopping by Woods | 144 |
| Alexander Scourby | Wordsworth | Upon Westminster Bridge | 145 |
| John Neville | Marlowe | The Passionate Shepherd | 145 |
| Claire Bloom | Shakespeare | It Was a Lover and His Lass | 147 |
| Dorothy Parker | Parker | The Red Dress | 149 |
| Alexander Scourby | Suckling | Encouragements to a Lover | 149 |
| Alexander Scourby | R. Browning | *My Last Duchess | 149 |
| Norman Rose | Thomas | *Do Not Go Gentle | 150 |
| Norman Corwin | Byron | She Walks in Beauty | 150 |
| Raymond E. Johnson | Lear | The Owl and the Pussy Cat | 151 |
| Basil Rathbone | Shakespeare | *When, in Disgrace | 152 |
| Norman Rose | E. B. White | Village Revisited | 153 |
| Arnold Moss | Goldsmith | Elegy on the Death of a Mad Dog | 153 |
| Edith Everett | E. B. Browning | How Do I Love Thee? | 155 |
| Alexander Scourby | Noyes | The Highwayman | 159 |
| John Gielgud | C. Rossetti | A Birthday | 159 |
| Basil Rathbone | Shelley | Ode to the West Wind | 161 |
| Robert Frost | Frost | *Birches | 169 |

| Reader | Poet | Poem | Rate (words per minute) |
|--------|------|------|-------------------------|
| John Gielgud | Byron | So We'll Go No More A-Roving | 171 |
| Raymond E. Johnson | Carroll | Father William | 173 |
| Alexander Scourby | Daly | Between Two Loves | 174 |
| Ogden Nash | Nash | Allow Me, Madam | 190 |
| Norman Rose | Nash | Lines to a World-Famous Poet | 203 |
| Edith Evans | Carroll | Father William | 210 |

2. If you have access to a tape recorder and a stop watch, time recordings of your own readings of various types of literature and compute your rates to determine if you make use of rate variety in reading aloud.

3. Read " A Subaltern's Love-Song " aloud and note the strong metrical structure. What kind of mood does the rhythm create?

## A SUBALTERN'S LOVE-SONG

JOHN BETJEMAN

Miss J. Hunter Dunn, Miss J. Hunter Dunn,
Furnish'd and burnish'd by Aldershot sun,
What strenuous singles we played after tea,
We in the tournament—you against me!

Love-thirty, love-forty, oh! weakness of joy,
The speed of a swallow, the grace of a boy,
With carefullest carelessness, gaily you won,
I am weak from your loveliness, Joan Hunter Dunn.

Miss Joan Hunter Dunn, Miss Joan Hunter Dunn,
How mad I am, sad I am, glad that you won.
The warm-handled racket is back in its press,
But my shock-headed victor, she loves me no less.

Her father's euonymus shines as we walk,
And swing past the summer-house, buried in talk,
And cool the verandah that welcomes us in
To the six-o'clock news and a lime-juice and gin.

The scent of the conifers, sound of the bath,
The view from my bedroom of moss-dappled path,

As I struggle with double-end evening tie,
For we dance at the Golf Club, my victor and I.

On the floor of her bedroom lie blazer and shorts
And the cream-coloured walls are be-trophied with sports,
And westering, questioning settles the sun
On your low-leaded window, Miss Joan Hunter Dunn.

The Hillman is waiting, the light's in the hall,
The pictures of Egypt are bright on the wall,
My sweet, I am standing beside the oak stair
And there on the landing's the light on your hair.

By roads "not adopted," by woodland ways,
She drove to the club in the late summer haze,
Into nine-o'clock Camberley, heavy with bells
And mushroomy, pine-woody, evergreen smells.

Miss Joan Hunter Dunn, Miss Joan Hunter Dunn,
I can hear from the car-park the dance has begun.
Oh! full Surrey twilight! importunate band!
Oh! strongly adorable tennis-girl's hand!

Around us are Rovers and Austins afar,
Above us, the intimate roof of the car,
And here on my right is the girl of my choice,
With the tilt of her nose and the chime of her voice,

And the scent of her wrap, and the words never said,
And the ominous, ominous dancing ahead.
We sat in the car-park till twenty to one
And now I'm engaged to Miss Joan Hunter Dunn.

4. Read "The Harlot's House" aloud, noting the mechanical rhythm and the purposeful monotony of the three-line stanzas. Notice how the last line, departing from metrical form by having only six syllables rather than eight, must receive careful treatment by the interpreter. How would you handle it?

## THE HARLOT'S HOUSE

OSCAR WILDE

We caught the tread of dancing feet,
We loitered down the moonlit street,
And stopped beneath the harlot's house.

Inside, above the din and fray,
We heard the loud musicians play
The "Treues Liebes Herz" of Strauss.

Like strange mechanical grotesques,
Making fantastic arabesques,
The shadows raced across the blind.

We watched the ghostly dancers spin
To sound of horn and violin,
Like black leaves wheeling in the wind.

Like wire-pulled automatons,
Slim silhouetted skeletons
Went sidling through the slow quadrille.

They took each other by the hand,
And danced a stately saraband;
Their laughter echoed thin and shrill.

Sometimes a clockwork puppet pressed
A phantom lover to her breast,
Sometimes they seemed to try to sing.

Sometimes a horrible marionette
Came out, and smoked its cigarette
Upon the steps like a live thing.

Then, turning to my love, I said,
"The dead are dancing with the dead,
The dust is whirling with the dust."

But she—she heard the violin,
And left my side and entered in:
Love passed into the house of lust.

Then suddenly the tune went false,
The dancers wearied of the waltz,
The shadows ceased to wheel and whirl

And down the long and silent street,
The dawn, with silver-sandaled feet,
Crept like a frightened girl.

5. In Féderico Garcia Lorca's "Lament for the Death of a Bullfighter," several different rhythms are to be found in the various sections. Note the "insistence" of the repetition in the first section quoted here:

# LAMENT FOR THE DEATH OF A BULLFIGHTER

FÉDERICO GARCÍA LORCA
*(Translated by A. L. Lloyd)*


I

Cogida[4] and Death

At five in the afternoon.
It was exactly five in the afternoon.
A child carried a white sheet
*at five in the afternoon.*
A rush-basket of slaked lime
*at five in the afternoon.*
The rest was death and death alone
*at five in the afternoon.*

The wind bore away the cottonwool
*at five in the afternoon.*
And the oxide scattered crystal and nickel
*at five in the afternoon.*
Now the dove and the leopard are struggling
*at five in the afternoon.*
And a thigh with a desolate horn
*at five in the afternoon.*
The refrain of a song strikes up
*at five in the afternoon.*
Bell-jars of arsenic and steam
*at five in the afternoon.*
Groups of silence in the corners
*at five in the afternoon.*

And, all heart, the bull charges!
*at five in the afternoon.*
Just as the sweat of snow was coming
*at five in the afternoon,*
when the bullring was covered in iodine
*at five in the afternoon,*

---

[4] *Cogida:* literally "the catching." The tossing of the bullfighter by the bull.

death laid its eggs in his wound
*at five in the afternoon.*
*At five in the afternoon.*
*At exactly five o'clock in the afternoon.*

A coffin on wheels is his bed
*at five in the afternoon.*
Bones and flutes sound in his ears
*at five in the afternoon.*
Already the bull is bellowing within his forehead
*at five in the afternoon.*
The room is iridescent with agony
*at five in the afternoon.*
Now from afar-off comes gangrene
*at five in the afternoon,*
a lily-trumpet through his green veins
*at five in the afternoon.*
His wounds blazed like suns
*at five in the afternoon,*
and the rabble shattered the windows
*at five in the afternoon.*
At five in the afternoon.
Ay, that terrible five o'clock in the afternoon!
It was five by all the clocks!
It was five in the shadow of the afternoon!

6. Many student readers have overlooked the rhythms of the speech
phrases as they are indicated in typography. Ferlinghetti has shown us in
print how to read his poem rhythmically:

## THE WORLD

### LAWRENCE FERLINGHETTI

The world is a beautiful place
        to be born into
if you don't mind happiness
        not always being
          so very much fun
   if you don't mind a touch of hell
        now and then
    just when everything is fine
        because even in heaven
     they don't sing

                              all the time
                  The world is a beautiful place
                                        to be born into
            if you don't mind some people dying
                                        all the time
                    or maybe only starving
                                    some of the time
                  which isn't half so bad
                                if it isn't you
            Oh the world is a beautiful place
                                        to be born into
                  if you don't much mind
                                a few dead minds
                    in the higher places
                                    or a bomb or two
                  now and then
                                in your upturned faces
              or such other improprieties
                                    as our Name Brand society
                          is prey to
                              with its men of distinction
                  and its men of extinction
                                    and its priests
                    and other patrolmen
                                        and its various segregations
            and congressional investigations
                                    and other constipations
                    that our fool flesh
                          is heir to
            Yes the world is the best place of all
                                        for a lot of such things as
              making the fun scene
                                    and making the love scene
          and making the sad scene
                                and singing low songs and having inspirations
              and walking around
                          looking at everything
                                        and smelling flowers
              and goosing statues
                              and even thinking
                                          and kissing people and
                  making babies and wearing pants
                                      and waving hats and
                          dancing

and going swimming in rivers
on picnics
in the middle of the summer
and just generally
'living it up'
Yes
but then right in the middle of it
comes the smiling
mortician

7. The accomplished writer uses words not only for their meaning values, but also for their sound values, even though there may be no exact relationship between the sound and the idea. In the following poem, the writer has expertly used both long and short sounds.

## BUT HE WAS COOL
## or: he even stopped for green lights

DON L. LEE

super-cool
ultrablack
a tan/purple
had a beautiful shade.

he had a double-natural
that wd put the sisters to shame.
his dashikis were tailor made
& his beads were imported sea shells
(from some blk/country i never heard of)
he was triple-hip.

his tikis were hand carved
out of ivory
& came express from the motherland.
he would greet u in swahili
& say good-by in yoruba.

woooooooooooo-jim he bes so cool & ill tel li gent
cool-cool is so cool he was un-cooled by
other niggers' cool
cool-cool ultracool was bop-cool/ice box
cool so cool cold cool
his wine didn't have to be cooled, him was

```
                air conditioned cool
            cool-cool/real cool made me cool—now
                ain't that cool
            cool-cool so cool him nick-named refrigerator.

cool-cool so cool
he didn't know,
after detroit, newark, chicago &c.,
we had to hip
                cool-cool/   super-cool/   real cool


    that
to be black
is
to be
very-hot.
```

8.   When prose is beautiful, as it is in this passage from Lawrence Durrell's *Clea*, it becomes rhythmical. What rhythmical elements can you find? While studying it, also be on the lookout for instances in which duration must be used for effective interpretation.

## *from* CLEA

### LAWRENCE DURRELL

It was still dark when we lay up outside the invisible harbour with its remembered outworks of forts and anti-submarine nets. I tried to paint the outlines on the darkness with my mind. The boom was raised only at dawn each day. An all-obliterating darkness reigned. Somewhere ahead of us lay the invisible coast of Africa, with its "kiss of thorns" as the Arabs say. It was intolerable to be so aware of them, the towers and minarets of the city, and yet to be unable to will them to appear. I could not see my own fingers before my face. The sea had become a vast empty ante-room, a hollow bubble of blackness.

Then suddenly there passed a sudden breath, a whiff like a wind passing across a bed of embers, and the nearer distance glowed pink as a sea-shell, deepening gradually into the rose-richness of a flower. A faint and terrible moaning came out across the water towards us, pulsing like the wing-beats of some fearful prehistoric bird—sirens which howled as the damned must howl in limbo. One's nerves were shaken like the branches of a tree. And as if in response to this sound lights began to prick out everywhere, sporadically at first, then in ribbons, bands, squares of crystal. The harbour suddenly outlined itself with complete clarity upon the dark panels of heaven, while long white fingers of powder-white light began to stalk about the sky in ungainly fashion, as if they were the legs of some awkward insect struggling to gain a purchase on the slippery black. A dense stream of coloured rockets now began to mount from the haze among the battleships, emptying on the sky their brilliant clusters of stars and diamonds and smashed pearl snuff-boxes with a marvelous prodigality. The air shook in strokes. Clouds of pink and yellow dust arose with the maroons to shine upon the greasy buttocks of the barrage balloons which were flying everywhere. The very sea seemed to tremble. I had had no idea that we were so near, or that the city could be so beautiful in the mere saturnalia of a war. It had begun to swell up, to expand like some mystical rose of the darkness, and the bombardment kept it company, overflowing the mind. To our surprise we found ourselves shouting at each other. We were staring at the burning embers of Augustine's Carthage, I thought to myself, we were observing the fall of city man.

It was as beautiful as it was stupefying. In the top left-hand corner of the tableau the searchlights had begun to congregate, quivering and sliding in their ungainly fashion, like daddy-long-legs. They intersected and collided feverishly, and it was clear that some signal had reached them which told of the struggles of some trapped insect on the outer cobweb of darkness. Again and again they crossed, probed, merged, divided. Then at last we saw what they were bracketing: six tiny silver moths moving down the skylanes with what seemed unbearable slowness. The sky had gone mad around them yet they still moved with this fatal languor; and languidly too curled the curving strings of hot diamonds which spouted up from the ships, or the rank lacklustre sniffs of cloudy shrapnel which marked their progress.

And deafening as was the roaring which now filled our ears it was possible to isolate many of the separate sounds which orchestrated the bombardment. The crackle of shards which fell back like a hailstorm upon the corrugated roofs of the waterside cafes: the scratchy mechanical voices of ships' signallers repeating, in the voices of ventriloquists' dummies, semi-intelligible phrases which sounded like "Three o'clock red, Three o'clock red". Strangely too, there was music somewhere at the heart of all the hubbub, jagged quartertones which stabbed; then, too, the foundering roar of buildings falling. Patches of light which disappeared and left an aperture of darkness at which a dirty yellow flame might come and lap like a thirsty animal. Nearer at hand (the water smacked the echo out) we could hear the rich harvest of spent cannon-shells pouring upon the decks from the Chicago Pianos: an almost continuous splashing of golden metal tumbling from the breeches of the skypointed guns.

So it went on, feasting the eye yet making the vertebrae quail before the whirlwind of meaningless power it disclosed. I had not realised the impersonality of war before. There was no room for human beings or thought of them under this vast umbrella of coloured death. Each drawn breath had become only a temporary refuge.

Then, almost as suddenly as it had started, the spectacle died away. The harbour vanished with theatrical suddenness, the string of precious stones was turned off, the sky emptied, the silence drenched us, only to be broken once more by that famished crying of the sirens which drilled at the nerves. And then, nothing—a nothingness weighing tons of darkness out of which grew the smaller and more familiar sounds of water licking at the gunwales. A faint shore-wind crept out to invest us with the alluvial smells of an invisible estuary. Was it only in my imagination that I heard from far away the sounds of wild-fowl on the lake?

We waited thus for a long time in great indecision; but meanwhile from the east the dawn had begun to overtake the sky, the city and desert. Human voices, weighted like lead, came softly out, stirring curiosity and compassion. Children's voices—and in the west a sputum-coloured meniscus on the horizon. We yawned, it was cold. Shivering, we turned to one another, feeling suddenly orphaned in this benighted world between light and darkness.

But gradually it grew up from the eastern marches, this familiar dawn, the first overflow of citron and rose which would set the dead waters of Mareotis a-glitter; and fine as a hair, yet so indistinct that one had to stop breathing to verify it, I heard (or thought I heard) the first call to prayer from some as yet invisible minaret.

Were there, then, still gods left to invoke? And even as the question entered my mind I saw, shooting from the harbour-mouth, the three small fishing-boats— sails of rust, liver and blue plum. They heeled upon a freshet and stooped across our bows like hawks. We could hear the rataplan of water lapping their prows. The small figure, balanced like riders, hailed us in Arabic to tell us that the boom was up, that we might enter the harbour.

9.  Granted that Howard Fast's biography *Citizen Tom Paine* is somewhat fictionalized, it still demonstrates that history can be eloquently written. Note the rhythmic elements of structure in this passage:

They had warned him in Thetford that London was a sinful city, but as he wandered wide-eyed among the sewer-like streets, he began to understand the difference between those who sin and those whose life is a sin. The lower-class Londoner of that time, the beast whose forest was a maze of alleyways, lived on cheap gin, cheap sin, and cheap robbery. For the first, the punishment was slow death, for the second horrible death, and for the last death by hanging or stoning or quartering. For a tupenny piece a man could get roaring, crazy drunk, and since drunkenness was the only way for the poor to forget that hell was now and not in the hereafter, gin had during the course of years come to replace almost every other food. Three-year-olds drank gin by the glassful, nursing mothers lived on gin and quieted their babies with it, working men took for their supper a can of gin, old folks hastened death with it, and adolescents made themselves insane with it. In some streets, at certain times of the day, the whole population would be screaming drunk with gin. Prostitutes lost their livelihood when any female from a child to a mother would sell herself for a penny to grind in the gin-mill.

In this, Tom Paine lived and drank and ran like a rat, and stole and cursed and fought, and slept in alleys and sheds and slimy basements. Until one day he took hold of himself, left Gin Row, and apprenticed himself to a staymaker.

There was no hope, he knew, no escape, no salvation.

Sixteen, a staymaker's assistant, he hadn't touched gin in over a year. His clothes were clean, if not good, and he read books. Night after night, he read books, all the books he could lay hands on—Swift and Addison and Pope and Defoe and Congreve and Fielding and Richardson, even Spenser, and sometimes Shakespeare; most of what he read he did not understand; Defoe and Fielding were somewhat plain to him, yet he rather resented that they should write of what he knew so well, instead of the dream world he fancied in print. He was a man, making his own way; it took him only a little while to completely expunge the Quaker "thee" from his speech. He swaggered through London, and with a rosy haze before his eyes, he would stand for hours before White's, the great Tory gambling house, or Brooks's, the Whig equivalent, and watch the bloods come to lay their thousands and their tens of thousands on the turn of a card. "That for me," he would say to himself, "that for me, by God!"

10. What words would you savor (dwell on, using duration of sound) in reading this poem? Why? If possible, contrast your work with John Gielgud's recording of the poem.

## PRELUDES

### T. S. ELIOT

I

The winter evening settles down
With smell of steaks in passageways.
Six o'clock.
The burnt-out ends of smoky days.
And now a gusty shower wraps
The grimy scraps
Of withered leaves about your feet
And newspapers from vacant lots;
The showers beat
On broken blinds and chimney-pots,
And at the corner of the street
A lonely cab-horse steams and stamps.
And then the lighting of the lamps.

II

The morning comes to consciousness
Of faint stale smells of beer
From the sawdust-trampled street
With all its muddy feet that press
To early coffee-stands.
With the other masquerades
That time resumes,
One thinks of all the hands
That are raising dingy shades
In a thousand furnished rooms.


III

You tossed a blanket from the bed,
You lay upon your back, and waited;
You dozed, and watched the night revealing
The thousand sordid images
Of which your soul was constituted;
They flickered against the ceiling.
And when all the world came back
And the light crept up between the shutters
And you heard the sparrows in the gutters,
You had such a vision of the street
As the street hardly understands;
Sitting along the bed's edge, where
You curled the papers from your hair,
Or clasped the yellow soles of feet
In the palms of both soiled hands.


IV

His soul stretched tight across the skies
That fade behind a city block,
Or trampled by insistent feet
At four and five and six o'clock;
And short square fingers stuffing pipes,
And evening newspapers, and eyes
Assured of certain certainties,
The conscience of a blackened street
Impatient to assume the world.
I am moved by fancies that are curled
Around these images, and cling:
The notion of some infinitely gentle
Infinitely suffering thing.

Wipe your hand across your mouth, and laugh;
The worlds revolve like ancient women
Gathering fuel in vacant lots.

11. If possible, listen to the poet's own recording of this poem. Thomas, probably better than any other reader, made maximum use of duration.

## IN MY CRAFT OR SULLEN ART

DYLAN THOMAS

In my craft or sullen art
Exercised in the still night
When only the moon rages
And the lovers lie abed
With all their griefs in their arms,
I labour by singing light
Not for ambition or bread
Or the strut and trade of charms
On the ivory stages
But for the common wages
Of their most secret heart.
Not for the proud man apart
From the raging moon I write
On these spindrift pages
Not for the towering dead
With their nightingales and psalms
But for the lovers, their arms
Round the griefs of the ages,
Who pay no praise or wages
Nor heed my craft or art.

# 10 *Audible Communication Through Loudness*

Have you ever attended an amateur play and had great difficulty hearing the actors' lines? You strained to comprehend but found the dialogue not loud enough to be heard. This kind of experience provides a most frustrating evening. Sufficient loudness for audibility is the first requirement for effective oral communication. Nothing else matters if speech is not heard. Careful timing, dramatic pauses, meaningful inflections, subtle use of vocal quality, and much visible communication are all wasted when loudness is inadequate. If you have tried to enjoy a television program when the volume was too low, you know how pathetic and even ludicrous it can be for an audience to *watch* speech and not be able to *hear* it. Spoken language must be heard to be understood and appreciated.

Apparently, however, there are people who have not grasped this obvious fact. Teachers and students are all too familiar with individuals who participate in discussion or rise publicly to speak or read in tiny, weak, muffled, or breathy voices that almost no one can hear. Usually such persons are offended when it is suggested that they repeat what they have said. Sometimes people protest that they cannot speak any louder, yet they can easily be heard in the halls, on the athletic field, or at a party.

Do not think that we advise you to shout. Nothing could be further from our intention. Overuse of loudness is no better than speaking too quietly. If you would develop and retain adequate control of the other vocal variables, which are time, pitch, and quality, you must avoid the strain of excessive loudness. Speaking with too much volume robs you of the ability to utilize adequate vocal duration, sustain phrases as the sense requires, employ delicate inflections, and vary the vocal quality so as to express the feeling. In addition, excessive loudness is distracting and, in extreme cases, even uncomfortable for your listeners.

While we wish to stress that loudness must be sufficient for audibility, we are no less emphatic in saying that *restraint* in the use of loudness is also essential. Without it, you tend to be inflexible and even crude. Too little loudness and your audience will not be able to listen to you; too much loudness and your audience will have no desire to listen to you.

The oral reader's obligation to achieve comfortably audible levels of loudness is the most rudimentary requisite to successful communication. Within acceptable limits, the interpreter must also achieve variations in loudness that contribute to the communication of ideas and emotions. Our treatment of loudness in this chapter will explore, first, how loudness is achieved in the speech production process; and, second, the different uses of loudness that assist the communication of literature. The two concerns are directly linked, because *efficient production* of loudness is essential for its *effective application* to the demands of literature and the performance setting.

## PHONATION: THE PRODUCTION OF SPEECH SOUND

Few of us ever give much thought to how speech sounds are produced. We have been speaking for a good number of years, and the process occurs naturally. Some of us, however, have "naturally" developed poor habits that limit expressiveness and place undue strain on the vocal mechanism. Few persons have developed the necessary efficiency of operation that allows them to sustain high levels of loudness over extended periods of time. Have you ever suffered from a sore throat after much cheering at a basketball game or singing too energetically? If so, you had strained unnecessarily to achieve loudness. A brief technical explanation of *phonation*, the process of creating speech sounds, will help to point out the physical requirements for creating and sustaining adequate loudness.

Currently the most widely accepted theory of phonation among speech scientists is the " myoelastic-aerodynamic " theory. It relates the movement of laryngeal muscles (*myo* means " muscle," and *elastic* refers to " movement ") to the force of the air being exhaled (*aero* means " air," and *dynamic* means " force ").[1] The theory states that when the pressure of air beneath the vocal folds equals the pressure of the muscles that hold the folds together, the folds open, are enervated by the vagus nerve, vibrate in the breath stream, and produce phonation. Of course, the phonatory pulsations are borne on gross puffs of breath. The puffs and the pulsations might seem synonymous. However, this is not true, for the puffs of breath do not move rapidly, and they persist only a few inches in front of the face, whereas the pulsations are rapid and continue to be exerted a long way. These pulsations, which are patterns of more and less pressure, push the molecules of air, which in turn push others, and the impact is continued over a considerable distance. These pulsations travel at approximately 1,120 feet per second in the atmosphere.

When this movement of molecules strikes the tympanic membrane of the ear, sound is heard. We speak of the loudness of that sound as the characteristic responsible for the impact on the membrane. *Loudness* may thus be called the inherent " weight " of sound. The same sound has different degrees of loudness when heard at ten feet from its source and at forty feet.

[1] See Robert G. King and Eleanor M. DiMichael, *Improving Articulation and Voice* (New York: The Macmillan Co., 1966), p. 123.

Loudness is dissipated as distance is increased. It diminishes inversely with the square of the distance from the source in the same way that the surface area of an expanding spherical balloon increases more rapidly than does the length of the radius within the balloon. A sound at twenty feet from its source is only one-fourth as loud as at ten feet.

The *intensity* of the voice is directly proportional to the *force* exerted on the vocal folds by the breath stream. Thus, the voice may be very intense at the point of origin because a great deal of force has been expended to produce it. At that point the sound will be heard as a very loud and intense sound, but at some distance it will be less loud although equally intense.

The term *loudness* refers to the effect upon the listener. Loudness is the perceptual product of *intensity*, which is a term to describe the physical nature of the sound wave, the magnitude of the molecular disturbance produced by the vibrating folds. *Force* is the motivating element that sets the vocal folds in vibration. To create an audible speech sound, then, a speaker exhales air from the lungs (force), which creates pressure on the vocal folds causing them to vibrate and displace air (intensity); this vibration and intensity travels to a listener's ear and is perceived as a degree of loudness.

Efficient phonation occurs as appropriate levels of loudness are created with minimal degrees of physical exertion at each stage of the process. A sufficient amount of air is available in the lungs; exhalation is controlled to avoid wasting air; vibration of the vocal chords is relaxed and smooth; amplification of the sound utilizes the full capacities of the throat, mouth, and nose as resonators; and transmission of the sound through the atmosphere is direct and unimpeded. Inefficient operation at any point in this process may result in inadequate levels of loudness, noticeable strain in the voice, and possible damage to the organs of speech.

**Abdominal Control of Exhalation.** Correct breathing is the most crucial necessity for efficient speech. Exhalation, as we said, provides the motivating element for the force of speech. Unfortunately, many persons have developed poor breathing habits. To test whether you are among them, take a deep breath. Inhale as much air as you comfortably can. Did you throw back your shoulders and expand the chest while holding in the abdomen? If so, you were trying to expand your lungs simply by expanding the rib cage.

The cage itself, however, is relatively rigid, and its expansion alone does not provide maximum room for inhalation. Inhalation requires that the chest cavity be enlarged to produce a partial vacuum, and the only way to achieve the necessary room is to expand the chest cavity downward as well as from front to back and side to side. The floor of that cavity is largely muscular and separates the chest from the vital organs in the abdomen. The contraction of the diaphragm, a dome-shaped structure, enlarges the room for the lungs by pushing the contents of the abdomen downward and outward. If you were to tighten the abdominal muscles and pull them in, you would restrict the area in which the lungs can expand and, thereby, lessen the amount of air you take in.

Exhalation for speech reverses the inhalation process. Control of the abdominal muscles is important to ensure that the breath is used economically. By slowly and smoothly drawing in the abdomen, you allow the diaphragm to return to a relaxed bell shape that pushes up into the chest region and forces air from the lungs. The work is done by the muscles in the abdomen, so the throat region can stay relaxed to produce full and resonant tones.

To observe genuine abdominal breathing, lie on your back and hold your chest high with a book resting just below the sternum or breastbone. Watch the book rise and fall as you breathe. In order to increase the " feel " of such breathing, increase the number of books. Remaining on your back and removing the books, place your hand just below the sternum or breastbone and feel the movement of the abdominal wall as you breathe. Then stand, put your hand in the same spot, and see if you continue to breathe in the same way.

The time you spend developing good breathing habits will prove well worth the effort. If you are a singer, ask your vocal teacher; if you are an athlete, ask your coach. Either one will assure you that abdominal breathing promotes vocal and bodily relaxation, provides more oxygen for the blood stream, makes for better control of exhalation, and permits greater and more sustained use of force. By taking in greater amounts of air and controlling, more efficiently, the release of air, you should find that you do not have to interrupt your speech for breath nearly so often. The relaxation of the chest and throat regions allowed by abdominal control of respiration helps you to utter relaxed speech sounds at great length, with little fatigue, and no loss of force. Finally, as a result of this relaxation, you will likely discover that the tensions of stage fright are also reduced.

**Projection.**    If you hold up before an audience a small glass slide that is meant for projection upon a screen, its detail will be almost indistinguishable because the size is inadequate. If, on the other hand, you place the slide in a projector and throw the image on a screen, everyone in the room will be able to appreciate the color, form, and detail, for the size is now adequate. Projection in public speaking or reading is much the same. It is enlargement of the normal visible and audible characteristics of conversational speech so as to communicate to the back row as well as to the front.

In projecting *visibly* you make facial expressions and bodily actions more obvious. A small sneer easily seen at a distance of a few feet becomes a somewhat larger one. A movement of the eyes becomes a movement of the head. A movement of the head becomes a movement of the entire body. A turn of the hand becomes a gesture of the hand and arm. The visible behavior used in communication is larger.

In projecting *audibly* you enlarge all vocal techniques. Loudness is increased without the strain and the distortion of a shout. The speaker may exert more force on the breath stream, but he also achieves vocal projection by means of increased resonance.

The chief resonators are the cavities and surfaces of the larynx, pharynx or throat, mouth, and nose. If these are not inflamed or if they are not obstructed by organic growth such as enlarged tonsils or adenoids, good reinforcement of tone can be achieved. For increased vocal projection, open your mouth somewhat more than usual and relax the muscles of the face and throat so that the cavities and walls will reinforce the vocal tones. Vocal projection also involves a slightly slower rate of utterance, perhaps slightly increased pauses before and after the most important thought centers, increased phonatory duration, an extended range of pitch, more pronounced inflectional patterns, and, of course, improved articulation. Each of these vocal elements is discussed elsewhere in this text. In short, projection is the enlargement of the whole process of visible and audible communication.

If you are to read in a large room or theater, the elements of projection will be necessary for you to reach listeners who are sitting in the back. More often, however, you will probably perform in relatively small, intimate settings. In such cases, you may not need to significantly enlarge vocal techniques in order to be heard, but you can still use the elements of projection to advantage. Thus, when a selection of literature calls for increased volume and intensity, you can provide your listeners with the impression of great force and loudness without blasting them out of the room.

## LOUDNESS AND EFFECTIVE COMMUNICATION

Acquisition of efficient speech production supplies the communicator with the tools for effective oral reading. Without judicious application to the demands of specific literature, however, the most pleasing speech sounds are empty and worthless. The effective oral reader must be sensitive to the many subtle variations of loudness inherent in language and responds accordingly.

**Syllabic Stress.**    Long acquaintance with English pronunciation and the intent to convey meanings enable us to employ unconsciously many different degrees of loudness—along with pitch and duration—to pronounce words correctly. Here, for example, are six common English words with their pronunciations. In each case the standard spelling is followed by the diacritical markings from the *American Heritage Dictionary* and the phonetic symbols from Kenyon and Knott's *A Pronouncing Dictionary of American English*. Read the words aloud, clearly pronouncing each several times:

livelihood, / lĭv′lē-hoŏd′ / [ˈlaɪvlɪˌhʊd]
indent, / ĭn-děnt′ / [ɪnˈdɛnt]
grimy, / grī′mē / [ˈgraɪmɪ]
fanatic, / fənăt′ĭk / [fəˈnætɪk]

cohesion, / kō-hē′zhən / [koˈhiʒən]
chiropractor, / kīr′ə-prăk′tər / [ˈkɑɪrəˌpræktər]

Which syllable of " livelihood " was made to stand out? Which syllable of "grimy?" Reread all six words; you will find that normally the accented syllable is the one spoken with the greatest degree of loudness, the highest pitch, and the longest duration.

Misplaced stresses on words sound unnatural and may, in some instances, alter meanings. " Rebel " changes from noun to verb when the stress is shifted from the first to the second syllable. " Incense " changes from a noun describing a fragrance to a verb meaning " to make angry " when the stress is shifted. As an accustomed speaker of the English language, you should not need to pay special attention to providing appropriate syllabic stress on words. But, when you are concentrating on a multitude of other expressive factors, be certain that you do not distort your normally correct placement of stress.

**Emphasis.** Loudness is the most common vocal element used to place emphasis on important words and thought centers. Just as the individual syllables within a word receive various degrees of stress, words within a phrase or sentence are accorded relative emphasis by the degree of force with which they are uttered. To illustrate the important role loudness plays in emphasizing key words and subordinating words of lesser significance, try reading the following passage with one unchanging level of loudness.

There is something feeble and a little contemptible about a man who cannot face the perils of life without the help of comfortable myths. . . . Moreover, since he is aware, however dimly, that his opinions are not rational, he becomes furious when they are disputed.

—BERTRAND RUSSELL

If you employed longer duration, heightened pitch, and pauses to give emphasis to the important words in the statement, then you were probably able to be communicative without noticeably varying the loudness. By using various degrees of force, however, along with changes in pitch and duration, the achievement of emphasis becomes much easier, sounds more natural, the achievement of emphasis. becomes much easier, sounds more natural, and is more effective.

Remember that loudness is only *one* way of giving emphasis. All too often, the beginning reader tends to rely almost exclusively on loudness to gain needed emphasis, and the result sounds unnatural. Like any element of expression that is overused, excessive reliance on loudness merely calls attention to the techniques of communication. Work to cultivate as many vocal and physical means of emphasis as you can, reserving overt changes in loudness for times when they are especially needed.

## TOUCH

When the principle of " varying the loudness according to the sense " is applied to extended phrases, sentences, paragraphs, or even to whole selections, it is called *touch*. We read " The rattling old Ford galloped by " with a different touch—that is, with a different overall use of loudness—than we apply on "Slowly and silently the funeral procession wound by." Another instance of how touch differs may be seen in the following two excerpts of speeches, both of which were delivered by Winston Churchill in June of 1940:

Come then; let us to the task, to the battle, to the toil. . . . We shall fight on the beaches, we shall fight on the landing grounds, we shall fight in the fields and in the streets, we shall fight in the hills; we shall never surrender.

Let us therefore brace ourselves to our duties, and so bear ourselves that, if the British Empire and its Commonwealth last for a thousand years, men will still say: "This was their finest hour."

In both passages Churchill was addressing the House of Commons regarding World War II; yet the ringing call to arms of the first excerpt would require a more forceful touch than would the inspirational prophecy of the second.

To distinguish among the various kinds of touch is extremely difficult, for touch is inextricably bound in the highly personalized nature of meaning. Different selections of literature do suggest decidely different kinds of touch, however, and the reader must respond with appropriate degrees of force and intensity.

We speak of three kinds of touch or attack: *gentle, conversational,* and *forceful*. These terms are by no means descriptive of all the possibilities in touch, but we use them for the sake of major distinctions. By beginning with these three rough distinctions, we have a starting point for determining more subtle shades of touch appropriate to specific selections.

The calm, soothing, and lullaby-like nature of the following poem suggests the use of *gentle* touch. Avoid any decided change in loudness, pitch or timing:

## WAKING

ARCHIBALD MACLEISH

The sadness we bring back from sleep
like an herb in the mouth . . .

                            sage?
                                    rosemary?

like a fragrance we can neither lose nor
keep . . .
   woodsmoke?
      oak-leaves?
like the closing
softly of a distant . . .
     distant? . . .
        door . . .


             Oh
like earth on our shoes from an unremembered journey . . .
What earth?
    What journey?


       Why did we return?


  The *conversational* touch is what we normally employ with direct conversation. The following poem is a good example of the kind of literature that you will probably want to read with a conversational touch. Try reading the selection as if someone is talking directly and sincerely but not dramatically. Employ much variety of loudness. To put it briefly, be conversational:

## PLAIN TALK

### WILLIAM JAY SMITH

"There are people so dumb," my father said,
"That they don't know beans from an old bedstead.
They can't tell one thing from another,
Ella Cinders from Whistler's Mother,
A porcupine quill from a peacock feather,
A buffalo-flop from Florentine leather,
Meatless shanks boiled bare and blue,
They bob up and down like bones in a stew;
Don't know their arse from a sassafras root,
And couldn't pour piss from a cowhide boot
With complete directions on the heel."

That's how *he* felt. That's how *I* feel.


  You know of course, that anger or excitement often prompts you to employ more loudness and to employ it more abruptly than normally. In this quotation from one of our very best murder stories, the nobleman Macduff is rousing the slumbering household to announce that the king has

been killed in his sleep. To convey the meaning, fill your lungs to capacity and
say the words with quick, heavy strokes of the abdominal muscles. Probably
you will want to use the most climactic intensity near the end of the third
line and again in the last three lines. We call this a *forceful* touch:

## *from* MACBETH

### WILLIAM SHAKESPEARE

Awake! Awake!
Ring the alarum-bell:—murder and treason!
Banquo and Donalbain! Malcolm! awake!
Shake off this downy sleep, death's counterfeit,
And look on death itself! up, up, and see
The great doom's image! Malcolm! Banquo!
As from your graves rise up, and walk like sprites,
To countenance this horror!

As seen in the increasingly forceful touch possible near the end of those
rousing lines from Shakespeare, there are truly more than three degrees of
touch; the possibilities are as infinite as the degrees of emotion.

Sometimes the language of a selection directly indicates how loud it should
be read. In the following lines, William Wordsworth tells us that the setting
for his poem is " calm " and " quiet ":

It is a beauteous evening, calm and free,
The holy time is quiet as a Nun
Breathless with adoration;
                    — *"It is a Beauteous Evening Calm and Free"*

Alfred, Lord Tennyson calls for a sharply contrasting touch to begin his
poem, " Morte D'Arthur ":

So all day long the noise of battle roll'd
Among the mountains by the winter sea;

In a third example, Stephen Spender directs a gradually increasing loudness
for his description of an express train's gathering speed:

It is now she begins to sing—at first quite low
Then loud, and at last with a jazzy madness—
The song of her whistle screaming at curves,
Of deafening tunnels, brakes, innumerable bolts.

                    — *"The Express"*

The language of any selection of literature may be said to have a particular texture. If we are to "feel" this texture, and to convey that feeling to an audience, then we must apply to the language a fitting touch. The imagery, the ideas presented, and the emotional state of the speaker contribute to this sense of texture, but it is more than that. The very sounds of the words contribute to the feel of the work. They may be smooth and relaxing, as in:

When to the sessions of sweet silent thought
I summon up remembrance of things past,

—WILLIAM SHAKESPEARE, Sonnet 30

or rough and coarse:

The hand that held my wrist
Was battered on one knuckle;
At every step you missed
My right ear scraped a buckle.

—THEODORE ROETHKE, "My Papa's Waltz"

or loudly booming:

Booth led boldly with his big bass drum—

—VACHEL LINDSAY, "General William Booth Enters into Heaven"

Effective employment of loudness, in conjunction with the other means of audible expression, preserves the texture of language in performance, providing an appropriate, audible setting in which ideas and emotions will thrive.

## EXERCISES

1. Practice the following exercises to increase the efficiency of your breathing:

a. Pant in quick breaths with the mouth open. You should be able to feel vigorous abdominal thrusts.

b. Inhale all the breath you can hold and then blow it out in a long whistle. As you reach the end of the whistle, prolong it by pressing with both hands against the abdomen just below the ribs. With proper breathing you should be able to whistle for fifteen or twenty seconds.

c. If you would like to see a mechanical illustration of abdominal breathing, study the action of a hand-operated bicycle or automobile tire pump. Hold the pump upside down so that you can visualize the force of the abdominal muscles pushing the air out of the lungs from below.

d. Using abdominal breathing, practice the extended phonation of some vowel sound for as long as one breath will permit. You ought to be able to hold the tone for twenty to thirty seconds. If you are unable to sustain it this long, practice the exercise repeatedly over a period of several days until you have substantially increased your time. Learn not to waste your breath on too rapid exhalation.

e. Instead of holding the same sound, try a succession of different vowel sounds with only one breath, beginning each one separately from the previous sound. You should be able to make twenty or thirty different sounds with one breath. Again, it may be necessary to practice repeatedly for several days.

f. With short quick strokes of the diaphragm and abdominal muscles, phonate a series of separate vowel sounds, each with a separate breath. Be sure you can feel the breathing action with one hand on the front of your body just below the sternum.

g. Now do the same exercise beginning each phonation with the sound of a consonant such as *p, b, k, g, t, d, s,* or *sh.* Try them all and try them often, making sure you employ abdominal action.

2. Reading to children is excellent practice in developing effective use of touch. Read the following selections to youngsters, employing more overt variations of loudness than you would use for adults:

## THE SWING

ROBERT LOUIS STEVENSON

How do you like to go up in a swing,
  Up in the air so blue?
Oh, I do think it the pleasantest thing
  Ever a child can do!

Up in the air and over the wall,
  Till I can see so wide,
Rivers and trees and cattle and all
  Over the countryside—

Till I look down on the garden green,
  Down on the roof so brown—
Up in the air I go flying again,
  Up in the air and down!

# THE PLAINT OF THE CAMEL

GUY WETMORE CARRYL

"Canary-birds feed on sugar and seed,
  Parrots have crackers to crunch;
And, as for the poodles, they tell me the noodles
  Have chickens and cream for their lunch.
    But there's never a question
    About MY digestion—
      ANYTHING does for me!

"Cats, you're aware, can repose in a chair,
  Chickens can roost upon rails;
Puppies are able to sleep in a stable,
  And oysters can slumber in pails.
    But no one supposes
    A poor Camel dozes—
      ANY PLACE does for me!

"Lambs are enclosed where it's never exposed,
  Coops are constructed for hens;
Kittens are treated to houses well heated,
  And pigs are protected by pens.
    But a Camel comes handy
    Wherever it's sandy—
      ANYWHERE does for me!

"People would laugh if you rode a giraffe,
  Or mounted the back of an ox;
It's nobody's habit to ride on a rabbit,
  Or try to bestraddle a fox.
    But as for a Camel, he's
    Ridden by families—
      ANY LOAD does for me!

"A snake is as round as a hole in the ground,
  And weasels are wavy and sleek;
And no alligator could ever be straighter
  Than lizards that live in a creek.
    But a Camel's all lumpy
    And bumpy and humpy—
      ANY SHAPE does for me!"

3.  In contrast to the simplicity of the preceding children's verses, the next two poems contain a multiplicity of images that crowd your senses and impose a rich mosaic of moods. To read either of these works effectively, you will certainly be compelled by the literature to employ many subtle variations of touch.

## THE HOLY INNOCENTS

### ROBERT LOWELL

Listen, the hay-bells tinkle as the cart
Wavers on rubber tires along the tar
And cindered ice below the burlap mill
And ale-wife run. The oxen drool and start
In wonder at the fenders of a car
And blunder hugely up St. Peter's hill.
These are the undefiled by woman—their
Sorrow is not the sorrow of this world:
King Herod shrieking vengeance at the curled
Up knees of Jesus choking in the air,
A king of speechless clods and infants. Still
The world out-Herods Herod; and the year,
The nineteen-hundred forty-fifth of grace,
Lumbers with losses up the clinkered hill
Of our purgation; and the oxen near
The worn foundations of their resting place,
The holy manger where their bed is corn
And holly torn for Christmas. If they die,
As Jesus, in the harness, who will mourn?
Lamb of the shepherds, Child, how still you lie.

## CHURCH GOING

### PHILIP LARKIN

Once I am sure there's nothing going on
I step inside, letting the door thud shut.
Another church: matting, seats, and stone,
And little books; sprawlings of flowers, cut
For Sunday, brownish now; some brass and stuff
Up at the holy end; the small neat organ;
And a tense, musty unignorable silence,
Brewed God knows how long. Hatless, I take off
My cycle-clips in awkward reverence,

Move forward, run my hand around the font.
From where I stand, the roof looks almost new—
Cleaned, or restored? Someone would know: I don't.
Mounting the lectern, I peruse a few
Hectoring large-scale verses, and pronounce
"Here endeth" much more loudly than I'd meant.
The echoes snigger briefly. Back at the door
I sign the book, donate an Irish sixpence,
Reflect the place was not worth stopping for.

Yet stop I did: in fact I often do,
And always end much at a loss like this,
Wondering what to look for; wondering, too,
When churches fall completely out of use
What we shall turn them into; if we shall keep
A few cathedrals chronically on show,
Their parchment, plate and pyx in locked cases,
And let the rest rent-free to rain and sheep.
Shall we avoid them as unlucky places?

Or, after dark, will dubious women come
To make their children touch a particular stone;
Pick simples for a cancer; or on some
Advised night see walking a dead one?
Power of some sort or other will go on
In games, in riddles, seemingly at random;
But superstition, like belief, must die,
And what remains when disbelief has gone?
Grass, weedy pavement, brambles, buttress, sky,

A shape less recognisable each week,
A purpose more obscure. I wonder who
Will be the last, the very last, to seek
This place for what it was; one of the crew
That tap and jot and know what rood-lofts were?
Some ruin-bibber, randy for antique,
Or Christmas-addict, counting on a whiff
Of gown-and-bands and organ-pipes and myrrh?
Or will he be my representative,

Bored, uninformed, knowing the ghostly silt
Dispersed, yet tending to this cross of ground
Through suburb scrub because it held unspilt
So long and equably what since is found

Only in separation—marriage, and birth,
And death, and thoughts of these—for whom was built
This special shell? For, though I've no idea
What this accoutred frowsty barn is worth,
It pleases me to stand in silence here;

A serious house on serious earth it is,
In whose blent air all our compulsions meet,
Are recognised, and robed as destinies.
And that much never can be obsolete,
Since someone will forever be surprising
A hunger in himself to be more serious,
And gravitating with it to this ground,
Which, he once heard, was proper to grow wise in,
If only that so many dead lie round.

4. Although both of the following selections would likely be best read with a predominantly forceful touch, they project widely divergent attitudes. Read them aloud. Do you find yourself using loudness in various ways to express the differing attitudes of the literature?

# DO NOT GO GENTLE INTO THAT GOOD NIGHT

DYLAN THOMAS

Do not go gentle into that good night,
Old age should burn and rave at close of day;
Rage, rage against the dying of the light.

Though wise men at their end know dark is right,
Because their words had forked no lightning they
Do not go gentle into that good night.

Good men, the last wave by, crying how bright
Their frail deeds might have danced in a green bay,
Rage, rage against the dying of the light.

Wild men who caught and sang the sun in flight,
And learn, too late, they grieved it on its way,
Do not go gentle into that good night.

Grave men, near death, who see with blinding sight
Blind eyes could blaze like meteors and be gay,
Rage, rage against the dying of the light.

And you, my father, there on the sad height,
Curse, bless, me now with your fierce tears, I pray.
Do not go gentle into that good night.
Rage, rage against the dying of the light.

## *from* SINNERS IN THE HANDS OF AN ANGRY GOD

JONATHAN EDWARDS

O Sinner! Consider the fearful danger you are in. 'Tis a great furnace of wrath, a wide and bottomless pit, full of the fire of wrath, that you are held over in the hand of that God whose wrath is provoked and incensed as much against you as against many of the damned in hell. You hang by a slender thread, with the flames of divine wrath flashing about it, and ready every moment to singe it and burn it asunder; and you have no interest in any Mediator, and nothing to lay hold of to save yourself, nothing to keep off the flames of wrath, nothing of your own, nothing that you ever have done, nothing that you can do, to induce God to spare you one moment. . . .

Therefore, let every one that is out of Christ now awake and fly from the wrath to come. The wrath of Almighty God is now undoubtedly hanging over a great part of his congregation. Let every one fly out of Sodom. "Haste and escape for your lives, look not behind you, escape to the mountain, lest ye be consumed."

5. In what ways do the following sonnet and public speech call for similar touch from the oral reader?

## SONNET 30

WILLIAM SHAKESPEARE

When to the sessions of sweet silent thought
I summon up remembrance of things past,
I sigh the lack of many a thing I sought,
And with old woes new wail my dear time's waste;
Then can I drown an eye, unused to flow,
For precious friends hid in death's dateless night,
And weep afresh love's long-since-cancell'd woe,
And moan the expense of many a vanish'd sight.
Then can I grieve at grievances foregone,
And heavily from woe to woe tell o'er
The sad account of fore-bemoanéd moan,
Which I new pay as if not paid before.
     But if the while I think on thee, dear Friend,
All losses are restored, and sorrows end.

# FAREWELL TO SPRINGFIELD NEIGHBORS UPON LEAVING FOR WASHINGTON, FEBRUARY 11, 1861

ABRAHAM LINCOLN

My Friends: No one, not in my situation, can appreciate my feeling of sadness at this parting. To this place, and the kindness of these people, I owe everything. Here I have lived a quarter of a century, and have passed from a young to an old man. Here my children have been born, and one is buried. I now leave, not knowing when or whether ever I may return, with a task before me greater than that which rested upon Washington. Without the assistance of that Divine Being who ever attended him, I cannot succeed. With that assistance, I cannot fail. Trusting in Him who can go with me, and remain with you, and be everywhere for good, let us confidently hope that all will yet be well. To His care commending you, as I hope in your prayers you will commend me, I bid you an affectionate farewell.

6. Each of the following selections undergoes significant transitions in idea, emotion, or image. Variation in touch is inherent in any physical realization of these pieces when expressed dynamically.

# WAR IS KIND

STEPHEN CRANE

Do not weep, maiden, for war is kind.
Because your lover threw wild hands toward the sky
And the affrighted steed ran on alone,
Do not weep.
War is kind.

Hoarse, booming drums of the regiment,
Little souls who thirst for fight,
These men were born to drill and die.
The unexplained glory flies above them,
Great is the battle-god, and his kingdom—
A field where a thousand corpses lie.

Do not weep, babe, for war is kind.
Because your father tumbled in the yellow trenches
Raged at his breast, gulped and died,
Do not weep.
War is kind.

Swift-blazing flag of the regiment,
Eagle with crest of red and gold,
These men were born to drill and die.
Point for them the virtue of slaughter,
Make plain to them the excellence of killing,
And a field where a thousand corpses lie.

Mother whose heart hung humble as a button
On the bright splendid shroud of your son,
Do not weep.
War is kind.

## JIM BLUDSO

JOHN HAY

Wall, no! I can't tell whar he lives,
    Because he don't live, you see;
Leastways, he's got out of the habit
    Of livin' like you and me.
Whar have you been for the last three year
    That you haven't heard folks tell
How Jimmy Bludso passed in his checks,
    The night of the *Prairie Belle?*

He weren't no saint,—them engineers
    Is all pretty much alike,—
One wife in Natchez-under-the-Hill
    And another one here, in Pike;
A keerless man in his talk was Jim,
    And an awkward hand in a row,
But he never flunked, and he never lied,—
    I reckon he never knowed how.

And this was all the religion he had,—
    To treat his engine well;
Never be passed on the river;
    To mind the pilot's bell;
And if ever the *Prairie Belle* took fire—
    A thousand times he swore
He'd hold her nozzle agin the bank
    Till the last soul got ashore.

All boats has their day on the Mississip,
    And her day come at last—

The *Movastar* was a better boat,
  But the *Belle* she wouldn't be passed.
And so she come tearin' along that night—
  The oldest craft on the line—
With a nigger squat on her safety valve,
  And her furnace crammed, rosin and pine.

The fire bust out as she clared the bar,
  And burnt a hole in the night,
And quick as a flash she turned, and made
  For that willer-bank on the right.
There was runnin' and cursin', but Jim yelled out,
  Over all the infernal roar,
"I'll hold her nozzle agin the bank
  Till the last galoot's ashore."

Through the hot, black breath of the burnin' boat
  Jim Bludso's voice was heard,
And they all had trust in his cussedness,
  And knowed he would keep his word.
And, sure's you're born, they all got off
  Afore the smokestacks fell,—
And Bludso's ghost went up alone
  In the smoke of the *Prairie Belle*.

He weren't no saint—but at jedgment
  I'd run my chance with Jim,
'Longside of some pious gentlemen
  That wouldn't shook hands with him.
He seen his duty, a dead-sure thing—
  And went for it thar and then;
And Christ ain't a goin' to be too hard
  On a man that died for men.

# THE EXPRESS

### STEPHEN SPENDER

After the first powerful plain manifesto
The black statement of pistons, without more fuss
But gliding like a queen, she leaves the station.
Without bowing and with restrained unconcern
She passes the houses which humbly crowd outside,
The gasworks and at last the heavy page

Of death, printed by gravestones in the cemetery.
Beyond the town there lies the open country
Where, gathering speed, she acquires mystery,
The luminous self-possession of ships on ocean.
It is now she begins to sing—at first quite low
Then loud, and at last with a jazzy madness—
The song of her whistle screaming at curves,
Of deafening tunnels, brakes, innumerable bolts.
And always light, aerial, underneath
Goes the elate metre of her wheels.
Steaming through metal landscape on her lines
She plunges new eras of wild happiness
Where speed throws up strange shapes, broad curves
And parallels clean like the steel of guns.
At last, further than Edinburgh or Rome,
Beyond the crest of the world, she reaches night
Where only a low streamline brightness
Of phosphorus on the tossing hills is white.
Ah, like a comet through flame she moves entranced
Wrapt in her music no bird song, no, nor bough
Breaking with honey buds, shall ever equal.

## *from* THE CONFESSIONS OF NAT TURNER

WILLIAM STYRON

An exquisitely sharpened hatred for the white man is of course an emotion not difficult for Negroes to harbor. Yet if truth be known, this hatred does not abound in every Negro's soul; it relies upon too many mysterious and hidden patterns of life and chance to flourish luxuriantly everywhere. Real hatred of the sort of which I speak—hatred so pure and obdurate that no sympathy, no human warmth, no flicker of compassion can make the faintest nick or scratch upon the stony surface of its being— is not common to all Negroes. Like a flower of granite with cruel leaves it grows, when it grows at all, as if from fragile seed cast upon uncertain ground. Many conditions are required for the full fruition of this hatred, for its ripe and malevolent growth, yet none of these is as important as that at one time or another the Negro live to some degree of intimacy with the white man. That he know the object of his hatred, and that he become knowledgeable about the white man's wiles, his duplicity, his greediness, and his ultimate depravity.

For without knowing the white man at close hand, without having submitted to his wanton and arrogant kindnesses, without having smelled the smell of his bedsheets and his dirty underdrawers and the inside of his privy, and felt the casual yet insolent touch of his women's fingers upon his own black arm, without seeing him at sport and at ease and at his hypocrite's worship and at his drunken vileness and at his lustful and adulterous couplings in the hay-field—without having known all these cozy and familial truths, I say, a Negro can only *pretend* hatred. Such hatred is an abstraction and a delusion. For example. A poor field Negro may once in a while be struck by the whip of an overseer riding on a tall white horse, that same Negro may be forced onto short rations for a month and feel his stomach rumble daily in the tight cramps of near-starvation, again this Negro might someday be thrown into a cart and sold like a mule at auction in pouring rain; yet if this selfsame Negro—surrounded from childhood by a sea of black folk, hoeing and scraping in the fields from dawn to dusk year in and year out and knowing no white man other than that overseer whose presence is a mean distant voice and a lash and whose face is a nameless and changing white blob against the sky—finds himself trying to hate white men, he will come to understand that he is hating imperfectly, without that calm and intelligent and unrepenting purity of hatred which I have already described and which is so necessary in order to murder. Such a Negro, unacquainted with white men and their smell and their blanched and bloodless actuality and their evil, will perhaps hate but with a hatred which is all sullen-ness and impotent resentment, like the helpless, resigned fury one feels toward indifferent Nature throughout long days of relentless heat or after periods of unceasing rain.

## THE LAUGHERS

### LOUIS UNTERMEYER

SPRING!
And her hidden bugles up the street.
Spring—and the sweet
Laughter of winds at the crossing;
Laughter of birds and a fountain tossing
Its hair in abandoned ecstasies.
Laughter of trees.
Laughter of shop-girls that giggle and blush;
Laugh of the tug-boat's impertinent fife.
Laughter followed by a trembling hush—
Laughter of love, scarce whispered aloud.
Then, stilled by no sacredness or strife,
Laughter that leaps from the crowd:
Seizing the world in a rush.
Laughter of life . . .

Earth takes deep breaths like a man who had feared he might smother,
Filling his lungs before bursting into a shout . . .

Windows are opened—curtains flying out;
Over the wash-lines women call to each other.
And, under the calling, there surges, too clearly to doubt,
Spring, with the noises
Of shrill, little voices;
Joining in "Tag" and the furious chase
Of "I-spy," "Red Rover" and "Prisoner's Base";
Of the roller-skates whir at the sidewalk's slope,
Of boys playing marbles and girls skipping rope.
And there, down the avenue, behold,
The first true herald of the Spring—
The hand-organ gasping and wheezily murmuring
Its tunes ten-years old . . .
And the music, trivial and tawdry, has freshness and magical swing
And over and under it,
During and after—
The laughter
Of Spring!

And lifted still
With the common thrill,
With the throbbing air, the tingling vapor,
That rose like strong and mingled wines,
I turned to my paper,
And read these lines:
    Now that the Spring is here,
    The war enters its bloodiest phase . . .
    The men are impatient . . .
    Bad roads, storms and the rigors of the winter
    Have held back the contending armies . . .
    But the recruits have arrived,
    And are waiting only the first days of warm weather . . .
    There will be terrible fighting along the whole line—
    Now that Spring has come.

I put the paper down . . .
Something struck out the sun—something unseen;
Something arose like a dark wave to drown
The golden streets with a sickly green.
Something polluted the blossoming day
With the touch of decay.
The music thinned and died;
People seemed hollow-eyed.
Even the faces of children, where gaiety lingers,

Sagged and drooped like banners about to be furled—
And Silence laid its bony fingers
On the lips of the world . . .
A grisly quiet with the power to choke;
A quiet that only one thing broke;
One thing alone rose up thereafter . . .
Laughter!
Laughter of streams running red.
Laughter of evil things in the night;
Vultures carousing over the dead;
Laughter of ghouls.
Chuckling of idiots, cursed with sight.
Laughter of dark and horrible pools.
Scream of the bullet's rattling mirth,
Sweeping the earth.
Laugh of the cannon's poisonous breath . . .
And over the shouts and the wreckage and crumbling
The raucous and rumbling
Laughter of death.
Death that arises to sing,—
Hailing the Spring.

# 11 *Audible Communication Through Pitch*

To describe an individual's expressiveness, we frequently refer to his use of pitch. When a speaker is particularly dull and listless, we say he speaks in a monotone. All the vocal variables contribute to this negative impression, but the lack of pitch variation stands out most prominently. In response to a magnificent performance, on the other hand, we may also refer to the use of pitch to describe the communicative success. The opening lines of Dufault's "Gielgud Reading Lear," for instance, focus largely on the actor's successful use of pitch to capture Lear's emotions:

He comes on with *keening moan*
as if all stops upon his pipe
but the last *falsetto* vent
were choked by grief,

The pitch of the human voice is its highness or lowness on a musical scale. Each of us has a habitual level of pitch at which we tend to speak, with the voice varying up and down from that pitch. When bored, our pitch tends to stay on one level in a monotone. When excited, our pitch tends to rise and fall greatly. Expressiveness without considerable changes in pitch is impossible.

## VARIATION IN PITCH

Variation of vocal pitch to communicate meaning is employed by most of the animal world, where the higher ranges of pitch usually indicate fear or excitement and the lower ones composure and sometimes aggressiveness. Human beings of all cultures use this same basic method of communicating meaning by varying vocal pitch. Every family with a baby can distinguish among wordless sounds that denote hunger, fear, pain, anger, contentment, and pleasure. In each case, the primary difference is one of pitch. Adults employ pitch levels in a multitude of ways. Increased loudness for syllabic stress is normally accompanied by a slight rise in pitch. Heightened pitch, again with added loudness, is also a frequently employed means of adding emphasis. Differing pitch variation of single words often means the difference between a statement of fact and a question. In the same way, it is employed in sentences. Here, however, we often adapt the primary level of pitch to the overall meaning of the sentence. For example, the quiet restrained "I hate you" suggests a pitch level that is different from that of the carefree invitation, "Let's go to the ball game." The same distinction applies to whole paragraphs or even more extended speech.

Two passages written by Mark Twain illustrate differences in the basic pitch level that may be called for. The first seems to call for a relatively low pitch to match the author's mockingly serious morality. Very possibly the interpreter might alter the pitch for the newspaper quotation and the grandmother's dialogue, but most of the selection should probably remain piously intoned at a low pitch. The succeeding passage, in stark contrast, seems to demand a higher overall pitch in response to the untempered enthusiasm of the speaker:

# HISTORY REPEATS ITSELF

### MARK TWAIN

The following I find in a Sandwich Island paper which some friend has sent me from that tranquil far-off retreat. The coincidence between my own experience and that here set down by the late Mr. Benton is so remarkable that I cannot forbear publishing and commenting upon the paragraph. The Sandwich Island paper says:

"How touching is this tribute of the late Hon. T. H. Benton to his mother's influence:—'My mother asked me never to use tobacco; I have never touched it from that time to the present day. She asked me not to gamble, and I have never gambled. I cannot tell who is losing in games that are being played. She admonished me, too, against liquor-drinking, and whatever capacity for endurance I have at present, and whatever usefulness I may have attained through life, I attribute to having complied with her pious and correct wishes. When I was seven years of age she asked me not to drink, and then I made a resolution of total abstinence; and that I have adhered to it through all time I owe to my mother.'"

I never saw anything so curious. It is almost an exact epitome of my own moral career—after simply subsituting a grandmother for a mother. How well I remember my grandmother's asking me not to use tobacco, good old soul. She said, "You're at it again, are you, you whelp? Now don't ever let me catch you chewing tobacco before breakfast again, or I lay I'll blacksnake you within an inch of your life!" I have never touched it at that hour of the morning from that time to the present day.

She asked me not to gamble. She whispered and said, "Put up those wicked cards this minute!—two pair and a jack, you numbskull, and the other fellow's got a flush!"

I never have gambled from that day to this—never once—without a "cold deck" in my pocket. I cannot even tell who is going to lose in games that are being played unless I deal myself.

When I was two years of age she asked me not to drink, and then I made a resolution of total abstinence. That I have adhered to it and enjoyed the beneficent effects of it through all, I owe to my grandmother. I have never drunk a drop from that day to this of any kind of water.

## *from* THE ADVENTURES OF HUCKLEBERRY FINN

### MARK TWAIN

It was a real bully circus. It was the splendidest sight that ever was when they all come riding in, two and two, a gentleman and lady, side by side, the men just in their drawers and undershirts, and no shoes nor stirrups, and resting their hands on their thighs easy and comfortable—there must 'a' been twenty of them—and every lady with a lovely complexion and perfectly beautiful, and looking just like a gang of real sure-enough queens and dressed in clothes that cost millions of dollars, and just littered with diamonds. It was a powerful fine sight; I never seen anything so lovely. And then one by one they got up and stood, and went a-weaving round the ring so gentle and wavy and graceful, the men looking ever so tall and airy and straight, with their heads bobbing and skimming along, away up there under the tent-roof, and every lady's rose-leafy dress flapping soft and silky round her hips, and she looking like the most loveliest parasol.

And then faster and faster they went, all of them dancing, first one foot out in the air and then the other, the horses leaning more and more, and the ringmaster going round and round the center pole, cracking his whip and shouting "Hi!—hi!" and the clown cracking jokes behind him; and by and by all hands dropped the reins, and every lady put her knuckles on her hips and every gentleman folded his arms, and then how the horses did lean over and hump themselves! And so one after the other they all skipped off into the ring, and made the sweetest bow I ever see, and then scampered out, and everybody clapped their hands and went just wild.

In addition to reading each of these passages in a different general level of pitch, you have probably distinguished them in another way. In order to express the excitement inherent in *Huckleberry Finn*, you have probably employed a greater range of pitch in reading it. Such variation of pitch to convey meaning is a normal part of oral expression.

## ORIGINS OF VOCAL PITCH

When you have become conscious of using different levels of pitch for different kinds of material, one of the questions you ultimately ask is, " How does it happen that my voice is higher (or lower) than other people's?" Like most of the aspects of personality, voice is derived basically from the two sources of heredity and environment.

The habitual level at which you speak is largely determined by your physical inheritance. Your vocal mechanism has pitch limits below and above which you cannot go. Place your finger on the point of your Adam's apple. Slide your finger upward slightly until you find the little groove just above. This marks the top of the *larynx*, often called the voice box. The larynx houses two muscular bands, which apparently were originally employed only as a valve in the breath stream. If you will again place your hands under the seat of your chair and try to lift both the chair and yourself, you will notice that you close this valve when you make a major bodily effort. Most animals have learned to control the *glottis*, or opening in the valve, to produce voice. The length and thickness of these muscular bands, which we call the *vocal folds*, limit the pitches at which they can vibrate in the breath stream. In this regard the vocal folds are analogous to the strings of a violin: the larger or longer the string, the lower the pitch. You know that as you shorten the vibrating length of the violin string by placing your finger nearer the bridge, a higher note is produced. You cannot, however, make a lower note than the size and length of the string permit. So it is that the thickness and length of your vocal folds set up broad limits for the pitches you can produce; the longer and heavier your vocal bands, the lower the possible pitch of your voice. On the other hand, we must recognize that few people employ the full range of their pitch possibilities. Therefore, you may be reasonably sure that you can learn to raise or lower your pitch beyond its habitual limits.

Another factor in the determination of the pitch at which you normally speak is your environment. If you live in an atmosphere of composure, quite probably your normal pitch will be lower than it would be if you were surrounded by excitement. Excitement produces tension; tension raises pitch. Even more influential than such environment is the pitch level employed by people with whom you associate. As a general rule we tend to copy the speech of other members of the family or of intimate friends. Girls often approximate the pitch of their mothers and boys, of their fathers. This tendency to imitate means that your pitch may or may not be a natural one within the limits your vocal mechanism has set for you.

A final factor in the determination of your pitch is your personality. Of course, personality itself is the product of heredity and environment, but your attitudes, tensions, and even health may cause you to use a characteristic pitch level. In this sense, pitch is often an indicator of the inner person.

## CHANGING YOUR PITCH

How do you change the pitch of your voice? What happens to result in a lower or higher pitch? Length and thickness of the vibrating vocal folds are the two variables that govern the pitch level of phonation. High-speed motion pictures have been taken of the vocal folds in action, and actual measurements of individual frames of film have revealed a progressive increase in the vibrating length of the folds as the pitch of phonation rises.[1] As the vibrating length increases, its thickness diminishes. Conversely, as the pitch falls, the length diminishes and the thickness increases.[2] The level of pitch is determined by the regulation of the length and thickness of that part of the vocal folds being vibrated to make the tone.

## HABITUAL PITCH

When we say that one person's vocal pitch is higher or lower than another's, we are speaking of *habitual pitch*. It is that pitch level we employ most often when sense or feeling does not require departure from it. It is the pitch at which we utter the unemphasized sounds. We tend to rise above the habitual level when centering on an idea. We tend to fall below it at ends of clauses. Perhaps the easiest way for us to communicate an understanding of what we mean by habitual pitch is to illustrate it in sentences such as the following. You will employ your own habitual pitch range as you read the sentences aloud, *except* on the *italicized* words and those at the ends of sentences.

1. I will try to *locate* my *habitual* pitch.
2. I must listen to the *pitch* of my voice.
3. The *unitalicized* words are spoken at my *habitual* pitch.

## OPTIMUM PITCH

Is your habitual pitch the one that is really best for you? There is no absolute answer to this question, for the limits of your *optimum pitch* are broad and indefinite. We define optimum pitch as the best or most favorable one for speaking. Your optimum may be quite different from that of others. It is by definition an ideal. Many people have attained the ideal quite unconsciously. Their habitual pitch is their optimum pitch.

There are some good reasons your habitual pitch *should* be your optimum one. First, the optimum is easiest to phonate. At optimum pitch, muscular adjustment is nearer to a point of rest than at any other pitch level. At the very high and very low levels of pitch, the muscular adjustment of the

---

[1] H. Hollien, "Some Laryngeal Correlates of Vocal Pitch," *Journal of Speech and Hearing Research*, III (1960), 52–58.

[2] Paul Moore and Hans von Leden, films: *The Larynx and Voice: The Function of the Normal Larynx*, January 1957; *The Larynx and Voice: Physiology of the Larynx Under Daily Stress*, Laryngeal Research Laboratory, William and Harriet Gould Foundation, Northwestern University, Chicago.

larynx is greater, and so the phonation easiest to make lies somewhere in between. Second, the optimum pitch permits greater intensity with less effort. When the folds are most nearly at a point of rest, they are more elastic and so more responsive to the force of the breath stream. Third, the use of optimum pitch permits effective use of your vocal range. It makes it easy for you to vary intonation above and below that level. Variations of pitch are most readily achieved when the point of departure is the optimum pitch.

How can you tell whether you normally speak or read at an optimum level of pitch? How can you tell what your optimum level is? One way is to sing to the highest and lowest limits you can comfortably reach, find those limits on the keys of the piano, and then locate the middle of the range. Generally speaking your optimum pitch should be about two notes below this middle point. One authority says that if you go through this routine to find your optimum, you may expect it to be somewhere between one-fourth and one-third above the lowest tone you can produce.[3] Another says that to find your optimum you can use a technique of vocalizing while chewing. He suggests that you chew with closed lips and nothing in your mouth, and observe your tongue moving continually during the process. Then he says that you should immediately open the mouth, vocalize, and chew with extensive movements of the lips and tongue. If the activity of jaw, lips, and tongue is sufficiently vigorous, a variety of sounds escapes the mouth. If the sounds are uniform in the sense of rhythmic identical syllables, the movement is not vigorous enough.[4] Jon Eisenson has found that persons who perform the above experiment in the manner described vocalize at or close to their optimum pitch. Another way to approximate your optimum pitch is to sing down the scale to the lowest note you can easily reach and then sing up again five notes to reach the optimum. An even simpler method is to produce an easy, open-mouthed "ah-h-h-h." This tone usually approximates the optimum. We suggest you try several of these five methods and see if you arrive at the same, or nearly the same pitch, every time. Almost certainly, you will be able to approximate your optimum level, the one to which you should return most often in speaking. If it is different from your habitual pitch, we suggest you try to speak more nearly at your optimum level.

## PITCH FAULTS

Although you may have achieved your optimum pitch in speaking or reading, your effective use of voice may still be hampered by one or more

[3] Jon Eisenson, *The Improvement of Voice and Diction* (New York: The Macmillan Company, 1965), pp. 103–104.

[4] E. Froeschels, "Hygiene of the Voice," *Archives of Otolaryngology*, XXXVIII (August 1943), 122–130.

pitch faults. The most serious of these is a *monopitch*, a lack of variety in pitch, which results in inattention and boredom. Very few people speak in one constant pitch, for the nature of English pronunciation requires some variety. Remember that "grimy" and "indent" have two pitch levels. To speak with no pitch variety is at best to sound as silly as some comedians; at worst it is to be almost completely unintelligible. Many persons, however, limit themselves to a monotonous range of only two or three halfnotes. The normally expressive voice encompasses a wide range of pitch levels that extends both above and below the optimum. Seldom would you wish to exercise the extremes of screech and growl, but the greater the range you have at your disposal, the greater the possibilities for effectiveness.

Almost as serious as a lack of pitch variety is the employment of a *pitch pattern*. Perhaps you have heard such a pattern in church when a minister read scripture. Or, you may have heard political figures in conventions and elsewhere speak in a pompously repetitive pattern of pitches that could be plotted on a musical scale. Other patterns include the "reading tone" adopted by some commercial announcers, the suspiciously overfriendly pattern of certain sales people, or the mechanical tour-guide monotony of persons who have repeated the same utterance so frequently that they have lost all interest in it. A very common pattern of pitch occurs as speakers conclude *every* sentence with a lowering of pitch. Not only does this result in a mechanical monotony, but the pattern breaks up the continuity of ideas by enforcing a completion of thought after every idea.

Surely if the utterance of ideas is to be meaningful, any noticeable pitch pattern must be avoided. Far from adding to communication, such regular repetitions of pitch lull the unsuspecting listener into slumber. Pitch patterns usually result from failure to experience the thoughts as the words are being uttered. They reveal a mind *not* involved with ideas or one that has selected a contrived, obviously insincere manner. Reading is thus sound without sense.

While a monopitch or a repetitious pattern causes dullness, the *over-employment* of pitch variety may just as definitely detract from the communication of the meaning. Probably you are familiar with the caricature of the elocutionist who so nimbly trips up and down the scale in a fantastic display of versatility that the listener sits in rapt admiration of his skill but never of his ideas. Actresses and actors sometimes exert such dynamic control over their voice ranges that they use them contrary to normal conversational restraints. Such performers apparently believe that if a little is good, a great deal is better. We deplore overuse of pitch variety as much as underuse. The employment of pitch should aid and never hinder communication.

## VOCAL MELODY

For interesting speaking or reading, the speech *melody* or arrangement of pitch changes should involve as much variation as is necessary for maximum communication of meaning. Listening to speech melody should be both a meaningful and a pleasant experience, unless of course full awareness of meaning is actually implemented by unpleasant listening. This next passage, for instance, is perhaps properly unpleasant to the ear:

A succession of loud and shrill screams, bursting suddenly from the throat of the chained form, seemed to thrust me violently back.
—EDGAR ALLAN POE, from *The Cask of Amontillado*

The reader of this passage would certainly refrain from screaming the words, but there would most likely be a tendency to use a higher pitch range than the optimum.

Whether the literature reflects harmony or discord, melodic flow or jangling cacophony, its effective reading involves speech melody that reflects the sense, so that the two coalesce into a unified, lifelike expression of idea and emotion. Not confined to the precise score of a musical composition, the sensitive reader responds to the melody that is inherent in the specific language act.

Vocal melody is an elusive but nevertheless significant index of a person's inner feelings. It suggests the degree to which a reader has achieved identification with his meaning. It reveals comprehension and sincerity. It may also reveal lack of understanding and insincerity. Thus, melody lends convincing support to the position that the single most important factor in effective reading or speaking is vivid awareness of meaning at the moment of utterance. You cannot depend on hiding your lack of understanding or your insincerity. Vocal melody provides a ready index to what is going on in the speaker's mind.

The mechanics of melody can be explained by means of three aspects of pitch: *key, step,* and *inflection.* These are the ingredients of melody, the fundamental requisites to effective use of pitch. We shall explore each of these briefly, but we should keep in mind that vocal melody (or any dimension of communication) is not reducible to a set of technical explanations.

## MAINTAINING A KEY

The term *key* indicates the general level of tone in an extended section of speech. It may be higher or lower than your optimum pitch and is determined by the emotions inherent in the literature. Earlier in this chapter, for instance, we noted that two passages by Mark Twain would probably be read at different overall pitch levels. Their meanings encourage different keys in performance.

To generalize about the choice of key in speaking or reading, it may be said that there are three main levels with different broad uses. Usually the higher keys are used to express excitement, fear, rage, delight, and other emotions characterized by great tension. The medium key (analogous to the optimum pitch discussed earlier) is commonly employed to suggest sincerity and calmness. The lower keys may be used to mean tragedy, worship, repressed hate, and despair. These three designations are not hard-and-fast rules but, rather, the broadest of generalities. There are many exceptions. Keys do overlap. You cannot catalogue the qualities of voice and say that if you speak in such and such a pitch, you will express a specific emotion.

Quite often the appropriate key for reading a piece of literature changes from one section to another. This change is especially important in reading drama or a story with dialogue, although much poetry also requires changes in key. The effective oral interpreter is sensitive to many subtle and overt changes in mood of a selection of literature and responds, thereby altering the key accordingly.

When you are experimenting with different keys for the performance of a work, keep in mind that your optimum level is the key that affords you the greatest freedom for pitch variation. If there is no strong reason for adopting a high or low key, you should normally use what is the most natural and the most easily expressive: the optimum.

## STEP

The vocal *step* in speaking or reading is most obviously illustrated by a similar practice in singing. In this bit of music there are pitch changes

between words and sometimes between syllables. This same phenomenon occurs in normal speech and is called the vocal step. Just as there are such changes of pitch in singing without a change of key, so there are steps in speech without a change of key.

Whereas your musical steps are dictated by the score, your steps in speaking and reading are determined entirely by your understanding of the meaning. Different people repeat the age-old crucial declaration, "I love you," in a variety of steps. Here are three of them. See if you can read the words aloud with the steps indicated.

love
I     you.

I
  love you.


      you.
I love

Shortly we shall see how " I love you " can be made more meaningful with the use of pitch slides, or inflections.

Copy the following verse to indicate appropriate steps, and practice reading it accordingly.

## THE DUCK

OGDEN NASH

Behold the duck.
It does not cluck.
A cluck it lacks.
It quacks.
It is especially fond
Of a puddle or pond.
When it dines or sups,
It bottoms ups.

Almost all intelligible speech employs pitch steps. The only exception is that speech in which monotony is deliberately sought. Sometimes the purpose of such monotony is humor, and sometimes it is the communication of the idea of sameness as in these lines:

Alone, alone, all, all alone,
Alone on a wide, wide sea!
            —SAMUEL TAYLOR COLERIDGE, *The Rime of the Ancient Mariner*

The step occurs most often on relatively unimportant monosyllables and the unstressed syllables in polysyllabic words. The meaning of very simple language, such as " The Duck," could be communicated with the step as the sole means of changing pitch; yet most readers would use inflections on the most significant words.

## INFLECTION

*Inflection* is the process of changing pitch within a syllable. Someone has called it bending pitch to make the sense. It is certainly the most versatile and the most difficult of all the pitch devices used to convey meaning. The word "yes" may be used to demonstrate the most common inflectional patterns.

upward inflection—yés

downward inflection—yès

varieties of the circumflex—yes

yes

By means of the upward inflection you say "Yes" and mean "What?" By means of the downward inflection you say "Yes" and express an affirmation. Using the first circumflex, you may convey the meaning "I *certainly* do!" By inverting the circumflex you may mean "I'm thinking about what you said and you *may* be right although I'm *not sure*." Depending on the length of the word and the complexity of the meaning intended, you may repeat these patterns, or you may alter them by beginning or ending the pitch at a different level, or by modifying the amount of pitch change. Experiment with the word *Oh-h-h* to see how many different meaningful patterns of inflection you can produce.

In Chapter 4, we found we could convey an almost infinite number of meanings with the words "I am going to Chicago." Many of those meanings were expressed primarily through inflections. Using the following sentence see how many meanings you can express through differing inflections. Remember that you have at least four inflectional patterns that you can use on each word. Then, of course, you can employ those patterns on the individual words in different combinations with other words. You should be able to express eight or ten distinctions in meaning without difficulty. Especially try the circumflex on the last word:

I am here.

The inflection is normally the most important characteristic of meaningful and melodic speech. Without it, speaking is monotonous, uninteresting, and even irritating. If you will listen to a radio or television show in which supposedly spontaneous remarks of guests are really memorized or read from the script, you will hear at once what is wrong. People repeat their lines in the most unnatural manner. They mouth sentimental ideas in a flat, insincere tone which simply says, "I'm embarrassed," nothing more. If speech is to be normal, interesting, and colorful, it must employ the inflection. The refined and complex meanings implicit in good literature are expressed primarily through the medium of the inflection. Theoretically at least, it permits you to transmit meaning with every single word you utter.

## INFLECTIONS IN USE

When we examine speech patterns, we find that even though inflections are personal and attitudinal, effective speakers and readers apparently show some basic agreements in using them. The rising inflection ($/$) generally indicates uncertainty, incompleteness, or a questioning frame of mind. For example, in asking the simple question "Are you sure?" we might very well use both two downward steps and a rising slide or inflection:

— — ╱
Are you sure?

The falling inflection ($\setminus$) usually indicates certainty, completion, or simple assertion. In confidently answering the question just asked, one might reply in one of these two patterns:

╱— ╲                                     — ╲
I am sure.                    or            I am sure.

The circumflexes ╱╲ and ╲╱ applied to the following word certainly communicate different meanings; do they not?

╱╲                                          ╲╱
No.                                         No.

The former seems to express assurance, but the latter communicates some doubt. The circumflex is commonly used when asserting or identifying, as in the following items that are contrasted:

_ — _ ╱╲ _ ╱╲
I didn't walk, I drove.

Since the circumflex that is indicated with the sign      ends with a rising inflection, it tends to suggest some doubt or lack of completion, as in the following case:

_ _ ╲╱
I am sure, but I admit I may be wrong.

To see how valuable inflections are in expressive speech, including oral reading, read aloud the following sentence in the two ways indicated. How do the meanings differ?

No, I don't think so.  No, I don't think so.

There are no rules for the use of inflections in speech. When the reader has command of the vocal instrument, and is empathically participating in the thought and emotion of the literature, the pattern of steps and inflections —the vocal melody—takes care of itself. If you are not as effective a speaker or reader as you would like to be, you may find that your speaking or reading lacks effective use of these devices. Fundamental to your improvement will be a realization of their importance in vocal expressiveness. A study of the following examples may convince you of this importance.

Here are some of the many melodies of the human heart and voice employed in the simple words *I love you.* We do not say that the use of pitch must be as indicated in order to communicate the meaning specified: No melodies can be prescribed for any meanings. This is only a demonstration of the fact that speech takes on different pitch melodies when the speaker has different meanings in mind. As you concentrate on the context of each example, your inflections may come out something like these indicated here:

Who loves you?    Why, I love you.    [A simple assertion.]

No one loves you?    I love you.    [Reassurance.]

I suppose there's really no hope for me, but    I love you.    [Speaker lacks confidence.]

No one else dares to love you because    I love you!    [A strong assertion.]

How do I feel about you?    Why, I love you.    [A simple assertion.]

I mean it!    I love you!    [A strong assertion.]

I don't hate you.    I love you.         [An intellectual distinction.]

I don't hate you.    I love you.         [But you burn me up sometimes!]

Quit pestering
me! All right,
I'll say it once
and for all.         I love you.         [Now, let me alone!]

## PITCH AND EMOTION

The strong relationship between a person's emotional state and the pitch of his utterance is physiologically based. The added energy that comes with tremendous enthusiasm is released in the form of wide pitch variations. The lethargy of boredom, conversely, simply does not produce the necessary energy for overt changes in pitch. Since higher ranges of pitch occur as the vocal chords are tense and constricted, they are the natural consequence of emotions that are characterized by greater tension.

Human emotions and corresponding pitches cannot be classified or specified. Emotions are as varied and complex as the individuals who experience them and the situations within which they find themselves. One person's fear may be expressed in shrill screams while another's is choked in a low key. Following, are two passages from poems written by Samuel Taylor Coleridge. The prevailing emotion of both is *grief*, yet they probably would require differing uses of pitch.

The tear which mourn'd a brother's fate scarce dry—
Pain after pain, and woe succeeding woe—
Is my heart destin'd for another blow?
O my sweet sister! and must thou too die?
—*"On Receiving an Account That His Only Sister's Death Was Inevitable"*

A grief without a pang, void, dark, and drear,
    A stifled, drowsy, unimpassioned grief,
    Which finds no natural outlet, no relief,
        In word, or sigh, or tear—

—*"Dejection: An Ode"*

The lines from the first poem might well be read in a relatively high key. In response to his sister's impending death, Coleridge hastily released his emotions into verse. The poet is crying out his grief; he is questioning without waiting to receive an answer; he is expressing emotion without pause for reasoned thought. The accurate reading of the poem would likely be in relatively high-pitched outbursts of feeling.

A lower overall pitch seems appropriate to "Dejection: An Ode," for the grief is "stifled, drowsy, unimpassioned." It is emotion for which there is no relief, no outlet. It bespeaks a pain that is pent up in the individual. Whereas Coleridge lashes out at circumstance in the first poem, in the second, he is held prisoner in his grief.

Examine any of the poems we have quoted throughout this text. They represent a broad range of contemporary as well as traditional verse. In most of them, you will note the presence of strong emotion, but few (if any) seem to call for extended use of high pitch. The same is true for narrative passages. In general, instances of highly impassioned emotion are confined to the drama and to characters' speech in prose. When the language of a lyric poem or narrative releases gushes of emotion, it usually means that the writer has sacrificed all else to feeling, that the writer lacks maturity, or both. Richard Eberhart's poem, which follows, offers some explanation in this regard:

## IF I COULD ONLY LIVE AT THE PITCH THAT IS NEAR MADNESS

RICHARD EBERHART

If I could only live at the pitch that is near madness
When everything is as it was in my childhood
Violent, vivid, and of infinite possibility:
That the sun and the moon broke over my head.

Then I cast time out of the trees and fields,
Then I stood immaculate in the Ego;
Then I eyed the world with all delight,
Reality was the perfection of my sight.

And time has big handles on the hands,
Fields and trees a way of being themselves.
I saw battalions of the race of mankind
Standing stolid, demanding a moral answer.

I gave the moral answer and I died
And into a realm of complexity came
Where nothing is possible but necessity
And the truth wailing there like a red babe.

The "pitch that is near madness" is confined to the poet's childhood, that died so that the adult could be born. The poet relives something of the simple delight of childhood in the poem, but it is held in check by the "realm of complexity," by the "necessity" he cannot escape. Mature literature explores this realm without childlike simplification, and its effective reading requires a similarly mature response. Just as the effective writer exercises emotive restraint, the oral interpreter should judiciously control the extent of pitch range used to convey emotion.

## PITCH AND PERSONA

The voices that speak within a literary selection are identified, first of all, by their ideas and emotions within the fictive setting. By vocally and physically participating in thoughts and feelings, the oral reader gives voice to personae. Often, no additional attempt at impersonation is necessary or advisable. At other times, characters may be so vividly portrayed in the literature that greater vocal and visible responses by the reader are forthcoming, and the reader may give separate consideration to those *selected* behavioral responses that may most efficiently accomplish imaginative suggestion in the listener. Analysis of pitch uses, then, may be helpful.

We can begin our consideration of pitch and persona by delineating common variations regarding age, sex, and personality. Naturally, unless our literature provides us with nothing more than one-dimensional cardboard figures, we cannot rely on these basic distinctions for any more than a tentative starting point to which there must be numerous exceptions. First, adults tend to speak in a lower pitch range than children. Look back to the quotations from Saroyan's *The Human Comedy* at the beginning of Chapter 3. When reading these passages, you would not foolishly try to imitate the higher voice pitches of the boys, yet you might effectively use a *slightly* higher key than your own conversational one, along with a suggestion of boyish intonations (melodies), while lightening your voice quality. Both the naive wonderment and the age of the boys would contribute to your decision to speak their dialogue at a higher pitch. Second, women tend to have higher-pitched voices and to exercise a wider range of pitch than do men. This distinction can be helpful, particularly when you are reading a dialogue between a male and a female character; but it can also be a dangerous course if relied upon too heavily. As Mrs. Malaprop and Sir Anthony converse in Sheridan's *The Rivals* (quoted in Chapter 6), the reader might helpfully suggest their differences by giving Mrs. Malaprop a higher and broader range of pitch. The differences in pitch use of the two is supported by the sex of the individuals, but *even more by their unique personalities*. Thus, our third point is that dimensions of a character's personality will often direct a particular sort of pitch. Mrs. Malaprop's erroneous excesses of language, for instance, make similar excesses of pitch (as well as other vocal features) seem appropriate. Sir Anthony, on the other hand, argues more calmly and rationally: his lower pitch range would reflect that contrasting trait. The combined features of a speaker's personality contribute to varying degrees of tension and relaxation, which find suitable expression in correspondingly higher or lower pitch and broad or narrow deviations in pitch. Remember that the best performances evolve from restrained animation that takes into account all facets of the character.

When narrative commentary directly describes the pitch of a speaker's voice, the oral performance should respond to the directive. In the passage from *Raintree County* quoted in Chapter 5, for instance, the narrator says that General Jackson's " voice blew like a horn of cracked brass, having no variations in pitch or volume between a hard bray and a hoarse whisper." If the interpreter disregards these attributes of pitch (as well as loudness and quality) in the utterance of the General's speech, the performance presents the audience with a glaring inconsistency.

So far, our discussion of pitch and persona has dealt with *who* is speaking, without taking into consideration *why* the individual speaks. In the following lines from William Shakespeare's play *Julius Caesar*, Cassius is attempting to sway Marcus Brutus from his allegiance to Caesar. How might Cassius employ variations in pitch to accomplish his end?

I cannot tell what you and other men
Think of this life; but, for my single self,
I had as lief not be as live to be
In awe of such a thing as I myself.
I was born free as Cæsar; so were you:
We both have fed as well; and we can both
Endure the winter's cold as well as he:
For once, upon a raw and gusty day,
The troubled Tiber chafing with her shores,
Cæsar said to me, 'Darest thou, Cassius, now
Leap in with me into this angry flood,
And swim to yonder point?' Upon the word,
Accoutred as I was, I plunged in,
And bade him follow: so, indeed, he did.
The torrent roar'd; and we did buffet it
With lusty sinews, throwing it aside
And stemming it with hearts of controversy:
But ere we could arrive the point proposed,
Cæsar cried, 'Help me, Cassius, or I sink!'
I, as Aeneas, our great ancestor,
Did from the flames of Troy upon his shoulder
The old Anchises bear, so from the waves of Tiber

Did I the tired Cæsar; and this man
Is now become a god; and Cassius is
A wretched creature, and must bend his body,
If Cæsar carelessly but nod on him.
He had a fever when he was in Spain,
And, when the fit was on him, I did mark
How he did shake: 'tis true, this god did shake:
His coward lips did from their colour fly;
And that same eye, whose bend doth awe the world,
Did lose his lustre: I did hear him groan:
Ay, and that tongue of his, that bade the Romans
Mark him, and write his speeches in their books,
Alas, it cried, 'Give me some drink, Titinius,'
As a sick girl. Ye gods, it doth amaze me,
A man of such a feeble temper should
So get the start of the majestic world,
And bear the palm alone.

Certainly, there is *no one right way* of using pitch to suggest Cassius' attempt to discredit Caesar, but we can mention a few possibilities. First, as he speaks the supposed words of Caesar, Cassius would very possibly use a strained high pitch. This would reinforce his claims of Caesar's weakness and cowardice. In contrast to his caricature of a feeble Caesar, Cassius' self-descriptions would likely be voiced in a relatively low key that strives to reflect strength and stability. Perhaps, also, he might raise his pitch in expressing his astonishment that "this man / Is now become a god" and that "A man of such feeble temper should / So get the start of the majestic world." When we add to these considerations all that Shakespeare reveals to us regarding Cassius' personality, we have a solid basis for selecting appropriate uses of pitch and for coordinating pitch with other vocal and physical variables.

## EXERCISES

1. The following short story by a famous humorist is a delicate and meaningful expression of an urge that most of us have experienced. The stars (*) indicate some of the places where the meaning suggests changes of key. Probably you will find other places. Do not hesitate to make the changes very obvious. They will add to the humour as well as emphasize the startling underlying seriousness.

# A BOX TO HIDE IN

### JAMES THURBER

I waited till the large woman with the awful hat took up her sack of groceries and went out, peering at the tomatoes and lettuce on her way. The clerk asked me what mine was.

*"Have you got a box," I asked, "a large box? I want a box to hide in."

*"You want a box?" he asked.

*"I want a box to hide in," I said.

*"Whatta you mean?" he said. "You mean a big box?"

*I said I meant a big box, big enough to hold me.

*"I haven't got any boxes," he said. "Only cartons that cans come in."

*I tried several other groceries and none of them had a box big enough for me to hide in. There was nothing for it but to face life out. I didn't feel strong, and I'd had this overpowering desire to hide in a box for a long time.

*"Whatta you mean you want to hide in this box?" one grocer asked me.

*"It's a form of escape," I told him, "hiding in a box. It circumscribes your worries and the range of your anguish. You don't see people either."

*"How in the hell do you eat when you're in this box?" asked the grocer. "How in the hell do you get anything to eat?" *I said I had never been in a box and didn't know, but that that would take care of itself.

*"Well," he said, finally, "I haven't got any boxes, only some pasteboard cartons that cans come in."

*It was the same every place. I gave up when it got dark and the groceries closed, and hid in my room again. I turned out the light and lay on the bed. You feel better when it gets dark. *I could have hid in a closet, I suppose, but people are always opening doors. Somebody would find you in a closet. They would be startled and you'd have to tell them why you were in the closet. *Nobody pays any attention to a big box lying on the floor. You could stay in it for days and nobody'd think to look in it, not even the cleaning-woman.

*My cleaning-woman came the next morning and woke me up. I was still feeling bad. I asked her if she knew where I could get a large box.

*" How big a box you want?" she asked.

*"I want a box big enough for me to get inside of," I said. *She looked at me with big, dim eyes. There's something wrong with her glands. She's awful but she has a big heart, which makes it worse. She's unbearable, her husband is sick and her children are sick and she is sick too. *I got to thinking how pleasant it would be if I were in a box now, and didn't have to see her. I would be in a box right there in the room and she wouldn't know. I wondered if you have a desire to bark or laugh when someone who doesn't know walks by the box you are in. Maybe she would have a spell with her heart, if I did that, and would die right there. The officers and the elevatorman and Mr. Gramadge would find us. *"Funny doggone thing happened at the building last night," the doorman

would say to his wife. "I let in this woman to clean up 10-F and she never come out, see? She's never there more'n an hour, but she never come out, see? So when it got to be time for me to go off duty, why I says to Crennick, who was on the elevator, I says 'what the hell you suppose has happened to that woman cleans 10-F.' He says he didn't know; he says he never seen her after he took her up. So I spoke to Mr. Gramadge about it. *'I'm sorry to bother you, Mr. Gramadge,' I says 'but there's something funny about that woman cleans 10-F.' *So I told him. So he said we better have a look and we all three goes up and knocks on the door and rings the bell, see, and nobody answers so he said we'd have to walk in so Crennick opened the door and we walked in and here was this woman cleans the apartment dead as a herring on the floor and the gentleman that lives there was in a box.". . .

  *The cleaning-woman kept looking at me. It was hard to realize she wasn't dead. *"It's a form of escape," I murmured. *"What say?" she asked, dully.

  *"You don't know of any large packing boxes, do you?" I asked.

  *"No, I don't," she said.

  *I haven't found one yet, but I still have this overpowering urge to hide in a box. *Maybe it will go away, maybe I'll be all right. Maybe it will get worse. It's hard to say.

    2.  The first of these two poems by Walt Whitman would probably require considerable changes of key to express the " varied carols " of " America singing." The second poem, however, focuses primarily on a single " live-oak growing." Would it, therefore, call for a less varied use of pitch?

# I HEAR AMERICA SINGING

### WALT WHITMAN

I hear America singing, the varied carols I hear,
Those of mechanics, each one singing his as it should be blithe and strong,
The carpenter singing his as he measures his plank or beam,
The mason singing his as he makes ready for work, or leaves off work,
The boatman singing what belongs to him in his boat, the deckhand singing
    on the steamboat deck,
The shoemaker singing as he sits on his bench, the hatter singing as he stands,
The wood-cutter's song, the plowboy's on his way in the morning, or
    at noon intermission or at sundown,
The delicious singing of the mother, or of the young wife at work, or
    of the girl sewing or washing,
Each singing what belongs to him or her and to none else,
The day what belongs to the day—at night the party of young fellows,
    robust, friendly,
Singing with open mouths their strong melodious songs.

# I SAW IN LOUISIANA A LIVE-OAK GROWING

## WALT WHITMAN

I saw in Louisiana a live-oak growing,
All alone stood it and the moss hung down from the branches,
Without any companion it grew there uttering joyous leaves of dark green,
And its look, rude, unbending, lusty, made me think of myself,
But I wonder'd how it could utter joyous leaves standing alone there
    without its friend near, for I knew I could not,
And I broke off a twig with a certain number of leaves upon it, and
    twined around it a little moss,
And brought it away, and I have placed it in sight in my room,
It is not needed to remind me as of my own dear friends,
(For I believe lately I think of little else than of them,)
Yet it remains to me a curious token, it makes me think of manly love;
For all that, and though the live-oak glistens there in Louisiana solitary
    in a wide flat space,
Uttering joyous leaves all its life without a friend a lover near,
I know very well I could not.

    3. Consider how you might use various inflections inherent in the advice in the following poem. Be sure to notice that the first three stanzas issue commands to "Go listen," "think no more," and "Practice your beauty"; while the last stanza recounts a story of beauty that has faded.

# BLUE GIRLS

## JOHN CROWE RANSOM

Twirling your blue skirts, traveling the sward
Under the towers of your seminary,
Go listen to your teachers old and contrary
Without believing a word.

Tie the white fillets then about your lustrous hair
And think no more of what will come to pass
Than bluebirds that go walking on the grass
And chattering on the air.

Practice your beauty, blue girls, before it fail;
And I will cry with my loud lips and publish
Beauty which all our power shall never establish,
It is so frail.

For I could tell you a story which is true:
I know a lady with a terrible tongue,
Blear eyes fallen from blue,
All her perfections tarnished—and yet it is not long
Since she was lovelier than any of you.

# 12 *Audible Communication Through Quality*

If a musician in the next room were to produce the same pitch on a violin, saxophone, trombone, and clarinet in succession, you would have no difficulty in distinguishing the instruments. You know that each has a characteristic sound. If two of your friends in the same room were to sing the same note, you would have little difficulty in telling one voice from the other. Finally, if the two friends were to utter a sentence in the same key, volume, and tempo, you could easily tell which voice was which. In each instance the sound is distinguished by a characteristic *quality*, which you would have no trouble in recognizing.

The fundamental quality (or *timbre*) of a musical instrument cannot be changed. Try as you will, you can never make a tuba sound like a clarinet. Its construction destines it always to sound like a tuba. The human voice, however, is much more flexible and is capable of producing a wide range of different qualities. Our basic voices change constantly. A voice sounds different in illness than in health, different in anger than in joy, different in deference than in arrogance. Any kind of physical tension affects the voice. The sound of a voice varies with age, health, emotions, moods, and your attitudes toward what you say and to whom you speak. Within the framework of your basic vocal tone, your voice is many voices.

As performers, we must learn to control voice quality in keeping with the literary meaning of the moment. As artists, we need to learn certain skills; however, we will make sure that the skills do not call attention to themselves. In this instance the voice quality must always be motivated by responses to the literature, not by an obviously poor job of pretending.

## ORIGINS OF VOCAL QUALITY

The quality of an individual's voice, like pitch, is determined largely by hereditary and environmental factors. The physical makeup of the larynx and vocal folds inherited by a person, as well as the size and shape of the resonators (throat, mouth, and nose), govern the range of quality that is possible. Environment, too, plays a role, as the individual tends to assimilate features of voices he hears around him. If a mother and daughter sound much alike, it is probably because of both their similar physical features and their

*293*

common environment. Perhaps you have noticed that you begin saying words and phrases commonly used by someone with whom you spend much time. Somewhat more subtly, you probably assimilate some of the quality of the person's voice as well.

A third influence on the quality of your voice may be your ability to hear pleasing tones and to distinguish them from less pleasing ones. Perhaps an "ear for sound" is inherited. Certainly, "tone deafness" seems to be innate. But for most of us the ability to recognize pleasing vocal quality depends on acquaintance with such quality in vocal or instrumental music or in speech. Whatever the reasons, people vary considerably in their ability to discriminate between various qualities. One person may enjoy the performance of a symphony orchestra, while another cringes at the unbearably "sour" notes. Your recognition of pleasing quality does not insure that you will be able to produce similar sound, but it can be a helpful first step.

Unfortunately, these factors are to a great extent outside your conscious control insofar as the limits of an oral interpretation class are concerned. You can do very little about the length, size, and contour of your vocal folds. The correction of defective voice quality, either given to a person by birth or developed by bad habits, is the work of the speech pathologist or the voice and diction instructor, rather than the teacher of the oral interpretation of literature.

On the other hand, given a satisfactory voice, one can always improve the use of it through attention and effort. Good literature deserves as expressive a voice as you can bring to it.


## OPTIMUM QUALITY

When all dimensions of the speech production process operate in a harmonious balance, the result is a quality that is *optimum*. Naturally, the optimum quality for different persons will vary according to their unique physical characteristics. There are, however, certain features they should have in common: a full, resonant sound that is easy and pleasant to listen to; a sustained control that stems from efficient employment of the vocal mechanism; and a seemingly effortless production of speech. Most important, the optimum quality is inconspicuous. The voice does not call attention to itself for any reason. When an oral reader strives to achieve a quality that his vocal mechanism was not meant to produce, the voice sounds strained and artificial.

Vocal quality is important in securing and focusing listener attention. A speaker is simply more "listenable" when his vocal quality is pleasing and varied. It was this listenable quality that characterized the speaking of Franklin D. Roosevelt. The recordings of Dylan Thomas and Alexander Scourby are also distinguished by an especially effective quality of voice. If possible, arrange to hear one of their records, and recognize for yourself that the quality is primarily responsible for your careful listening. Your acquisition of optimum quality allows you comfortably to engage your audience's attention, and it provides a point of departure from which maximum flexibility is possible for the communication of attitude and emotion.

In order to understand vocal quality and to consider the improvement of your own, it may be helpful to more precisely understand the nature of *vocal tone* and its amplification through *resonance*. Optimum quality results from their efficient and cooperative interaction.

## VOCAL TONE

Vocal tone is the sound produced when the breath stream causes the vocal folds to vibrate and they in turn set the molecules of air in motion. Tone as perceived by the listener is the interpretation of these vibrations after they impinge upon his eardrum.

Many vibrators, such as violin strings and the vocal folds, are able to produce several modes of vibration simultaneously. The total result is a *tone complex*. It consists of the lowest audible pitch, called the *fundamental*, and additional frequencies produced as the vibrating body divides into halves, thirds, fourths, fifths, and so on. These additional frequencies, sounding above and simultaneously with the fundamental pitch, are called *overtones*. The halves involve vibration at twice the frequency of the whole vibrator, and produce a pitch one octave higher than the fundamental; the fourths, two octaves higher; and so forth. The tone complex is heard by the ear as a single pitch.

The fundamental, or the lowest frequency, is the one you hear consciously because it has the greatest amplitude. If we could remove all overtones and retain only the fundamental, we would be unable to distinguish the tones of the violin, saxophone, trombone, clarinet, and the human voice—provided, of course, that the same fundamental were being produced in each case. When we say that middle C on a perfectly tuned piano has 261.626 vibrations per second, we mean that the fundamental of that pitch has that many vibrations in one second. We know, however, that a violin and a trumpet, or often two pianos, differ in the quality of middle C. The reason is simple: each produces a different set of overtones simultaneously with the fundamental.

In the human voice, quality is determined not only by the purity of the vibrations produced in the larynx but, also, by their relative amplitudes and their harmonious relationships with each other. This pattern of overtones results primarily from physical traits beyond the control of the individual. Within the limits of your own speech mechanism, however, you can insure the best results by relaxed and controlled vibration of the vocal folds at your optimum pitch.

# RESONANCE

The second and more controllable aspect of quality in sound is *resonance*. The notes of some musical instruments differ in quality primarily because of resonance. It is the length and shape of the air column rather than the nature of the mouthpiece that is mainly responsible for the difference in the quality of the trumpet and the trombone. So it is also that the saxophone and clarinet produce different qualities because of different resonating chambers. Likewise, people's voices differ in quality because of different resonating chambers and different employment of them.

What is resonance? Perhaps it can best be explained by illustrations. Borrow from your speech, music, or physics instructor a tuning fork. Remove the fork from its sounding box and strike it hard enough to produce a loud tone. While the fork is still making sound, apply the shank to the top of a table or desk. The whole surface will pulsate, and the sound can be heard throughout a large room. The vibrations are transmitted directly to the sounding board in a process called *forced vibration*. The resonance of forced vibration is nonselective and merely amplifies the sound.

*Sympathetic vibration* can be demonstrated by sitting at the piano, depressing the " loud " pedal so that all strings are free to vibrate, and then singing various tones up and down the scale. Soon you will produce a tone that will easily set up audible sympathetic vibration in one of the strings. You have struck a pitch that corresponds to that of the string, and the sound waves have set the string in vibration.

So-called cavity resonance is in reality merely another manifestation of sympathetic vibration, but a slight distinction is possible. Cavity resonance is the concentration and reflection of sound waves. Take up the tuning fork again. Let us assume for convenience that it represents middle C. This time we will use a collection of bottles and jars of various shapes and sizes. If the collection is extensive, you will find at least one bottle or jar that will greatly amplify the tone when the vibrating fork is held over the opening. Now take a large jar with a relatively small opening, and, as you hold the vibrating fork over the opening, slowly pour water into the jar. As the volume of the open cavity in the jar diminishes, you will find a size that corresponds to the pitch of the fork.

If you had another fork that vibrated at twice the frequency of the first, you would have to use more water to reduce the size of the resonance cavity. The smaller cavity resonates the higher pitch. This principle is illustrated in the various resonating cavities of the marimba: long brass tubes for low tones, small and short ones for the high tones. Thus we are speaking of tuned resonance, which is selective.

Resonance is both amplification of sound and the mechanism by which a given combination of partials is selected for emphasis and subordination. It emphasizes some overtones and subordinates others. The frequencies to which the resonator is "in tune" pass freely; those to which the resonator is not "in tune" do not. It is selective transmission. The selectivity of the resonator is determined by its size, mass, and texture. Since the resonance capacity of the nose, mouth, and throat is variable, we can adjust our resonators so that they are "in tune" and, therefore, functioning at peak efficiency.

## VOCAL RESONANCE

To discover how resonance is employed in voice, produce a sustained monotone with your own vocal folds—say "ah"—and, without interrupting the flow of sound or changing the pitch, alter the sound to produce the following long vowel sounds.

e  [i]  (ee)
a  [e]  (ay)
o  [o]  (oh)
u  [u]  (oo)

The difference you hear in these four sounds is essentially one of resonance.

You may feel this resonance in your speech by applying your finger tips to certain parts of your body. Repeat aloud the first few words of the Gettysburg Address while you touch your forehead. Do the same things as you place your finger tips to the bridge of your nose, your teeth, your Adam's apple, and finally your ribs. The vibration you feel is resonance.

According to *Webster's Third New International Dictionary*, resonance is "the intensification and enrichment of a musical tone by supplementary vibration." Such intensification or amplification takes place in the air within cavities and on hard and soft surfaces. In the case of the tuning fork, resonance takes place in the box, its hollow interior, and its walls. When the vibrating fork is held over the partially filled glass of water, resonance occurs in the column of air and in the walls of the glass. In the human voice, resonance occurs theoretically in every cavity and surface of the body. Practically speaking, resonance takes place in the cavities and bones of the head, in the mouth, in the throat or pharynx, in their respective walls, and in the chest cavity and walls.

In the proper production of speech sounds, resonance plays a major role. In the formation of all vowel and diphthong sounds, the tongue and the palate serve to modify the shape and size of the oral resonance chamber. *Diphthongs* are combinations of two vowel sounds pronounced consecutively without a break in phonation. The so-called long "i" [aɪ] as in "ice" is such a sound. Resonance is not, however, confined to the formation of vowels and diphthongs. It is employed in the making of all voiced sounds, including the voiced consonants: b [b], m [m], w [w], v [v], th [ð], z [z], d [d], n [n], r [r], l [l], zh [ʒ], j [dʒ], y [j], g [g], ng [ŋ]. In these sounds, the role of resonance is primarily one of amplifying the sounds produced as the articulators change the shape of the oral cavity.

In order to complete the picture of vocal resonance, we must mention an additional specialized form without which normal speech is impossible. The consonants m [m], n [n], and ng [ŋ] are resonated in the nasal cavity. In fact, the major difference between the *m* and the *b*, the *n* and the *d*, and the *ng* and the *g*, is that the former in each instance is resonated nasally. If you will pronounce "come" and "cub," you will see that the same mouth positions are employed except that in "come" the passageway between the mouth and nose is kept open while in "cub" it is closed. Try the same experiment and you will recognize the same difference between "bun" and "bud" and "rang" and "rag." When this normal *nasal* resonance is not present for these consonants and their neighboring vowels, we speak of *denasal* speech. When you have a severe cold in your head, so that the nasal passages are blocked, your sentence "I am not going to come again" becomes "I ab dot goig to cub agaid." Usually the correction of such speech, whether it results from a cold infection or some more serious structural malformation, is achieved only through the removal of the blockage.

While a degree of nasal resonance is necessary for normal speech, we must hasten to observe that it can be, and often is, overdone. To "talk through your nose," as we say, is to overuse nasal resonance. Such speech is readily recognizable to the listener, but many of us have habitual *nasality* ourselves and often are not aware of it. Nasality is monotonous and unpleasant to the listener. You may discover whether you are guilty of such nasality by doing the following simple experiment. With thumb and forefinger pinch the bridge of your nose about where the supports of eyeglasses ordinarily rest. Now feel the resonance as you say the following sentence: "My nasal resonance is usually adequate." While speaking the first three words, you should feel much more vibration than during the last three. If you feel much vibration during all of the sentence, you may be sure that you employ an excessive amount of nasal resonance.

Nasality results from failure to reduce the opening between the mouth and the nasal cavity when making sounds other than m [m], n [n], and ng [ŋ]. In normal speech, except the formation of the three sounds just mentioned, the soft palate and the uvula rise and meet the back wall of the throat, which comes forward, almost to close off the nasal passages. When this closure is not adequate, the voice is nasal. Usually the condition can be corrected with persistent practice in the acceptable formation of sounds. Sometimes, however, structural difficulties must have the care of a surgeon. If you discover that you have a nasal voice and, if you can consciously reduce the nasality, you may be assured that persistent practice will result in diminishing it appreciably.

## VOCAL RESONANCE FOR PROJECTION

In Chapter 10 we observed that increasing the resonance of any sound results in its greater projection. Obviously you can enlarge the sound of the tuning fork by striking it with more force, but you can also enlarge it by attaching the sounding box. With the trumpet mouthpiece alone, you can produce any pitch you desire; but when you also use the rest of the instrument, you are able to project the tone by increasing the resonance.

So it is that vocal tones can be projected. Open your mouth and throat in a huge yawn to produce greater relaxation, greater resonance, and greater projection. If you relax your mouth, throat, and chest structures to provide a maximum opportunity for resonance, and if you employ a limited but not offensive degree of nasal resonance, coupled with adequate breath support, your speech tones will have an optimum projection.

Resonance not only contributes to projection, but it also enriches speech by amplifying harmonious overtones so that the resultant sound is more pleasing to the ear. Thus, resonation both enlarges and selectively shapes vocal tones for the projection of quality.

## KINDS OF VOCAL QUALITY AND THEIR USES

Quality is the most comprehensive indicator of an individual's physical characteristics, environmental influences, and emotions. The oral interpreter should employ an optimum quality as a point of departure, but he will deviate considerably in response to the many subtle changes of attitude and feeling in a work of literature. In the days of the elocutionist, the student made a catalogue of these vocal qualities and learned to apply them on demand. We know today that any classification of vocal qualities is about the least scientific aspect of voice work, because the significance of quality depends on the subjective reaction of the listener. Who can say how another will react to the taste of okra? Who can say that a certain vocal quality will positively produce a certain reaction in a listener? Although we no longer believe that vocal qualities can be adequately categorized and used on demand, it is often helpful for the student to learn to recognize a few basic types of voices.

**Breathy.** In the employment of this kind of vocal quality, the vocal folds fail to approximate along their entire length, and so there is a mixture of vibrating and nonvibrating air. The whisper is the extreme of this quality.

Sometimes a *breathy* quality is used to express a confidential manner. It is also employed to communicate fear, surprise, or even horror. In reading Poe's " The Cask of Amontillado," you might want in some places to use such a vocal quality. After the vengeful Montressor has entombed Fortunato alive in a remote recess of the catacombs, the victim suddenly sheds his drunkenness and in mortal terror calls, "For the love of God, Montressor!" This line might require a *breathy* quality or "stage whisper."

**Throaty.**   When the breath stream is forced roughly between tense vocal folds and through a tense pharynx, the result is a harsh quality we call *throaty* or guttural. It is frequently expressive of coarseness, crudity, or roughness. Occasionally you find a brutish, Frankensteinian character who will be best expressed with this quality. For example, if in Shakespeare's *The Tempest* you were reading the following lines spoken by Caliban, the savage and deformed slave, you might speak with a throaty quality:

As wicked dew as e'er my mother brush'd
With raven's feather from unwholesome fen,
Drop on you both! a south-west blow on ye,
And blister you all o'er.

You might use a little less of much the same quality in reading the following speech of Captain Keeney in Eugene O'Neill's *Ile:*

Hell! I got to git the ile, I tell you . . .
I got to get me the ile! I got to git it
in spite of all hell, and I ain't agoin' home
till I do git it!

To a much more limited degree you might use some *throaty* quality in these lines from "The Man with the Hoe" by Edwin Markham.

Down all the caverns of Hell to their last gulf
There is no shape more terrible than this—

Frequently an isolated word or phrase will be best expressed with a touch of throaty quality. Because of sound combinations and connotations, some words require a bit of this quality for normal utterance. Practice the following as examples: *gruesome, gruff, grumble, awful, horror.*

**Hollow.**   When you have a maximum of pharyngeal resonance you can produce a *hollow*, barrel-sounding quality. Sometimes we call it a funereal or sepulchral tone. It often suggests remoteness or morbidity. Readers and actors use it for such characters as the ghost in *Hamlet* and Marley's ghost in *A Christmas Carol* by Charles Dickens. Some readers make limited use of this quality in the following lines from "Break, Break, Break" by Alfred, Lord Tennyson.

Break, break, break,
   On thy cold gray stones, O Sea!

And I would that my tongue could utter
  The thoughts that arise in me.

" The Laughers " by Louis Untermeyer, which is included in the exercises at
the end of Chapter 10, may in places need some *hollow* quality for full
communication. Look up these lines in that poem and see if you agree.

A grisly quiet with the power to choke;
A quiet that only one thing broke;
One thing alone rose up thereafter. . . .
Laughter.

**Nasal.** The twangy sound produced by too much *nasal* resonance often
expresses ignorance or rusticity, and is frequently used to suggest a humorous
response. The whine, which may indicate an ingratiating attitude, is nasality
coupled with slow rate of utterance and prolonged duration of sounds. The
*nasal* quality should be used with great discretion.

**Denasal.** Earlier in this chapter we recognized that the absence of nasal
resonance, especially on m [m], n [n], and ng [ŋ], produces a *denasal* quality.
Of course, this quality is most immediately suggestive of some nasal stoppage,
but is sometimes used to indicate stupidity. It may be useful for humor, but
even for that purpose it should very seldom be employed.

**Oral.** When resonance is held to a bare minimum and is kept largely in
the mouth, the result is a relatively weak, confined quality that we call *oral*.
When the speaker or reader wishes to convey quietness, gentleness, weakness, fatigue, illness, or age, this quality may be an effective one to use. It is
frequently employed when circumstances permit doing so without loss of
audibility. Try reading the following poem with an *oral* quality.

## I'M NOBODY

EMILY DICKINSON

I'm nobody! Who are you?
  Are you nobody, too?
Then there's a pair of us—don't tell!
  They'd banish us, you know.

How dreary to be somebody!
  How public like a frog
To tell your name the livelong day
  To an admiring bog!

**Falsetto.** Etymologically, *falsetto* may be translated as "little false voice." The falsetto is thin, shrill, and unnaturally high. It is uttered with the glottis completely closed at the front.

It is also sometimes employed for broad comic effect. In serious reading or speaking it occasionally characterizes great wonder or surprise. It is also sometimes used to a very limited extent in distinguishing voices in comic dialogue, but only the broadest farce!

**Tremulous.** Voice in which the force and resonance are uncertainly maintained in a wavering pattern is generally designated as *tremulous*. It seems to suggest extreme uncertainty, perhaps great pain or great age. It may sometimes be used in the portions of dialogue that are meant to communicate these conditions. Used discretely, it may sometimes be meaningful in the reading of delicate verse. When used generously, it results in melodrama.

**Full.** If both the volume and the resonance of the normal tone are increased, a speaker or reader may produce a so-called *full* quality. This quality is often thought to be suggestive of dignity and confidence, but may easily degenerate into the melodramatic. When we speak disparagingly of "ministerial tone," this quality is usually what we mean. The *full* quality is frequently necessary, but its excessive use will appear unnatural. (The nineteenth-century elocutionist cultivated this quality and called it "orotund.")

Other words we could use to describe vocal quality are *sharp, metallic, harsh, bored, tired,* and *passionate,* to mention only a few. Hundreds of adjectives are available to describe particular voices; however, these may well refer only to special uses of the vocal qualities already described. For example, the breathy quality may suggest passion.

## Use of Voice Quality in Communication

By striving to achieve your own optimum quality and experimenting with other types of vocal quality, you should gain increased command of a vitally important aspect of communicative speech. The more varied the types of quality you are able to produce, the greater the range of your expressive potential. During the performance of a specific literary work, however, the employment of quality should reflect adherence to one simple principle: *to feel like is to sound like.* The teacher of acting speaks of *kinesthetic* tone, telling the player that any particular word, "rose" for example, lacks real significance until its utterance gives some intimation of the speaker's feelings toward the entity being named. Feelings involve an inclination to do something about the entity—to seek it, to avoid it, to foster it, to sense it more fully, or to eliminate it from the mind. Whatever mental, emotional, and bodily activity is implicit in the speaker as he says the word is reflected in the quality of the sound of the word. Thus it is that whatever imagery is being experienced by the speaker will be shown in the quality of voice. If you feel scared, you will sound scared. If you wish to convey fright in reading, you must recall at least the image of fear. To convey anger in reading, you must recall the image of anger. So it is with any emotion: First feel it, and then you can express it—provided, of course, you have the faculty for doing so.

Because of the principle *to feel like is to sound like*, vocal quality must ever spring from within the reader. Quality should always result from intellectual and emotional stimulation. To impose a specific quality is to create the artificiality we deplore in the elocutionist and the ham. Furthermore, the imposition of vocal quality without comprehension inevitably calls attention to the vocal technique and not to the meaning.

When you read aloud to others, adjust all your body tensions to the nature of the meaning being expressed. Feel the meaning with all of yourself, down to your finger tips. When you have succeeded in doing so, your most suitable vocal quality is most likely to ensue.

## EXERCISES

1. Read aloud the following words, holding the nasals for full resonance:

| rang | tongue | win   | mass | hymn  |
|------|--------|-------|------|-------|
| sang | clung  | bone  | main | rhyme |
| bang | ran    | cone  | made | time  |
| ring | ban    | flown | dam  | dime  |

2. Practice reading the following story, using loudness, pitch, time, and quality to achieve a maximum communication of meaning. (If possible, listen to Charles Laughton's recording of this passage and note the many voice qualities he uses.)

### THE FIERY FURNACE

DANIEL 3:1–30, KING JAMES VERSION

1  Nebuchadnezzar the king made an image of gold, whose height was three-score cubits, and the breadth thereof six cubits: he set it up in the plain of Dura, in the province of Babylon.

2  Then Nebuchadnezzar the king sent to gather together the princes, the governors, and the captains, the judges, the treasurers, the counsellors, the sheriffs, and all the rulers of the provinces, to come to the dedication of the image which Nebuchadnezzar the king had set up.

3   Then the princes, the governors, and captains, the judges, the treasurers, the counsellors, the sheriffs, and all the rulers of the provinces, were gathered together unto the dedication of the image that Nebuchadnezzar had set up, and they stood before the image that Nebuchadnezzar had set up.

4   Then an herald cried aloud, To you it is commanded, O people, nations, and languages,

5   That at what time ye hear the sound of the cornet, flute, harp, sackbut, psaltery, dulcimer, and all kinds of musick, ye fall down and worship the golden image that Nebuchadnezzar the king hath set up:

6   And whoso falleth not down and worshippeth shall the same hour be cast into the midst of a burning fiery furnace.

7   Therefore at that time, when all the people heard the sound of the cornet, flute, harp, sackbut, psaltery, dulcimer, and all kinds of musick, all the people, the nations, and the languages fell down and worshipped the golden image that Nebuchadnezzar the king had set up.

8   Wherefore at that time certain Chaldeans came near, and accused the Jews.

9   They spake and said to the king Nebuchadnezzar, O king, live for ever.

10   Thou, O king, hast made a decree, that every man that shall hear the sound of the cornet, flute, harp, sackbut, psaltery, and dulcimer, and all kinds of musick, shall fall down and worship the golden image:

11   And whoso falleth not down and worshippeth, that he should be cast into the midst of a burning fiery furnace.

12   There are certain Jews whom thou hast set over the affairs of the province of Babylon, Shadrach, Meshach, and Abednego; these men, O king, have not regarded thee: they serve not thy gods, nor worship the golden image which thou hast set up.

13   Then Nebuchadnezzar in his rage and fury commanded to bring Shadrach, Meshach, and Abednego. Then they brought these men before the king.

14   Nebuchadnezzar spake and said unto them, Is it true, O Shadrach, Meshach, and Abednego, do not ye serve my gods, nor worship the golden image which I have set up?

15   Now if ye be ready that at what time ye hear the sound of the cornet, flute, harp, sackbut, psaltery, and dulcimer, and all kinds of musick, ye fall down and worship the image which I have made; well: but if ye worship not, ye shall be cast the same hour into the midst of a burning fiery furnace; and who is that God that shall deliver you out of my hands?

16   Shadrach, Meshach, and Abednego, answered and said to the king, O Nebuchadnezzar, we are not careful to answer thee in this matter.

17   If it be so, our God whom we serve is able to deliver us from the burning fiery furnace, and he will deliver us out of thine hand, O king.

18   But if not, be it known unto thee, O king, that we will not serve thy gods, nor worship the golden image which thou hast set up.

19   Then was Nebuchadnezzar full of fury, and the form of his visage was

changed against Shadrach, Meshach, and Abednego: therefore he spake, and commanded that they should heat the furnace seven times more than it was wont to be heated.

20 And he commanded the most mighty men that were in his army to bind Shadrach, Meshach, and Abednego, and to cast them into the burning fiery furnace.

21 Then these men were bound in their coats, their hosen, and their hats, and their other garments, and were cast into the midst of the burning fiery furnace.

22 Therefore because the king's commandment was urgent, and the furnace exceeding hot, the flame of the fire slew those men that took up Shadrach, Meshach, and Abednego.

23 And these three men, Shadrach, Meshach, and Abednego, fell down bound into the midst of the burning fiery furnace.

24 Then Nebuchadnezzar the king was astonished, and rose up in haste, and spake, and said unto his counsellors, Did not we cast three men bound into the midst of the fire? They answered and said unto the king, True, O king.

25 He answered and said, Lo, I see four men loose, walking in the midst of the fire, and they have no hurt; and the form of the fourth is like the Son of God.

26 Then Nebuchadnezzar came near to the mouth of the burning fiery furnace, and spake, and said, Shadrach, Meshach, and Abednego, ye servants of the most high God, come forth, and come hither. Then Shadrach, Meshach, and Abednego, came forth out of the midst of the fire.

27 And the princes, governors, and captains, and the king's counsellors, being gathered together, saw these men, upon whose bodies the fire had no power, nor was an hair of their head singed, neither were their coats changed, nor the smell of fire had passed on them.

28 Then Nebuchadnezzar spake, and said, Blessed be the God of Shadrach, Meshach, and Abednego, who hath sent his angel, and delivered his servants that trusted in him, and have changed the king's word, and yielded their bodies, that they might not serve nor worship any god, except their own God.

29 Therefore I make a decree, That every people, nation, and language, which speak anything amiss against the God of Shadrach, Meshach, and Abednego, shall be cut in pieces, and their houses shall be made a dunghill: because there is no other God that can deliver after this sort.

30 Then the king promoted Shadrach, Meshach, and Abednego, in the province of Babylon.

3. This excerpt from a famous play requires many changes in vocal quality in order to express the meaning. The character whose lines we are quoting is valiant and romantic in the extreme, but he is desperately sensitive about the length of his enormous nose. Read the play to appreciate fully Cyrano's personality. Listen to José Ferrer's recording if possible. Practice

reading aloud the " Nose Speech " with such vocal qualities as best express the meaning. Cyrano is telling a fool how he might have been clever in insulting Cyrano's nose.

## *from* CYRANO DE BERGERAC

EDMOND ROSTAND

CYRANO:    Ah, no, young sir!
   You are too simple. Why, you might have said—
   Oh, a great many things! Mon dieu, why waste
   Your opportunity? For example, thus:—
   [*Aggressive*]  I, sir, if that nose were mine,
   I'd have it amputated—on the spot!
   [*Friendly*]  How do you drink with such a nose?
   You ought to have a cup made specially.
   [*Descriptive*]  'Tis a rock—a crag—a cape—
   A cape? say rather, a peninsula!
   [*Inquisitive*]  What is that receptacle—
   A razor-case or a portfolio?
   [*Kindly*]  Ah, do you love the little birds
   So much that when they come and sing to you,
   You give them this to perch on?  [*Insolent*]
   Sir, when you smoke, the neighbors must suppose
   Your chimney is on fire.  [*Cautious*]  Take care—
   A weight like that might make you topheavy.
   [*Thoughtful*]  Somebody fetch my parasol—
   Those delicate colors fade so in the sun!
   [*Pedantic*]  Does not Aristophanes
   Mention a mythologic monster called
   Hippocampelephantocamelos?
   Surely we have here the original!
   [*Familiar*]  Well, old torchlight! Hang your hat
   Over that chandelier—it hurts my eyes.
   [*Eloquent*]  When it blows, the typhoon howls,
   And the clouds darken.  [*Dramatic*]  When it bleeds—
   The Red Sea!  [*Enterprising*]  What a sign
   For some perfumer!  [*Lyric*]  Hark—the horn
   Of Roland calls to summon Charlemagne!—
   [*Simple*]  When do they unveil the monument?
   [*Respectful*]  Sir, I recognize in you
   A man of parts, a man of prominence—
   [*Rustic*]  Hey? What? Call that a nose? Na, na—
   I be no fool like what you think I be—

That there's a blue cucumber!   [*Military*]
Point against cavalry!   [*Practical*]   Why not
A lottery with this for the grand prize?
Or—parodying Faustus in the play—
"Was this the nose that launched a thousand ships
And burned the topless towers of Ilium?"
These, my dear sir, are things you might have said
Had you some tinge of letters, or of wit
To color your discourse. But wit,—not so,
You never had an atom—and of letters,
You need but three to write you down—an Ass.
Moreover,—if you had the invention, here
Before these folk to make a jest of me—
Be sure you would not then articulate
The twentieth part of half a syllable
Of the beginning! For I say these things
Lightly enough myself, about myself,
But I allow none else to utter them.

4.  Experiment with a wide range of qualities that match the spirit of the following humorous verse. In private, try out extremes that may contribute to the humor, but be selective.

## THE CLEAN PLATTER

OGDEN NASH

Some painters paint the sapphire sea,
And some the fathering storm.
Others portray young lambs at play,
But most, the female form.
'Twas trite in that primeval dawn
When painting got its start,
That a lady with her garments on
Is Life, but is she Art?
By undraped nymphs
I am not wooed;
I'd rather painters painted food.

Food,
Yes, food,
Just any old kind of food.
Pooh for the cook,
And pooh for the price!

Some of it's nicer, but all of it's nice.
Pheasant is pleasant, of course,
And terrapin, too, is tasty,
Lobster I freely endorse,
In pâté or patty or pasty.
But there's nothing the matter with butter,
And nothing the matter with jam,
And the warmest of greetings I utter
To the ham and yam and clam.
For they're food,
All food
And I think very highly of food.
Though I am broody at times
When bothered by rhymes,
I brood
On food.

Food,
Just food,
Just any old kind of food.
Let it be sour,
Or let it be sweet,
As long as you're sure it is something to eat.
Go purloin a sirloin, my pet,
If you'd win a devotion incredible;
And asparagus tips vinaigrette,
Or anything else that is edible.
Bring salad or sausage or scrapple,
A berry or even a beet,
Bring an oyster, an egg, or an apple,
As long as it's something to eat.
For it's food,
It's food;
Never mind what kind of food.
Through thick and through thin
I am constantly in
The mood
For food.

Some singers sing of ladies' eyes,
And some of ladies' lips,
Refined ones praise their ladylike ways,
And coarse ones hymn their hips.
The Oxford Book of English Verse

Is lush with lyrics tender;
A poet, I guess, is more or less,
Preoccupied with gender.
Yet I, though custom call me crude,
Prefer to sing in praise of food.

5. The speakers in these next four poems are vague and abstract, yet the attitudes presented are vivid. Careful use of vocal quality can convey these attitudes while preserving the universality of the poems.

## FOUR POEMS

STEPHEN CRANE

I

In the desert
I saw a creature, naked, bestial,
Who, squatting upon the ground,
Held his heart in his hands,
And ate of it.
I said, 'Is it good, friend?'
'It is bitter—bitter,' he answered;
'But I like it
Because it is bitter,
And because it is my heart.'

II

Once there came a man
Who said,
'Range me all men of the world in rows.'
And instantly
There was terrific clamour among the people
Against being ranged in rows.
There was a loud quarrel, world-wide.
It endured for ages;
And blood was shed
By those who would not stand in rows,
And by those who pined to stand in rows.
Eventually, the man went to death, weeping.
And those who stayed in bloody scuffle
Knew not the great simplicity.

III

A man said to the universe:
'Sir, I exist!'

'However,' replied the universe,
'The fact has not created in me
A sense of obligation.'


    IV
A man adrift on a slim spar
A horizon smaller than the rim of a bottle
Tented waves rearing lashy dark points
The near whine of froth in circles.

                              God is cold.


The incessant raise and swing of the sea
And growl after growl of crest
The sinkings, green, seething, endless
The upheaval half-completed.

                              God is cold.


The seas are in the hollow of The Hand;
Oceans may be turned to a spray
Raining down through the stars
Because of a gesture of pity toward a babe.
Oceans may become grey ashes,
Die with a long moan and a roar
Amid the tumult of the fishes
And the cries of the ships,
Because The Hand beckons the mice.
A horizon smaller than a doomed assassin's cap,
Inky, surging tumults
A reeling, drunken sky and no sky
A pale hand sliding from a polished spar.

                              God is cold.


The puff of a coat imprisoning air:
A face kissing the water-death
A weary slow sway of a lost hand
And the sea, the moving sea, the sea.

                              God is cold.


    6. As you read the following short story, notice how it seems to direct a
change in vocal quality from the opening portion to the close. Very possibly,
a breathy quality might be used in the last two paragraphs in response to the
narrator's strong identification with Tergvinder's peace.

# TERGVINDER'S STONE

### W. S. MERWIN

One time my friend Tergvinder brought a large round boulder into his living room. He rolled it up the steps with the help of some two-by-fours, and when he got it out into the middle of the room, where some people have coffee tables (though he had never had one there himself) he left it. He said that was where it belonged.

It is really a plain-looking stone. Not as large as Plymouth Rock by a great deal, but then it does not have all the claims of a big shaky promotion campaign to support. That was one of the things Tergvinder said about it. He made no claims at all for it, he said. It was other people who called it Tergvinder's Stone. All he said was that according to him it belonged there.

His dog took to peeing on it, which created a problem (Tergvinder had not moved the carpet before he got the stone to where he said it belonged). Their tomcat took to squirting it, too. His wife fell over it quite often at first and it did not help their already strained marriage. Tergvinder said there was nothing to be done about it. It was in the order of things. That was a phrase he seldom employed, and never when he conceived that there was any room left for doubt.

He confided in me that he often woke in the middle of the night, troubled by the ancient, nameless ills of the planet, and got up quietly not to wake his wife, and walked through the house naked, without turning on any lights. He said that at such times he found himself listening, listening, aware of how some shapes in the darkness emitted low sounds like breathing, as they never did by day. He said he had become aware of a hole in the darkness in the middle of the living room, and out of that hole a breathing, a mournful dissatisfied sound of an absence waiting for what belonged to it, for something it had never seen and could not conceive of, but without which it could not rest. It was a sound, Tergvinder said, that touched him with fellow-feeling, and he had undertaken—oh, without saying anything to anybody—to assuage, if he could, that wordless longing that seemed always on the verge of despair. How to do it was another matter, and for months he had circled the problem, night and day, without apparently coming any closer to a solution. Then one day he had seen the stone. It had been there all the time at the bottom of his drive, he said, and he had never really seen it. Never recognized it for what it was. The nearer to the house he had got it, the more certain he had become. The stone had rolled into its present place like a lost loved one falling into arms that had long ached for it.

Tergvinder says that now on nights when he walks through the dark house he comes and stands in the living room doorway and listens to the peace in the middle of the floor. He knows its size, its weight, the touch of it, something of what is thought of it. He knows that it is peace. As he listens, some hint of that peace touches him too. Often, after a while, he steps down into the living room and goes and kneels beside the stone and they converse for hours in silence—a silence broken only by the sound of his own breathing.

7. The following short story is a vivid satirical commentary on commercialization of sentimentality. Perhaps you would call it melodrama. Although it is to be read as if serious, the listener must always remember that it is ridiculous. Constant attention to both vocal quality and inflections will serve to depict the significance to the listener.

## A DEATH IN THE STADIUM

ROBERT NATHAN

My friend approached me with these words: "How are you?" Before I could reply, he exclaimed: "I am on my way to attend the public death of Principus, the great actor, at the stadium. Come, we will go together, for it is sure to be an interesting spectacle." And he added: "He was the greatest actor in the world."

I turned and went with him, for I had heard of this affair. Indeed, it seemed as if the whole city were hurrying in that direction; nevertheless, we managed to squeeze ourselves into the subway. As we jogged slowly up-town, with many stops and waits, my friend told me a little more about Principus, whose death was convulsing the entire nation. "He was a great hero. Now he is dying; with a showman's instinct, and also in order to provide for his family, he has determined to die in public, comforted during his last moments by the groans of his admirers."

It was a peaceful evening; the roof-tops of the city towered upward into the sky stained by the sunset and lighted by a few pale stars. The great actor lay dying in a field ordinarily given over to prize-fights or baseball, and rented or this occasion; the seats which rose in concrete tiers all about him were entirely filled, while crowds of men and women at the gates gazed with gloomy interest at the ushers, who gazed back at them with a lofty expression.

After some delay, due to the crowds, we bought our tickets, and also two small straw mats to sit on, and ascended to our seats. Next to us sat an Englishman, an aquaintance of my friend's. "How do you do?" he said; "this is extraordinary."

The death-bed was in the center of the field, under a bright light, and surrounded by doctors, nurses, reporters, and newspaper photographers. We were a little late; when we arrived, the mayor had already been there: assisted by the doctors, he had given Principus the first injection of strychnine, after which he had retired amid applause. Thereafter the dying man had received visits from the Fire Commissioner, a committee from the Actor's Equity, three State Senators, and a Mr. Cohen, of Hollywood. The President of the United States had been invited, and had sent a small cake.

The audience gazed at the dying man with anxious enthusiasm. Now and then a sigh, like a gust of wind on a hill, rippled up and down the aisles where venders of lemonade, peanuts, sausages, and pennants moved about, calling their wares. On the pennants, which were arranged with black mourning borders, were printed the names of the most important plays in which Principus had taken the part of hero. Spectators bought their favorites, and waved them at the dying man.

"Ah!" they cried. "Oh!"

"Principus."

"Don't let them kill you."

And they shouted advice, interspersed with jeers at the doctors.

Suddenly, in the row in front of us, a man stood up, and turned around to glare at me. "I am a friend of his," he exclaimed with energy. "I am also a member of the Rotary Club of Syracuse, N.Y. Who are you pushing?"

"Nobody," I answered firmly; and after some hesitation he sat down again.

The Englishman gave me a gloomy glance. "The trouble with America," he said, "is that you do nothing original. This reminds me of the ancient festivals at Rome under Diocletian. You are always borrowing something. Why don't you strike out for yourself?"

He had hardly finished speaking when a woman rose in her seat in a far corner of the stadium, gave a scream and fell forward on her face. At once there was a rush for her, she was lifted up, examined by some police matrons, photographed, and her name and address taken; after which she was carried out, with an expression of satisfaction on her face. A moment later, in another part of the great circle, another woman repeated this performance. She also was photographed and carried out, looking very pleased. As a result of this incident, all over the stadium women rose screaming, and fell in various attitudes, some with their noses pointed to the sky, others on their stomachs. These, however, were left where they fell, and presently got up again and sat down, waving their flags.

"You Americans," said the Briton, "you are like everybody else. Why should I watch this sort of thing, which was done very much better by the Druids in England centuries ago?" And leaning forward with a strained expression, he shouted: "Look here, are you going to die, or not?"

The sick actor lay gazing at his public with weary eyes. In the bright light above his bed, he looked pale and thin; I wondered how it felt to die. The doctors moved anxiously about the bedside, conferring with the nurses and with each other; but they did not seem to agree with each other, or to notice the cheers with which the audience greeted each bulletin, regardless of its content.

An hour later extras were for sale in the aisles. "Woman Swoons at Principus Death," shouted the newsboys. "All about the big death." These editions already had photographs of the first woman to faint, whose pet name was Pinky. The Englishman bought one.

"We also," he observed, "have women in England."

"They have also been known to faint."

The man in front of us looked back at him angrily. "This is the largest death," he said, "there has ever been."

"It is a triumph," agreed my friend.

All at once a hush fell upon the stadium. All eyes were directed at the doctors; huddled around the bedside of the dying actor, they made it plain by their expressions that a crisis had arrived. The audience held its breath; the lemonade venders were silent. At last the head doctor stepped back, and held up his hand. Pale, but with a noble look, he exclaimed: "He will live."

A few cheers broke out, but they were immediately drowned in a storm of hisses. Men and women rose to their feet; flags were waved, peanuts, sausages, and pop bottles were hurled at the doctors and at the dying man. "We want to see him die," shouted the crowds who had bought tickets for this event. Led by the two women who had been photographed, they broke into jeers and catcalls.

"Cowards," they shrieked; "idiots."

"Let us have some new doctors."

The dying man raised himself warily; he seemed to be searching for the sky, already dark with night. His eyes scanned with amazement the stormy sea of faces around him and above him. The desire of so many people for his death descended upon him in an overwhelming compulsion, fell upon him in an irresistible wave; with a sigh he lay down and died. At once flashlights went off, a procession was formed with Pinky at the head, and pieces of the bed were broken off for souvenirs. Several men threw their hats into the air; and an old woman who happened to fall down in the excitement, was trampled upon.

"We also die in England," said the Englishman bitterly. "Can't you be original?"

And he went home, first stopping to buy a small piece of cotton cloth from the death-sheet of Principus, the world's greatest lover.

# Four

## Interpreting the Basic Forms of Literature

# 13 Suggestions on the Interpretative Reading of Prose

*Good Heavens! For more than forty years I have been speaking prose without knowing it.*

So speaks a character in Molière's play *The Would-Be Gentleman*. Though we all speak prose, we usually have not stopped to think about it as we have considered other forms of verbal expression. Definitions of prose almost always employ such words as " ordinary " or " commonplace." They describe prose as the kind of language we use in speaking and writing. As a result, we probably assume that the author of prose literature creates something inferior, compared to writers of such unordinary or uncommon forms as verse and poetry. Not so! A prominent poet once said in the authors' presence that the reason he writes poetry is that he doesn't have time to write prose! He meant that while prose writing necessarily consumes long periods of writing time, he can compose a line of verse while walking to work, write it on an envelope, stick it in his pocket, take it out a week later, write a line to follow it while waiting in the dentist's outer office, and perhaps " make a poem " in a week, a month, or a year, but in convenient time periods that were otherwise wasted moments. George Bernard Shaw, a magnificent writer of prose plays, once wrote a blank verse burlesque of blank verse plays. Then, he wrote to his public:

It may be asked why I wrote the Admirable Bashville in blank verse. My answer is that the operation of the copyright law of that time . . . left me only a week to write it in. Blank verse is so childishly easy and expedient (hence, by the way, Shakespear's copious output), that by adopting it I was enabled to do within the week what would have cost me a month in prose.[1]

To Shaw, verse was nothing to be worshipped just because it was verse, and prose was a form of writing that required real skill. We are not suggesting that prose is better than verse. We are contending that it is not to be considered inferior to any other form, just because of its *form*. Either prose or verse may range from the trivial to the poetic. Writings include not only mundane letters but also beautiful ones; not only common diaries but also

[1] Bernard Shaw, Preface to *The Admirable Bashville* published in *Bernard Shaw: Collected Plays with their Prefaces*, Vol. II, New York: Dodd, Mead & Company, 1971, p. 433.

eloquent ones; not only ordinary run-of-the-mill newspaper and magazine articles but also expository passages of the most inspired sort; not only corny jokes to be quickly forgotten but also memorable humorous essays and sketches; not only crass commercials but also eloquent public speeches; and not only cheap stories but the greatest narrative fiction. Oral interpreters are interested in the best of each type of prose. Each is different, and each has its own problems for oral interpretation.

According to Jeremy Bentham, prose is characterized by lines which run to the margin, while in verse "some of them fall short!" Prose is arranged in sentences and paragraphs, not lines and stanzas. Prose can contain anything verse can. As we have suggested, the better prose is, the more it possesses poetic qualities. We shall say more about this matter in the following chapter.

Some prose serves us in everyday spontaneous communication, such as conversation, where language is used to exchange information or just to pass the time of day. Prose also serves more exciting functions such as the recording of human events in journalism and history. Still other prose is instructional, or inspirational, or both, such as the works of the anthropologist Loren Eiseley. Read this one:

## *from* THE BIRD AND THE MACHINE
## Taken from *The Immense Journey*

LOREN EISELEY

Everything worked perfectly except for one detail—I didn't know what kind of birds were there. I never thought about it at all, and it wouldn't have mattered if I had. My orders were to get something interesting. I snapped on the flash and sure enough there was a great beating and feathers flying, but instead of my having them, they, or rather he, had me. He had my hand, that is, and for a small hawk not much bigger than my fist he was doing all right. I heard him give one short metallic cry when the light went on and my hand descended on the bird beside him; after that he was busy with his claws and his beak was sunk in my thumb. In the struggle I knocked the lamp over on the shelf, and his mate got her sight back and whisked neatly through the hole in the roof and off among the stars outside. It all happened in fifteen seconds and you might think I would have fallen down the ladder, but no, I had a professional assassin's reputation to keep up, and the bird, of course, made the mistake of thinking the hand was the enemy and not the eyes behind it. He chewed my thumb up pretty effectively and lacerated my hand with his claws, but in the end I got him, having two hands to work with.

He was a sparrow hawk and a fine young male in the prime of life. I was sorry not to catch the pair of them, but as I dripped blood and folded his wings carefully, holding him by the back so that he couldn't strike again, I had to admit the two of them might have been more than I could have handled under the circumstances. The little fellow had saved his mate by diverting me, and that was that. He was born to it, and made no outcry now, resting in my hand hopelessly, but peering toward me in the shadows behind the lamp with a fierce, almost indifferent glance. He neither gave nor expected mercy and something out of the high air passed from him to me, stirring a faint embarrassment.

I quit looking into that eye and managed to get my huge carcass with its fist full of prey back down the ladder. I put the bird in a box too small to allow him to injure himself by struggle and walked out to welcome the arriving trucks. It had been a long day, and camp still to make in the darkness. In the morning that bird would be just another episode. He would go back with the bones in the truck to a small cage in a city where he would spend the rest of his life. And a good thing, too. I sucked my aching thumb and spat out some blood. An assassin has to get used to these things. I had a professional reputation to keep up.

In the morning, with the change that comes on suddenly in that high country, the mist that had hovered below us in the valley was gone. The sky was a deep blue, and one could see for miles over the high outcroppings of stone. I was up early and brought the box in which the little hawk was imprisoned out onto the grass where I was building a cage. A wind as cool as a mountain spring ran over the grass and stirred my hair. It was a fine day to be alive. I looked up and all around and at the hole in the cabin roof out of which the other little hawk had fled. There was no sign of her anywhere that I could see.

"Probably in the next county by now," I thought cynically, but before beginning work I decided I'd have a look at my last night's capture.

Secretively, I looked again all around the camp and up and down and opened the box. I got him right out in my hand with his wings folded properly and I was careful not to startle him. He lay limp in my grasp and I could feel his heart pound under the feathers but he only looked beyond me and up.

I saw him look that last look away beyond me into a sky so full of light that I could not follow his gaze. The little breeze flowed over me again, and nearby a mountain aspen shook all its tiny leaves. I suppose I must have had an idea then of what I was going to do, but I never let it come up into consciousness. I just reached over and laid the hawk on the grass.

He lay there a long minute without hope, unmoving, his eyes still fixed on that blue vault above him. It must have been that he was already so far away in heart that he never felt the release from my hand. He never even stood. He just lay with his breast against the grass.

In the next second after that long minute he was gone. Like a flicker of light, he had vanished with my eyes full on him, but without actually seeing even a premonitory wing beat. He was gone straight into that towering emptiness of light and crystal that my eyes could scarcely bear to penetrate. For another long moment there was silence. I could not see him. The light was too intense. Then from far up somewhere a cry came ringing down.

I was young then and had seen little of the world, but when I heard that cry my heart turned over. It was not the cry of the hawk I had captured; for, by shifting my position against the sun, I was now seeing further up. Straight out of the sun's eye, where she must have been soaring restlessly above us for untold hours, hurtled his mate. And from far up, ringing from peak to peak of the summits over us, came a cry of such unutterable and ecstatic joy that it sounds down across the years and tingles among the cups on my quiet breakfast table.

I saw them both now. He was rising fast to meet her. They met in a great soaring gyre that turned to a whirling circle and a dance of wings. Once more, just once, their two voices, joined in a harsh wild medley of question and response, struck and echoed against the pinnacles of the valley. Then they were gone forever somewhere into those upper regions beyond the eyes of men.

I am older now, and sleep less, and have seen most of what there is to see and am not very much impressed any more, I suppose, by anything. "What Next in the Attributes of Machines?" my morning headline runs. "It Might Be the Power to Reproduce Themselves."

I lay the paper down and across my mind a phrase floats insinuatingly: "It does not seem that there is anything in the construction, constituents, or behavior of the human being which it is essentially impossible for science to duplicate and synthesize. On the other hand . . ."

All over the city the cogs in the hard, bright mechanisms have begun to turn. Figures move through computers, names are spelled out, a thoughtful machine selects the fingerprints of a wanted criminal from an array of thousands. In the laboratory an electronic mouse runs swiftly through a maze toward the cheese it can neither taste nor enjoy. On the second run it does better than a living mouse.

"On the other hand . . ." Ah, my mind takes up, on the other hand the machine does not bleed, ache, hang for hours in the empty sky in a torment of hope to learn the fate of another machine, nor does it cry out with joy nor dance in the air with the fierce passion of a bird. Far off, over a distance greater than space, that remote cry from the heart of heaven makes a faint buzzing among my breakfast dishes and passes on and away.

One can easily see the wide difference between the uses of words in everyday speaking and writing, and Mr. Eiseley's efforts to provide us with an *experience* by the use of word cues to our imaginations! While the ordinary politician may use words in prose form called a speech, occasionally a skilled politician comes along and writes a speech that lives as a great piece of literature. We don't need to quote one here. We can merely mention the Gettysburg Address as an example and not waste words. The point is that

Eiseley and Lincoln have used prose exquisitely while most of us do not. They elevated prose to a creative level that appeals to our hearts as well as to our intellects.

## On Reading Narrative Literature

Most prose "creative writing" comes to us in forms we feel are both narrative and fictional in scope. Of course, there are other forms of narrative —travel, biography, autobiography—but we tend to think primarily of the novel, novella, and short story as the interpreter's gold mines of narrative prose. While telling a story, an author may at the same time do other things: He may, for example, be descriptive, as Lawrence Durrell was in the passage from *Clea* you have already read in Chapter 9. While creating fictive worlds for us, an author may also excite, transport, delight, inspire, or enlighten us on the universals of human existence.

Read the following short excerpts from two novels and note the facility of the authors in depicting poignant moments experienced by two women who never actually existed in the real world.

### *from* TELL ME THAT YOU LOVE ME, JUNIE MOON

MARJORIE KELLOGG

Being a sensitive person, Junie Moon smelled trouble in the air almost before Warren manufactured it. She was certain that Warren had changed his mind about them living together, or at least her living with them. In a way, she felt relieved. The thought of the three of them outside of the protective walls of the hospital was appalling to her. And the thought of she herself being seen by outsiders was one which she had postponed.

Minnie, who lay dying in the next bed, was the only one to mention it. They talked mostly at night while the others slept.

"He got you real bad, Junie Moon," Minnie said one night. Her voice sounded far away, like a lonely train going across the fields. "A man that would do a thing like that ought never to be born."

"I didn't think he was mean," Junie Moon said.

"I never knew a mean man who looked it," Minnie sighed. "It's the sweet baby-faced ones you got to step aside for. Did it hurt?"

"What?"

"When he poured on the acid."

She tried to remember. "A terrible stink, like something burning. I don't remember much about the pain. There was so much of it, it was like drinking too much—after a while everything gets fuzzy and in slow motion. Later it hurt. I'll tell you that for a fact."

"He sure got you real bad. Have you seen yourself?"

"Why should I go around looking at myself, can you tell me that?" She wanted to tell Minnie to mind her own damned business, but then she looked at the thin little woman, her hair in tiny pigtails all over her head, her abdomen full of tubes and drains and incisions. At last she said: "It was pretty bad."

Minnie's voice was almost a whisper. "Of course I didn't know you before, Junie Moon. You probably was a good-looking woman, that would be my guess."

"But now, Minnie?"

"Now it's like you say: pretty bad."

There. The words fell like stones. She did not think she could tolerate the sound. Later that night she went into the bathroom, bolted the door, and turned on the glaring overhead light. She walked straight to the mirror.

When she first saw herself, she tried to scream, but no sound came. She stood watching the horrible face in the mirror trying to scream, the mouth cavernous despite the fact that the lips could barely open. "Help," she cried soundlessly, "help." She moved her bottom jaw up and down and it reminded her of a marionette's mechanical mouth. "Help." No one came. The bathroom light seemed to get brighter. The crimson trench where the nose had been gave her face a bloody jack-o'-lantern look. It was worse than she had thought.

When she went to bed, Minnie was still awake, staring up at the ceiling.

"You went to look?" Minnie asked. Junie Moon didn't answer. "It won't ever be so bad as it was in there," Minnie said. Then she turned to Junie Moon. "Let Minnie see your hand. Come on now. I heard you smash the mirror." She took a towel from her nightstand and wrapped it around Junie Moon's bleeding hand. "No more blood for you, missy. The worst part is over."

"The hell you say, Minnie." It was hard to tell if Minnie heard or not. She was in and out of her dreams so much. And when she slept she talked as if she were awake.

Later that night Minnie cried: "Come and get me, I'm tired of waiting."

"Turn over, Minnie."

"I dreamed I was falling. Falling off a big mountain to the bottom of the sea."

"Turn over, Minnie."

"My mama wore a bright green dress and carried Easter lilies. Nurse! Nurse!"

"It's all right, Minnie."

They tried to comfort each other.

## *from* ARE WE THERE YET?

DIANE VREULS

A round loaf rising, from behind the farthest hill. Then the body, bulging and gingham. Two massive arms and the plump, oiled hands. The wide lap. Swaddled legs ending in—there they are—those shoes, men's leather shoes without laces. She is standing against the blue wall of the sky, holding a bowl.

Now she seems to be coming towards me, floating from crest to crest, her head gently nudging the clouds. She picks her way through a forest, bending to weed. She pulls up beets, carrots, turnips, twists them into bunches and waves them. Clumps of soil from the roots rain down on the counties.

"Why don't you come when I call?"

"I didn't hear."

"How many times I told you not to lie in the mud. What you doing here, girl?"

"I'm floating."

"Um hmm. Tomatoes are rotting. Chickens aren't fed. And she's floating."

She plucks me up, another vegetable, fills the zinc tub and scrubs, her bosom swaying. I'm wrapped up tight in a towel and set out to dry.

"Lying in puddles like swine, you're spoiled, that's what you are." Spoiled. Better an orphan left at her door, better a thief. I've been both. Spoiled is the worst.

"I should whip you and put you to bed, you know that."

I know it's Saturday night, deep-dish chicken pie and the Game. We lived alone then and she hated to play by herself, I'm safe: without me she's a cart with one wheel. Nothing, no muddy vices of mine, could come between her and the Game. Sunday to Friday she's straight as a row; accounts never lag, and it's cash on the line. But Saturday night we wash up the pots, shake the cloth and fold it away. It's the only time the table is bare, in fact the only time any wood shows in that house with its crocheted doilies, antimacassars, small braided rugs. I gaze at that table, naked and shining under the lamp, a magic pond.

Soon it's filled with the game. Oma's rummy takes three decks of cards, a six-pack of Barq's and a pound of beans for chips, which she counts like a pirate, black eyes gleaming. Ten is her lowest bid. She's not much on her feet, but set at a table she travels till dawn. Scoops up my discards saying "Old Emma, you shouldn't ought to have done that," and lays out a seven-card run. Soon she's got half the decks in her hands and mountains of beans. Lacking skill I play thin and sometimes can catch her with fifty-eight cards. But she always wins, wins any way she can. She carelessly spills the deck and it comes up aces. Loses cards in the folds of her skirt. Leaning heavily over the board she sweeps my lays to the floor—or hers, depending. When her chips are down she invents: the eight of diamonds is wild, ace can only be low. It's the oral tradition, altered from week to week. I have never found out all the rules.

When the cards shuffle against her, when the luck of the innocent rules, she becomes more innocent still. "Oh well, we don't want to keep SCORE now, do we, Emma. One thing I hate, it's a calculating critter. It's the fun of the game!"

And it was. Watching her mischief, catching her sly, I'd laugh so hard I'd collapse on the table, exposing my entire hand. Skunked every week, but I loved it. Her zeal, her clumsy maneuvers, her delight at winning were so huge I never felt I'd been cheated. She'd given me, Emma Benson, at the mere age of seven, the power to make her rich.

**Time in Narrative Prose.**   One of the distinguishing features of narrative literature is the fact that the story comes to us through a narrator. Unlike dramas, which happen NOW, as we watch them upon a stage or screen, narratives happened THEN, and the storyteller is the filter through which we " hear " of them. The *Junie Moon* excerpt is written, as narratives usually are, in past tense. In *Are We There Yet?* we find an effort to bridge the gap between the past and present. The past is told in present tense, which makes it seem vitally alive now. The last paragraph of the passage, however, reminds us that the persona, Emma Benson, remembers her grandmother as she had been years before, when Emma was only seven. The present tense used throughout the narrative is a distinctive characteristic of this novel. We are aware that the events occurred in the past, but it *seems* as if they are happening now, as in a drama. This technique, however, is unusual in the narrative form. We must readily acknowledge that the world of narrative is the past-tense world, in most narratives; that a narrator is the medium by which we get the story; and that what we are told may be only what the narrator chooses for us to know. We are in the hands of another being; therefore, in reading narratives aloud, we face problems not faced by actors in their direct depiction of dramatic works: problems in preserving the narrative filter of events already concluded before our reading.

**Point of View in Narratives.**   Since we are at the mercy of the narrator, whoever he or she may be, we must figure out his or her angle. We can ask the usual questions: *Who* is the narrator? *What* is the narrator relating? to *whom*? *when*? under *what circumstances*? for what *reasons*? and with *what attitude*? We can observe that narrators reveal an attitude toward characters and events. They seem to be indifferent to what is happening in the story, perhaps coldly objective, or they may be openly subjective, as is Emma Benson, telling of the Saturday night cardgames with her grandmother; or, they may be more objective but sympathetic, as is the narrator of *Tell Me That You Love Me, Junie Moon*, who is kindly predisposed to Junie's physical condition but never is maudlin. (The beauty of this book is that persons with physical handicaps are treated as human beings, so much so that we can even laugh at their very human foibles in spite of their handicaps. This is made possible by the narrator's particular predisposition. Another narrator with the same tale might have been cruel.)

A second aspect of point of view is scope: omniscient, personal, or reportorial. The narrator in *Junie Moon* is never identified as a character in the story. Yet he knows what many of the characters think and feel. In the episode you have just read, the narrator knows how Junie thinks and feels about Warren, about Minnie, and about her own face. In other episodes of that book, the narrator chooses also to look inside other characters. This we call an omniscient viewpoint; such a narrator is truly godlike in the power to read the minds and anticipate the actions of a book's characters. In *Are We There Yet?*, on the other hand, we have a book about the personal life of the character who tells the story. We do not know any facts when we read this book, except for the facts Emma Benson knows and wishes to disclose to us. Finally, the reportorial narrator may not have omniscient powers and may not be personally involved in the story. This narrator may only "report" what happened, from his point of view, of course, but without much personal involvement.

A third way to classify point of view is to indicate the grammatical "person" of the point of view. *Tell Me That You Love Me, Junie Moon* is clearly *third*-person: "she," "he," and "they" are the pronoun subjects and objects of all events. In *Are We There Yet?*, we have *first*-person: "I" and "we" are the predominant pronouns. Even here, the third person is frequently used by the first-person narrator; Emma refers in this passage to Oma as "she" and "her." Third-person narration may be used by an un-identified narrator, as is the case in *Junie Moon*, or it may be used by a secondary character in the story. The latter is exemplified by Huck Finn, who relates *Tom Sawyer Abroad*:

Do you reckon Tom Sawyer was satisfied after all them adventures? I mean the adventures we had down the river, and the time we set the darky Jim free and Tom got shot in the leg. No, he wasn't. It only just p'isoned him for more. That was all the effect it had. You see, when we three came back up the river in glory, as you may say, from that long travel, and the village received us with a torchlight procession and speeches, and everybody hurrah'd and shouted, it made us heroes, and that was what Tom Sawyer had always been hankering to be.[2]

The first-person narrator may be the main character in the story, as Emma Benson is, or as Huck Finn is in the book primarily about him, *The Adventures of Huckleberry Finn*:

You don't know about me without you have read a book by the name of *The Adventures of Tom Sawyer*; but that ain't no matter. That book was made by Mr. Mark Twain, and he told the truth, mainly. There was things which he stretched, but mainly he told the truth. That is nothing. I never seen anybody but lied one time or another, without it was Aunt Polly, or the widow, or maybe Mary. Aunt Polly—Tom's Aunt Polly, she is—and Mary, and the Widow

[2] Mark Twain, *Tom Sawyer Abroad, Tom Sawyer, Detective, and Other Stories, Etc., Etc.*, New York: Harper & Brothers Publishers, 1904.

Douglas is all told about in that book, which is mostly a true book, with some stretchers, as I said before.[3]

Apparently, then, Twain considered himself the narrator of *The Adventures of Tom Sawyer:*

"Tom!"
No answer.
"Tom!"
No answer.
"What's gone with that boy, I wonder? You TOM!"
No answer.
The old lady pulled her spectacles down and looked over them about the room; then she put them up and looked out under them. She seldom or never looked *through* them for so small a thing as a boy; they were her state pair, the pride of her heart, and were built for "style," not service—she could have seen through a pair of stove-lids just as well. She looked perplexed for a moment, and then said, not fiercely, but still loud enough for the furniture to hear:
"Well, I lay if I get hold of you I'll—"[4]

All too often we are likely to ignore narrators in our everyday reading for pleasure. Yet, they are there, telling us what they want us to know, or what they are *able* to tell us, playing upon our imaginations, perhaps even our prejudices, without our being aware of them. Perhaps the casual silent reader can afford inattention to sources of narration, but the oral interpreter is always obligated to be aware. When we read a story, the narrator is our eyes and ears, our memory and our imagination. Without careful attention to the narrative point of view, our perspective is left to chance or possibly reduced to chaos. We should be interested in the story that is told, of course, but we must also be concerned with the *telling*. That is the function of the narrator; that is the point of view for our receiving the story; and that is the role the interpreter primarily adopts. Authors very carefully select appropriate points of view for their stories in the form of narrators, and the oral interpreter strives to become the embodiment of that point of view.

Some scholars have catalogued points of view more precisely. For example, Moffett and McElheny distinguish between interior monologue, dramatic monologue, letter narration, diary narration, subjective narration, detached narration, memoir, biography—anonymous single person, anonymous—

---

[3] Mark Twain, *The Adventures of Huckleberry Finn*, New York: Harper & Brothers Publishers, (1899).
[4] Mark Twain, *The Adventures of Tom Sawyer*, New York: Harper & Brothers Publishers, (1920).

dual character, multiple character, and no character point of view.[5] Booth offers ten variables by which narrators may be delineated: They speak in first or third person; they may be dramatized (involved in the related events) to some extent; they select varying degrees of detail or summary; they allow themselves certain amounts of commentary about events; they reflect varying levels of awareness that they are in a speaking situation; they control distance between themselves, their subject matters, and their audiences; they may introduce quoted materials that agree with or seek to undermine their position; they reveal varying degrees of knowledge about persons and events; and they may express psychological insights into themselves or other persons.[6]

When you have ascertained the essential characteristics of a narrator's point of view, do not think that he or she will necessarily remain consistent. Characters in a story or play may change during the course of events, and so at times do narrators. A new persona may take over, or the former narrator whose style we are accustomed to may depart from an earlier pattern of observation. In *Moby Dick*, for instance, the author apparently made no effort to maintain consistency. (Who was it that said a foolish consistency is only for small minds?) The wandering sailor, Ishmael, is clearly the narrator at the beginning, the end, and throughout much of the novel; yet other characters soliloquize their most intimate thoughts and feelings, and we read of events that Ishmael could not possibly have witnessed, but which are described for us by *someone*! An objective narrator may, without explanation, suddenly explain a character's motivation, or a narrator who has been revealing a character's thoughts and feelings may suddenly clam up and refuse to continue to do so. An omniscient narrator may limit his powers to only one or two characters and show no interest in the workings of other minds. The reader of prose fiction must be on his toes *all* the time. Recognizing these complexities, we can appreciate the challenges of reading narrative literature.

## OTHER PARTS OF NARRATIVE PROSE

In this section we offer a concise catalogue of some other terms and parts of narrative prose. Examples are taken from Herman Melville's classic novel *Moby Dick* with some brief suggestions on how to cope with them orally.

**Narrative Commentary.**  A narrator makes personal observations that, at least momentarily, attract the reader's attention away from the story to himself:

[5] Moffett, James, and Kenneth R. McElheny, *Points of View: An Anthology of Short Stories.* New York: Mentor—New American Library, 1966.
[6] Wayne C. Booth, *The Rhetoric of Fiction.* Chicago: University of Chicago Press, 1961, pp. 149–65.

Chief among these motives was the overwhelming idea of the great whale himself. Such a portentous and mysterious monster roused all my curiosity. Then the wild and distant seas where he rolled his island bulk; the undeliverable, nameless perils of the whale; these, with all the attending marvels of a thousand Patagonian sights and sounds, helped to sway me to my wish.

Such commentary should be read in the personality of the persona, directly to the listeners. Sometimes, the narrator openly admits the presence of the audience, as this one does at the very beginning of the book: "Call me Ishmael."

**Summary.**   The narrator sums up actions that may have taken longer to happen than it takes to relate them:

I stuffed a shirt or two into my old carpet-bag, tucked it under my arm, and started for Cape Horn and the Pacific. Quitting the good city of old Manhatto, I duly arrived in New Bedford. It was on a Saturday night in December.

In storytelling form the reader addresses his listeners directly. When the narrator chooses to condense events into a brief summary, he suggests that these events are not as important as those he describes in detail or delineates with dialogue. For the reader, it is important to note that there is a major transition in time. The narrator places himself and the characters suddenly into a new time, place, or mood. In stories where plot is dominant, a precise reading of an important summary is extremely important. Where plot is not dominant, narrative commentary may be more significant than summary.

**Dialogue.**   Dialogue is conversation between characters:

"Landlord! I've changed my mind about that harpooner.—I shan't sleep with him. I'll try the bench here."
"Just as you please; I'm sorry I can't spare ye a table-cloth for a mattress; and it's a plaguy rough board here. . . ."

Personalities of characters should be suggested. However, keep in mind that the preceding conversation happened in the past and comes to us, in this case, through Ishmael, and Ishmael tells it later, perhaps even years after it happened. When the narrator gives us dialogue, he shifts from *telling* us what happened to *showing* us what happened, to some degree. He allows us to focus much more directly on the characters in action, and his narrative filter becomes much thinner. This, then, justifies a degree of impersonation for the characters.

**Tag lines.**   Tag lines are phrases identifying speaker and the manner of speaking. (We have italicized the tags that follow.)

"But avast," *he added, tapping his forehead,* "you hain't no objections to sharing a harpooner's blanket, have ye?"

. . .

"My boy," *said the landlord,* "you'll have the nightmare to a dead sartainty."

. . .

"Landlord," *I whispered,* "that ain't the harpooner, is it?"

. . .

"Oh, no," *said he, looking a sort of diabolically funny. . . ."*

When tags are unnecessary, because they are obvious in context, or because the reader's method of reading them suggests the manner, they may usually be deleted. Often, the manner of speaking described in the tag can be suggested by the reader; such elimination keeps the continuity of dialogue moving and lessens the intrusion of the narrator. We must urge caution, however: Sometimes, the presence of the narrator is vital to retain, and sometimes the tags function strongly in the rhythmic structure of the prose. In such cases, tags should be cut only with great care. We usually advise the beginning student to consider eliminating them where possible, and the advanced student to consider the desirability for retaining them!

**Direct Discourse.** The character tells what he *thinks*, at times in quotation marks, at times not:

The devil fetch that harpooner, thought I, but stop, couldn't I steal a march on him—bolt his door inside, and jump into his bed, not to be wakened by the most violent knockings?

This passage should be read in the personality of the speaker, but clearly as a revelation of thoughts, not as dialogue. It can be read directly to the audience.

**Indirect Discourse.** The narrator reports in his own words what a character has said. Quotation marks are not used:

He answered no, not yet; and added that he was fearful Christianity, or rather Christians, had unfitted him for ascending the pure and undefiled throne of thirty pagan Kings before him. But by and by, he said, he would return,—as soon as he felt himself baptized again.

To know how Queequeg—the "He" of the above quotation—really spoke, we quote a bit of his actual speech:

"Kill-e," cried Queequeg, twisting his tattooed face into an unearthly expression of disdain, "ah! him bevy small-e fish-e; Queequeg no kill-e so small-e fish-e; Queequeg kill-e big whale!"

The manner of reading indirect discourse is to keep the character of the narrator, with the narrator suggesting to some degree the personality of the person he " quotes." Narrators are more impersonative in indirect discourse to the degree that they approximate the actual words of the character.

**Soliloquy.**   The inner thoughts of a character other than the narrator are revealed as if the character were speaking aloud:

My soul is more than matched; she's over-manned and by a madman! Insufferable sting, that sanity should ground arms on such a field! But he drilled deep down and blasted all my reason out of me! I think I see his impious end; but feel that I must help him to it. Will I, nill I, the ineffable thing has tied me to him; tows me with a cable I have no knife to cut. Horrible old man!

Read such material in the personality of the character with no narrative filter affecting it, and suggest that the character is speaking only to himself. Do not acknowledge the presence of the audience. Think it aloud, but keep eyes usually in the realm of the audience, not down on the floor, and certainly not to the audience's eyes.

**An Extended Speech by a Character.**   Father Mapple's sermon in *Moby Dick* is one of the most renowned sermons—or speeches of any kind, for that matter—in all American literature. In reading it, one would address the audience as if it were Father Mapple's congregation, and one would also have ample time to suggest the good preacher's character while doing so.

**Description.**   Description of persons, places, and objects that provide imaginative materials for a narrative tale is an important skill of the narrative writer. It can occupy a place of prime magnitude in depicting action, as in this passage:

Like noiseless nautilus shells, their light prows sped through the sea; but only slowly they neared the foe. As they neared him, the ocean grew still more smooth; seemed drawing a carpet over its waves; seemed a noon-meadow, so serenely it spread. At length the breathless hunter came so nigh his seemingly unsuspecting prey, that his entire dazzling hump was distinctly visible, sliding along the sea as if an isolated thing, and continually set in a revolving ring of finest, fleecy, greenish foam. He saw the vast, involved wrinkles of the slightly projecting head beyond. Before it, far out on the soft Turkish-rugged waters, went the glistening white shadow from his broad, milky forehead, a musical rippling playfully accompanying the shade; and behind, the blue waters interchangeably flowed over into the moving valley of his steady wake; and on either hand bright bubbles arose and danced by his side. But these were broken again by the light toes of hundreds of gay fowls softly feathering the sea, alternate with their fitful flight; and like to some flag-staff rising from the painted hull of an argosy, the tall but shattered pole of a recent lance projected from the white whale's back; and at intervals one of the cloud of soft-toed fowls hovering, and to and fro skimming like a canopy over the fish, silently perched and rocked on this pole, the long tail feathers streaming like pennons.

A gentle joyousness—a mighty mildness of repose in swiftness, invested the gliding whale. Not the white bull Jupiter swimming away with ravished Europa clinging to his graceful horns; his lovely, leering eyes sideways intent upon the maid; with smooth bewitching fleetness, rippling straight for the nuptial bower in Crete; not Jove, not that great majesty Supreme! did surpass the glorified White Whale as he so divinely swam.

Imagery is the major effect of description, and it is imagery the reader must experience while reading. Without the inner experience of the images, the words will only be words, and the images will not be created in the audience's imaginations.

Images and the attitudes and moods in which they are presented are closely related; therefore, the reader should give careful consideration to the mood or attitude of the persona. Descriptions are not photographic representations, but selective or even emotional impressions. In the description we have just quoted, the persona recalls a marvelous and beautiful moment during a whale hunt.

**Plot and Action.** Plot is the sequence of actions, the storyline, in prose fiction. It is a matter of major interest to most people who read fiction. (Unfortunately, it is too often the item of *sole* interest.) Plot is too long to illustrate here, and only in the case of the short story would you probably read narrative material to an audience primarily for plot interest, simply because of time limitations. Therefore, the reader may have time only for reading portions of plot. For this reason, he may choose the interesting actions of longer narratives. These may be mental or emotional developments rather than physical ones. Inherent in the entire plot will be the development of the climax. Audiences like climactic buildups; consequently, these should be considered in choosing portions of narratives to read. Their recreations must be accomplished by heightened imagery and communicative techniques discussed in earlier chapters. Without some climactic development and release of tension, a reading is likely to be bland. This is *not* to suggest that you always read action-packed materials, for even in the quiet description of the surfaced whale, the mention of the lance projecting from it would constitute a climactic moment in that description. The image of the bird perching upon the moving pole is a unique release of the tension of the paragraph. The second paragraph builds another and stronger climax to the release of the persona's admiration for the scene and the sense of majesty which the whale instills in him. Good writing builds larger climaxes upon smaller ones.

**Character.**    The actions of plot are impossible without human beings (or other characters like Eiseley's hawk or Melville's whale) who enact them. Short story writers create characters for us with carefully selected samples of information and action that enable the characters to develop in our imaginations. Novelists have more time and space in which to create characters. We learn of them through what they say and do; through what other characters say of them; and also through the words of the narrator. Characters may cause action; action may develop or destroy characters. It is with these characters *in actions* that the oral interpreter usually is involved. Father Mapple reveals himself in his sermon. The author uses the entire novel to reveal Ahab's character, yet we still do not fathom him fully. Queequeg, the harpooner from the South Pacific islands, appears first as a mysterious savage, but later proves to be a human being of utmost simplicity and love.

**Style.**    Style, one of those abstractions that persons often use, is defined in a thousand different ways (including " Style is the man "), and is difficult to identify precisely. The writers of *A Handbook to Literature* define style as " The arrangement of words in a manner which at once best expresses the individuality of the author and the idea and intent in his mind."[7] The best style, they conclude, would be the one which best expresses the particular idea of the particular person. Therefore, style is a combination of the person's ability to be expressive and the person's ideas. A humorous idea produces a different style from a serious one. A philosophical person has a different style from a nincompoop, and so forth. To accomplish the best expression and communication of one's ideas (Remember: " idea " encompasses feelings about the idea!) would be accomplished by the best arrangements; the best syntax; the best words; the best images; the best figurative and symbolic content; the best uses of sound, flow, and rhythms of language.

Consider these elements as they appear in a quotation from Hemingway's *The Old Man and the Sea* and contrast them with the preceding description of the whale from *Moby Dick*:

Then the fish came alive, with his death in him, and rose high out of the water showing all his great length and width and all his power and his beauty. He seemed to hang in the air above the old man in the skiff. Then he fell into the water with a crash that sent spray over the old man and over all of the skiff.

The old man felt faint and sick and he could not see well. But he cleared the harpoon line and let it run slowly through his raw hands and, when he could see, he saw the fish was on his back with his silver belly up. The shaft of the harpoon was projecting at an angle from the fish's shoulder and

---

[7] William Flint Thrall, Addison Hibbard, and C. Hugh Homan, *A Handbook to Literature*, New York: The Odyssey Press, 1960, p. 474.

the sea was discolouring with the red of the blood from his heart. First it was dark as a shoal in the blue water that was more than a mile deep. Then it spread like a cloud. The fish was silvery and still and floated with the waves.[8]

Anyone who would compare these writings from two such classics of the American novel would soon come to the subjective conclusion that they are quite different, although they are about relatively similar subjects. Trying them out aloud would give one a physical sensation of their differences in style. *The Old Man and the Sea* seems to be very modern and simple; *Moby Dick*, older and more ornate. The former flows from the modern tongue more readily than the other, but both are successful in stimulating imaginary responses with their imagery. Specifically, though, what are their differences? Concretely, how is Hemingway's writing different from Melville's? We know no better way to demonstrate these differences than to count various elements and give you some quantitative measurements of their individual characteristics.

First, let us look at vocabulary. Hemingway used monosyllables, almost exclusively (even in his title): 87 per cent, with only 11 per cent, bisyllables and 2 per cent, trisyllables. Melville, by contrast, used longer words: 67 per cent, monosyllables, 24 per cent, bisyllables, 8 per cent, trisyllables, and 1 per cent each, of four- and five-syllable words. Looking at vocabulary a different way, we may wish to see which piece used the *larger* vocabulary, not for any qualitative judgments, but simply because we want to know another characteristic of style. For this, we can count the number of words in the passage, count the number of different words used, and divide the former into the latter. This gives us what is called a type-token ratio, which indicates the size of vocabulary used. We find in these cases proof of what we might have suspected: The *Moby Dick* passage has a ratio of .74, which seems significantly higher—implying a larger vocabulary—than the selection from *The Old Man and the Sea*, which has a ratio of .59. Still another way of approaching vocabulary would be to count the various word types and compute the percentage of the whole selection for each type; then, compare the figures for the two selections. In doing so, we find that the two authors used almost identical percentages of nouns, prepositions, and pronouns (*OMS* 21, *MD* 22; *OMS* 14, *MD* 14; *OMS* 7, *MD* 6, respectively). They use notably different percentages of conjunctions (*OMS* 9, *MD* 5), articles (*OMS* 14.5, *MD* 11), verbs (*OMS* 14.5, *MD* 10), adjectives (*OMS* 14, *MD* 22), and adverbs (*OMS* 6, *MD* 10). We can summarize these differences by stating that the *Moby Dick* passage used fewer nonsubstantive connectives and modifiers and far more descriptive words. Because of *Moby Dick's* considerable use of gerunds and present participles (verb forms ending in -*ing*), we made one more computation in vocabulary,

[8] Ernest Hemingway, *The Old Man and the Sea*. New York: Charles Scribner's Sons, 1952, p. 104.

finding that *Moby Dick* used 16 of these forms to only 3 for *The Old Man and the Sea*.

A second way to approach style is to look at sentence structure. Hemingway's sentences averaged 19.6 words in length; Melville's, 38.5, almost *double*! There is more to sentence structure, however. What about *type* of sentence? Each used 2 simple sentences. Hemingway used 4 compound sentences; Melville, 1. Hemingway used 2 complex sentences; Melville, none. Hemingway used 1 compound-complex sentence; Melville, 5! We can conclude that Hemingway's style here is simple and straightforward; Melville's, involved and involuted. Hemingway's compound sentences are fundamentally groupings—connected by " and "—of simple assertions of fact, while Melville's contain many inverted arrangements of clauses involved with the persona's impressions.

Another structural feature is the use of metrical beats, which we shall examine more fully in the section on prose rhythm following this one, but we can give here a quantitative summary of metrical differences between these two selections. *The Old Man and the Sea* selection is primarily iambic, containing (according to *our* scansion—yours may be different): 31 iambs ($\cup/$), 4 anapests ($\cup\cup/$), 9 trochees ($/\cup$), and 1 dactyl ($/\cup\cup$). The first two types of meter are called " rising " meter, and the second two are " falling "; thus, this is a piece with a rising rhythm. *Moby Dick*, with 47 iambs, 10 anapests (totaling 57 rising feet), and 48 trochees and 18 dactyls (totaling 66 falling feet), is almost evenly divided between the two kinds of meter. Iambic is the characteristic beat of " conversational " speech. For this reason, you will find the Hemingway selection easy and flowing in oral reading, and most emphatic and demonstrative when a falling beat takes over, as in the final feet of this sentence:

$$\ldots \text{he saw} \mid \text{the fish} \mid \text{was on} \mid \text{his back} \mid \text{with his} \mid \text{silver} \mid \text{belly} \mid \text{up.}$$

You will also find the noniambic portions of Melville's writing least conversational, demanding more familiarity and practice for effective oral reading.

We do not suggest that the reader do this type of arithmetic computation. We only wish to confirm concretely what a sensitive reader will *feel* about style, particularly when reading aloud.

Third, we can consider uses of figurative, allusional, or symbolic language. Both pieces use simple similes such as: Hemingway's *like a cloud* and *as a shoal*, and Melville's *like noiseless Nautilus shells*. Both also use more skillful figures: Hemingway's *with his death in him* and Melville's *drawing a carpet, seemed a noon meadow*, and *Turkish-rugged sea*. Hemingway used no allusions, but Melville sends us to classical mythology with references to *the bull Jupiter* abducting the *ravished Europa* and headed for the *nuptial bower in Crete*. These raise the passage to something more than description, perhaps even to symbolic significance. (We do *not* deny symbolic significance in *The Old Man and the Sea*!) We see Hemingway accomplishing a conversational directness, while Melville effects a literary style uncharacteristic of conversation. One piece may ring more true to modern ears accustomed to conversational language, but who knows how literary posterity will judge the two for excellence? *Moby Dick* still holds its own after a century and a quarter. *The Old Man and the Sea* may also. Actually, we *want* books to be different, as different as people. Style *is* the person speaking, or writing!

**Prose Rhythm.** In Chapter 9, we dealt briefly with the subject of rhythm. In doing so we indicated that both verse and prose have rhythm. When we can scan, with some assurance of accuracy, the meters of verse, we find the identification of rhythm there relatively easy to understand, for it is similar to the beats of various kinds of music. With prose, however, we have greater difficulty in comprehending rhythm because we are dealing with rhythms which are quite irregular, unpatterned, and often intangible. Consequently, we cannot come up with precise delineations of rhythms in prose. But rhythm is there. The better the prose is, the more likely it is to be rhythmic.

In our earlier discussion, we noted that rhythm is largely recurrence, and we noted the alliterative recurrence of initial consonants in Ingersoll's speech on Napoleon. In the passage from *Moby Dick* there are 20 alliterative groups: *noiseless-Nautilus, sped-sea, still-smooth, seemingly-unsuspecting, so-serenely-spread, sliding-sea, revolving-ring, finest-fleecy-foam, vast-involved, behind-blue, bright-bubbles, softly-sea, fowls-(softly)-feathering-flagstaff, fitful-flight, white-whale, perched-pole, mighty-mildness, whale-white,* and *lovely-leering.* In reading these aloud in context, one is aware—at least subconsciously— of the pulsations of repetition. Then, there can be the recurrence of words: In the passage from *The Old Man and the Sea,* " old man " is used three times, " he," five times, and " his," eight times. Think how many times they must appear in the entire book! We can also note the repetition of structure, which we have already termed " parallel structure." In Hemingway's paragraphs, the style of the sentences is repetitive, straight, simple assertion. Three of his sentences begin with the adverb " Then." Furthermore, note that the author connected many clauses and words together with the conjunction " and "— ten times, to be exact. Read the passage aloud and note the almost wavelike pulsation of the parts connected in this way. As to recurrent structure, look also at the final sentence from *Moby Dick,* with the repeated clause openings of " Not . . . ." The parallelism is rhythmic in building an impressive climax.

Rhythm is also inherent in speech. Peoples have their own tongues, and the rhythms of languages and dialects are distinctive features to be captured by anyone wishing to master them. Mastery of vocabulary and sound-system is one thing, but mastery of the rhythms is quite another, achieved by comparatively few foreigners. The rhythms of speech become apparent in cadences, or speech units. One can layout on paper the cadences of good prose so that it is similar to free verse in appearance. Look at the opening of our passage from *The Old Man and the Sea*, for example:

Then the fish came alive,
with his death in him,
and rose high out of the water
showing all his great length and width
and all his power and his beauty.
He seemed to hang in the air
above the old man in the skiff.
Then he fell into the water with a crash
that sent spray over the old man
and over all of the skiff.

When you read aloud in these cadences, you cannot help but feel the speech rhythms. Try another exercise: Layout the first two sentences of the *Moby Dick* passage, as we have just done, and note the cadences of speech in a more elaborate style of writing. Speech rhythms are there, too, although they may not be the rhythms of modern conversational speech.

Although prose cannot have consistent metrical patterns, for then it would be verse, prose can have moments of metrical pulsations very much like the meter in verse. Note again the predominance of iambs and the strength of the final feet in this line:

... he saw | the fish | was on | his back | with his | silver | belly | up.

Note the effects of the anapests and the effect of the meter which is almost totally rising:

First | it was dark | as a shoal | in the blue | water

that was more | than a mile | deep.

Then | it spread | like a cloud.

In *Moby Dick*, also, we find examples of regularity in beats. In the first part of this sentence, they first rise, then fall, and are almost entirely falling in the last three lines:

At length | the breath|less hunt|er came

so nigh | his seem|ingly | unsus|pecting | prey,

⏑ ／ ⏑ ／ ／ ⏑ ／
that his | entire | dazzling | hump

⏑ ⏑ ／ ⏑ ／⏑⏑
was dis|tinctly | visible,

／⏑ ⏑ ／ ⏑ ／ ⏑ ／⏑ ／⏑／⏑ ／
sliding | along | the sea | as if an | isolated | thing,

⏑ ⏑ ／⏑⏑⏑ ／⏑⏑ ⏑ ／⏑ ／ ⏑
and con|tinu|ally | set in a | revolving | ring (of)

／⏑ ／⏑ ／ ⏑ ／
finest, | fleecy, | greenish, | foam.

Such stresses and slacks are implicit in words and phrases. In *Moby Dick*, note the dactyls in the following: *Feathering, hull of an argosy, one of the, hovering, canopy,* and *silently.*

We should like to stay on this subject because we find it rather fun, but space does not permit us to. Scan other passages, for yourselves. Try sentence No. 6 of *The Old Man and the Sea* and note still different rhythms in: *was projecting at an angle from the fish's, and the sea was discolouring with the red of the blood from his heart.* Try, also, the first few sentences of Eiseley's essay at the beginning of this chapter or the selection from *Clea* in Chapter 9. Note that Eiseley, following some very flowing alternation of stresses and slacks, jars the reader with a series of consecutive heavy stresses. The recurrence of these becomes rhythmic too! Rhythm is intended in good prose. The effective reader is either naturally sensitive to its existence or must consciously look for it before feeling it. Try scanning good prose, not for any arbitrary right way to do it, but to enable you to see it on paper and then to feel its presence. Rhythm is a delight, once you experience it.

## ON READING EXPOSITORY PROSE

The oral interpretation of expository prose—prose that sets forth ideas—involves a few special considerations relating primarily to our understanding of what we read. First, look at the organization; discover the overall plan of the whole selection. The general patterns of exposition are few and clearly identifiable. To explain a process or a procedure, a *chronological* order is used. For some content, a *space* order is employed. More-abstract content is explained in a *topical* arrangement, perhaps with items in an order of climax. Exposition achieved by *comparison* or *contrast* may consist of two major blocks, or of perhaps a series of topics each of which is treated in two subtopics. Sometimes exposition is arranged in a sequence of *cause and effect*, or perhaps effect and cause. Many an explanation is in an order of *problem and solution.* Whatever the pattern in your selection, find it, and, if desirable, outline it on paper. Then, examine the structure of each paragraph. Make sure you see the relationship of every sentence to the topic sentence. Then, analyze each individual sentence. Which parts are major and which, minor? What relationship does each part have to some other part? In exposition, word grouping and centering are especially important. Finally, you may have to define some troublesome words. The objective in exposition is maximum clarity, and so a single word may be crucial.

It is quite easy to make your reading of exposition suffer from over-emphasis, for much of the content is really subordinate: Much of it is proof material intended to substantiate larger contentions. The subordinate parts properly receive less emphasis than the larger ideas they serve to make clear. With a faster rate, fewer and shorter pauses, and perhaps less volume, subordinate the unimportant. The following quotation is a good illustration of material in which the effective reader will use much subordination:

> Philosophically, Don Juan is a man who, though gifted enough to be exceptionally capable of distinguishing between good and evil, follows his own instincts without regard to the common, statute, or canon law; and therefore, whilst gaining the ardent sympathy of our rebellious instincts (which are flattered by the brilliancies with which Don Juan associates them) finds himself in mortal conflict with existing institutions, and defends himself by fraud and force as unscrupulously as a farmer defends his crops by the same means against vermin.[9]

Since this is a single sentence, the reader will first have to find the main ideas, then tie them to the subordinate ideas in proportions equal to their relative significance. Of course, the silent reader has to do this, too, in order to read intelligently. Try to find the main and subordinate ideas, then try to read them aloud with various degrees of interest and importance.

Expository writing is sometimes not the most dynamic writing to read to audiences simply because it is often devoid of images. This is especially so when it deals with abstract thought. Your choice of expository prose to read aloud will usually take into consideration its imagistic powers, although there are times when one must read thought-provoking materials which do not contain the concreteness of images. Then, the reader must get and maintain audience interest by reading interestingly. He must provide the attraction of attitude where images are absent. We have dealt with the subject of empathy in Chapter 7. Using your present knowledge of it, consider how you might introduce the subject of empathy to an audience, thereby motivating listening before reading the following passage, which is the opening of a philosophical examination of empathy:

[9] Bernard Shaw, "Preface to *Man and Superman*," *Ibid.*, p. 497.

# EMPATHY, INNER IMITATION, AND SENSE-FEELINGS*

THEODOR LIPPS

I direct my attention in the following to empathy in general. What I shall say applies to empathic projection into definite sorts of objects, especially into the movements, postures, and positions of man, whether real or represented as in sculpture; also into the forms of architecture.

Esthetic enjoyment is a feeling of pleasure or joy in each individual case colored in some specific way and ever different in each new esthetic object—a pleasure caused by viewing the object. In this experience the esthetic object is always sensuous, that is, sensuously perceived or imagined, and it is only this. I have a feeling of joy before a beautiful object: this means that I have this feeling in viewing the sensuous perception or image, in which form the beautiful object immediately presents itself to me. I have it while I view this object, *i.e.,* bring it into clear attention, apperceive it. But only the sensuous appearance of the esthetic object, for example, of the work of art, is attended to in esthetic contemplation. It alone is the "object" of the esthetic enjoyment; it is the only thing that stands "opposite" me as something distinct from myself and with which I, and my feeling of pleasure, enter into some "relationship." It is through this relationship that I am joyous or pleased, in short, enjoying myself.

# ON READING THE HUMOROUS ESSAY

Essayists frequently employ witty ideas, satire, burlesques, and comic sketches. These may be in the form of narratives, or they may be imitations of serious prose. We quote in full the following parody of serious literary scholarship. White's medium for satire is the " minor poets." What is a " minor " poet, as opposed to a " major " one? (Some of each may be found in this textbook, if one can really make such a distinction!)

## HOW TO TELL A MAJOR POET FROM A MINOR POET

E. B. WHITE

Among the thousands of letters which I received two years ago from people thanking me for my article "How to Drive the New Ford" were several con-

---

\* *Einfühlung, innere Nachahmung, und Organempfindungen. "Organempfindungen,"* here translated as " sense-feelings," refers to the feelings localized in the body, to kinesthetic sensations, motor disturbances, physical cravings such as hunger, and so forth.[10]

[10] Quoted in Melvin M. Rader, *A Modern Book of Esthetics: An Anthology.* New York: Holt, Rinehart and Winston, 1935.

taining the request that I "tell them how to distinguish a major poet from a minor poet." It is for these people that I have prepared the following article, knowing that only through one's ability to distinguish a major poet from a minor poet may one hope to improve one's appreciation of, or contempt for, poetry itself.

Take the first ten poets that come into your head—the list might run something like this: Robert Frost, Arthur Guiterman, Edgar Lee Masters, Dorothy Parker, Douglas Fairbanks, Jr., Stephen Vincent Benét, Edwin Arlington Robinson, Lorraine Fay, Berton Braley, Edna St. Vincent Millay. Can you tell, quickly and easily, which are major and which minor? Or suppose you were a hostess and a poet were to arrive unexpectedly at your party—could you introduce him properly: "This is Mr. Lutbeck, the major poet," or "This is Mr. Schenk, the minor poet"? More likely you would have to say merely, "This is Mr. Masefield, the poet"—an embarrassing situation for both poet and hostess alike.

All poetry falls into two classes: serious verse and light verse. Serious verse is verse written by a major poet; light verse is verse written by a minor poet. To distinguish the one from the other, one must have a sensitive ear and a lively imagination. Broadly speaking, a major poet may be told from a minor poet in two ways: (1) by the character of the verse, (2) by the character of the poet. (Note: it is not always advisable to go into the character of the poet.)

As to the verse itself, let me state a few elementary rules. Any poem starting with "And when" is a serious poem written by a major poet. To illustrate— here are the first two lines of a serious poem easily distinguished by the "And when":

And when, in earth's forgotten moment, I
Unbound the cord to which the soul was bound. . .

Any poem, on the other hand, ending with "And how" comes under the head of light verse, written by a minor poet. Following are the *last* two lines of a "light" poem, instantly identifiable by the terminal phrase:

Placing his lips against her brow
He kissed her eyelids shut. And how.

All poems of the latter type are what I call "light by degrees"—that is, they bear evidences of having once been serious, but the last line has been altered. The above couplet, for example, was unquestionably part of a serious poem which the poet wrote in 1916 while at Dartmouth, and originally ended:

Placing his lips against her brow
He kissed her eyelids shut enow.

It took fourteen years of knocking around the world before he saw how the last line could be revised to make the poem suitable for publication.

While the subject matter of a poem does not always enable the reader to classify it, he can often pick up a strong clue. Suppose, for instance, you were to run across a poem beginning:

When I went down to the corner grocer
He asked would I like a bottle of Welch's
                    grape juice
    And I said, "No, sir."

You will know that it is a minor poem because it deals with a trade-marked product. If the poem continues in this vein:

"Then how would you like a package of Jello,
A can of Del Monte peaches, some Grape Nuts,
And a box of Rinso—
Or don't you thin' so?"

you may be reasonably sure not only that the verse is "light" verse but that the poet has established some good contacts and is getting along nicely.

And now we come to the use of the word "rue" as a noun. All poems containing the word "rue" as a noun are serious. This word, rhyming as it does with "you," "true," "parvenu," "emu," "cock-a-doodle-doo," and thousands of other words, and occupying as it does a distinguished place among nouns whose meaning is just a shade unclear to most people—this word, I say, is the sort without which a major poet could not struggle along. It is the hallmark of serious verse. No minor poet dares use it, because his very minority carries with it the obligation to be a little more explicit. There are times when he would like to use "rue," as, for instance, when he is composing a poem in the A. E. Housman manner:

When drums were heard in Pelham,
The soldier's eyes were blue,
But I came back through Scarsdale,
And the . . .

Here the poet would like to get in the word "rue" because it has the right sound, but he doesn't dare.

So much for the character of the verse. Here are a few general rules about the poets themselves. All poets who, when reading from their own works, experience a choked feeling, are major. For that matter, all poets who read from their own works are major, whether they choke or not. All women poets, dead or alive, who smoke cigars are major. All poets who have sold a sonnet for one hundred and twenty-five dollars to a magazine with a paid circulation of four hundred thousand are major. A sonnet is composed of fourteen lines; thus the payment in this case is eight dollars and ninety-three cents a line, which constitutes a poet's majority. (It also indicates that the editor has probably been swept off his feet.)

All poets whose work appears in "The Conning Tower" of the *World* are minor, because the *World* is printed on uncoated stock—which is offensive to major poets. All poets named Edna St. Vincent Millay are major.

All poets who submit their manuscripts through an agent are major. These manuscripts are instantly recognized as serious verse. They come enclosed in a manila folder accompanied by a letter from the agent: "Dear Mr.——: Here is a new group of Miss McGroin's poems, called 'Seven Poems.' We think they are the most important she has done yet, and hope you will like them as much as we do." Such letters make it a comparatively simple matter for an editor to distinguish between serious and light verse, because of the word "important."

Incidentally, letters from poets who submit their work directly to a publication without the help of an agent are less indicative but are longer. Usually they are intimate, breezy affairs, that begin by referring to some previously rejected poem that the editor has forgotten about. They begin: "Dear Mr.——: Thanks so much for your friendly note. I have read over 'Invulnerable' and I think I see your point, although in line eight the word 'hernia' is, I insist, the only word to quite express the mood. At any rate, here are two new offerings. 'Thrush-Bound' and 'The Hill,' both of which are rather timely. I suppose you know that Vivien and I have rented the most amusing wee house near the outskirts of Sharon—it used to be a well house and the well still takes up most of the living room. We are as poor as church mice but Vivien says, etc., etc."

A poet who, in a roomful of people, is noticeably keeping at a little distance and "seeing into" things is a major poet. This poet commonly writes in unrhymed six-foot and seven-foot verse, beginning something like this:

When, once, finding myself alone in a gathering of people,
I stood, a little apart, and through the endless confusion of voices . . .

This is a major poem and you needn't give it a second thought.

There are many more ways of telling a major poet from a minor poet, but I think I have covered the principal ones. The truth is, it is fairly easy to tell the two types apart; it is only when one sets about trying to decide whether what they write is any good or not that the thing really becomes complicated.

How would you approach the reading of this essay? Well, first *you* must see it as funny. You must know enough about the major and minor poets, yourself, to see how ridiculous White's classifications and assertions really are! Once you enjoy it, then you are ready to consider your listeners. They, too, must be prepared to see the absurdity of the essay; therefore, your introduction must do for an audience what only time, reading, and study have done for you. The content of the introduction is vital, but so is your manner of speaking. Then, your manner of reading the piece is also vital. Will you laugh while reading it, or will you serve it better by adopting the same mock-serious academic tones that exist in White's manner of writing?

The figure of speech called *hyperbole*, gross exaggeration, is used by many comedians. By exaggerating something out of all proportion they make a matter absurd and therefore funny. It is the device used by the impressionist on stage and the caricaturist on paper. One can read this essay by suggesting the manner of a lofty professor in the very first sentence and his " thousands of letters." Hyperbole would also be shown in a slightly " hammy " way of reading the verses quoted in the essay, since they are parodies of serious verse. Surprise is another prime ingredient of humor; therefore, the surprise in " How to Drive the New Ford " will be increased by a slight pause before it. The audience, expecting something truly world-shaking (after " thousands of letters "), will laugh at this absurdity. Such is also the case near the end of the first paragraph, where we expect a more sensible reason for knowing the difference between the two kinds of poets than " improving our appreciation of, or contempt for, poetry itself! " Then, too, look at the structure of the *end* of that sentence. " Appreciation of, or contempt for, poetry itself " is funny, because of its careful imitation of a pedantic, qualifying structure. Pauses at the commas will help in reading it aloud.

Continuing our discussion of comic elements in reading the humorous essay, we must note the importance of timing. Sudden changes of rate can be funny. Such a change might be used for the last phrase of the second paragraph. In the third paragraph, one might be ripping through the middle, then slow down in enumerating the two "characters," and speed up suddenly for the end of the parenthetical remark. The comedian and comic actor will tell you that timing is everything. It is the timing of the expert performer that controls audience behavior. It is this same skill that is extremely difficult for the amateur to learn. Look also for opportunities to create humorous surprises by sudden changes in loudness, pitch, and voice quality as well, even facial expression or other nonverbal cues. While it is not our intention to make a comedian of you, we do recommend that you try to learn to enjoy good humorous prose. It would seem that the ultimate in your full appreciation of a comic piece would be for you to read it to an audience successfully. As a start, try to read White's essay aloud for your own amusement. Plan *how* you would try to achieve chuckles or laughs at certain points. Since everyone in your class is studying " How to Tell a Major Poet from a Minor Poet," you may choose another audience for it, but we are confident that your class would like to hear some worthwhile humorous literature from you.

## ON READING PERSONAL WRITINGS

Sometimes, letters, diaries, and journals rise to the level of public interest and literary quality because of the fame of their authors or because of their style and universal content. A main consideration when reading them is the audience each was intended for. A letter is usually addressed to a single person, whereas diaries and journals may be addressed to the writer himself, to no one in particular, to the diary as if it were a person, or to posterity. Even a letter may be written with the knowledge that it will be preserved and read by thousands of persons in the future. The implied, or anticipated, audience will affect how one reads personal writings as well as the actual audience. The very personal nature of an intimate letter should be preserved in public communication. Let the audience feel the privilege of " listening " to something private. The letter will be read to an imaginary recipient, not to the audience. For communications clearly prepared for the historical record, the reader should address the listeners directly, for they are clearly a part of the intended audience. Another important factor is attitude, as affected by the apparent purpose of the communication : factual-informative, persuasive, jocular or friendly chitchat, confession, argument, devotion, or other postures. How does attitude in this context affect the style of the writer? In a formal journal, used to record events as they happen (perhaps for history or perhaps merely for the writer's own reference), the style may be scholarly, scientific, factual, or objective. The diary may have abbreviated clauses or phrases rather than full sentences, initials for names of persons and places, or a gossipy style. In either style the writer may disclose or try to hide his real self.

A series of letters between two persons can make for fascinating reading. We think immediately of the correspondence between Bernard Shaw and Ellen Terry, or between the poet Marianne Moore and the officer of the Ford Motor Company. When both sets of letters are available, you can read from them at your performance, with the two personalities indulging in dialogue. When only one side of the correspondence is available, biographical research may reveal the effect of the letters on the other person, which can be related in transitional commentary. One would need to understand and explain the context in a series of events and letters between Lawrence Durrell and Henry Miller to make sense of the following excerpt from one of Durrell's letters:

I have met Eliot who is a very charming person, believe it or not. Had an impertinent note from Shaw saying that *Tropic* must wait its turn—which may be months. Alors, I wrote and asked him to return the one copy to me, the old bugger. Seeing MacCarthy on Wednesday, about *Tropic*—hasn't yet read it, by the way. Pringle reading *Max*.[11]

[11] George Wickes, ed. *Lawrence Durrell and Henry Miller: A Private Correspondence.* New York: E. P. Dutton & Co., Inc., 1964, p. 118.

In contrast to this very private statement, we offer a public letter by Bernard Shaw—a letter he wrote to the editor of a newspaper, for everyone to read:

My dear T. P.,—

All autobiographies are lies. I do not mean unconscious, unintentional lies: I mean deliberate lies. No man is bad enough to tell the truth about himself during his lifetime, involving, as it must, the truth about his family and friends and colleagues. And no man is good enough to tell the truth to posterity in a document which he suppresses until there is nobody left alive to contradict him.

I speak with the more confidence on the subject because I have myself tried the experiment, within certain timid limits, of being candidly autobiographical. But I have produced no permanent impression, because nobody has ever believed me. I once told a brilliant London journalist [A. B. Walkley] some facts about my family. It is a very large family, running to about forty first cousins and to innumerable second and thirds. Like most large families, it did not consist exclusively of teetotalers; nor did all its members remain until death up to the very moderate legal standard of sanity. One of them discovered an absolutely original method of committing suicide. It was simple to the verge of triteness; yet no human being had ever thought of it before. It was also amusing. But in the act of carrying it out, my relative jammed the mechanism of his heart—possibly in the paroxysm of laughter which the mere narration of his suicidal method has never since failed to provoke—and, if I may be allowed to state the result in my Irish way, he died about a second before he succeeded in killing himself. The coroner's jury found that he died "from natural causes"; and the secret of the suicide was kept, not only from the public, but from most of the family.

I revealed that secret in private conversation to the brilliant journalist aforesaid. He shrieked with laughter, and printed the whole story in his next *causerie*. It never for a moment occurred to him that it was true. To this day he regards me as the most reckless liar in London.[12]

We hope that you noticed the considerable difference in writing style in those letters, both written by extremely gifted writers.

A style, falling between the fragmentary intimacy of Durrell's letter and the consciously public letter of Shaw, is apparent in a diary written by a little-known Irish nationalist, Joseph Holliway. Holliway went to hear Shaw lecture in Dublin and wrote about the experience later in his journal, perhaps only for his own record, perhaps also for later public reading:

Saturday, October 26. ... I went down to hear Shaw's discourse on "Literature in Ireland" at the little theatre.... His discourse was quite Shavian in

[12] Bernard Shaw, "In the Days of My Youth," from *Selected Non-Dramatic Writings of Bernard Shaw* (Dan H. Lawrence, ed.) Boston: Houghton Mifflin Company, 1965, p. 433.

his findings, and he kept nagging all the while he spoke; he afterwards said he knew he was nagging but once set going he could not stop. Only those who don't succeed in art or literature make good critics was his opinion; therefore, he was no critic. He didn't read critically. It was only when they went to Paris Irishmen could write, and then he spoke of George Moore's and Joyce's works and their indecencies. He also said that Synge got his local colour in Paris, and that there is nothing Irish about The Playboy. The central idea is that the worship of crime is universal; in fact, the Irish people don't understand it. Then he went on to say that the Irish should be conscripted out of their own country so that they would learn to know what Ireland was really like. He also said they could never get anything until they ceased to have a grievance. Nobody liked people with a grievance; they were generally bores. The men who didn't leave Ireland wouldn't write like Synge. The plays that were written by Irishmen who never travelled were generally those that lacked poetic outlook and were sordid and abusive in character. . . . Shaw is always stimulating and entertaining and never dull. He mixed all he said with a very nimble wit, and his words came ever ready to his lips. He speaks excellently well always, and his delivery is clear and telling![13]

We should make one more statement about the reading of personal writings: The unique qualities of the person and the situation under which the writing was done are vital and are usually essential to any understanding or appreciation of what is said. If you are not familiar with Shaw, you cannot appreciate these quotations fully, but we hope you understand our main points.

## ON READING THE SPEECH

The public speech is an oral utterance for a specific audience and occasion. The oral nature of speeches likens them to dramatic writings: Both are intended primarily for a listening audience, and only secondarily for a reading audience. For this reason, the *best* public speeches often provide excellent material for the oral interpreter. They can be dramatic, enlightening, or entertaining. They employ language that is engaging and stimulating, and they progress with a clear sense of direction and purpose.

Public speeches differ from other prose because of their inescapable context in an historical situation. The writer of novels, short stories, or other imaginative literature speaks to a general reading audience. These works appeal to contemporaries of the writer, but they often find appreciative readers from other cultures and in succeeding generations. Imaginative literature makes it own context in a fictive world that it creates.

[13] Quoted from Introduction to *Bernard Shaw's Nondramatic Literary Criticism* (Stanley Weintraub, ed.) Lincoln, Nebraska: University of Nebraska Press, 1972, pp. xix–xx.

Public speakers, on the other hand, address themselves to situations immediately at hand. Whereas novelists might write *about* their world, public speakers address themselves to audiences *within* the ongoing progress of world history. Their messages are responses to social or political conditions; to local, national, or international events; to situations existing at that moment and in that location. The public speaker's audience is an inherent part of the circumstances that motivated the speech. Consequently, the speaker can assume a degree of involvement on the part of listeners before starting to speak. Since the audience is already a part of the speech context, there is no need to create a fictive world into which an audience must be lured.

The distinction we have made between imaginative literature and public speeches is tenuous, and we do not wish to enforce a rigid rule. But, when we consider that speeches are usually inextricably bound in a specific historical moment, we can draw some conclusions regarding the interpreter's performance.

When you select a public speech to perform, be careful that you do not choose one that is "time-bound." There are a lot of speeches which may have been successful when delivered, but do not offer sufficient meaning for an audience removed in time and place. Try to find speeches that attend to more universal concerns, which have meaning that transcends the specific circumstances of the original utterance. For example, Pericles, speaking in Athens, 430 B.C.; Martin Luther, defending himself before the Diet of Worms, 1521; Patrick Henry, preparing Virginia for war against England, 1775—each of these addresses was directed to a situation long since past, yet each speaks to human circumstances and attitudes that have no time or place restrictions.

Even though you carefully select material that is pertinent to a contemporary audience, your introduction usually plays an important role in the interpretation of a public speech. Public speakers have no need to tell their audience the time and place of their addresses. Often they will acknowledge certain details at the beginning, but they generally assume that their listeners are already aware of the relevant situations. The interpreter, who reads the speech outside of its intended context, must explain the situation if the audience is going to understand and empathize with its content, such as growing strife and civil war, for speeches of Lincoln; World War II, for Churchill; changing attitudes of the early 1960's, for Kennedy. The introduction should be specific so that the interpreter's audience can understand and participate imaginatively in the circumstances that led to the speech's delivery, influencing its style and content. Ideally, the interpreter should sensitize his audience so that it is in a frame of mind consistent with the original listeners and can, therefore, respond similarly.

In performance the interpreter should respond to the public speech just as he would to any other literature. The language seeks to communicate ideas and feelings, and the oral reader becomes the embodiment of the message.

Especially when performing modern speeches by persons, whose vocal and physical features are well known, some oral readers feel as if they must impersonate the original speaker's voice and mannerisms. We suggest that you resist this temptation. You probably would not try to reproduce Truman Capote's rather distinctive voice when reading from either "A Christmas Memory" or *In Cold Blood*; similarly there is no need for you to try to duplicate Kennedy's Massachusetts accent when reading his Inaugural Address. Some suggestion of the speaker's regional dialect can be helpful if these origins have a bearing on the speech itself. Otherwise, direct impersonation is unnecessary and generally distracting. As you read, work to assimilate the *role* of the original speaker, but do not worry about portraying the individual's physical traits. Your objective is not so much dramatic impersonation of an historical figure as it is dynamic sharing of ideas and emotions with an audience.

## A Reading Program of "Island of Fear"

*The following sample reading program illustrates many of the problems faced by the interpreter in reading narrative prose. It includes a demonstration of how to cut a story that would otherwise be too long for the time allotment. The copy is heavily annotated to provide the student assistance in understanding the story and in actually reading it aloud. In order to present this reading program publicly, one must obtain the necessary permission from the copyright owner whose name may be found among the Acknowledgments at the beginning of this book.*

### Introduction

Like millions of other readers, I am addicted to literary fantasies, including, of course, science fiction. While my addiction often results in a waste of time as I read worthless stories devoid of skill, it frequently rewards me with intriguing literary experiences: The impossible and ridiculous become real, vivid, and breathtaking.

The secret of this literary capacity to become momentarily believable often lies in the meticulous employment of realistic details and in the use of a frame of reference already somewhat familiar to the reader. The writer weaves his fascinating tapestry out of threads that seem individually genuine.

Such is the case in "Island of Fear," by William Sambrot. The central figure of the story is a modern and apparently young man who has sufficient money and leisure to pursue an intense search for relics of the ancient past. You find him on an island in the Aegean Sea. It was in this ancient sea that Ulysses wandered for twenty years after the Trojan War, and it was here that he encountered the strange creatures about whom you read as a child.[14]

---

[14] Please notice that the introduction attempts to achieve at least three purposes: to interest the listeners, to assist them in understanding, and to give them some idea of what to look for.

## ISLAND OF FEAR[15]

WILLIAM SAMBROT

Kyle Elliot[16] clutched the smooth tight-fitting stones of the high wall, unmindful of the fierce direct rays of the Aegean sun on his neck, staring, staring through a chink.

He'd come to this tiny island, dropped into the middle of the Aegean like a pebble on a vast blue shield,[17] just in the hope that something ~~something like what lay beyond that wall~~ might turn up. And it had.[18] It had.

Beyond,[19] in the garden behind the wall, was a fountain, plashing gently. And in the center of that fountain, two nudes, a mother and child.

A mother and child, marvelously intertwined, intricately wrought of some stone that almost might have been heliotrope, jasper or one of the other semi-precious chalcedonies[20]—although that would have been manifestly impossible.

~~He took a small object like a pencil from his pocket and extended it. A miniature telescope. He gasped, looking once more through the chink.~~[21] Heavens, the detail of the woman! Head slightly turned, eyes just widening with the infinitestimal beginning of an expression of surprise[22] as she looked—at what? And half sliding, clutching with one hand at the smooth thigh, reaching mouth slightly rounded, plump other hand not quite touching the milk-swollen breast—the child.[23]

His professional eye moved over the figures, his mind racing, trying to place

---

[15] The complete story would require about twenty-eight minutes to read. The short version, employing the deletions indicated here, can be read in nineteen or twenty minutes. In your study of this program, first read the story in its entirety and then reread, leaving out the deletions.

[16] Because Elliot is not directly described or characterized by the author, you must picture him for yourself. His apparent financial circumstances, his interests, his actions, and his thoughts will give you many clues. He seems intelligent, educated, curious, and brave, perhaps foolhardy. He has an overpowering obsession for antiquities, so powerful that his final action is dictated by his curiosity for the "old."

[17] Note the rich, romantic flavor that the author executes with a minimum of verbiage.

[18] Foreshadowing such as this seems a favorite device of the author. Upon reading the story aloud, you will want to recognize these shadows for what they are: seeds of suspense, as in this instance, and subtle hints that the listener may later remember as the events unfold.

[19] The next four paragraphs describe a lovely statue, intricate and beautiful in its detail, a supreme work of art. The description, typical of good writing, leaves much to the imagination: It is rich in suggestion. Give your imagination free reign so that you see infinitely more than a literal interpretation of the words would provide. You can further enhance the beauty of this portion by providing full utterance to the ear appeal of the lines, especially the cadences, the liquid consonants, the syllables of inherently long duration, and the metrical pulsations.

[20] The three terms *heliotrope, jasper,* and *chalcedonies* may be new to you. What are their meanings? Why "would have been manifestly impossible?" Since the author has a vocabulary of the story's locale and of ancient mythology, you will probably have some research to do.

[21] Deletions such as this remove small elements from the action of the story without diminishing the mood or handicapping the plot.

[22] Indirect discourse. This omniscient persona knows what Kyle is thinking.

[23] Visualize these wonderful images!

the sculptor, and failing. It was of no known period. It might have been done yesterday; it might be millenniums old. Only one thing was certain—no catalogue on earth listed it.[24]

Kyle had found this island by pure chance.[25] He'd taken passage on a decrepit Greek caïque[26] that plied the Aegean, nudging slowly and without schedule from island to island. From Lesbos to Chios to Samos, down through the myriad Cyclades, and so on about the fabled sea, touching the old, old lands where the gods had walked like men.[27] The islands where occasionally some treasure, long buried, came to light, and if it pleased Kyle's eyes, and money obtained it, then he would add it to his small collection. But only rarely did anything please Kyle. Only rarely.[28]

~~The battered caïque's engine had quit in the midst of a small storm which drove them south and west. By the time the storm had cleared, the asthmatic old engine was back in shape, coughing along. There was no radio, but the captain was undisturbed. Who could get lost in the Aegean.~~[29]

They had been drifting along, a small water bug of a ship lost in the greenish-blue sea, when Kyle had seen the dim purple shadow that was a tiny island in the distance. The glasses brought the little blob of land closer and he sucked in his breath.[30] An incredible wall, covering a good quarter of the miniature island, leaped into view,[31] a great horseshoe of masonry that grew out of the sea, curved, embraced several acres of the land, then returned, sinking at last into the sea again, where white foam leaped high even as he watched.

He called the captain's attention to it. "There is a little island over there."[32] And the captain, grinning, had squinted in the direction of Kyle's pointing finger.

"There is a wall on it," Kyle said, and instantly the grin vanished from the captain's face; his head snapped around and he stared rigidly ahead, away from the island.[33]

[24] Here is an element essential to the story: It explains Collector Elliot's fascination.

[25] Now the author backtracks to summarize how Elliot happened to be on the island looking through the chink in this strange wall: Indeed, the next nineteen paragraphs summarize while he remains fascinated with the sight of the statue.

[26] Consult the dictionary for both meaning and pronunciation.

[27] Do not miss the romantic allusions. The author assumes they will be meaningful to you. Refresh your memory of them by referring to Bullfinch's *Mythology*.

[28] Here you learn more about the collector: discriminating and apparently wealthy enough to buy anything he wanted.

[29] In the interest of brevity this paragraph has been omitted: The action herein does not seem essential to the plot. No later portion of the story depends on this for understanding.

[30] Here is the first element of mystery Kyle encountered in his adventure. It is another source of suspense for the reader. Strive to speak the lines with a suggestion of the awe and amazement Kyle must have experienced.

[31] Be sure you understand the arrangement of the wall.

[32] The first dialogue in the story. Remember that your manner of uttering Elliot's lines can help to communicate his personality. Perhaps his eager interest will be demonstrated with eyes and a gesture as well as with voice. We suggest you direct your eyes and face slightly to the right of center as you read Elliot's lines.

[33] The reason for the captain's response is a mystery at this point and is another source of suspense. The role of the narration here is to communicate both the nature of the captain's response and the storyteller's surprise and wonder.

"It is nothing," the captain said harshly.[34] "Only a few goatherders live there. It has no name, even."

"There is a wall," Kyle had said gently. "Here"—handing him the glasses—"look."

"No." The captain's head didn't move an iota. His eyes remained straight ahead. "It is just another ruin. There is no harbor there; it is years since anyone has gone there. You would not like it. No electricity."

"I want to see the wall and what is behind it."

The captain flicked an eye at him. Kyle started. The eye seemed genuinely agitated. "There is nothing behind it. It is a very old place and everything is long since gone."

"I want to see the wall," Kyle said quietly.

They'd put him off, finally,[35] the little caïque pointing its grizzled snout to sea, its engine turning over just enough to keep it under way, its muted throbbing the only sound. They'd rowed him over in a dinghy,[36] and as he approached he'd noticed the strangely quiet single street of the village, the lone inn, the few dories with patched lateen sails, and on the low, worn-down hills the herds of drifting goats.

~~Almost, he might have believed the captain; that here was an old tired island, forgotten, out of the mainstream of the brilliant civilization that had flowered in this sea—almost, until he remembered that wall. Walls are built to protect, to keep out or keep in. He meant to see what.~~

After he'd settled in the primitive little inn,[37] he'd immediately set out for the wall, surveying it from the low knoll, surprised again to note how much of this small island it encompassed.

He'd walked all around it,[38] hoping to find a gate or a break in the smooth, unscalable wall that towered up. There had been none. ~~The grounds within sprawled on a sort of peninsula that jutted out to where rock, barnacled, fanged, resisted the restless surf.~~

And coming back along the great wall, utterly baffled, he'd heard the faint musical sound of water dropping within, and, peering carefully at the wall, had seen the small aperture, no bigger than a walnut, just above his head.

And looked through the aperture,[39] and so stood, dazed at so much beauty,

---

[34] If you will direct the captain's lines slightly to the left of center, you will help the listeners to distinguish his words from those of Elliot. In addition, contrasting his harshness with the eagerness of Elliot will make such tag lines as, "the captain said harshly," unnecessary. In this instance and in most other cases we have omitted such phrases.

[35] There is a minor climax here, and the line should be spoken clearly and quietly.

[36] Here is the beginning of a new segment of the story. It provides an excellent opportunity for imagery.

[37] This is still summary.

[38] This paragraph, as well as the following one, also seems to require slow utterance: They cover so much action and time in few words.

[39] The summary has brought us back to the action.

staring at the woman and child, unable to tear away, knowing that here, at last, was the absolute perfection he'd sought throughout the world.[40]

How was it that the catalogues failed to list this master work? These things were impossibly hard to keep quiet. And yet, ~~not a whisper,~~ not a rumor had drifted from this island ~~to the others of what lay within those walls~~. Here on this remote pinprick of land, so insignificant as to go unamed, here behind a huge wall ~~which was itself a work of genius~~, here was this magic mother and child glowing all unseen.

He stared, throat dry, heart pumping with the fierce exultation of the avid connoisseur who has found something truly great—and unknown. He must have it[41]—he would have it. ~~It wasn't listed, possibly—just possibly—its true worth was unknown. Perhaps the owner of this estate had inherited it, and it remained there, in the center of the gently falling water, unnoticed, unappreciated.~~

He reluctantly turned away from the chink in the wall and walked slowly back toward the village, scufflling the deep, pale immemorial dust.[42] Greece. Cradle of western culture. He thought again of the exquisite perfection of the mother and child back there. The sculptor of that little group deserved to walk on Olympus. Who was it?

Back in the village he paused before the inn to take some of the dust off his shoes,[43] thinking again how oddly incurious, for Greeks,[44] these few villagers were.

~~"Permit me?"~~

A boy,[45] eyes snapping, popped out of the inn with a rag in one hand and some primitive shoe blacking in the other, and began cleaning Kyle's shoes.

Kyle sat down on a bench and examined the boy. He was about fifteen, wiry and strong, but small for his age. He might have, in an earlier era, been a model for one of Praxiteles'[46] masterpieces: the same perfectly molded head, the tight curls, two ringlets falling over the brows, like Pan's snubbed horns, the classic Grecian profile. But no, a ridged scar ran from the boy's nose to the corner of the upper lip, lifting it ever so slightly, revealing a glimmer of white teeth.

---

[40] This paragraph and the next one. too. express the collector's wonder and ecstasy as he stares at this object that he feels he must have. You must study this portion well in order to experience his emotions vicariously.

[41] Apparently the summit of his appreciation. and incidentally the climax of another portion of the story. is the desire to acquire: Perhaps we can begin to sense here that Elliot's acquisitiveness will bring him only tragedy. Note that the succeeding lines. which have been deleted. reveal his sudden hope that he can get the statue for less than it is worth.

[42] Although dust is normally insignificant. it is in this instance essential to subsequent action. It is foreshadowing. Make it clear without undue or obvious emphasis.

[43] " Immemorial dust " and essential to the plot!

[44] Your inflection will say. in effect. "Why should these Greeks be so different?" More suspense.

[45] The second major character in the story. an appealing lad and somehow pathetic. too. His significance is not to be revealed for a time. but he is extensively characterized now. Excellent visual imagery. Try to construct a detailed mental picture.

[46] Check on this allusion. Perhaps some readers would like to refer to it in the introduction.

No, Praxiteles would never have used him for a model—unless, of course, he had a slightly flawed Pan in mind.

"Who owns the large estate beyond the village?"[47] ~~he asked in his excellent Greek~~. The boy looked up quickly and it was as if a shutter came down over his dark eyes.[48] He shook his head.

"You must know it," Kyle persisted.[49] "It covers the whole south end of this island. A big wall, very high, all the way to the water."

~~The boy shook his head stubbornly.~~[50] "It has always been there."

~~Kyle smiled at him. "Always is a long time," he said. "Perhaps your father might know?"~~[51]

~~"I am alone," the boy said with dignity.~~

~~"I'm sorry to hear that." Kyle studied the small, expert movement of the boy.~~ "You really don't know the name of the persons who live there?"

The boy muttered a single word.

"Gordon?"[52] ~~Kyle leaned forward.~~ "Did you say 'The Gordons'? Is it an English family that owns that property?" He felt the hope dying within.[53] If an English family owned it, the chances were slim indeed of obtaining that wonderful stone pair.

"They are not English,"[54] ~~the boy said.~~

"I'd like very much to see them."

"There is no way."

"I know there's no way from the island,"[55] ~~Kyle said~~, "but I suppose they must have a dock or some facilities for landing from the sea?"

The boy shook his head, keeping his eyes down. Some of the villagers had stopped, and now were clustered about him, watching and listening quietly. Kyle knew his Greeks, a happy boisterous people, intolerably curious sometimes; full of advice, quick to give it. These people merely stood, unsmiling, watching.[56]

[47] Elliot should be the same character who engaged in conversation with the captain earlier. Give him the same character placement. He looks down to the boy.

[48] The same inexplicable response the captain made! Your manner of utterance should reveal Elliot's mystification: an occasion perhaps for circumflex inflections.

[49] He fears his search is to be thwarted, and so perhaps he will emphasize " must," " whole," " big," " very," and " all the way."

[50] Supply the action as you speak the line. Does not the boy's answer really say, " I refuse to tell you about the wall"?

[51] These lines that reveal that the boy is alone in the world are useful but probably not essential to the plot, and so we have omitted them, allowing Elliot's interrogation of the boy to proceed without interruption.

[52] The boy has been so reluctant to answer and so unclear that Elliot cannot be sure he has said, " Gordon." Probably these three questions are uttered rapidly and in quick succession. Elliot's anxiety is very evident in his manner of speaking.

[53] He senses that his acquisitiveness is about to be thwarted. The lines bespeak dejection, which perhaps you can express with downward inflections.

[54] This is an answer to only the last of Elliot's questions, but apparently the collector is unaware of the fact and assumes, as you will see in his reply, that the name is " Gordon," that the family is not English, and that he still has a chance to persuade them to part with the statue.

[55] The same persistence and emphasis he used in saying the boy must know the wall.

[56] More mystery. Why are these Greeks so different?

The boy finished and Kyle flipped him a fifty-lepta coin.[57] The boy caught it and smiled, a flawed masterpiece.

"That wall,"[58] Kyle said to the spectators, ~~singling out one old man,~~[59] "I am interested in meeting the people who own that property."

~~The old man muttered something and walked away.~~

~~Kyle mentally kicked himself for the psychological error. In Greece, money talks first.~~ "I will pay fifty—one hundred drachmas," he said loudly, "to anyone who will take me in his boat around to the seaward side of the wall."

It was a lot of money, he knew, to a poor people ~~eking out a precarious existence on this rocky island, with their goats and scanty gardens. Most of them wouldn't see that much in a year's hard work. A lot of money~~[60]—but they looked at one another,[61] then turned and without a backward glance they walked away from him. All of them.

~~Throughout~~[62] ~~the village he met the same mysterious refusal, as difficult to overcome as that enigmatic wall that embraced the end of the island. They refused even to mention the wall or what it contained, who built it, and when. It was as though it didn't exist for them.~~

At dusk he went back to the inn, ~~ate *dolmadakis*~~[63] ~~minced meat, rice, egg and spices—surprisingly delicious;~~ drank *retsina*, ~~the resinated, astringent wine of the peasant;~~ and wondered about the lovely mother and child, standing there behind that great wall with the purple night clothing them.[64] A vast surge of sadness, of longing for the statues swept over him.

~~What a rotten break!~~[65] ~~He'd run into local taboos before. Most of them were the results of petty feuds, grudges going back to antiquity. They were cherished by the peasants, held tight, jealously guarded. What else was there of importance in their small lives? But this was something entirely different.~~

He[66] was standing on the outskirts of the darkened village, gazing unhappily out to sea, when he heard a soft scuffling. He turned quickly. ~~A small boy was~~

---

[57] What's a fifty-lepta coin? Apparently this action is to give the impression of removing the boy from the story.

[58] A little subterfuge here: He makes no reference to the statue, which is his real object.

[59] The incident of the old man is being omitted, and so this remark and the next one are directed to the whole group of villagers.

[60] The deletion results in condensation: A generous pause may make the lines more believable and heighten the contrast between the first clause and the second. Note that we have made one sentence where the author had three.

[61] Here's some effective though unconventional style. Beginning with "but" there are five groups of words that show the slow and complete rejection of Elliot: They can be read in steps of diminishing emphasis. Do some experimenting with the method of utterance.

[62] Another sizable portion of the story is being removed. Show the passage of time with a long pause.

[63] This deleted portion seems to lend authenticity; we will risk the loss.

[64] Imagery here for Elliot and for you.

[65] Indirect discourse.

[66] There is a quality of reverie here.

~~approaching~~. It was the shoeshine boy,[67] eyes gleaming in the starshine, shivering slightly,[68] though the night was balmy.

The boy clutched his arm. "~~The others—tonight,~~ I will take you in my boat," ~~he whispered.~~[69]

Kyle smiled, relief exploding within him.[70] Of course, he should have thought of the boy. A young fellow, ~~alone, without family~~, could use a hundred drachmas, whatever the taboo.

"Thank you," ~~he said warmly~~. "When can we leave?"

"Before the ebb tide—an hour before sunrise," ~~the boy said. "Only"—his teeth were chattering~~—"I will take you, but I will not come any closer than the outer rocks between the walls. From there, you must wait until the ebb tide and walk—and walk—" ~~He gasped, as though choking.~~[71]

"What are you afraid of?" ~~Kyle said. "I'll take all the responsibility for trespassing, although I don't think—"~~

~~The boy clutched his arm. "The others~~—tonight, when you go back to the inn, you will not tell the others that I am rowing you there?"

"Not if you don't want me to."

"Please do not!" ~~he gasped~~. "They would not like it if they knew—after, that I—"[72]

"I understand," ~~Kyle said~~. "I won't tell anyone."

"An hour before sunrise," ~~the boy whispered~~. "I will meet you at the wall where it goes into the water to the east."[73]

The stars were still glowing, but faintly, when Kyle met the boy,[74] a dim figure sitting in a small rowboat that bobbed up and down, scraping against the kelp and barnacles that grew from the base of the monolithic wall. ~~He realized suddenly that the boy must have rowed for hours to get the boat this far around the island. It had no sails.~~

He climbed in and they shoved off, the boy strangely silent. The sea was rough, a chill predawn wind blowing raggedly. The wall loomed up alongside, gigantic in the mist.

"Who built this wall?" he asked, once they were out onto the pitching water, heading slowly around the first of a series of jagged, barnacled rocks, thrusting wetly above the rapidly ebbing tide.

"The old ones," the boy said. His teeth were chattering, he kept his back steadfastly to the wall,[75] glancing only seaward to measure his progress. "It has always been there."

[67] Both pleasure and surprise.
[68] Suspense. We wonder why he shivers.
[69] Read the dialogue with a suggestion of a whisper.
[70] His relief will show in the manner in which you read, probably with a faster rate and heightened vocal enthusiasm.
[71] Again we delete the unnecessary. Suggest the choking yourself.
[72] Suspense!
[73] A long pause before you begin the last major section of the story.
[74] A fine opportunity for imagery.
[75] What would happen if he looked at the wall? This is foreshadowing.

Always. And yet, studying the long sweep of the wall beginning to emerge in the first light, Kyle knew that it was very old. Very old. It might well date back to the beginning of Greek civilization.[76] And the statues—the mother and child. All of it an enigma ~~no greater than the fact that they were unknown to the outside world~~.

As they drew slowly around until he was able to see the ends of the thick walls rising out of the swirling, sucking sea,[77] he realized that most certainly he could not have been the first ~~not even one of the first hundred~~. This island was remote, not worth even being on a mail route, but surely, over the many, many years that wall had towered, it must have been visited by people as curious as he. Other collectors. And yet, not a rumor.[78]

The boat rasped up against an enormous black rock, its tip, white with bird droppings, startling luminous in the half light.[79] The boy shipped[80] his oars.

"I will come back here at the next tide," ~~he said, shaking as though with a fever~~. "Will you pay me now?"[81]

"Of course." ~~Kyle took out his billfold.~~ "But aren't you at least going to take me farther in than this?"

"No," the boy said shrilly. "I cannot."

~~"How about the dock?" Kyle surveyed the considerable expanse of shallow, choppy surf between the rocks and the narrow sloping beach. "Why, there isn't a dock!"~~

~~There was nothing between the walls but sand, dotted with huge rocks, and inland, a tangled growth of underbrush with an occasional cypress rearing tall.~~

"I'll tell you what. I'll take the boat in and you wait here," ~~Kyle said~~. "I won't be long. I just want to get a chance to meet whoever owns the place and arrange—"

"No!"[82] There was sharp panic in the boy's voice, "If you take the boat—" He half rose, leaning forward to shove off from the rock. At that instant a swell raised the boat, then dropped it suddenly out from under the boy. Overbalanced, he swayed, arms waving wildly, then went over backwards, hitting his head on the rock. He slipped under the water like a stone.

Kyle made a quick lunge, and missing, immediately dived out of the rowboat after him, rasping his chest on the barnacled shelf of rock a few feet beneath the boat.[83] He got a good handful of the boy's shirt, but it tore like paper. He grabbed again, got a firm grip on his hair and stroked for the surface. He held him

[76] Foreshadowing, too.
[77] Imagery again! Perhaps a hint of disaster, too. Get sound values out of the alliterative words.
[78] Why? Suspense.
[79] More images—both audible and visual.
[80] Be sure you know the meaning of the word.
[81] Why should he be paid now? Foreshadowing of disaster for Elliot?
[82] The boy's reaction is violent. Your reading of this paragraph should reveal the climax when the boy sinks into the water.
[83] The excitement of the rescue should be revealed in the voice of the reader, fast, tense.

easily, treading water, looking for the rowboat. It was gone, ~~kicked away by his~~ ~~powerful dive, perhaps behind one of the other rocks.~~ No time to waste looking for it now.

He swam to shore, pulling the boy easily. ~~It was only a hundred yards or so~~ ~~to the smooth white beach, curving between the two arms of the wall that sloped~~ ~~out and down into the ocean. When he came out of the water the boy was~~ ~~coughing weakly, salt water dribbling from his nose.~~

Kyle carried him well above the tide mark and sat him down on the sand. The boy opened his eyes and peered at him, puzzled.

"You'll be all right," ~~Kyle said.~~ "I'd better get your boat before it drifts too far."

He walked back down to the surf line, kicked off his shoes and stroked off to where the boat rose and fell, nuzzling another of the large rocks that littered the space between the towering walls. He rowed the boat back, facing the sea and the swift-rising sun.[84] The wind had dropped to a whisper.

He beached the boat and gathered up his shoes. The boy was leaning against a rock, locking inland over his shoulder in an attitude of rigid watchfulness.[85]

"Feeling better now?" Kyle called cheerfully. ~~It occurred to him that their~~ ~~little mishap was an excellent excuse for being here, on property belonging to~~ ~~someone who obviously valued his privacy highly.~~

The boy didn't move.[86] He remained staring back into the tangle of trees, back to where the massive walls converged in the distance, stark, white, ancient.

Kyle touched him on the bare shoulder. He pulled his hand away, fists tightly clenched.[87] He looked at the sand. Here were the marks where the boy had risen, here the dragging footsteps where he'd come to lean against this rock. And here he still stood, glancing over his shoulder toward the trees, lips barely parted, a look of faint surprise just starting on his face.[88]

And there, coming out of the tangled trees, a delicate tracery of footsteps led towards this rock, and behind.[89] Footsteps, slender, high-arched, as though a woman barefooted, scarcely touching the sand, had approached for just an instant. Looking at the strange footprints, Kyle understood completely[90] what he should have guessed when first he'd peered through that chink in the wall, gasping at the unimaginable perfection of the woman and her child.

Kyle knew intimately all the ancient fables of early Greece. And now, looking at the footprints in the sand, one of the most terrible leaped into his mind: the Gorgons.[91]

[84] Why should the author note that Elliot faces the sea and sun as he rows back to the boy?

[85] The boy's "rigid watchfulness" constitutes foreshadowing, but it receives only a little attention in order that the climax be saved for a few more seconds.

[86] You wonder why, and so the author builds suspense for the climax.

[87] He begins to sense what has happened and seeks confirmation or denial in the circumstances.

[88] Remember the expression on the face of the woman in the statue.

[89] His awe, fear, and comprehension slowly grow.

[90] Now he knows, but the listener is kept wondering a bit longer. Indeed, Elliot's awareness only serves to enhance the suspense of the listener.

[91] Climax for those who know "the Gorgons."

The Gorgons were three sisters, Medusa, Euryale and Stheno,[92] with snakes writhing where their hair should have been. Three creatures so awful to look upon, the legend said, that whosoever dared gaze upon them instantly turned to stone.[93]

Kyle stood on the warm sand, with the gull cries, the restless Aegean sea sounds all about him, and he knew, at last, who the old ones were who'd built the wall; why they'd built it to lead into the living waters—and whom—what—the walls were meant to contain.

Not an English family named the Gordons. A much more ancient family, named—the Gorgons. Perseus had slain Medusa, but her two hideous sisters, Euryale and Stheno, were immortal.

Immortal.[94] Oh, God! It was impossible! A myth![95] And yet—

His connoisseur's eyes,[96] even through the sweat of fear, noted the utter perfection of the small statue that leaned against the rock, head turned slightly, an expression of surprise on the face as it peered over one shoulder in the direction of the trees. The two tight ringlets, like snubbed horns above the brow, the perfect molding of the head, the classic Grecian profile. Salt water still flecked the smoothly gleaming shoulders, still dripped from the torn shirt that flapped about the stone waist.

Pan in chalcedony.[97] But Pan had a flaw. From the nose to the corner of the upper lips ran a ridge, an onyx scar that lifted the edge of the onyx lip slightly, so that, faintly, a glimmer of onyx teeth showed. A flawed masterpiece.

He heard the rustle behind him,[98] as of robes, smelled an indescribable scent, heard a sound that could only have been a multiple hissing[99] and though he knew he mustn't, he turned slowly. And looked.[100]

---

[92] Pronounce them accurately and confidently. " Medusa " will serve as the climax for still other listeners.

[93] This is the moment of recognition for many modern listeners. Give your audience just a moment to grasp it.

[94] Set off the word with a pause before and another after. Each of the following three exclamation marks calls for a meaningful pause, too.

[95] He wants to deny the truth of what has happened—indeed, he does. A myth is only a *fiction*!

[96] This paragraph describes beauty, and the manner of reading it must reveal the beauty of the lines. Even in the midst of tragedy, Elliot remains a lover of the beautiful.

[97] The story is to be complete by tying in the earlier description of the boy with his appearance as a statue.

[98] After a dramatic pause, this seems a kind of postscript, an anticlimactic ending to a story that has already ended. The surprise of Elliot is reflected in the surprise of the reader. Build to another major climactic ending.

[99] Images of repulsion: Sense them. Let the audience image them!

[100] Retain the suspense to the very last word. It's a remarkable story that permits you to do this.

# 14 Suggestions on the Interpretative Reading of Poetry and Verse

Many kinds of people write poems; they write many kinds of poems; and they write them for many different reasons. Poems are written by the lover, certainly, and by the bereaved; but also by the New England farmer, the wandering vagabond, the insurance company vice-president, the college professor, the housewife, the fifth-grader, the astronaut, the presidential candidate, the drug taker, the physician—in short, by almost everyone. When we group all the many and varied poems that have been written and that are yet to be written into a class, we have *poetry*.

What is poetry? What is the common feature that characterizes those writings that we call poems? Robert Frost once offered a simple response: "Poetry is the kind of thing poets write." This is true enough, but poets must also write letters, interoffice memos, grocery lists, and a host of other scribblings that surely aren't poetry. Attempts to separate what is poetry from what is not have resulted in numerous definitions. Our exploration of a few of these may shed some light on the matter.

A large number of definitions seek to separate poetry from other forms of literature as the highest literary form, the finest writing of which man is capable, demanding the reverence of all:

*Samuel Taylor Coleridge:* "Prose: words in their best order. Poetry: the best words in the best order."

*Matthew Arnold:* "Poetry is simply the most beautiful, the most impressive, and the most effective mode of saying things."

*Michael Roberts:* "If a piece of writing achieves something impossible for prose, you had better call it poetry."

*Louis Untermeyer:* "It [poetry] is the height of literature, and its enjoyment is the greatest of literary joys."

Other attempts at definition concentrate on the achievement of poetry, which goes beyond the normal levels of our consciousness and transcends in words what cannot be said in words:

*Carl Sandburg:* "Poetry is a series of explanations of life, fading off into horizons too swift for explanations."

*Edwin Arlington Robinson:* "Poetry is language that tells us, through a more or less emotional reaction, something that cannot be said."

359

*Dylan Thomas:* ". . . the rhythmic, inevitably narrative, movement from an overclothed blindness to a naked vision."

*Emily Dickinson:* "If I read a book and it makes my whole body so cold no fire can ever warm me, I know that it is poetry. If I feel physically as if the top of my head were taken off, I know that it is poetry."

Poetry is an essence that defies a definitive explanation. It is an abstraction —an ideal—much like *truth, beauty,* or *art.* While we could rigidly limit the scope of writings we call poetry, in so doing we would merely narrow its potential for eliciting meaningful experiences. In a sense, poetry is redefined with every new creation of a poem and with every new experiencing of a poem.

We can, however, set down some of the characteristics of poetry. Poetry tends to be concentrated-condensed-squeezed; it says much in a few words. Poetry tends to be figurative and symbolic; it often speaks of matters other than those it seems to speak about. Poetry depends to a great extent on sound and is meant to be read aloud and heard; the words are important for their sound values as well as for their meanings. Poetry deals in strong imagery. Poetry is usually rhythmical. Poetry is nearly always emotional in content. Poetry is concrete and yet possesses ambiguity. Poetry is — — —.

If, like many people, you approach the experience of poetry with some reservations, you may take comfort in the knowledge that poets themselves sometimes share your skepticism.

## POETRY

MARIANNE MOORE

I, too, dislike it: there are things that are important beyond
        all this fiddle.
  Reading it, however, with a perfect contempt for it, one
        discovers in
  it after all, a place for the genuine.
    Hands that can grasp, eyes
    that can dilate, hair that can rise
      if it must, these things are important not because a

high-sounding interpretation can be put upon them but be-
        cause they are
  useful. When they become so derivative as to become
        unintelligible,
  the same thing may be said for all of us, that we
    do not admire what
    we cannot understand: the bat
      holding on upside down or in quest of something to

eat, elephants pushing a wild horse taking a roll, a tireless
        wolf under
    a tree, the immovable critic twitching his skin like a
        horse that feels a flea, the base-
    ball fan, the statistician—
        nor is it valid
            to discriminate against "business documents and
school-books"; all these phenomena are important. One
        must make a distinction

however: when dragged into prominence by half poets,
        the result is not poetry,
    nor till the poets among us can be
        "literalists of
        the imagination"—above
            insolence and triviality and can present
for inspection, "imaginary gardens with real toads in them,"
        shall we have
    it. In the meantime, if you demand on the one hand,
the raw material of poetry in
    all its rawness and
    that which is on the other hand
        genuine, you are interested in poetry.

Most persons think of poetry and verse as being identical, but it is useful to make a distinction between the two. Certainly, poetry occurs frequently in verse form, but we also find poetic language in prose. Verse may exist without any poetic value whatsoever. Poetry is an elusive, abstract, ideal quality about which we can reach only the most tentative conclusions and imprecise agreements. Verse, like prose, is a form within which poetic language may be cast.

Verse is a highly structured form of writing, tending to use lines of arbitrary length and number, a somewhat tight pattern of rhythm (usually in the form of meter), and often rhyme. Of course, there are different forms: regular rhymed verse, blank verse, and free verse. The first contains all three elements: line form, meter, and rhyme. Blank verse uses a very regular metrical form but does not use rhyme. Free verse, containing no meter and no rhyme, may sometimes be so far from regular verse as to be hardly distinguishable from prose, and yet it still may be fine poetry.

The distinction we make between poetry and verse is amply illustrated by a familiar couplet:

Early to bed and early to rise,
Makes a man healthy, wealthy, and wise.

This is verse: it contains a regular pattern of metrical rhythm in rhymed lines of equal syllabic length. But who would wish to call it *poetry*?

## THE POEM AS A COMMUNICATIVE ACT

Why do people write poetry? Probably most often to express something they feel or think. Some of them do so whether or not they think anyone will ever read what they have written. They just want to "put it into words" and to "get it down on paper." Perhaps most published poets do expect someone to read their poems, and they acknowledge that they are thus trying to communicate with other human beings.

But, it is not quite that simple. What does the poet want *us* as interpreters to communicate? That question may get us into trouble, for some poets seem to know what they have tried to say in their poems, and they want us to communicate exactly the same thing or stay out of the act. Others freely acknowledge that they do not know exactly what their poems say because they cannot recall exactly what they were trying to say when they wrote them, and also because a good poem takes on a life and significance of its own that enables it to say something more than—or something slightly different from—the original intention of the writer! Still others claim that they have no conscious intention. They write not to say something but, rather, to find out what they have to say. Poets often disavow any control over the meanings of their poems once they have written them. And yet, these poets are trying to communicate something to someone, in some instances only to themselves. We said in earlier chapters that the oral interpreter must do all he can to discover what the author intended but, also, realize that the meaning for him is in his own response.

Just to complicate the whole field for us, though, is a school of critical thought that maintains that at least some poems are *not* intended as communicative or expressive acts; rather, they may be products of pure creativity. One poet said in a lecture that he was trying neither to express himself nor to communicate anything but, instead, was building *objects* with words, as other artists might build objects with clay, wood, metal, or other materials. We would argue that as the oral interpreter gives verbal shape to these objects and evokes listener responses, communication (while it may not be the central aim of the work) does, indeed, occur. Expression may not be the objective of a poem, but it is still the means by which the poem becomes accessible to the silent reader or listening audience.

Archibald MacLeish tells us:

A poem should not mean
But be.

                                        —*"Ars Poetica"*

However, before a poem can *be anything*, it must *mean something*: It must elicit responses from its readers. The oral interpreter's communicative challenge is to express the meanings inherent in a poem so that it can exist—can " be "—in the experience of the listeners.

Most of the poetry you are likely to encounter does seek directly to communicate. A poet may wish to philosophize, as Jeffers did in " Science "; to teach a lesson as Pope did in " An Essay on Criticism "; to persuade, as Markham did in " The Man with the Hoe "; to sing a song about an emotional experience, as Keats did in " Ode to a Nightingale "; to tell a story, as Robert Penn Warren did in " The Ballad of Billie Potts "; to reveal a character, as Robinson did in " Mr. Flood's Party "; to present a dramatic situation between two characters, as Frost did in " Home Burial "; to create a mood, as Walter de la Mare did in " The Listeners "; to write word music, as Lanier did in " The Song of the Chattahoochie " or as Poe did in " The Bells "; to sing a song of nonsense, as Carroll did in " Jabberwocky." There are *many* communicative purposes for poetry. The interpretative reader of poetry must discover the communicative nature of the poem, be it simple or a complex combination of several purposes, in order to determine the communicative requirements for its performance.

## ENCOUNTERING A POEM

*Student:*   I spent three hours last night trying to find a poem to read for the poetry reading assignment.
*Instructor:*   Good. What did you finally select?
*Student:*   I couldn't find one I liked. I must have read over a hundred poems, and none of them did anything for me!

The instructor immediately recognizes the problem. The student evidently skimmed through poem after poem, waiting for the language of one to jump off the page and proclaim itself as THE SELECTION to be performed.

There is no one right way to approach the reading of poetry, but there are some basic guidelines that will help. First, the reading of a poem takes time. The true poet condenses experience and imagination into a tightly knit verbal space. If you read poems the same way you might consume the evening newspaper, you will surely miss the *poetry* in the *poem*. Don't be in a hurry. Give yourself time to know the poem intimately; to respond to questions it raises; to immerse yourself in the experience it makes possible.

Second, approach the poem with an open mind. Don't rush to judgment concerning its mood, ideas, or theme. Allow the poem to be simple or complex; to be concrete or abstract; to agree or disagree with your own views. Every reading of a poem is personal, and you should certainly apply your own personality and experiences to its exploration. But, as you do so, take care that you do not force poetry to correspond to any preset expectation.

Third, read the poem with both your eyes and your ears. Involve your whole body in the process of uncovering its meaning. The experience of a poem requires full bodily participation if you are to feel its emotions; hear its music; sense its images; and comprehend its ideas.

By exercising an unhurried, open-minded, full employment of your capacities, you provide favorable conditions for establishing meaningful relationships with individual poems. Notice, however, that we have not been talking about analysis—about *studying* poetry. That comes later. All too often people take apart the poem and study its mechanics without first experiencing the poem itself:

Our meddling intellect
Misshapes the beauteous forms of things,—
We murder to dissect.

> —WILLIAM WORDSWORTH, *"The Tables Turned"*

The dissectable parts of poetry—meter and rhyme, image and idea—are inert when separated from the whole. We should study them carefully after we have gained an initial appreciation of the whole. Then, their study increases and intensifies our appreciation. Then, we are experiencing poetry and not merely the materials out of which a poem is made.

In the spirit we have described, read the following modern poem. Respond as fully as you can, without worrying about whether your response is "right" or "wrong," without any goal beyond sharing an experience with the poet.

## MERRITT PARKWAY

DENISE LEVERTOV

As if it were
forever that they move, that we
keep moving—

Under a wan sky where
as the lights went on a star
pierced the haze and now
follows steadily
a constant
above our six lanes
the dreamlike continuum . . .

And the people—ourselves!
the humans from inside the
cars, apparent

only at gasoline stops
                    unsure,
        eyeing each other

            drink coffee hastily at the
            slot machines and hurry
        back to the cars
            vanish
            into them forever, to
        keep moving—

Houses now and then beyond the
sealed road, the trees / trees, bushes
passing by, passing
        the cars that
            keep moving ahead of

        us, past us, pressing behind us
                            and
                over left, those that come
            toward us shining too brightly
moving relentlessly

            in six lanes, gliding
        north and south, speeding with
        a slurred sound—

We believe that this poem both deserves and requires careful analysis for effective oral performance. What is the relationship between "they" and "we" in line two? Who is "we"? Is Levertov primarily interested in describing cars on a highway? Commenting on some aspect of human nature? Revealing her own personal feelings? What is the prevailing attitude of the poem? Does the attitude change? Does the poem, like the cars, proceed "relentlessly," "speeding with a slurred sound"? These are but a few of many questions we might wish to apply toward analysis of the poem. But the initial encounter need not go beyond engaging in an experience out of which questions will be raised and answered.

## AMBIGUITY AND OBSCURITY

The complex of sound, feeling, and idea that makes up a poem often contains more meanings than meet the casual eye. These meanings may be ambiguous and obscure. Perhaps this explains the reluctance of many to read poems. In frustration we demand: "Why didn't he say it simply so that I couldn't help but get his meanings?" But to ask this of the poet is to deny poetry its inherent power of distilling into a *few* words aspects of the human experience which are not simple, not ordinary, and not intended to be digested easily. Greatness is seldom simple, be it a human life or a work of art derived from human life. The best of literature may at times be frustratingly difficult to fathom but, also, correspondingly rewarding to one who makes the effort.

This is not to suggest that simple poems may not be good poems or that obscurity is in itself a virtue; rather, it is to say that complex human experiences cannot be fully expressed in simple language. Like real life, real literature is seldom simple. Earlier, in Chapter 6, we observed that ambiguity in J. P. Donleavy's story "One for Yes" stimulates the reader to a rewardingly complex response. We find ambiguity worthwhile for further discussion here, because poems frequently possess multiple possibilities of meaning that challenge the interpreter's analytical and expressive capabilities. The oral reader who does not perceive ambiguity, or who chooses to disregard that element in a poem, reduces its meanings, thereby lessening its potential impact on an audience.

The valid question does arise, however, about the feasibility of communicating ambiguous or obscure meanings to audiences. To expect instant communicative success with literature requiring several silent readings for understanding seems unrealistic at best. Well, of course, that is a function of the interpreter: to probe the depths of meaning and find the means for making possible at least a partial understanding and appreciation in the listener. Good oral interpretation can send the listener back to the written poem with an increased capacity to understand and appreciate it, even when communication of full meaning is impossible. The oral interpreter's insights, enthusiasm, and informative remarks hopefully lead to understanding and eventual appreciation by the audience. The interpreter's introduction to the reading of an obscure poem is especially important preparation for insightful reading. And, of course, we should never underestimate the power of the expressive human voice, face, and body to communicate meanings that may not be transparent.

Traditionally, the speaker tries to *make clear* the meanings behind words. If meaning is "ambiguous" in the worst sense, it must be cleared up for the listener. But ambiguity in the best sense—the device of saying more than one thing at once with one set of words—is to be found in abundance in great poetry. It is unlikely that an oral interpreter will succeed in communicating at once *all* the possible meanings that a silent reader may eventually find in the lines after hours of scrutiny. Some attempts to do so may result, not in exciting multiplicities of meaning, but in confusion. On the other hand, there is no excuse for diluting a complex poem into a superficial clarity.

Well, then, how can an interpreter give more than one meaning in the same utterance? This is an easy question to answer if we return to our definition of meaning as response. The interpreter does not *give* meanings but, rather, elicits responses (meanings) from an audience. The successful reading often preserves the possibility of multiple meanings so that they can be realized by attentive listeners. A deliberately *inexpressive* recitation that allows for *any* meaning or meanings is inconsistent with the communicative purposes of interpretation. But, a controlled performance that is responsive to simultaneous connotations of idea and feeling encourages a similarly productive ambiguity in the listener.

Look back to Theodore Roethke's poem, " My Papa's Waltz," at the end of Chapter 4. Its attitude seems somewhat ambiguous. Separate critics have described it both as a pleasant reminiscence and as a recollection of terror. Well, which is it? Within the limits of ethical responsibility and good scholarship, you are entitled to your own " interpretation " of this or any poem. (Many different Hamlets have legitimately been brought to life on the stage.) You might (justifiably, we believe) read Roethke's poem with either attitude as the predominant emotion. But, it seems also possible to adopt a somewhat ambiguous posture toward the father that bespeaks a " bittersweet " love-hate feeling.

The attitude of this next poem seems consistently contemplative, but there is ambiguity.

## ON A SQUIRREL CROSSING THE ROAD IN AUTUMN, IN NEW ENGLAND

RICHARD EBERHART

It is what he does not know,
Crossing the road under the elm trees,
About the mechanism of my car,
About the Commonwealth of Massachusetts,
About Mozart, India, Arcturus,

That wins my praise. I engage
At once in whirling squirrel-praise.
He obeys the orders of nature
Without knowing them.
It is what he does not know
That makes him beautiful.
Such a knot of little purposeful nature!

I who can see him as he cannot see himself
Repose in the ignorance that is his blessing.

It is what man does not know of God
Composes the visible poem of the world.
                    . . . Just missed him!

Look to the last line of the poem as the driver realizes he "Just missed him!" " " Him " clearly refers to the squirrel—the car narrowly avoids running over the animal. But, "him" seems also to be God. This ambiguity contributes to an essential comparison between the squirrel (as viewed by man) and man (in relationship to God). Other ambiguities occur as we consider ourselves very much like and, at the same time, different from the squirrel, as we think how our ignorance can be a blessing, and as we resolve how what we don't know can be a " *visible* poem."

Ambiguity in literature can be rewarding when the reader *reveals* multiple meanings, but it can be frustrating when the reading itself is ambiguous. We can offer no prescription for success, because every successful performance results from a delicate balance of simultaneous performer and listener responses. The interpreter needs to be receptive to ambiguities in literature and, at the same time, responsive to the needs and capabilities of the audience.

## PRIME ELEMENTS OF POETIC LANGUAGE

Figurative language and conscious constructions in sound are frequently employed by poets. These elements of poetic language are important stimulants to the sensory and kinesthetic imagery essential for poetry to make an instant impact, in contrast to the general discursiveness of prose.

**Figures of Speech.** James Thurber wrote an amusing character sketch called " Here Lies Miss Groby," about a former teacher whose chief delight in life was identifying figures in literature. Thurber's story illustrates that anyone holding such a distorted view of what is important in literature "can't see the forest for the trees" (as the figure of speech goes!). One of your authors has a volume published in 1875 that is entirely devoted in its *534 pages* to the identification, discussion, and illustration of *225 different* figures of speech![1] Metonymy alone is shown (in 19 pages) to have 39 varieties! Our modern study of figurative language is meager, indeed, compared with that book's vast effort or to classroom exercises required of students in previous eras of literary study. Although Miss Groby and a writer of a hundred years ago may have been preoccupied with figures of speech to the point of absurdity, it is important for us to know the values of figurative language, particularly in poetry, and to recognize some of the most common forms we shall encounter. Figures of speech are not just something academic for only the Miss Grobys to appreciate. Figures of speech abound in our daily conversation. We suspect that you cannot, in a normal day's conversing, refrain from speaking figuratively. In a literal world, all of us seem to delight

[1] John Walker Vilant Macbeth, *The Might and Mirth of Literature* (New York : Harper & Row, Publishers, 1875).

in words and phrases that intensify meaning by drawing likenesses between seemingly dissimilar things.

We are most familiar with the *simile*, which is an obvious comparison using *like* or *as* to state a specific reference. For example, we say, "When she heard that, she took off like a flying saucer." The poet may write:

The worlds revolve like ancient women
Gathering fuel in vacant lots.

—T. S. ELIOT, *"Preludes"*

As idle as a painted ship
Upon a painted ocean . . .

—SAMUEL TAYLOR COLERIDGE, *The Rime of the Ancient Mariner*

But I hung on like death:

—THEODORE ROETHKE, *"My Papa's Waltz"*

The *metaphor* is a more direct comparison, in which the comparative word is omitted and an assertion of identity is made. For example, we may say, "The boss is an old bear this morning; he just ate me alive." The poet may write:

My vigor is a new-minted penny,
Which I cast at your feet.

—AMY LOWELL, *"A Lady"*

Sometimes the verb *to be* is omitted but the metaphor is still there, as in:

Yet he weeps for her,
with seeming-helpless hands conducts
a whole mighty orchestra of eyes
to weep for her . . .

—PETER KANE DUFAULT, *"Gielgud Reading Lear"*

An *apostrophe* is direct address to an object or an idea as if it were a person. We sing songs of adoration of our nation or our alma mater. We speak coaxingly to a sluggish automobile on a subzero morning: "Come on, Bessie, don't fail me now!" The poet writes:

Death, be not proud . . .

—JOHN DONNE, *"Death Be Not Proud"*

O Holy Night! from thee I learn to bear
What man has borne before.

—HENRY WADSWORTH LONGFELLOW, *"Hymn to the Night"*

*Personification* is the comparison of an object, animal, or idea to a human being by giving it human qualities. Donald Duck and Snoopy are favorite, simple, examples of personification, but less obvious uses give pleasure in both conversation and in literature. The golfer complains, " The ball absolutely refused to drop today." The poet writes:

This Sea that bares her bosom to the moon . . .
    —WILLIAM WORDSWORTH, *"The World is Too Much With Us"*

When duty whispers low, *Thou must,*
  The youth replies, *I can.*
    —RALPH WALDO EMERSON, *"Voluntaries"*

. . . nothing sighs except the river . . .
    —GABRIELA MISTRAL, *"Night"*

*Hyperbole* is obvious and gross exaggeration to produce such effects as humor, impressiveness, or terror. To brighten conversation, we exaggerate all the time—without intending to lie. A mild social faux pas in the retelling is followed by the comment, " I fell flat on my face!" The caricaturist exaggerates certain aspects of the physiognomy, and the impressionist similarly takes a single presidential trait and builds a whole act on his exaggeration of it.

Poets, too, use hyperbole. Look back to Andrew Marvell's "To His Coy Mistress," in Chapter 2, and George Barker's "To My Mother," in Chapter 6. The phrase " Sitting as huge as Asia," from Barker's poem, is both hyperbole and simile. Other examples are:

Here once the embattled farmers stood
And fired the shot heard around the world.
    —RALPH WALDO EMERSON, *"The Concord Hymn"*

. . . the whole world goes to sleep
to the sway of my cradle swinging.
    —GABRIELA MISTRAL, *"Night"*

*Metonymy* is a figure in which the speaker or writer uses one word for another related to it. The speaker may employ the cause for the effect, the effect for the cause, the sign for what it signifies, or the container for what it contains: *Uncle Sam* or *Columbia* may suggest the United States, *table* may suggest food, or *purple and gold* may suggest a particular college.

In *synecdoche*, a form of metonymy, the speaker employs the name of a part to represent the whole: a " sail" represents a ship, " heads " represent cattle, " noses " people, or " hands" workers. Some metonymies in literature quoted in this text are:

From my mother's sleep I fell into the State . . .
> —RANDALL JARREL, *"The Death of the Ball Turret Gunner"*

So was I once myself a swinger of birches.
> —ROBERT FROST, *"Birches"*

if you don't mind a touch of hell
> now and then

>           .   .   .

> as our Name Brand Society

>           .   .   .

and its men of extinction
> and its priests

> and other patrolmen

>           .   .   .

> comes the smiling

> mortician
>> —LAWRENCE FERLINGHETTI, *"The World"*

. . . she will move from mourning into morning.
> —GEORGE BARKER, *"To My Mother"*

Give me high noon—and let it then be night!
> —JOHN G. NEIHARDT, *"Let Me Live Out My Years"*

In reading a poem, indeed any literature, that employs figures of speech, the interpreter needs to be aware not only of the literal meaning implied, but of the figurative as well. In Sara Teasdale's simile,

One by one, like leaves from a tree,
All my faiths have forsaken me.
> —*"Leaves"*

the reader should remember that leaves fall slowly, that they never return to their former places, and that we associate the falling of leaves with sadness.

**Sound Devices.** Poetry also employs sound devices, because it is usually an attempt to form a perfect union of sense and sound. This is one of the main reasons a poem is *orally* communicative and *aurally* satisfying. In order for this perfect union to be effected, a poem should be given voice. It should be read aloud. The oral reader must give special attention to the formation and combination of sounds as the poet planned them.

*Onomatopoeia* or sound symbolism, already mentioned in Chapter 9, is the use of words whose sounds suggest their sense. It is natural correspondence between sound and sense. Simple examples are *buzz*, *hiss*, *clack*, *bang*, and *twitter*. Onomatopoeia is employed in poetry in single words such as the preceding, in phrases, and in extended pieces such as "The Bells" by Poe. The following are instances of onomatopoeia that extend beyond a single word:

And thumping and plumping, and bumping and jumping,
And dashing and flashing, and splashing and clashing,
   And so never ending,
   And always descending,
Sounds and motions for ever and ever are blending,
   All at once and all o'er,
   With a mighty uproar,
And this way the water comes down at Lodore.
      —ROBERT SOUTHEY, *"How the Water Comes Down at Lodore"*

And the plashing of waterdrops
In the marble fountain
Comes down the garden paths.

                    —AMY LOWELL, *"Patterns"*

Discover the instances of onomatopoeia in the poetry you are to read. Try fully to recognize the correspondence between sound and sense. Then when you read aloud, try to utter the words in such a way as to make the most of the sound values. In reading the last lines quoted, you would adjust rhythm, pitch, loudness, and quality so as to suggest the actual sound of waterdrops. Perhaps a warning is necessary. Do not allow the way you read it to seem more important than what you read.

*Alliteration* is the device of beginning syllables in close succession with the same consonantal sound. It is a means to the musical quality in poetry, and quite often the reader will want to emphasize it—but never to the exclusion of the sense. Examples are quite common; here are a few:

The fair breeze blew, the white foam flew.
The furrow followed free.
      —SAMUEL TAYLOR COLERIDGE, *The Rime of the Ancient Mariner*

The moan of doves in immemorial elms,
And murmuring of innumerable bees.
              —ALFRED, LORD TENNYSON, *"The Princess"*

Both of these instances of alliteration achieve an onomatopoetic effect that contributes to the poem's meaning. Denise Levertov uses alliteration to the same end in describing the movement of cars on "Merritt Parkway":

in six lanes, gliding
north and south, speeding with
a slurred sound—

Alliteration can also be used for comic effect, as in the following:

With blade, with bloody blameful blade,
He bravely broached his boiling bloody breast.
—SHAKESPEARE, *A Midsummer Night's Dream*

*Assonance* is the repetition of vowel or diphthong sounds, especially in stressed syllables, as in *freedom, sleep, free*. One of the purposes of assonance in poetry is to provide pleasure to the ear. The device may be used, however, for other purposes. It helps to fuse the poetic unit into an integrated whole; and it may serve to emphasize certain elements of meaning. The following examples may help you to identify assonance:

I arise from dreams of thee,
In the first sweet sleep of night.
—PERCY BYSSHE SHELLEY, *"Lines to an Indian Air"*

The curfew tolls the knell of parting day,
The lowing herd wind slowly oe'r the lea.
—THOMAS GRAY, *"Elegy Written in a Country Churchyard"*

Assonance may not be consciously recognized by the reader—even by the oral reader—but if you will look at Stephen Spender's poem "The Express" in Chapter 10, you will find a significant use of the long *e* [i] sound in: queen, she, leaves, she, speed, she, she, screaming, aerial, underneath, meter, wheels, steaming, she, speed, clean, steel, she, reaches, streamline, she, equal, aerial. One can hardly feel that the sound thus constantly heard in this poem does not have a constructive, communicative purpose to play, whether or not Spender consciously thought of it in the composing.

## STRUCTURE OF VERSE

Underlying the surface of a poem lie evidences of the poet's labors to create a particular sound structure. As architect of the verse, a poet may construct his poem using a *fixed* or an *organic* form. The fixed-form poem begins with conventional patterns of line and stanza length, meter, and sometimes rhyme. To write a sonnet, for instance, the poet begins with a formula of fourteen iambic pentameter lines with a prescribed rhyme scheme. Using this conventional pattern as a skeleton, the poet may elect to adhere closely to the norm or to depart through changing rhythms, line lengths, or rhyme patterns. Modern poets tend to break away from uniformity to a much greater extent than poets of other ages. Today, poets experiment with lines of various lengths, in terms of syllables, feet, and numbers of stresses per line; they are inventive in their handling of variety in metrical feet; and they depart freely from accustomed employment of rhyme.

Organic forms of poetry, more commonly referred to as *free verse* or *vers libre*, are constructed without prearranged conventional patterns. Some poets who write in organic forms suggest that a line of their verse corresponds to a thought unit; others claim that the line is a unit of breath, and still others say they do not adhere to any one means of determining line lengths. But a free verse poem is not really *free*: it creates its own form, its own confinement, in a structure that grows organically with the creation of the work.

Whether the poem we read rigidly adheres to a fixed form, departs considerably from a traditional pattern, or creates its own wholly unique structure, it is beneficial to understand the fundamental ingredients of conventional verse. An awareness of the principles of stanzaic structure, meter, and rhyme opens us to the raw materials of the fixed-form poet and, also, to patterns that may often be lurking within what seems to be the freest of free verse.

The common denominator of each of the elements we shall discuss is *recurrence*, which builds expectations in the reader or listener. As a poem begins to conform to a more or less regular meter, and as its rhymes occur in regular patterns, we expect that the pattern will continue. Whoever composed the following limerick capitalized on our expectations that a familiar metrical pattern will be carried forth:

A decrepit old gasman, named Peter,
While hunting around his gas heater,
   Touched a leak with his light;
   He rose out of sight—
And, as everyone who knows anything about poetry can tell you, he
    also ruined the meter.

                                              —ANONYMOUS

This blatant departure from an expected rhythm serves as a joke. More subtle deviations combine the expected and the unexpected, fixity and flux, pleasurable variations within a comfortably familiar frame. We shall examine some instances of artistic variation as we explore meter and rhyme in the following sections.

**Stanzaic Structure.**   Whereas prose combines sentences into paragraphs, verse binds lines within stanzas. The stanzaic structure may correspond to phrase and sentence structures of the language, but a thought group may carry over from one line or stanza to the next. In either case, the interpreter should respect line and stanza divisions as significant elements of the poem's form. Although it is nearly impossible to generalize about the significance of stanza form, it is often true that simple stanzaic structure best communicates simple content and that more complicated structure is appropriate for complicated content. Limericks exemplify the first and sonnets, the second. Emily Dickinson used simple stanzaic forms, and Eliot used complicated ones.

**Meter.**   Arrange syllabic stresses into a planned structural form and you have what is called *meter*. In all verse except free verse, meter is a prime element of structure. Meter is a distinguishable pattern of recurrent vocal stresses, a trellis against which the poet trains a rose. The trellis is of no significance in itself, yet it affects the rose, by supporting it, and, in a sense, controlling it. Supported by the framework of the trellis is an interesting " message " of shape and color. Supported by the time pattern of the meter is an interesting " message " of sound and silence. Although it is to the " message " that we attend, that basic form behind it also makes a contribution to the message. Meter alone is mechanical and dull. One can enjoy a poem without *consciously* attending to the meter. But because the meter is often a directive force contributing to the poem's impact, the oral interpreter must often study it in some detail.

Meter is sometimes a very simple matter, such as you find in nursery rhymes, light verse, and limericks. In these, the meter is instantly recognized. On the other hand, the mass of our great poetry has less-pronounced meters, or to put it more accurately, meters that are subordinate to more-significant subtle rhythms of speech and meaning than the mere mechanical alternations of vocal stresses in a basic pattern. In other words, the rose becomes much more important than the trellis! In preparing to read such poems, one should still be aware of the supporting-disciplining form of the metrical pattern and so increase his sensitivity to the poem's total meaning. *Prosody*, the science of versification, begins with a recognition of mere alternations of light and heavy beats, but continued study involves such complex and subtle variations that only persons specializing in that science—indulging in lifetime scholarship—can comprehend its full ramifications.

There are four basic forms in which the stresses and unstresses occur in English verse. The most common form—because it is the native accentual rhythm of English—is the *iambic foot* ($\cup$ /), in which an unstressed syllable is followed by a stressed one, as in:

$\cup$ / $\cup$ / $\cup$ / $\cup$ / $\cup$ /
The cur/few tolls / the knell / of part/ing day,

$\cup$ / $\cup$ / $\cup$ / $\cup$ / $\cup$ /
The low/ing herd / wind slow/ly o'er / the lea, . . .

—THOMAS GRAY, *"Elegy Written in a Country Churchyard"*

The other two-element foot is the *trochaic foot* ( / ∪ ), in which the stressed syllable occurs first, as in:

/ ∪ / ∪ / ∪ / ∪ / ∪ / ∪
Once up/on a / mid-night / dreary, / while I / pondered, / weak and /

/ ∪
weary / . . .

—EDGAR ALLAN POE, *"The Raven"*

There are two forms of three-syllable feet: (1) the *anapestic* (∪∪/), in which the stressed syllable follows two unstressed ones, as in:

∪ ∪ / ∪ ∪ / ∪ ∪ / ∪ ∪ /
'Twas the night / before Christ/mas, when all / through the house / . . .

—CLEMENT CLARKE MOORE, *"A Visit from St. Nicholas"*

and (2) the *dactyllic* (/∪∪), in which the stressed syllable occurs initially, as in:

/ ∪ ∪ / ∪ ∪
Cannon to / right of them, /

/ ∪ ∪ / ∪ ∪
Cannon to / left of them, / . . .

—ALFRED, LORD TENNYSON, *"The Charge of the Light Brigade"*

These meters seldom occur in pure forms. In good poems of any age there are substitutions of one kind of foot where you might expect another. A meter with no variation would become intolerable if carried very far.

In good poems, the poet deliberately creates a tension between his meter and his meaning as it is to be manifested in speech. This is like syncopation in music, which we enjoy. We quickly tire of the metronomic monotony of honky-tonk piano, the steadily revolving music of the merry-go-round, the consistent pattern of the suave hotel orchestra playing the "businessman's bounce," and the persistent beat of early rock 'n' roll. These never surprise the listener; they merely grind away without syncopation; and, although they may prove pleasant for a time, ultimately they wear us out. Eventually, more sophisticated—complex—forms of rhythm must assert themselves to satisfy us.

The rhythmic tensions created in a poem can only be fully revealed in performance. We can, however, gain some notion of how this is achieved by noting syllables that are stressed ( / ), unstressed ( ∪ ), or that fall somewhere in between ( ? ). We have indicated how *we* hear the metrical stresses in a familiar poem by Robert Frost, yet the stresses, slacks, and the metrical feet that we should be inclined to use are certainly not the only way to analyze the poem. (The better the poem, the greater the opportunity for divergent interpretations.) Read Frost's poem according to our markings and see if you agree. While your analysis of the rhythm may depart somewhat from ours, it surely will still expose rhythmic tensions that surprise and satisfy.

## STOPPING BY WOODS ON A SNOWY EVENING

ROBERT FROST

Whose woods / these are / I think / I know. /                          1

His house / is in / the vil/lage though; /                            2

He will / not see / me stop/ping here /                               3

To watch / his woods / fill up / with snow. /                         4

My lit/tle horse / must think / it queer /                            5

To stop / without / a farm/house near /                               6

Between / the woods / and froz/en lake /                              7

The dark/est eve/ning of / the year. /                                8

He gives / his harn/ess bells / a shake /                             9

To ask / if there / is some / mistake, /                              10

The on/ly oth/er sound's / the sweep /                                11

Of eas/y wind / and dow/ny flake. /                                   12

The woods / are lovely, / dark / and deep, /                          13

But I / have prom/ises / to keep, /                                   14

And miles / to go / before / I sleep, /                               15

And miles / to go / before / I sleep.                                 16

The poem can be thumped out in steady iambics: " whose WOODS these ARE i THINK i KNOW " and so on. But Frost *forces* us away from monotony, chiefly by altering vocal stresses, arranging or allowing for internal pauses, and skillfully using carry-overs. Unlike some modern poets, Frost is a strong believer in metrical structure. He is supposed to have said one time that he would as soon play tennis without a net as write poetry without meter. Yet he never lets his meters dominate his message; in fact, he is one of the most conversational of poets.

Let us now give close attention to how Frost has achieved his marvelous tension, or syncopation, between the meter and the idea in "Stopping by Woods on a Snowy Evening." First, the basic pattern is iambic with four feet and four stresses per line. This pattern remains intact in lines 5, 7, 9, 11, 12, 15, and 16, and possibly also in lines 2 and 10. In line 13 the occurrence of the internal pause after "lovely" simply shifts the marking of the foot and adds weight to the heavy stress on "dark." Lines 2, 8, 10, and 14 may each have only three stresses because of the unimportance in normal speech of such words as "in," "of," and "there," and the final syllable of "promises." *Here* is a good example of that syncopation we were speaking of. The anticipated metrical structure calls for four stresses in each of these lines; conversational naturalness does not. To stress them strongly would be to create singsong; to ignore the metrical tendency to stress them would be to run the danger of reading in too prosy a manner. In reality, because of the anticipated pattern, we may read "in," "of," "there," and "—es" with slight stresses, recognizing that although Frost may have designed four stresses per line, he does not expect them to be *equal* stresses. In speech, we have several levels of stress according to the emphatic importance of what we are saying. Take an example from the poem. In line 5, is not "queer" more emphatic than "lit—", or "think"?

The impulse for natural emphasis causes many variations from the pattern. Let us look at a few lines together, and you can analyze the rest of the poem for yourself. In the first line, "Whose," which falls on a normally light syllable in the basic pattern, is an important emphatic word. On the other hand, "are," which falls upon a stressed part of a metrical foot is not significant, being a form of the verb *to be*, which is rarely emphasized in normal speech; therefore, any stress on it will be very light. We have already shown how "in" in line 2 is perhaps unstressed entirely. Line 3 offers interesting possibilities for variation either for emphasizing "He" rather than the unimportant auxiliary verb "will" in the first foot or unstressing both of these and stressing both "not" and "see" in the next foot. In line 4, "woods" is an echo of the same word in the first line and therefore is so obvious that it should not receive any stress other than what is unavoidable, whereas both words in the following foot, "fill" and "up," do receive natural stress in conversational speech.

In the second stanza, lines 5 and 7 are straightforward iambic, but lines 6 and 8 break up the possibilities for monotony. "Farmhouse" has two stressed syllables, which means that the last foot has two stressed beats. To compensate for this, the reader can well avoid giving major stress to the second syllable of "without." In line 8, as we have already indicated, "of" should *not* be stressed or very slightly at most.

The poet may emphasize particular meaning by his use of metrical variation. Look at George Cuomo's fine little poem "On the Death of a Student Hopelessly Failing My Course," in Chapter 1. If you will scan it, simply by marking the normally (in conversation) stressed syllables ($/$), and those normally unstressed ($\cup$) on a separate sheet of paper, you will find that it is blank verse, with an iambic ($\cup/$) pattern. The first line is strictly iambic: $\cup/\ \cup/\ \cup/\ \cup/\ \cup/$. With the second line, you will run into trouble if you insist on retaining the iambic beat, for you will find it is fundamentally trochaic: $/\cup\ /\cup\ \cup/\ /\cup\ /\cup$. The introduction of trochees does more than add an interesting variety; it introduces a whole new atmosphere: a change in rhythm from the simple assertion of the boy's death to a new element—the feelings of his parents. In the third line you will find an extraordinary thing happening in the last five syllables; they are all heavy beats, giving a great deal of accented emphasis:

"... poor boy!' Poor boy, he"!

If you count the syllables in the lines, you find that all the lines have ten syllables except line 12, which has only nine, and it, too, ends with several heavy beats:

"... fire-red sports car."

The absence of the extra anticipated tenth beat adds significance by giving time for a pause at this climactic point. If you divide the lines into five feet each and then count the various types of feet, you may come up with some figures like ours: iambs ($\cup/$) 40, trochees ($/\cup$) 13, spondees ($//$) 12, pyrrhics ($\cup\cup$) 4, and one partial foot (end of line 12) with a heavy beat and an understood pause filling it out, making a total of 70 feet. Iambic meter is most like our conversational speech. When the poet has changed to trochaic feet, he usually accomplishes a shift in attention or emphasis. When he uses spondees, he accomplishes strong emphasis. An example of emphasis accomplished with trochees occurs in line 11:

"Failure / themed his / small life."

Putting some unaccented syllables together speeds up the line, as in

"Quickness / of hand," /

"Soaring / from the / mountain" /

or softens it,

"comfort/ing him." /

The beauty of poetry is derived chiefly not from the meter but from the rhythm of meaning, that is, the rhythm of speech superimposed upon the meter (the rose on the trellis). It is possible for a sensitive reader to be subconsciously aware of the rhythm and to read rhythmically without having studied the meter. However, we contend that the potential understanding and appreciation resulting from analysis of metrical structure is frequently, if not always, valuable. We must study what a good poet *does* in order to realize as fully as possible what he *says*. We may shudder while reading some of the academic arguments between prosodists about the " only valid " reading of a specific poetic line, for these discussions become esoteric and remote from the *total* impact of the poem as a *whole* piece of literature. However, we do suggest that you try scanning some poems, with the realization that how you do it and how others do it will be different. The reason for scanning is simply to discover the poet's design and the role of the design in his act of communication. From such study, you can discover the basis for the syncopation we seek to find wherever the poet has provided it. From it, we also seek clues to his meaning, not discovered elsewhere or by other means. From it, we can observe the skeletal framework that supports the living " flesh " of the poem.

**Rhyme.**    Traditional verse employs more or less regular rhyme. Because, in the following lines (" Jenny Kiss'd Me "), the first ends in the same syllable as the third, the second the same as the fourth, the fifth the same as the seventh, and the sixth the same as the eighth, we say that the rhyme scheme is *ababcdcd*.

## JENNY KISS'D ME

LEIGH HUNT

Jenny kiss'd me when we met,
   jumping from the chair she sat in;
Time, you thief, who love to get
   Sweets into your list, put that in!
Say I'm weary, say I'm sad,
   Say that health and wealth have miss'd me,
Say I'm growing old, but add,
   Jenny kiss'd me.

The rhyme scheme in Leigh Hunt's little poem is quite simple, but much of our best literature employs a far more complicated rhyme scheme. For example, the format of the English sonnet requires precisely fourteen rhymed lines in the following scheme: *ababcdcd efef gg*. The beauty and intricacy of the sonnet, involving the rhyme scheme and other standards of form, are perhaps best illustrated in the poems of Shakespeare. Notice that the following lines adhere exactly to the prescribed rhyming pattern. In doing so, they contribute to the unity of the poem.

## SONNET 116

### WILLIAM SHAKESPEARE

Let me not to the marriage of true minds
Admit impediments. Love is not love
Which alters when it alteration finds,
Or bends with the remover to remove:
O, no! it is ever-fixed mark.
That looks on tempests and is never shaken;
It is the star to every wandering bark,
Whose worth's unknown, although his height be taken.
Love's not Time's fool, though rosy lips and cheeks
Within his bending sickle's compass come;
Love alters not with his brief hours and weeks,
But bears it out even to the edge of doom.
 If this be error, and upon me prov'd,
 I never writ, nor no man ever lov'd.

In the fixed-form poem, rhyme contributes a kind of musical punctuation to the sound structure. When the rhymes occur regularly at the ends of lines and stanzas, they serve to separate them as significant units of the poem's form. Like metrical patterns, rhyme schemes provide a basic format to which the poet need not always rigidly adhere. Look back to Philip Larkin's poem, " Church Going," at the end of Chapter 10. You will notice that he employs a rhyme scheme of *ababcadcd* throughout, but many of the rhymed words are *near rhymes* which only approximate the normal correspondence between the final vowel and consonant. In the first stanza, for instance, Larkin rhymes " on," " stone," and " organ;" and " stuff " and " off. " In the second, he rhymes " font," " don't," and " meant;" and " pronounce " and " six-pence." These near rhymes are accompanied by traditional rhymes in the stanzas, such as " shut " and " cut," and " new " and " few." Subtle variations from the precise sound correspondence still fulfill our expectation of rhyme, but with an often pleasing modification.

Free verse poems often contain rhyme, even though it is not so regularly structured. In " The World," for instance, Lawrence Ferlinghetti made extensive use of rhyme:

if you don't much *mind*
                a few dead *minds*
    in the higher pla*ces*
                    or a bomb or two
        now and then
                    in your upturned fa*ces*

or such other impropr*ieties*
                    as our Name Brand soc*iety*
          *is* prey to
                    with its men of dist*inction*
     and its men of ext*inction*
                         and its priests
          and other patrolmen
                         and its various segreg*ations*
and congressional investig*ations*
                         and other constip*ations*


Notice the unusual effect created by " soc*iety*/*is* " as it carries forth in two lines to complete the rhyme with " impropr*ieties*." Ferlinghetti has exercised freedoms in his use of rhyme, unrestricted by the constraints of conventional schemes. Other instances of rhyme in free verse can be found in Marianne Moore's " Poetry," at the beginning of this chapter. Most of the line end-rhymes in the poem occur during phrases that carry over a thought group to the succeeding line, such as:

*"*literalists *of*
the imagination*"*—above
     insolence and triviality . . .


The rhymes provide a subtle strain of verse structure to language that might otherwise sound more like prose.

While the primary contribution of rhyme is to the sound structure of verse, it sometimes bears a direct influence on meaning. As the reader sounds the second word of a rhyming pair, the first is also called to mind. The resulting sound correspondence suggests the possibility that words' meanings may also be related in some significant way. In Ferlinghetti's poem, for instance, " improprieties " are characteristic of what " society is," " distinction " is the opposite pole of " extinction," and the " segregations " and " investigations " are " constipations." The first rhyming pair in Theodore Roethke's " My Papa's Waltz " matches " breath " (the basis of life) and " death." Robert Herrick employs a similar contrast in the final couplet of " Corinna's Going a Maying "·

Then, while time serves, and we are but dec*aying,*
Come, my *Corinna*, come, let's goe a M*aying*


The contrast is heightened by the presence of the rhyme. The sound reinforces the sense.

## IDENTITY OF FORM AND MEANING

Whatever be the type of poetry or verse, the author's relationship to the meaning, and the techniques or the structure employed, these features and the meaning itself are one. The mode of expression and the meaning are one. Any really good poem or verse will demonstrate this fact, and any effective performance preserves the coalescence of sound and sense. We suggest that in addition to other things you may do with a poem, you also give due consideration to the way it is built. Read it metrically, beating out the stresses for all they are worth! Separate each of the lines and stanzas by noticeable pauses, and emphasize the rhyme. Although such singsong reading is abhorrent to you (and others!), your physical experience with the metrical pattern will guide your oral reading to an artistic " dimension " that you may not otherwise achieve. Your awareness of a poem's raw materials—its stanzaic structure, meter, and rhyme—is an important first step in reconstructing the oral shape of the work.

The successful performance of a poem grows out of the interpreter's responses to the individual elements of the language. To experience a poem fully, however, we must go beyond the separate parts of the poem. We must savor its sounds and feel its rhythms. Understanding of stanzaic structure gives way to an " oral shape " that separates and emphasizes thought groups. Singsong metrical reading matures into a rhythmical experience that blends idea and attitude into speech rhythms that (though often heightened) are consistent with the accustomed phrasing and intonation of the English language. Recognition of alliteration, assonance, and rhyme resolves into a mosaic of sound combinations that gives varying textures to the flow of meaningful sound. An oral interpreter who cannot *hear* the music of a poem will be unable to communicate its full act of language to an audience.

Following, is the first stanza of " The Tyger," by William Blake. Note the stanzaic structure, the metrical pattern, and the rhyme scheme; and read the lines aloud to hear how the form and meaning coalesce to create a distinctive word music:

Tyger! Tyger! burning bright
In the forests of the night,
What immortal hand or eye
Could frame thy fearful symmetry?

As you listen to your reading of the stanza, do you hear a " fearful symmetry " in the sound? There are four lines with a basic pattern of four stresses in each line. Try accentuating the meter and the rhymes to the point of chanting while considering the awesome power of the tiger. You should probably feel constrained by the symmetry of the language, for this containment leads to power. By struggling against the fetters of the language, your strength (like the tiger's) is compressed, your muscles, tightened and poised.

Let us turn to another poem which adheres to a fixed-form of stanzaic structure, meter, and rhyme. As you read it, you should experience a distinctly different texture of sound from the word music of "The Tyger."

## I KNEW A WOMAN

### THEODORE ROETHKE

I knew a woman, lovely in her bones,
When small birds sighed, she would sigh back at them;
Ah, when she moved, she moved more ways than one:
The shapes a bright container can contain!
Of her choice virtues only gods should speak,
Or English poets who grew up on Greek
(I'd have them sing in chorus, cheek to cheek).

How well her wishes went! She stroked my chin,
She taught me Turn, and Counter-turn, and Stand;
She taught me Touch, that undulant white skin;
I nibbled meekly from her proffered hand;
She was the sickle; I, poor I, the rake,
Coming behind her for her pretty sake
(But what prodigious mowing we did make).

Love likes a gander, and adores a goose:
Her full lips pursed, the errant note to seize;
She played it quick, she played it light and loose;
My eyes, they dazzled at her flowing knees;
Her several parts could keep a pure repose,
Or one hip quiver with a mobile nose
(She moved in circles, and those circles moved).

Let seed be grass, and grass turn into hay:
I'm martyr to a motion not my own;
What's freedom for? To know eternity.
I swear she cast a shadow white as stone.
But who would count eternity in days?
These old bones live to learn her wanton ways:
(I measure time by how a body sways).

The lines of Roethke's poem are longer than Blake's and much more fluid. The sounds are relaxed and sensual as they move (like the woman they describe) "more ways than one." In the last line the poet tells us: "I measure time by how a body sways." As interpreters of the poem, sharing in the poet's adoration of the woman, we, too, should measure time in swaying, flowing rhythms.

Both " The Tyger " and " I Knew a Woman " are fixed-form poems, so our rhythmic responses are guided by the underlying frame of a flexibly recurrent meter and rhyme. With a free verse poem, though, we are without a recognizable starting point from which to discover the appropriate flow of sound. As you read the following free verse poem, keep in mind the sort of rhythms we associate with " blues " music and see if you hear a *spoken* blues in its language:

## CRACKED RECORD BLUES

KENNETH FEARING

If you watch it long enough you can see the clock move,
If you try hard enough you can hold a little water in the palm of
      your hand,
If you listen once or twice you know it's not the needle, or the tune, but a
      crack in the record when sometimes a phonograph falters and repeats, and
      repeats, and repeats, and repeats—

And if you think about it long enough, long enough, long enough,
      long enough then everything is simple and you can understand
      the times,
You can see for yourself that the Hudson still flows, that the
      seasons change as ever, that love is always love,
Words still have a meaning, still clear and still the same;
You can count upon your fingers that two plus two still equals,
      still equals, still equals, still equals—
There is nothing in this world that should bother the mind.

Because the mind is a common sense affair filled with common
      sense answers to common sense facts,
It can add up, can add up, can add up, can add up earthquakes
      and subtract them from fires,
It can bisect an atom or analyze the planets—
All it has to do is to, do is to, do is to, do is to start at the beginning
      and continue to the end.

We know of no way to describe the rhythms of Fearing's poem in a few words. Unless we perform it for you the way we *think* it sounds, all we can say is that you either hear it or you don't. But, if you *can* hear it, you can perform it, and you can help others to hear and appreciate it as well.

Fearing's technique of repeating phrases to suggest the cracked record is intriguing, and his often pulsating rhythms draw the reader into the syncopation of sound. Naturally, you would not wish to get so enraptured with the music that you undermine the sense of the poem, but a careful reading can reveal that the sound and the sense are inextricably bound up as one. They create word music that is at once pleasurable and enlightening.

This last poem is, according to the poet, a "roughed up" sonnet. It conforms to the stanzaic pattern and rhyme scheme of the sonnet form, yet its rhythms clearly avoid metric regularity.

## A SONNET FOR BIG NOSE GEORGE PARROTT

### RICHARD HAAS

But what about that mean one, Big Nose George Parrott?
They got him real good in Rawlings Wyoming.
They were all on their furies, "We oughta gut-
shoot'm." The mob had no hurry: "You're gonna swing,

George, from the telegraph pole." And he did, but
as folks tell of it, Big Nose's rope broke.
So, they tried him again, and do you know what?
He'd worked his hands free; Big Nose wouldn't croak

'cause he love-hugged that pole—then slowly slid down:
"Go down bad Big Nose to your final measure!"
'Cept the gov'nor, who then was the doctor in town,
dissected and skinned him, and turned him to leather.

He was walked in for years, or so the tale goes,
"The best of good boots" was that bad man, Big Nose.

The charm of this narrative poem comes largely from its unique persona. The colloquial speech of the storyteller combines with elements of the fixed sonnet form to create a uniquely structured experience. To discover the identity of form and meaning in " A Sonnet for Big Nose George Parrott," we suggest you have fun with it, just as the poet seems to have done. Experiment with various rhythms, dialects, and gestures that help you to capture the personality of the storyteller. Be aware of the sonnet structure, but do not let that hinder your dramatic response.

## THE DRAMATIC NATURE OF POETRY

When we listen to many poets read, we are struck by what seems to us an expressionless form of reciting, perhaps even a sort of chanting, which would indicate that they are more concerned with the structural framework than we tend to be. One famous poet congratulated a student who had read poetry at a dinner in his honor: " Bill, you're a fine actor!" The poet knew what he was saying, and it was not all a compliment. He felt that Bill was stressing the dramatic elements of the poems and neglecting the musical features. Thus, we have two divergent schools of thought as to how a poem should be read. The critic Yvor Winters, for example, asserts that poetry is formal and should not be read conversationally or dramatically: " A formal reading which avoids dramatic declamation will necessarily take on something of the nature of a chant." We can understand Mr. Winters' point of view—it is not uncommon in literary circles—but to us, it is disturbing (but consistent) for him to write, also, that " actors " just cannot read poetry either in poems or in plays: " I have never witnessed a performance of Shakespeare without more of pain than of profit or of pleasure."[2]

Now, one might contend that the poets ought to know best how a poem should be read. We cannot deny that it is always interesting and often illuminating to hear a poet read his own works. But, ability at composition does not guarantee quality in performance. Many a musical composer is a respectable instrumentalist without being sufficiently talented for public concerts. And many a good poet is a poor reader. " Actors " have often neglected form, but they are learning to study it. As oral interpreters, we do have confidence in our ability to embody the human experience in the poem and to communicate it to our listeners.

There is drama in good poetry: A person is talking (the persona, not necessarily the author). He is speaking about something that has happened or is happening, somewhere, sometime, somehow, to someone. Determining these factors will bring the experience in the poem alive. Certainly, the interpreter's dramatic response to the persona should not obscure the music of the poem, but neither should the poem's sound overshadow the fictive experience. Poetic structure sets in motion human communication that grows out of, and is inseparable from, the music.

## A Reading Program: Poetry of John Ciardi

*The following sample reading program combines poems and critical commentary written by John Ciardi. The introduction and transitions present some of Ciardi's critical observations regarding poetry that offer insight into six of his own poems. In order to publicly present this reading program, one must obtain the necessary permissions from copyright owners whose names may be found among the Acknowledgments at the beginning of this book.*

[2] Yvor Winters, " The Audible Reading of Poetry," in *The Structure of Verse: Modern Essays on Prosody* Harvey Gross (ed.), (Greenwich, Conn.: Fawcett Publications, Inc., 1966), p. 135.

Those who speak *in* verse we call poets. Those who speak *of* verse we call critics. John Ciardi *does* and *is* both. His many volumes *in* and *of* verse have earned him a respected place as both poet and critic. At times, he combines his two roles to speak at once *of* and *in* poetry. By sharing in a few of these poems, we gain a better notion of what it is to write poetry and how it can be to experience poetry. As we do so, let us follow Ciardi's advice when he says: "The way to read a poem is with pleasure—with the child's pleasure in tasting the syllables on his tongue, . . . with the child's hand clapping rhythmic joy."[1] In that spirit, let us begin by asking Mr. Ciardi what he does while writing a poem. He offers some measure of response in "Advertisement for a reader":

## ADVERTISEMENT FOR A READER

This itch to sit at paper and to say
a midnight into fact, a flesh to rhyme,
is what I do instead of doing. May
the life I do not live in the still time
I sit here scratching, by some grace
there is in words, be justified. At best
nothing does better by the untold race
than its own tongues. So have all men been blest
by deeds of words from dead men who took time
they have no longer, but were glad to take
when they were rich, to make into a rhyme
they have forgotten, what they itched to make.

So it appears that what the poet does is to scratch a persistent itch. Surely, Mr. Ciardi, you can be more clear than that. What you say makes some sense, but—

## ARE WE THROUGH TALKING, I HOPE?

Why do I have to make
sense? What sense is
there to make unless
our senses make it? I
don't want to make
sense. I want sensibly
to make you because any
thing else is nonsense
and what sense is there
  in that?

[1] John Ciardi, *Mid-Century American Poets* (New York: Twayne Publishers, Inc., 1950), p. xv.

The title of that last short poem is " Are We Through Talking, I Hope?" Ciardi explains that a poem doesn't necessarily want to make sense: "if you mean to enjoy the poem as a poem, stop cross-examining it, stop trying to force it to 'make sense.' The poem *is* sense."[2] Already, we can see that Mr. Ciardi is not going to come out directly and explain poetry to us. Perhaps we have been confronting the issue too directly. Perhaps we would do better if we looked at a poem that doesn't say it is talking about poetry. Ciardi asserts that "Whenever a poem seems to be saying two things at once, it is saying two things at once, and should be so understood."[3] Well, this next poem, "One Jay at a Time," talks of blue jays. But could it also be talking about poetry?

## ONE JAY AT A TIME

I have never seen a
generalized blue jay.
I have never heard a
specific one utter a
denial. Blue jays are
one at a time and they
are always screamers
of an assertion. Look
at that stiff dandy on
the sill-box. YES! YES!
YES! he screams forever
on a launching pad in-
side himself. I AM! I AM!
I AM! AND HERE I GO!

If Ciardi really is speaking of poetry, here, then he is saying that poets are "screamers of an assertion." Indeed, he has said: "There is no such thing as a poem that does not affirm."[4] But, we might counter, what if the poet has nothing to affirm? In his poem "Nothing Would Come of This," Ciardi speaks of a death (we don't know whose) and the night he tried to find poetry in his response to that death. But, as he tells us, there was "no poem/in it to say if from all nights.": No sound of affirmation would come.

## NOTHING WOULD COME OF THIS

Nothing would come of this
night I sat to. "This is the
night you died," I kept saying

[2] Ciardi, *Mid-Century American Poets*, p. xvii.
[3] Ciardi, *Mid-Century American Poets*, p. 250.
[4] Ciardi, *Mid-Century American Poets*, p. 250.

to you, thinking I might make
the night speak its difference
from all others. It said, and I
listened: frog-burr, traffic-buzz,
cricket-rub, but no sound of
whatever your dying must mean to
make and remember I loved you
and that nothing would come of
it. It was a night, and no poem
in it to say if from all nights.
"Damn poetry," I said and took to
vodka-and-tonic and you stayed
dead to the end of the bottle and
I threw it away and it made some
sound, technically, but the cold
clinic of fact aside, none in any
meaning that could say: "I loved you
and no sound will come of it now."

Ciardi says he could not find poetry to describe his feelings. Like many of us, he simply couldn't find the words. Maybe he couldn't write the poem because he wanted only to talk *about* what happened. "The poet's trade," Ciardi says as critic, "is not to talk about experience, but to make it happen."[5] The death had already happened, and he couldn't make it happen any other way.

When Ciardi is successful in making poetry happen, he does so by exercising his freedom to choose: "Nothing in a good poem happens by accident; every word, every comma, every variant spelling must enter as an act of the poet's choice. A poem is a machine for making choices."[6] In "A Man Came Tuesday," Ciardi confronts that vital freedom to choose as he engages in a dialogue with his own future.

## A MAN CAME TUESDAY

A man came Tuesday.
Wanted what I didn't owe yet.
"By Friday you will. Pay now
and I'll discount 10%." That
made sense . . . would have . . .
except. . . . "Anything off

---

[5] John Ciardi. *Dialogue With an Audience* (Philadelphia: J. B. Lippincott Company. 1963). p. 228.

[6] Ciardi. *Dialogue*. p. 225.

for good intentions?" I asked.
"I," he said, "am not
the Parole Board. I'm your
nonnegotiable future
come to a take it or leave it."
"If I had the price of a choice."
"Exactly." "But if I had,
I'd have a different future."
"That," he said, "is what I'm trying
to get you to." "Who the devil
are you?" He shrugged:
"I have no contract with the truth
but I like to be persuasive—
what are you prepared to believe?"

What are we prepared to believe? Should we believe in itching? In the sense of our senses? In blue jays? In the silence that refuses to become sound? In anything the poem believes in? What if we don't agree? In this final poem, entitled "Poetry," Ciardi fields our questions by directing them back to us. The answers are in the poetry, but we must find them for ourselves.

## POETRY

Whether or not you like it is not my
business/whether or not you can take
it is, finally, yours/whether or not
it makes any difference to you it does
make its own, whether or not you see it.

Whether or not you see it is not your
business alone/whether or not it tells
you the difference between yourself and
busyness, it does tell whether or not.

# 15 Suggestions on the Interpretative Reading of Drama

Most of us enjoy plays as they unfold on stage, television, or film, but comparatively few persons enjoy reading a play from a book. Play reading requires a greater imaginative effort than story reading. Whereas the story writer or novelist *tells* a story, the dramatist *presents* it, in dialogue form, without much descriptive, expository, or analytical embellishment.

A good play script is really a carefully prepared scenario for the collaboration of all the various arts of the theater. (It is also an effective scenario for audience response!) As silent readers of dramatic literature, we must apply our imaginations to the words of the characters, to the author's brief stage directions, and permit the characters to enact their story on an imaginary stage within ourselves. We must actively visualize the play rather than passively permit a writer to tell it to us. We must be especially creative. Thus, the silent reading of a play requires more time and effort than most persons are willing to give during their recreational hours.

We might well ask, then: Why read plays? The reason is simply stated by John Gassner, in the volume *The Wonderful World of Books:* "Some of the greatest minds and spirits have expressed themselves in plays." This critic and scholar points out that the best-known writers in English, French, German, and Scandinavian are the dramatists: Shakespeare, Shaw, T. S. Eliot, O'Neill, Molière, Goethe, Schiller, and Ibsen, to name only a few. Not only have the greatest minds spoken to us in drama, but some of man's best thoughts, finest expressions of feeling, and most brilliant imaginative characters appear in drama.

The next question to answer is: Why read plays to other persons? There are many good reasons. First, plays are written to be spoken and to be heard; they are intended to receive audible and visible communicative treatment rather than to lie inert as mere symbols on the printed page. Second, plays have a definite audience appeal. Good plays come to us tested by audiences. Given an adequate presentation, they obtain favorable responses. Third, plays are—and there seems to be no other way of saying this!—plays are *dramatic*. They are concise, concrete, and suspenseful. They possess colorful characters and interest-holding conflicts and situations. Fourth, the greatest plays contain the greatest of man's poetry. It is in this fine combination of poetry and drama that we recognize the supremacy of Shakespeare. Fifth, the oral interpreter can "produce" a play upon the imaginative stages of his listeners' minds without having to use the physical stage. Instead of being burdened with scenery, costume, make-up, properties, and lighting, he needs only a manuscript, himself, and an audience. We do not say that drama should be read aloud rather than acted; we merely contend that it is excellent for interpretative reading as well as for the theater. Furthermore, many persons who are unable to see plays enacted in the theater will enjoy hearing them read well aloud. Sixth, practice in the interpretative reading of plays is the best possible oral training for the student actor. Of course, he should learn to read all kinds of literary materials, but experience in reading dramatic lines will enable him to deal more effectively with them on the stage.

The basic techniques for the reading of drama are largely the same as those for reading other forms of literature; however, the reading of drama does require much skill and technical preparation not discussed elsewhere in this text. The following suggestions should prove helpful:

## SELECTING THE DRAMATIC SCENE

Select scenes from plays that are strong in plot, character, mood, thought, and/or language, for these are aspects that the oral reader can handle with some degree of efficiency. Dialogue that advances the plot is interesting to listen to. Character and mood are elements that can be developed as easily by the reader as by the actor. Plays that communicate considerable thought make excellent material for the oral reader, and those that are rich in language, particularly poetry, cannot be surpassed as literature for oral communication.

You should avoid selecting plays that are highly dependent on physical activity and/or the visible trappings of the stage, such as costumes, properties, or scenery. It should be apparent that the reader has difficulty in suggesting more than a minimal amount of action. It is also obvious that the reader cannot supply scenic and other technical effects necessary for the appreciation of some plays. Spectacles, costume dramas, and period pieces do not make good material for the reader.

Three other suggestions about the selection of dramatic materials should be heeded. Simplify your task immeasurably by selecting scenes in which only one, two, or three characters appear, as it is quite difficult for the reader to handle more than this number. Read good plays that meet the requirements for good literature, discussed in Chapter 3, rather than the insignificant ones produced on many high school stages. Hundreds of good plays are available. Finally, select a scene to read that offers some satisfaction to your listeners, for they deserve to receive an experience from your reading. Because a dramatic scene is only part of a whole work, it is easy for the reader mistakenly to lift out a scene that has no satisfying ending in itself;

yet listeners find it disturbing to listen to an inconclusive snatch of drama.
Choose a scene that " gets somewhere " because it has a climactic movement
of its own.

## STUDYING THE PLAY

Dramatic structure is among the most difficult of literary forms for the
writer to master, and it is not simple for the student to study. It should not
be necessary for us to remind you that one must study the whole play in order
to fathom the intricacies of character and motivation in any scene. We do so,
not because we think *you* might make this error, but because it is our experience as teachers that students sometimes try to understand the characteriza-
tions and plot development by reading only a part of the drama. The reading
itself usually reveals such willful ignorance; questioning later confirms it.

Of particular significance is a study of organization: the development of
dramatic action in acts and scenes. An essential element of drama is conflict:
increasing tensions that create climaxes. Not only does the play as a whole
have a major climax, or turning point, but also each act and each scene within
the act has a climax. You should prepare to build one in your reading and also
to be aware of the relationship of the scene you are reading to the play as a
whole. No interpreter can hope to read an individual scene well without
possessing a thorough knowledge of the entire play. The formal analysis of
a play's organization is extremely vital. For example, the interpreter of the
scene from *Tiger at the Gates* included at the end of this chapter can really
understand and appreciate the motivations and moods of the two characters
only when he has full knowledge of the entire play and of the function of
this scene within the play. Almost at the end of Act I, Hector is revealed as
completely baffled by a discussion with Helen in which he had anticipated
success in convincing her that she should return to Greece to avert war.
The act opens with a conversation between his wife, Andromache, and his
sister, Cassandra, about the inevitability of war. Cassandra, having pro-
phetic powers, bets Andromache that there will be war, that Destiny, the
Tiger, waits at the gates of Troy and cannot be kept out. Ironically, it is
Hector, the great soldier, now tired of war and determined to avoid further
wars, who is identified by Cassandra as the Tiger. In spite of the odds
against him, Hector succeeds in obtaining an agreement from Paris to give
up Helen if she can be persuaded to return to Greece. It is at this point that
Hector tries to use logic with Helen. The scene and the act conclude with
Hector's realization that neither argument nor demands are accomplishing
much when opposed by Helen's femininity. The results of his efforts are
clearly left in doubt, but strongly intimated, in this scene.

Of course, it is not enough to stop with a study of the climactic part that
the scene fulfills in the entire play. The reader must also sense the climactic

builds and releases of tension within the individual scene. We recommend that you search the scene we have provided you for climactic lines, both intellectually and emotionally of greatest significance, and for lines that indicate that the character speaking is relaxing or changing the subject for the purpose of starting a new tactical approach. You will learn more by doing this for yourself than if we were to point them out for you.

Mood is another major consideration in drama. Every good dramatic scene has a predominant mood and also subtle momentary moods wrought by the interaction of the characters. These must be related to the predominant mood of the play as a whole. *Tiger at the Gates* is an ironic drama. Fatalism and impending doom are opposed, with frustration, by the determined battle of reason waged by Hector. In the play are sharp intellectual exchanges of maxims, often delivered with great wit. The words of fools are set off against the ardent wisdom of such persons as Hector, Andromache, Cassandra, and Hecuba. Irony is quite evident in the scene we quote here. In it also are wit, sarcasm, playfulness, and frustration.

Probably the most important factor in the understanding of a play is an understanding of the characters. As opposed to narrative fiction—where we receive so much assistance from a persona in our understanding of what is happening, what the characters *mean* when they speak, and perhaps even what the characters are thinking—when reading a play, aside from the usually terse stage directions, we learn everything from the oral expression and actions of the characters in the story. Consequently, the analysis of characters and the successful suggestion of the characters to the audience become extremely vital for the interpretative reader. In essence, the interpreter assumes an apparent role of implicit narrator, structuring the experience for the audience. Fortunately, several avenues are available for the study of characterization: not only what the characters say and do, but also what the author says in his play directions and what the characters say about each other. One might also learn from what the critics have said in their reviews of the play in production. In *Tiger at the Gates*, the author does not describe his characters in stage directions. Hector, although admirable, is not a complex figure: a man of action, grown tired of the folly of killing, energetically and stubbornly setting about negating the role of fate in the cause of war. Although he is guilty of losing his temper in frustration, he also proves able to remain remarkably cool for a man of his background and strong inclinations. On the other hand, Helen is a complex figure. There is no doubt of her beauty, her seductiveness, and her charms. Even though Ulysses describes her as having "the shallowest brain, the hardest heart, [and] the narrowest understanding of sex," her own fatalism and cleverness in repartee cannot help but make one wonder if he has not somewhat underrated her. It is clear from what she says and from what other characters say of her that she is the epitome of the coquette: She is without genuine emotion, either love or pity, and her only pleasure is in her physical power over whatever man interests her; yet even then, she is not fully possessed, being as Paris says, "remote." But, even though Ulysses is right in his assessment of her selfishness, he is incorrect in his assessment of her brain: It is certainly not "shallow." The woman is quite clever.

Therefore, let us reiterate: No oral reader should make the mistake of undertaking to read to others a scene from a play that he has not studied in its entirety.

## ADAPTING THE SCENE FOR READING

As a reader of dramatic literature, you will almost certainly be faced with the necessity for cutting the selection. Nonessential, confusing, or unnecessarily time-consuming material will have to be pruned from the play script. Easiest to cut are the author's play directions. Anything essential in them will usually be presented to the audience in an introduction or in transitions between scenes. (We must admit that a few dramatists—Shaw, for example—have written play directions of literary quality, worth reading aloud, but these are somewhat rare.) Some matters included in stage directions are important for the audience to know. For example, the setting of the action is sometimes very significant, but only as it is the locale for the fictive events, not its nature as a *stage setting*. The conventional theater uses its stage to represent a fictive locale, whereas the interpreter "stages this locale in the imagination." If you were to refer to a theatrical stage, through lines such as "exit stage left" or "cross down right," you would force your audience to translate your stage description into a fictive setting. Instead of saying that a character enters or exits the stage, then, say that he walks into the room or leaves the fictive setting. Furthermore, some internal commentary may be desirable to clarify what is happening and, thereby, assist the audience in visualizing occurrences. These interjected comments that do not come directly from the author's stage directions may be necessary to explain or summarize segments you have left out. In doing either, you must be careful not to relax the pace, tension, or mood of the drama. Other items fairly easy to omit are lines that are meaningful only to the entire play and meaningless in a short scene prepared for oral reading. Similarly, lines and even characters who do not advance the scene or are likely to confuse the listener can be deleted. One should be careful, however, not to distort the playwright's intentions or impair the action of the play. Each cut should have a sound reason behind it, and the final product should be consistent with the purpose of the original play. Although the beginner usually feels that the cutting of a single line constitutes a butchery of the play, limitations in time, space, and activity often require the interpretative reader to cut the dramatic scene for reading to an audience.

## SUGGESTING THE DRAMA

You will recall that in Chapter 2, we said that the short psychic distance of the usual reading situation forces the reader to suggest, rather than to portray, in order to be most effective. The reading of dramatic scenes offers a great temptation to the reader to forget the powers of imaginative suggestion and to try to *show* the characters to the audience. Of course, dramatic literature does permit a relatively high degree of impersonative treatment, with more pronounced audible and visible characterization than is suitable with other materials. As readers we should consider ourselves purveyor's of *interior* rather than *exterior* drama. We should be effective reporters of a dramatic scene, we see in our " mind's eye," and which the listener will also see in his " mind's eye."

This means that the reader will never turn a profile to the audience to make one character appear to talk to another character on the platform. The audience would then logically expect to see the other character also on the platform. Instead, the reader may use the technique, previously described in Chapter 2, of directing each character's lines over the heads of the audience in one specific direction: Character A, slightly to the left of the center of the back wall of the room; Character B, slightly to the right; and so on. Sometimes, accomplished readers will choose not to separate the characters in this way and assume a responsibility for suggesting each character vividly in other ways, audible and visible.

## SUGGESTING CHARACTER

The chief problem of the interpretative reader of drama is usually the suggestion of character. Unlike the actor, who has plenty of time with no distractions, the reader must be able to suggest two or more characters instantly, switching from one character to another, and without the assistance of make-up, costumes, gross pantomime, or scenic effects. This is accomplished through much practice and through developing the ability to shift concentration instantaneously. The techniques for suggesting characters are the use of characteristic body and facial attitudes, facial expression, slight suggestive actions, and characteristic voice variables for each character: pitch key and pitch patterns, rate and rhythm of speaking, uses of pauses and duration, habitual degree of loudness and touch, and suggestion of voice quality. To use these techniques suggestively or with restrained impersonation requires a skill as great as, and probably greater than, the skill expected of an actor who uses them with complete facility. We think you can easily see why training in interpretative reading should be good for aspiring actors.

A common pitfall of the reader of drama is to seize on some distinctive visual or vocal characteristic and to depend on it alone to communicate a character rather than to develop a deep interior conception of the character and to suggest the character in depth. The result is a stereotype—or stock character—a flat cardboard figure, rather than a rounded, breathing being. Of course, sometimes good dramatists will create stock characters purposely, but most characters in good plays have three dimensions instead of two. Any reader who treats Brady in *Inherit the Wind* as merely a stereotyped political windbag will fail to suggest the intended tragedy of his breakdown in the courtroom. We cannot feel sorry for a piece of cardboard. The reader, as well as the actor, must make the characters human by developing the suggestive means only after having a vivid *inner* realization of each character.

## INTERACTION OF CHARACTERS

Characters in plays, like persons in actual life, not only speak to each other but also *listen* to each other: One may react to another while he is speaking. Whereas the poor reader of drama merely speaks lines, the effective reader reads dialogue in a way to suggest that characters react to other characters. This reaction comes fleetingly, just as the character begins to speak, reacting to the previous line. This must be planned, practiced, and then strongly experienced during the reading. It is comparatively easy for one actor to react to another actor; it is much harder for the inter- pretative reader to suggest multiple characters reacting to each other; and yet this suggestion in interaction is essential if the scene is to seem real to a listener. Characters in a solo reading of drama *do* speak to each other and hear each other if the reader is proficient. We in the audience can recognize this interaction easily, and we miss it when the interaction is not occurring. It happens easily, naturally, but it must be practiced. A danger in the reader's adoption of character action that is too overt makes this impossible, and is another reason why action should be suggestive rather than explicit.

## KEEPING IT MOVING

A dramatic scene must *move*, not bog down. Actors learn to pick up their cues by starting to speak as the last word of the preceding line is uttered. Similarly, the interpretative reader must also pick up cues quickly, or the scene will drag. Avoid a deadening series of pauses between characters' lines. Keep it moving. The reader who has to look back at the script for every line can hardly be effective. Therefore, you will have to know your drama script well. Study thoroughly and practice much. This advice should not, however, cause you to ignore a dramatist's deliberate use of silence. Such modern playwrights as Pinter, Beckett, and Ionesco often write with silence as much as with words. In such cases, verbal cues should *not* be picked up rapidly.

In keeping the scene moving, you will do well not to place the characters too far apart, making a time-lapse in going from one focus to another, creating a virtual "no-man's land" between them. Avoid a repetitive pattern of cues. Various persons react at various speeds and in different ways. An extremely nervous, or angered, or defensive character, for instance, might respond quickly and hurriedly; while a character who is calm and collected would be in less of a hurry to react verbally. Occasionally, you might make use of those paralinguistic factors mentioned in Chapter 6. You can verbalize a pause, a sigh, and so on, as these elements are appropriate to the character, of course. Nor should there be a constant "V" as you look back at the book everytime you move from one character to another. If the scene is a fast-moving one, you may need to make several transitions in dialogue before referring to the script. All of these elements for effective performance add up to a good deal of technical practice in reading drama, but the technique never rules the scene; it only serves the imaginative fiction in good reading.

## A FINAL WORD

Unfortunately, competent readers sometimes shun the individual interpretative reading of dramatic materials. They do this for perhaps one or more of three reasons: First, they mistakenly feel that drama should be left for stage production, alone. Second, they wish to avoid the extensive preparation required for effective communication of drama. Third, some readers, recognizing the importance of impersonation in the reading of plays, do not feel personally qualified to use impersonation well. We have already said that the great wealth of fine literature in play form is admirably suited to interpretative reading and should not be neglected by the reader. We do acknowledge that the intensive analysis of the *whole* drama and the extensive practice essential to read it well place additional burdens of preparation on the reader. And, we do recognize that the reader with little of the dramatic spirit in his personality may not excel at first in the reading of drama. And yet, we urge the student of oral interpretation not to ignore drama as a source for reading materials even in the beginning course in interpretative reading. To do so would be to neglect an important facet of his training in communicative reading.

## A READING PROGRAM OF A SCENE FROM
## *Tiger at the Gates*

*The following is a sample reading program prepared by your authors. It is intended only for purposes of illustration and instruction. Its inclusion in this textbook gives no one the right to read it publicly without permission from Samuel French, Inc. (25 West 45th Street, New York, New York 10036).*

As World War II began in Europe, the French playwright, Jean Giraudoux, wrote a new version of the events leading to the Trojan War, in which he compared war to a tiger lurking at the gates. No matter how hard man tries (and sometimes he does not try very hard), he cannot keep the tiger out: War is inevitable. The play, translated into English by Christopher Fry and titled *Tiger at the Gates*, contains many memorable characters in brilliantly conceived scenes. One of the most interesting scenes is the one in which Hector, son of King Priam, who is trying to avert war with the Greeks, attempts to convince Helen to leave her lover, Paris, and return to her Greek husband, Menelaus.

Hector is a sensitive, peace-loving, modern soldier in ancient armor. Helen, traditionally the ultimate in feminine seductiveness, seems in this play to be a mixture of the beautiful-but-dumb and the beautiful-and-intelligent woman.

*Hector*:   Is Greece a beautiful country?[1]
*Helen*:   Paris found it ravishing.[2]
*Hector*:   I meant is Greece itself beautiful, apart from Helen?[3]
*Helen*:   How very charming of you.[4]
*Hector*:   I was simply wondering what it is really like.[5]
*Helen*:   Well, there are quite a great many kings, and a great many goats, dotted about on marble.[6]
~~*Hector*:   If the kings are in gold, and the goats angora, that would look pretty well when the sun was rising.~~
~~*Helen*:   I don't get up very early.~~
~~*Hector*:   And a great many gods as well, I believe? Paris tells me the sky is crawling with them; he tells me you can see the legs of goddesses hanging down from the clouds.~~
~~*Helen*:   Paris always goes about with his nose in the air. He may have seen them.~~
~~*Hector*:   But you haven't?~~

---

[1] Hector is merely starting a conversation.
[2] Helen begins to play with Hector, immediately, with her reference to her own beauty and power over men. A pause before "ravishing" and a good deal of attention to the meaning of the word could help to make the line quite effective.
[3] Is Hector gracious, patronizing, or sarcastic? It makes a great deal of difference in how the line is read.
[4] The meaning of "charming" depends on Hector's specific meaning in the preceding line, for Helen is reacting to Hector's words.
[5] Are the sparks flying already?
[6] Helen continues to play with Hector.

*Helen*: ~~I am not gifted that way. I will look out for them when I go back there again.~~[7]

*Hector*:  You were telling Paris you would never be going back there.

*Helen*:  He asked me to tell him so. I adore doing what Paris wants me to do.[8]

*Hector*:  I see. Is that also true of what you said about Menelaus? Do you not, after all, hate him?[9]

*Helen*:  Why should I hate him?

*Hector*:  For the one reason which might certainly make for hate. You have seen too much of him.

*Helen*:   Menelaus? Oh, no! I have never seen Menelaus. On the contrary.[10]

*Hector*:  You have never seen your husband![11]

*Helen*:  There are some things, and certain people, that stand out in bright colours for me. They are the ones I can see. I believe in them. I have never been able to see Menelaus.[12]

*Hector*:  ~~Though I suppose he must have come very close to you sometimes.~~

*Helen*:  ~~I have been able to touch him. But I can't honestly tell you I saw him.~~

*Hector*:  ~~They say he never left your side.~~

*Helen*:  ~~Apparently. I must have walked across him a great many times without knowing it.~~[13]

*Hector*:  Whereas you have seen Paris.[14]

*Helen*:  Vividly; in the clearest outline against the sky and the sun.[15]

*Hector*:  Does he still stand out as vividly as he did?[16] Look down there: leaning against the rampart.

*Helen*:  Are you sure that's Paris, down there?[17]

*Hector*:  He is waiting for you.

*Helen*:  ~~Good gracious! He's not nearly as clear as usual!~~

*Hector*:  ~~And yet the wall is freshly whitewashed. Look again: there he is in profile.~~[18]

*Helen*:  It's odd how people waiting for you stand out far less clearly than people you are waiting for.[19]

---

[7] These lines are cut because they do not significantly advance the scene. In order to condense a scene to fit time limits, the reader cuts nonessential material, while taking care not to distort the author's purpose.

[8] Is Helen teasing Hector, or could she already be a bit bored with Paris?

[9] Hector asks a leading question with all the finesse of a trial lawyer.

[10] Helen seems casual in this reply, but she has a subtle meaning for " seen."

[11] Hector knows she has seen him. He is not shocked, surprised, or confused. Rather, he is making a sarcastic statement, not asking a question.

[12] Now, Helen puts the full meaning into " see Menelaus."

[13] These lines are cut for the same reason as the previous cutting.

[14] " Paris " receives the emphasis of contrast with " Menelaus."

[15] Helen continues to play with words. Her excessive gusto reveals her insincerity.

[16] Hector senses that she has lost her enthusiasm for Paris.

[17] Mockingly?

[18] A small pruning of the script.

[19] Which " you " and which " for " receive the major emphasis of the sentence? Again, she is being clever.

Hector:   Are you sure that Paris loves you?[20]

Helen:   I don't like knowing about other people's feelings. There is nothing more embarrassing. Just as when you play cards and you see your opponent's hand. You are sure to lose.

Hector:   What about yourself? Do you love him?

Helen:   I don't much like knowing my own feelings either.

Hector:   But, listen: when you make love with Paris, when he sleeps in your arms, when you are circled round with Paris, overwhelmed with Paris, haven't you any thoughts about it?[21]

Helen:   My part is over. I leave any thinking to the universe. It does it much better than I do.[22]

Hector:   Have there been many others, before Paris?[23]

Helen:   Some.[24]

Hector:   And there will be others after him, wouldn't you say, as long as they stand out in clear relief against the sky, or the wall, or the white sheets on the bed? It is just as I thought it was. You don't love Paris particularly, Helen; you love men.[25]

Helen:   I don't dislike them. They're as pleasant as soap and a sponge and warm water; you feel cleansed and refreshed by them.[26]

Hector:   ~~Cassandra! Cassandra!~~

~~Cassandra (entering):   What do you want?~~[27]

Hector:   ~~Cassandra,~~ Helen [you are][28] going back this evening with the Greek ambassador.

Helen:   I? What makes you think so?

Hector:   Weren't you telling me that you didn't love Paris particularly?

Helen:   That was your interpretation. Still, if you like.[29]

Hector:   I quote my authority. You have the same liking for men as you have for a cake of soap.

Helen:   Yes; or pumice stone perhaps is better. What about it?

Hector:   ~~Well, then, you're not going to hesitate in your choice between going back to Greece, which you don't mind, and a catastrophe as terrible as war?~~

Helen:   ~~You don't understand me at all, Hector. Of course I'm not hesitating. It would be very easy to say 'I will do this or that, so that this can happen~~

---

[20] What is the important word?

[21] Hector is boring in on his cross-examination.

[22] An extreme effort to be casual.

[23] Hector is becoming ruthless.

[24] She admits no more than is necessary.

[25] Nasty. Hector builds one climax at the end of the first sentence and an even bigger one at the end of the speech.

[26] Helen answers very quickly and gets a laugh from the audience. Then, she pauses and philosophizes, again.

[27] This cut and the redirection of the next speech enable us to eliminate a character who is not vital to this scene.

[28] A slight liberty taken to redirect the line because of the deletion of the previous lines.

[29] On which word would extended duration be most effective?

~~or that can happen.' You've discovered my weakness and you are overjoyed. The man who discovers a woman's weakness is like the huntsman in the heat of the day who finds a cool spring. He wallows in it. But you mustn't think, because you have convinced me, you've convinced the future, too. Merely by making children behave as you want them to, you don't alter the course of destiny.~~

~~Hector: I don't follow your Greek shades and subtleties.~~

~~Helen: It's not a question of shades and subtleties. It's no less than a question of monsters and pyramids.[30]~~

Hector: Do you choose to leave here, yes or no?[31]

Helen: Don't bully me. I choose what happens in the way I choose men, or anything else. I choose whatever is not indefinite and vague. I choose what I see.[32]

Hector: I know, you said that: what you see in the brightest colours. And you don't see yourself returning to Menelaus in a few days' time?[33]

Helen: No. It's very difficult.[34]

Hector: We could no doubt persuade your husband to dress with great brilliance for your return.[35]

Helen: All the purple dye from all the murex shells in the sea wouldn't make him visible to me.[36]

~~Hector: Here you have a rival, Cassandra. Helen can read the future, too.~~

~~Helen: No, I can't read the future. But when I imagine the future some of the pictures I see are coloured, and some are dull and drab. And up to now it has always been the coloured scenes which have happened in the end.[37]~~

Hector: We are going to give you back to the Greeks at high noon, on the blinding sand, between the violet sea and the ochre-coloured wall. We shall all be in golden armour with red skirts; and my sisters, dressed in green and standing between my white stallion and Priam's black mare, will return you to the Greek ambassador, over whose silver helmet I can imagine tall purple plumes. You see that, I think?[38]

Helen: No, none of it. It is all quite sombre.

Hector: You are mocking me, aren't you?[39]

Helen: Why should I mock you? Very well, then. Let us go, if you like! Let us go

---

[30] Another cut, merely to shorten the scene. It is regrettable that good lines must be sacrificed, but this is inevitable.

[31] Almost a violent outburst. Hector's intellectualism is nearly lost in his exasperation.

[32] Helen blasts back at him, losing her composure, momentarily. Then, she speaks emphatically.

[33] Very sarcastic on the first sentence. The last sentence gets back to the argument.

[34] A pause before " difficult " emphasizes the inadequacy of the word.

[35] The sarcasm now becomes almost playful.

[36] Very dramatic manner.

[37] Pruning, as before.

[38] This is Hector's big speech, emphasizing all the colors. Climax is reached in the last sentence. Hector is probably visibly tired when he asks the question at the end.

[39] Helen's obstinacy has finally got the best of him.

and get ready to return me to the Greeks. We shall see what happens.[40]

~~Hector: Do you realize how you insult humanity, or is it unconscious?~~

~~Helen: I don't know what you mean.[41]~~

Hector:   You realize that your coloured picture-book is holding the world up to ridicule? While we are all battling and making sacrifices to bring about a time we can call our own, there are you, looking at your pictures which nothing in all eternity can alter. What's wrong? Which one has made you stop and stare at it with those blind eyes? I don't doubt it's the one where you are standing here on the ramparts, watching the battle going on below. Is it the battle you see?

Helen:   Yes.[42]

Hector:   And the city is in ruins or burning, isn't that so?

Helen:   Yes. It's a vivid red.

Hector:   And what about Paris? You are seeing his body dragged behind a chariot?

Helen:   Oh, do you think that is Paris? I see what looks like a flash of sunlight rolling in the dust. A diamond sparkling on his hand. Yes, it is! Often I don't recognize faces, but I always recognize the jewelry. It's his ring, I'm quite certain.[43]

Hector:   Exactly. Do I dare to ask you about Andromache, and myself, the scene of Andromache and Hector? You are looking at us. Don't deny it. How do you see us? Happy, grown old, bathed in light?[44]

Helen:   I am not trying to see it.[45]

Hector:   The scene of Andromache weeping over the body of Hector, does that shine clearer?

Helen:   You seem to know. But sometimes I see things shining, brilliantly shining, and they never happen. No one is infallible.[46]

Hector:   You needn't go on. I understand. There is a son between the weeping mother and the father stretched on the ground?[47]

Helen:   Yes. He is playing with his father's tangled hair. He is a sweet boy.[48]

Hector:   And these scenes are there in your eyes, down in the depths of them. Could I see them there?[49]

Helen:   I don't know. Look.[50]

Hector:   Nothing. Nothing except the ashes of all those fires, the gold and the

---

[40] A sudden reversal: an " All right. I'll prove it! " manner.

[41] More pruning.

[42] She pretends to see something she really does not see.

[43] Helen is apparently becoming entangled in Hector's net.

[44] A fast rate. He is boring in.

[45] She balks at playing the game further.

[46] The emptiness of her answer proves she sees nothing.

[47] Hector is revealing his *own* visions of the future.

[48] Embellishing a scene she does not see.

[49] A climax of tension.

[50] " Look " must convey a tremendous amount of meaning. possibly: " Look for yourself, Hector. So many men have found something in my eyes."

emerald in dust. How innocent it is, this crystal where the future is waiting. But there should be tears bathing it, and where are they? Would you cry, Helen, if you were going to be killed?[51]

Helen: I don't know. But I should scream. And I feel I shall scream if you go on at me like this, Hector. I am going to scream.[52]

Hector: You will leave for Greece this evening, Helen, otherwise I shall kill you.[53]

Helen: But I want to leave! I'm prepared to leave. All that I'm trying to tell is that I simply can't manage to distinguish the ship that is going to carry me there. Nothing is shining in the least, ~~neither the metal on the mast, nor the ring in the captain's nose, nor the cabin-boy's eyes, nor anything.~~[54]

Hector: You will go back on a grey sea under a grey sun. But we must have peace.

Helen: I cannot see peace.

~~Hector: Ask Cassandra to make her appear for you. Cassandra is a sorceress. She can summon up shapes and spirits.~~

~~A Messenger (entering): Hector, Priam is asking for you. The priests are opposed to our shutting the Gates of War. They say the gods will consider it an insult.~~

~~Hector: It is curious how the gods can never speak for themselves in these difficult matters.~~

~~Messenger: They have spoken for themselves. A thunderbolt has fallen on the temple, several men have been killed, the entrails of the victims have been consulted, and they are unanimously against Helen's return to Greece.~~

~~Hector: I would give a good deal to be able to consult the entrails of the priests . . . . I'll follow you.~~

~~(The MESSENGER goes)~~[55]

Well, now, Helen, do we agree about this?

Helen: Yes.[56]

Hector: From now on you will say what I tell you to say? You will do what I tell you to do?

Helen: Yes.

Hector: ~~Do you hear this, Cassandra?~~ Listen to this solid wall of negation which says Yes! They have all given in to me. Paris has given in to me, Priam has given in to me, Helen has given in to me. And yet I can't help feeling that in each of these apparent victories I have been defeated. You

---

[51] A long pause before "Nothing." A slow rate during the second sentence. His manner changes abruptly with "But there should be tears . . . ." He ends with a hint of the threat to come.

[52] Near panic.

[53] Strong, virile, commanding.

[54] Helen begins to break. The cutting was also made in the professional-acting edition of the play.

[55] These lines are essential to the play as a whole but not to this scene as a psychological unit.

[56] Helen's meanings for this and the following "Yes" may be far from simple. A short word with complex meanings is among the most difficult of lines to interpret. The final sentence of Hector's last speech in this scene may give a clue.

set out, thinking you are going to have to wrestle with giants; you brace yourself to conquer them, and you find yourself wrestling with something inflexible reflected in a woman's eye. ~~You have said yes beautifully, Helen, and you're brimful of a stubborn determination to defy me~~![57]

## A SUGGESTED LIST OF PLAYWRIGHTS FOR ORAL INTERPRETATION

*Note:* Do not regard this list as all-inclusive, because new writers are continually producing plays worthy of oral interpretation.

Aeschylus
Albee, Edward
Anderson, Maxwell
Anderson, Robert
Anouilh, Jean
Aristophanes
Beckett, Samuel
Behan, Brendan
Brecht, Bertolt
Capote, Truman
Chase, Mary
Chayefsky, Paddy
Chekhov, Anton
Coward, Noel
Crowley, Mort
Delaney, Shelagh
Dürrenmatt, Friedrich
Durrell, Lawrence
Elder III, Lonnie
Eliot, T. S.
Euripides
Friel, Brian
Fry, Christopher
Giraudoux, Jean
Guare, John
Hart, Moss and George S. Kaufman
Hellman, Lillian
Ibsen, Henrik
Inge, William

Ionesco, Eugène
Kopit, Arthur
Kops, Bernard
Lorca, Féderico García
Laurents, Arthur
Lindsay, Howard and Russel
    Crouse
MacLeish, Archibald
McCullers, Carson
Marlowe, Christopher
Miller, Arthur
Miller, Jason
Molière
Nash, N. Richard
O'Casey, Sean
O'Neill, Eugene
Osborne, John
Pinẽro, Miguel
Pinter, Harold
Saroyan, William
Sartre, Jean-Paul
Schisgal, Murray
Shaffer, Peter
Shakespeare, William
Shaw, George Bernard
Sheridan, Richard Brinsley
Simon, Neil
Sophocles
Stoppard, Tom

[57] Hector realizes he has won an intellectual fray, but that fate has ruled him the loser in his struggle for peace. His last sentence is cut because it points ahead to additional dialogue and dramatic action. The previous sentence provides a potent ending to this scene.

Storey, David
Strindberg, August
Synge, John Millington
Ustinov, Peter
Weiss, Peter

White, Theodore H.
Wilde, Oscar
Wilder, Thornton
Williams, Tennessee
Zindel, Paul

# Five

## Group Reading and Interpretative Theater

# 16

# Suggestions on the Forms of Group Reading and Interpretative Theater

An inevitable result of the popularity of individual interpretative reading has been that two or more readers have eventually wanted to read together, sometimes for their own amusement only and sometimes for the communication of literary experience to audiences. Of course, there is nothing really new in this. In ancient Greece the rhapsodes read the epics in relays; in ancient Rome a primitive form of what we now call "readers theater" apparently existed; and Gilbert Austin, in 1806, acknowledged that groups of persons might wish to gather to read plays to each other in a nontheatrical way or to read them in a semidramatic style for an audience.[1] Since the early 1950's, oral readers have been exploring several forms of group reading, to their own profit and to the delight of their audiences.

The reasons for current experimentation seem to lie in two facts: (1) Group activity is usually pleasurable; (2) The use of two or more readers permits a greater opportunity for the expression of the dramatic impulses in literature. Group activity in oral reading is very much with us, particularly in college and university settings and, increasingly, upon the professional scene. Of course, the academic successes have not achieved great fame, but such professional productions as *Don Juan in Hell, John Brown's Body, In White America, Brecht on Brecht,* and *Spoon River Anthology* received widespread approval. As a student of interpretative reading, you may wish to try group reading in one or more forms.

By extending our interpretative performances from the individual reader to the group, we open up new avenues for discovery. Sometimes, a group treatment of a work can vitalize our responses to a selection so that a solo interpretation will actually be improved upon. Experimentation with various forms of group reading tests the often tenuous ground between traditional theater and oral interpretation, contributing refreshingly new possibilities for our appreciation of both. Of course, we cannot, in this short chapter, attempt any complete coverage of the subject. Under the terms *readers theater* or

---

[1] Gilbert Austin, *Chironomia; or a Treatise on Rhetorical Delivery* (London: 1806), pp. 201–204.

*interpretative theater*, it is treated in specialized textbooks that we recommend
for your study if you should wish to explore the subject further.[2]

## FORMS OF GROUP READING

Let us look at six basic forms of group reading: informal group reading,
duo-reading, choral reading, collected scripts, traditional readers theater, and
chamber theater. We hope that these brief descriptions will stimulate you to
try some group reading for pure recreation, if not for your class or for a
public audience.

**Informal Group Reading.** " Informal group reading " refers to occasions
when friends or family read to each other from literature they all enjoy. For
example, they might choose a novel, with each person reading a short section
or chapter and then passing the book on to another person. They might select
a book of poetry, with each person reading his favorites. They might read a
play, with each person assuming responsibility for a particular character's
lines. One of your authors was informed by a former student, now a
distinguished professor of sociology, that he was still doing interpretative
reading. He said: " Doc, once a month, my wife and I have a group of close
friends over. We open a keg of beer and a novel. We drink the beer and we
read the novel to each other. We have a ball! " Such sharing of literature
through oral reading was very common before the pressures of modern life
so nearly eliminated intimate gatherings. Perhaps people will find their way
back to the social recognition of literature and the practice of sharing it
personally. Why only talk *about* a book when friends can participate *in*
experiencing it together?

**Duo-reading.** Students in oral interpretation classes stressing solo reading
often find it enjoyable and profitable to work with another reader when
presenting a selection to the class. It might be a scene from a play, a short
story, or an episode from a novel. An amazing range of literature can be
divided between two readers and presented effectively. Two men chose
sequences from Stanley Elkins' novel *The Dick Gibson Show*. In them a
nine-year-old boy calls a late-night telephone-talkshow radio announcer and
tells him of his desire to use the three-quarters of a million dollars he has
" in his piggybanks " for charitable purposes. The conversation made up

---

[2] Coger, Leslie Irene, and Melvin R. White. *Readers Theatre Handbook: A Dramatic Approach
to Literature*, 2nd ed., Chicago: Scott, Foresman and Company, 1973; Haas, Richard.
*Theatres of Interpretation*. Ann Arbor, Mich.: Roberts-Burton Publication, 1976 (Two of your
authors participated in the writing and editing of this book.); Long, Beverly Whitaker, Lee
Hudson, and Phillis Rienstra Jeffrey. *Group Performance of Literature*. Englewood Cliffs,
New Jersey: Prentice-Hall, Inc., 1977; Maclay, Joanna Hawkins. *Readers Theatre: Toward a
Grammar of Practice*. New York: Random House, Inc., 1971.

twenty minutes of fascinating listening. As they are radio-telephone conversations, there was no physical interaction between the characters, who focused directly forward, but each character spoke " to " the other vocally and reacted both vocally and visually. Since the small amount of narration in these passages is from the announcer's point of view, it was delivered by the man who read the announcer's lines. Audience focus is especially valuable for such duo-readings. Two women students read a scene between Amanda and Laura from *The Glass Menagerie*, and they focused toward the back wall, with their lines of focus crossing in the realm of the audience. They were alive physically and vocally, and they talked and reacted to each other imaginatively. The scene was as vivid for an audience in the classroom as it ever was on a stage. No one thought of either the men or the women as actual fictive characters, for they created the fictions effectively in the audience's imaginations.

**Choral Reading.** Choral reading is simultaneous group reading structured to accomplish a communicative effect on listeners. It should not be confused with the uninspired droning of the so-called responsive reading we hear sometimes in church, although choral reading is sometimes also reading in unison. It is done by a carefully organized and trained speech chorus. Places are assigned through auditions, not only by reading ability but also by voice type: male, female; light, dark. Readings are appropriately arranged, as music is arranged for a singing choir. Parts are assigned to particular sections or even to individual voices, and the group is directed in detail and rehearsed for precise, designed effect.

The speech chorus has had a somewhat spotty acceptance in academic circles, ignored by many but enthusiastically embraced on a few campuses. It has proved popular particularly in the church-related institutions where choirs specialize in religious-oriented literature. This is quite understandable, as it is with the musical choir: The " literature " is most suitable. The voice choir's forte lies in the performance of inspirational materials: of strength, awe, and excitement, nicely achieved when many voices are heard together. A group of voices has the same relationship to the solo voice as the orchestra has to the solo instrument. It is obvious, is it not, that a full chorus or orchestra has power possessed by no single voice or instrument? However, it is also obvious that the full chorus or orchestra cannot match the subtleties that can be communicated by the single voice or instrument. Even two pianos lack the capability for subtlety and refinement in meaning possessed by one piano's voice. Twenty human voices, blended and rehearsed, can create impressive effects, but the good speech chorus also makes use of the solo voice when it is needed.

A speech chorus may present an arrangement of many pieces of literature to constitute either a highly varied or an intensely unified program. It may also present a single work, of fiction, epic poetry, or even drama. For example, Professor I. Blaine Quarnstrom, of Central Michigan University, produced a full-length presentation of Eugene O'Neill's drama *Lazarus Laughed* with a speech chorus of twenty-five readers. Leading characters in the play moved in and out of the chorus to enact scenes on the forestage. The production was enhanced by modern costume and extensive use of sound, music, and lighting effects.

Sometimes choric speaking may be used in other productions to create suspense, as in the chase sequence from Ray Bradbury's *Fahrenheit 451*; or for comic atmosphere, as in a production of John Cheever's novel *Wapshot Chronicle*. In the former, the protagonist is chased by a futuristic mechanical hound with a deadly needle in his proboscis. In the latter, a young man leaves home for the first time, viewing places of interest from a train window. As the train speeds up, the choral enumeration of these images is accelerated.

The speech chorus cannot do everything that oral readers should do, but it offers tremendous rewards for students and audiences when directed by a capable person, properly rehearsed and presenting the right material.

**Collected Script.** Collected script refers to a variety of types of group and/or individual readings structured into a program format for public performance. A program may consist of several selections on a given theme, and perhaps even incorporates some readers-theater or chamber-theater scenes. In a program called "The Battle of the Sexes," four female readers and four male readers fought the famous battle with appropriate pieces of literature, ranging from the ancient to the modern, from poetry to prose, from the sublime to the ridiculous. The women were on one side of the platform; the men, on the other; and a jazz drummer sat between the sexes to set mood, to establish tempo, to punctuate, and to emphasize. Other collected script programs with titles indicating the nature of the materials collected, were entitled: "Communication Breakdown," "Hamlet in the Wings," "What is Bad Poetry?," and "We Shall Overkill."

A completely suggestive production, which made severe demands on the imaginations of the audience to unravel its meaning, was the program called "Communication Breakdown." In this presentation, the attempt was made to explore the major theme with various types of literature illustrating breakdowns in communication and also to frustrate the audience by actually producing communication breakdowns. This was accomplished by constantly interrupting the enactment of a short story that served as a backbone for the production, as if a radio or television drama was frequently interrupted by switching from station to station, occasionally reverting to the one carrying the drama. The program began with five readers holding "radio" scripts and standing before a microphone stand (holding no actual microphone). After singing a couple of verses of a popular song on communication breakdown, they read a snatch of the story as if it were a radio drama. One of the readers held a toy "clicker" and clicked it to suggest the switches in stations. Various items—light verse, gags, commercials, newspaper columns, serious poetry, and so on—interrupted the drama. It was not long before the "radio actors" abandoned their scripts, pushed the "mike" aside, and acted the main story, thus turning the radio drama into a television drama. It was several minutes before the audience became aware of what was really being suggested on the platform, but the director felt that this frustration added to the significance and impact of the program's theme of communication breakdowns.

"Hamlet in the Wings" was a collection of over ninety quotations from, or about, the play *Hamlet* gathered from over thirty sources. The effort was to provide information, illumination, and entertainment. "What Is Bad Poetry?" was an amusing consideration of verse that some persons might consider to be "poetry," but just did not measure up. It was purely for fun. "We Shall Overkill" set out to deal with our culture's apparent obsession for violence. Rather than being deadly serious, "We Shall Overkill" was shockingly flippant and comic, to impress an audience with the real seriousness of the situation. Each of these programs used three performers and only a few stools for properties. Manuscripts were used in the first two, but all were virtually memorized.

Students in the beginning courses in interpretative reading can often get together group programs of the concert variety for class presentation. The opportunities for creative experimentation in such programs are endless and often exceedingly rewarding.

Perhaps the titles of some collected programs done in an interpretative theater class will start you off with an idea for a program:

"Sing me a Song of Social Significance"
"Vespuccia the Beautiful"
"This Day"
"The Humor of Mark Twain"
"Shakespeare's Women"
"Zodiac"
"dada"
"101 Introductory to Cats"
"The Woman's View"
"The Art of Dying"
"Art Buchwald on Marriage"
"A Portrait of Prévert"
"The Hawk or the Dove"
"Fables for Fun"
"The Berrigans"
"War: Peace and Protest"
"Voices from the Insane Asylum"
"Forever Man"

**Traditional Readers Theater.**   By far the most common form of group reading used is called *readers theater*. So many other forms have developed with their own specialized characteristics that it is helpful to refer to the original variety as "traditional readers theater." Thus, the most familiar variety contains such elements as the use of reading stands, tall stools, audience focus, and very little movement, costumes, properties, or other stage trappings. Reading is usually from manuscript, or at least appears to be. Let's look at a few examples of traditional readers theater to help clarify this performing mode.

In a production of the Christopher Fry–Jean Giraudoux play *Tiger at the Gates* (the English version), fourteen readers, each associated with one of the characters in the play, stood behind individual reading stands located at various positions on platforms of various heights and sizes. Characters entered or existed on cue. Dress was modern and semiformal. Impersonative suggestion of character was accomplished by vocal and facial means. Staging did not assist pictorially in any literal way, except for the psychological arrangement and relationship of characters. There was no literal movement, no pantomime; thus, the scene tended to become static, although certain scenes were effectively suggested to the imagination by the more able readers. There was comparatively little "theater" involved in the performance.

A readers-theater presentation of John Cheever's novel *Wapshot Chronicle* was an experiment to see how well a small group of readers (five) could communicate a novel written predominantly in narrative form rather than in dialogue. Each reader handled the narration and dialogue of at least two distinct characters. Positions were static, yet they were rearranged at the intermission. All the readers were on the platform during the entire performance, using five stools and five lecterns. The constant change of voice in a choric approach to the material brought a variety that kept the performance dynamic. Additional variety was furnished by one scene that, because it was "acted," provided a dramatic interlude in the middle of the show: This scene was an uproarious satire in crisp dialogue form. Two readers moved to chairs facing the audience on opposite sides of a small table and enacted a burlesque of a psychological interview. Whereas the focus in the rest of the production was indirect (in the realm of the audience rather than directly between the characters), it became semidirect in this scene, with the two characters sometimes looking at each other, but playing primarily *to* the audience as vaudeville comedians used to indulge in open conversation primarily for the benefit of the audience. The change in focus did not seem unwarranted; proving consistent with the purpose, it added humor to the author's scene.

In a production of Bradbury's futuristic *Fahrenheit 451*, a chorus of four female and four male voices shared the narration of the novel. Dialogue scenes were primarily for duo-voices. These pairs of readers stood at lecterns at the sides of the small chorus. Downstage center, in front of the chorus, were three low stools with swivel seats. In a hilarious scene in which Bradbury has three women watching an absurd television drama on three walls of a living room, the women sat on the low stools, with their manuscripts in hand, and turned as if they were watching the TV scenes on first one wall then another. The production took place on an orchestra platform in a ballroom. Very simple lighting added a little to the theatricality, with red being an essential color in some important scenes. The production, although performed by amateurs, had a power over its audience through imaginative suggestion more potent than that of the realistic movie later made of the same book.

Another readers-theater program in which narration was presented similarly to the method used in *Wapshot Chronicle* was the program "Three Men from *Raintree County*," taken from the novel by Ross Lockridge, Jr. The production was read by three male readers, each one associated with one of the three major figures in the novel. The program was divided into three parts, of course, entitled "Johnny Shawnessy," "Jerusalem Webster Stiles," and "Garwood B. Jones." The program evolved from the director's desire to produce a readers-theater effort using this particular book and using materials suitable to three specific readers. The intent was that the theme of the entire book be suggested by the portions used, that each character be firmly developed in a short period of time, and that a strong attribute of the program be the communication of the lush language and images of the book. Again, the material was primarily narrative, yet all three readers read narrative concerning each of the major figures. Highly subjective narration and dialogue were assigned to the one reader identified with that character. Staging was very simple, consisting of only three reading stands and two chairs, with each being slightly shifted in position for each major part of the program, to focus attention on the character emphasized in that part. The major figure in each part stood, and the other two readers stood or sat as seemed most effective in the scene. An entertaining innovation was what was called "audience participation readers theater." Two of the scenes called for crowd participation: one, a congregation in a small country church singing a hymn; the other, a Fourth of July crowd applauding a senator's speech. This was explained to the audience at the start of the performance; copies of the hymn were distributed, and the audience was requested to sing along with the performers at the appropriate time when cued. They did this with great pleasure on three different occasions. Because the material at those junctures was humorous, everyone had fun.

In the programs just described, there was no attempt to embellish the platform with any kind of setting, make-up, costumes, properties, or lighting, except where previously noted. Those we shall describe from here on will reveal greater efforts to create a theatrical environment.

One of the great joys of readers-theater production is the opportunity it affords for experimentation in the form of production, with, of course, the style deriving from the literature to be communicated. Friedrich Dürrenmatt's little-known play, *The Marriage of Mr. Mississippi*, is a grotesque drama. The chief element of grotesqueness is incongruity. The director chose to adopt "consistent incongruity" as one of two keys to the style of his production; the other key was the verb *to play*. The performance became a sort of crazy romp, jumping without notice from obvious manuscript reading to a form of acting, without scripts, that children use when they *play at* acting. As dictated by the drama, there were also sudden changes in the relationship of the characters to members of their audience, as they stopped and talked to the audience. Focus shifted from the audience, to the performers, and back to the audience. Other incongruities suggested by the text were exploited: the utilization of three women to play one role (each in a different act of the three acts); the full but outlandish costuming of one character only, who tells the audience the author has deliberately made him ridiculous; and the abrupt shifts from sensitive to absurd moments.

Because of the suggestive powers of readers theater and the consequent advantage of doing without full staging, directors seldom produce it in large theaters or with much scenery. Although a few directors have experimented with sumptuous staging, not many bother with attempts at any realism. For one reason or another not necessarily related to the literature, sometimes a production may have to be given under conditions not exactly considered ideal. Such was the case with a production of Lawrence Durrell's *An Irish Faustus*, scheduled for showing in a large auditorium. Some of the rhetoric and bombast of the play could certainly be projected well to a large audience, but the communication of the abundant thought without much action to hold interest was a problem to be overcome in a "barn" of a theater. To reach the audience, participants worked without scripts most of the time and used a "skeletal" degree of acting. A designer-technician's desire to experiment with rear-screen projection brought about an interesting series of visual backgrounds for the action: abstractions and symbolic environmental suggestions. In one scene, where the author had provided only stage directions for important action but virtually no dialogue to accompany it, the readers moved to reading stands and read the stage directions while the screen suggested the action: As a stake was driven through the heart of a vampire in the forest, a wedge appeared at the top of the forest and as it reached the bottom of the screen, on cue, the screen suddenly filled with blood-red. In a scene taking place in Faustus's cabinet, the screen held a medallion with alchemist's symbols on it. When Mephisto appeared, the medallion was suddenly surrounded by a ring of fire. As Faustus dragged Mephisto to Hell (an interesting switch on the old story), the medallion faded and the ring of fire became a Hellmouth against which were seen the silhouettes of the determined Faustus and the cringing Mephisto. Such effects seemed consistent with the author's purposes and were a fortunate aid to communication under the circumstances of this production.

Traditional readers theater received a big boost in popularity in the 1950s, with such professional productions as " Don Juan in Hell," and " John Brown's Body." It has proved to be very popular on college campuses since that time. In the last decade it has also caught on in the high schools. Almost any kind of literature can receive a traditional form of production, even drama, as we have seen.

At this point, we should like to emphasize that whoever produces in readers theater should feel at liberty to experiment with literature and productions that do not assure " socko " audience response. Unfortunately, regular theater productions, which often cost a good deal to stage, must try to please sizable audiences.

**Chamber Theater.** Chamber theater is a particular form of narrative theater devised by Professor Robert Breen, of Northwestern University, for the dramatic presentation of narrative fiction, the short story, and the novel. Breen has defined chamber theater in this way:

The techniques of the Chamber Theater were devised to present the novel, or narrative fiction, on the stage so that the dramatic action would unfold with full and vivid immediacy, as it does in a play, but at the same time allowing the sensibility of the narrator, or the central intelligence in the form of a character, to so condition our view of that action that we who listen and watch would receive a highly organized and unified impression of it.[3]

The reader should keep in mind that chamber theater is *not* a rewriting of nondramatic fiction into play form. The original narrative form of the fiction is preserved, and the narrator of the story or novel remains the teller of the story. In fact, the narrator becomes a major performer in the production. This is not to suggest that narration is simply assigned to one reader who then stands at a lectern and reads. He becomes very much a part of the stage picture or action because the narrator's point of view in the novel or story is made apparent in the " drama " on stage. Since the narrator is such an important element in prose fiction, detailed study of the narrative positions and thoughtful consideration of how to communicate them in the production are essential.

Consider how narration was handled in one chamber theater production. The novel produced was *The Dissent of Dominick Shapiro* by Bernard Kops. The narrator of this book sees its events from the points of view of two characters, and he shifts his attention between these throughout the book. He tells about three-fourths of the story from Dominick's viewpoint and the other fourth from the viewpoint of Dominick's father, Lew. Never does the narrator go inside the mind of any other character in the novel. The

[3] Robert Breen, as quoted in Charlotte I. Lee, *Oral Interpretation* (4th ed.; Boston: Houghton Mifflin Company, 1971), p. 230.

narration is primarily third-person, but a considerable portion is in the form
of subjective opinion from one or the other of the two major characters. At
any time he may go inside the mind of either Dominick or Lew, whichever
one he happens to be standing beside, and he is always clearly beside one or
the other. Thus, the narration in the production can be divided between the
person established as the narrator and the persons established as Dominick
and Lew. The narrator can relate *events*, as seen by either character, and the
two characters can speak the narrative lines that communicate their thought
processes. In addition, the readers established as the characters will, of course,
handle the characters' dialogue. When the narrator is telling " Dominick's "
story, he stands on Dominick's side of the platform; when he tells " Lew's "
story, he stands on Lew's side. When either Lew or Dominick speak to other
characters, he addresses the actor involved; when either expresses his own
thoughts, he speaks in the direction of the audience.

Let us see how this worked in two different courtroom scenes, approximately twenty pages apart in the novel. The author has chosen to have the
narrator tell the first one, which we shall call " Scene A," from Dominick's
point of view and the second, " Scene B," from Lew's. We here quote
portions of each, revised from the novel in script form to show reading
assignments to the narrator and various characters. (There has been no
revision of the author's words.) In Scene A, we show " *Dom. Narr.*" to
indicate what narration would be handled by the Dominick actor and
" *Dominick* " for those lines spoken by Dominick to other characters. In
Scene B, we have done the same for " *Lew Narr.*" and " *Lew.*" Note
that any narration in the third person, referring to either Dominick or Lew
as " he " or " him " is handled by the narrator. Study the lines assigned to
" *Dom. Narr.*" and " *Lew Narr.*" to see how these seem to come from within
the character rather than from a narrator without.

## SCENE A

*Narr.:*   When Dominick saw them he smiled. Naturally they misconstrued and
thought he was being friendly. How little they knew him!

*Paula:*   Are you all right?

*Narr.:*   —his mother mouthed. He nodded back. His father looked solemn, as
if attending a religious ceremony.

*Dom. Narr.:*   She took out a small scent bottle and started spraying herself. The
smell permeated the whole room. The three magistrates did not take very
kindly to that.

*Narr.:*   He was pleased. He wanted no mercy from these people.

*Dom. Narr.:*   One of the magistrates was a woman.

*Narr.:*   He was sure she was, despite the moustache and the hands full of
thick veins.

*Dom. Narr.*:  The magistrate in the middle was obviously the boss. He was quite good looking with silver hair, but the mouth revealed signs of sexual sadism. The third magistrate was a fat blob, a successful tobacconist or a wet-fishmonger. So;

*Narr.*:  —his parents had come.

*Dom. Narr.*:  Trust them to spoil everything.

*Narr.*:  Why could they not allow him to hurtle into the pit of oblivion? He would not be saved. He could not allow himself to be rescued from these dark judges.

*Dom. Narr.*:  The constable droned the history of events to the three vultures, who hungrily were waiting to taste for themselves. Then the constable finished. They had stuck to the vagrancy charge;

*Narr.*:  —they hadn't said anything about him raping the whole female population of the town, from the age of eleven onwards.

*Judge*:  Shapiro? Shapiro? A strange sounding name. Is it Spanish or Italian?

*Lew*:  Your honour. We are of the Hebrew persuasion.

*Narr.*:  Lew stood up to speak while Dominick cringed, curled up inside, and boiled with rage.

*Lew*:  Oh, excuse me. I am his father, your honour.

*Narr.*:  Lew sat down again. The magistrate took off his glasses.

*Judge*:  Really! How interesting! It's very rarely we come up against a member of your race.

*Narr.*:  He smiled.

*Judge*:  So you are his parents?

*Narr.*:  His parents nodded gravely.

*Judge*:  And you come from—where?

*Narr.*:  He consulted some papers.

*Judge*:  From London? All the way from London for the sake of your son?

*Narr.*:  He replaced his glasses and scrutinized Dominick.

*Judge*:  I hope you appreciate your parents; who seem decent, honourable people.

*Narr.*:  He nodded.

*Dom. Narr.*:  What a miserable Sodswine! With a droplet of snot hanging from his left nostril.

*Lew*:  Your Lordship, may I speak?

*Narr.*:  —Lew said. So his father was trying the usual flattery;

*Dom. Narr.*:  —calling a meagre Magistrate "Lord." The way he called a Policeman "Officer," or a Parking Meter Attendant "My dear fellow." What's more they fell for it. This old swine was smiling, benignly, right now.

*Narr.*:  If he was not careful he would not even spend seven days in prison. He needed a week desperately, to scratch his name into the brickwork and to finalize his divorce from the whole of nauseating humanity.

*Dominick*:  Please! I must say something.

*Narr.*:  He shot to his feet but the magistrate glared at him.

*Judge*:   Silence! Sit down!
*Dom. Narr.*:   The Sodswine shouted—
*Narr.*:   —and then he turned to Lew and said nicely,
*Judge*:   You may speak presently Mr.—er—Shapiro.[4]


## SCENE B

*Narr.*:   Lew couldn't help feeling rather proud when he saw the morning papers.
*Lew Narr.*:   Shattered but proud.

*Lew Narr.*:   And there were three magistrates again; a woman and two men. This lot were practically interchangeable with the others at St. Ives.
*Narr.*:   They were poring over papers and sometimes glancing over at his son.
*Lew Narr.*:   It looked none too healthy.
*Narr.*:   Then his lawyer arrived.
*Lawyer*:   Lew, don't worry,
*Narr.*:   —he whispered, as he sat down beside him. He didn't like his lawyer to call him Lew; he would have liked a bit more respect from a lawyer who practiced in John Street; he had been a jolly good customer these last fifteen years and had paid through the nose. On top of that, never once had he had the discourtesy to call his lawyer by his first name.
*Lew*:   I am worried Mr. Simmonds. I'll be frank.
*Lawyer*:   Not a thing to worry about; even with that other thing in Cornwall. But please see that he doesn't do it again.
*Lew Narr.*:   All very well for these geezers to speak. His sons were all at boarding schools, being pushed down and suppressed into nice English Gentlemen.
*Lawyer*:   Leave it to me. I've used this speech often. It always works.
*Narr.*:   The lawyer rose to speak.
*Lew Narr.*:   Well, no doubt with all his confidence and all his papers he knew what he was about.
*Lawyer*:   . . . this young man is the inarticulate voice of our new society; a product of affluence, an enigma that occurs when class and social barriers break down. A bubble on the surface of change, trying to form identity out of the nihilism of our troubled time . . .
*Lew Narr.*:   And so on. It was that sort of speech.
*Narr.*:   And Lew was glad when Mr. Simmonds finally sat down. And so apparently were the magistrates.
*Magistrate*:   To all that phut! Phut and phooey! I reject all your glib and modernistic nonsense.
*Narr.*:   Then the magistrate went through his papers again.

[4] Bernard Kops, *The Dissent of Dominick Shapiro* (New York: Coward-McCann, Inc., 1966), pp. 161–163.

*Magistrate*: I see he has been in trouble recently. Two days ago as a matter of fact.

*Narr.*: The lawyer sat down.

*Magistrate*: For vagrancy. Conditional discharge!

*Narr.*: —the magistrate said.

*Magistrate*: Well, well. You haven't learned much of a lesson. Perhaps we should teach you a real one.

*Narr.*: Lew felt a flutter of panic within him.

*Lew Narr.*: All was lost. The shame! The sorrow! The sleepless nights!

*Narr.*: If only his heart would not let him down he might be able to save the situation.

*Lew Narr.*: A seizure here would not draw an ounce of sympathy from these judges.

*Narr.*: As he got up he could see Dominick cursing under his breath.

*Lew Narr.*: It was too late to take his fine feelings into consideration.

*Lew*: Your honour—if you will forgive a humble father pleading for his son?

*Narr.*: The old man nodded.

*Lew*: If you study statistics . . .

*Narr.*: He dare not look at his son for fear of seeing the look of derision that usually came when he mentioned this word.

*Lew Narr.*: And Dominick was dead right; for some reason people believed you if you mentioned the magic word "Statistics."

*Lew*: . . . Statistics prove that you rarely find a young Jewish boy who is a delinquent. Furthermore I say unto you, adolescents of the Hebrew persuasion are never drunks or dope fiends, or wife beaters. How often do you meet a Jewish prostitute?

*Narr.*: The magistrate wriggled uncomfortably in his chair and shook his head to show that he rarely met any sort of prostitute.[5]

The narrator, situated in the wide aisle between the platform and the audience, established himself at the beginning of the production as an intermediary between the action and the audience by reading from a manuscript, which he held in his hands. He moved from side to side as the viewpoints shifted, always remaining close to the action. He read to the audience, as a storyteller should, but he turned and watched the action with the audience and even took a few short speaking roles, as did the Stage Manager in Thorton Wilder's *Our Town*. One can easily see the great importance of this narrator: In such a production, one is likely to cast a highly qualified, authoritative reader as the narrator. After the show, discerning audience members commented upon a belated realization of how much the narrator had contributed to the production. An audio tape revealed this very readily to the ear. But visually the narrator blended so well with the action that one

[5] Bernard Kops, *The Dissent of Dominick Shapiro* (New York: Coward-McCann, Inc., 1966), pp. 186–189.

tended to forget his presence, and yet the audience unconsciously depended on him for a major portion of the total story.

The production of *The Dissent of Dominick Shapiro* took place on a bare platform in a lecture hall. The platform contained one manuscript on a reading stand on stage right, surrounded partially by a semicircle of colored boxes of various heights upon which the cast of readers sat when not in the action. In some cases, rather than leaving their stools to participate in the scene, they simply called their lines from their sitting positions. Upstage left was a high platform, suggesting Dominick's upstairs bedroom, in which he spent considerable time. In center stage were two low stools on which actors sat when called on to sit in the living room, dining room, banquet hall, office, courtroom, and so on. Because the story is primarily Dominick's, the reader playing him never joined the "chorus" of readers but always remained a distinct visual identity. Other characters left the group of readers only when they came into close psychological association with Dominick, or, with Lew when the story was told from his point of view. Then, the reader involved would leave the group (and the script) and assume a visual identity in the action. Action took place on the platform, in front of it, and in the aisles of the auditorium. Every door in the hall was used for exits and entrances.

From the foregoing description, we hope that you can readily see that chamber theater is distinguished from readers theater primarily by the presence of the narrator as a distinct person or persons, either as an omniscient figure or as a character or characters within the story. This is much different from the methods for handling narration in the readers-theater productions described earlier. However, both forms may present prose fiction. Both forms are based on the principles of interpretative reading. Both are suggestive and theatrical in flavor, with chamber theater usually becoming more theatrical than readers theater, even using complete staging if desired. Both forms, when dealing with narrative literature, can be called "narrative theater."

**Literature for Group Reading.**   The principles of selection for individual interpretation apply also in the selection of materials for group reading, except that one should be careful to correlate the literature with the appropriate form of production. Almost any type or combination of types of materials can be incorporated into a collected script performance. We have already suggested that inspirational literature, passages building suspense or excitement, and selections emphasizing power or humor make good choral reading materials. Sometimes, literature written specifically for choric treatment, such as ancient or modern plays written with choruses in them, are available. Of course, readers theater requires characterization and dialogue, so that fiction and drama are obvious materials, but narrative and dialogue poetry are also good. Some persons seem to feel that readers theater should not concern itself with plays written for stage production but should leave those to the theater; yet we disagree with such a limitation. Obviously, plays having a great deal of important action or those dependent on scenic values are no better for readers theater than they are for solo interpretation. Plays strong in idea, language, character, and mood are conducive to imaginative suggestion. Some directors choose to produce plays of an experimental nature and plays not likely to be produced in the theater. Last, narrative theater, by definition, is limited to narrative fiction.

**Preparation of Script.** Directors of group-reading productions will seldom find a ready-made script but will usually prepare a specific script for a specific production. Seldom will they produce a long show without spending countless hours choosing materials, fitting them together, editing or otherwise adapting them. A collected script on a theme will require much reading simply to find the literature. About three hours of materials were gathered for the program "Battle of the Sexes" before it was eventually shortened to an hour and a quarter in playing time. Furthermore, the arrangement of the selections for maximum effect required much planning and experimentation. The program "Three Men from *Raintree County*" evolved (after a great deal of despair of ever getting an integrated forty-five minute program out of such an epic!) from pages 97–119, 143–152, and 259–270 of a thousand-page edition. Then, it required much cutting of these forty-five pages, for they would have required at least three times the forty-five minute period allowed for reading aloud.

Time limitations are an important consideration in any form of group reading. Because heavy demands are made on the imaginative participation of the audience, the total time for the performance is commonly thought to be comparatively short, with most directors preferring a show of considerably less than two hours. Often an hour to an hour and a half may be best for highly concentrated, imaginative recreation. Therefore, to produce a full-length play or novel in a short period requires much editing. To do this, one must decide what it is he wishes to emphasize, because it is obvious he cannot produce the whole work. Is it the main plot, or story line, or is it only an episode or two? Is it primarily characterization? mood? It is probable that subplots and minor characters will often be sacrificed in order to deal effectively with the major ones. Whatever is done, the director should *not* attempt to rewrite the author. The only rewriting should be a very few—if any—necessary transitions, for fluent movement of the edited script. Occasionally, and only occasionally, it may prove advantageous or essential to change the order of materials slightly to make sense to hearers when other materials are deleted.

**Analysis of Literature.** The director will obviously conduct the same thorough analysis of the literature that the oral interpreter or the director of any play will give. We need not repeat what we have said elsewhere or try to cover analytical principles discussed in hundreds of good books dealing with this subject.

**Rehearsal of Production.**   Because group-reading productions do not always require full memorization, complete action, or elaborate staging, no one should make the grievous error of assuming that they can be hastily prepared or rehearsed, for they should be executed as thoroughly as all good stage productions. Rehearsal periods for an hour presentation should usually be as extensive as for a three-act play. No production should receive shoddy consideration by either director or reader.

**Permission to Produce.**   The director of group-reading productions must assume responsibility for obtaining permission from holders of copyrights on all literature not in the public domain that he wishes to present to the public, whether or not the show is for educational purposes, profit, or both. (Classroom performances have not customarily been considered public performances.) Producers of group-reading performances of plays will probably have to pay the same royalty fees they would pay for regular stage production. Novels and short stories may sometimes be produced without payment of royalty fees, but permission must be obtained in advance, preferably before the director begins his preparation, and certainly before performance. Copyright holders deserve a thorough explanation from the director of his intentions and also payment for the use of their materials if required.

**Staging.**   The staging for a group-reading production can be anything from a bare platform containing only the proverbial stools and stands, which have become almost the trademark of readers theater, to a fully accoutered stage for a chamber theater production. Directors have experimented with stage settings, and the trend has been from the bare platform to some degree of theatrical setting on a small stage in an intimate theater, particularly for longer readers-theater and chamber-theater performances. This does not imply *realistic* settings. Because suggestion is a prime advantage of all multiple reading, suggestion in setting is also to be desired. Another trend has led away from a static arrangement of the readers to the use of movement. This has shocked some theatrical purists who have contended that a major difference between the interpreter's theater and the actor's theater is that the interpreter cannot, or should not, *move*, whereas the actor may. (Directors of one state high school forensic league foolishly " ruled " movement *out* of the high school group-reading event.) The answer to this would seem to be that there is no logical reason why the interpreter's body should be prevented from being as expressive as the actor's body. Most college directors call for movement from their readers any time they think it desirable.

Another trend in staging has been noticeable since about 1960. It was once felt that each reader should have his own manuscript and *use* it! This has changed in the practice of those most active in the field, who now feel that *the* manuscript (actually, one or more of them) may be in evidence somewhere upon the platform or stage as a symbol of the source of the literature, or it may be omitted entirely. Readers today, particularly in highly theatrical readers- and chamber-theater productions, do considerably more memorizing than they used to. When a reader is using impersonative techniques, including movement, to suggest character, he often limits his effectiveness if he is highly dependent on a manuscript. Readers should never appear to be "acting with book in hand," which is both poor reading and poor acting—a form of activity suitable only for a period of rehearsals before lines are learned, and to be deplored any other time.

A characteristic of group-reading has usually been the indirect focus used by the interpretative reader rather than the direct focus of the actor. In other words, in a traditional readers-theater production, for example, readers will not appear to speak to each other on the platform, but will establish the locus of the action in the realm of the audience, where it can more easily be formed in the listener's imagination. Two readers might well present a duo-scene, standing at lecterns, facing the audience somewhat squarely, but directing their eyes so that their two lines of vision cross, over the heads of the audience, in this manner:

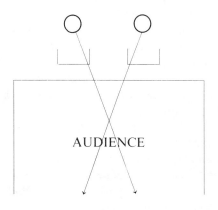

This is good practice. Although at first it may seem a bit strange to the novice, it works. When this sort of indirect, or "offstage," focus is used, there is no need for any staging. But, there are many occasions when a more direct relationship between the performers is needed or desired—for some constructive purpose, of course—and, in these instances, we must accept the fact that the reader then tends to come into the scene as the character rather than strictly as himself. Such literal and direct focus requires that the performer do *more* for the audience because the imagination of the viewer is called on to do *less*. Therefore, one should realize that although the shift from audience focus to platform focus may have certain advantages on occasion, it also places more responsibility on the reader to provide more thorough picturization and also to be more free from the manuscript. These may turn out to be disadvantages in themselves. Such shifts, therefore, should be undertaken only with care.

Properties are usually kept to a minimum in any form of multiple reading. When the readers are located on stools or behind lecterns, or both, the use of hand props becomes ludicrous; however, when the reader is permitted the use of movement, because he is bodily free, we see him in many productions pantomiming the handling of selected imaginary props, such as the frequent drinking of coffee from an imaginary cup and saucer in *The Marriage of Mr. Mississippi*, or Mephisto's eloquent extraction of a glass of wine from thin air, or Dominick's pretended eating and drinking at the wedding reception while the narrator describes his gluttony. Environmental properties may be more in order, as long as they are primarily suggestive to the imagination. Few props so often are as handy as a table and a couple of straight chairs. A good test for the director is to ask himself of every property he considers using: "Is this thing really necessary?" If it isn't, he ought to throw it out. Two necessary props in *Mississippi* were Don Quixote's dishpan helmet and broken lance, for Count Bodo's final speech. Specified in the stage directions, these items enabled the audience to recognize that the author saw the idealist as a ridiculous figure. Three highly desirable props for character delineation in the same show were Bodo's medical forehead mirror, stethoscope, and antique dark glasses.

Literal costuming is as infrequent as are literal props. A good policy is to keep it simple, meeting only the basic requirements for suggestion. Bodo wore a white physician's jacket. The three Vanessas wore black (mourning), white (purity), and red (carnality), but the dresses were modern and appropriate to the readers as well as to the characters. Modern dress, appropriate to the tone of the production, the mood of the literature, and, perhaps, suggestive to the character, is about as explicit as one can get in traditional readers-theater productions. Occasionally, the use of some realistic costume is obligatory, as was the case of the old Russian overcoat and fur hat that Dominick found in the closet and insisted on wearing through most of the book. These furnished the necessary visual stimuli to make him as absurd to the adult world as the book indicated.

Lighting, of course, can be a tremendous aid to any staged reading, for nothing can contribute more to focus attention or create mood than good lighting. It need not be complete or complex, but where conditions permit controlled lighting, the director should not overlook its possibilities.

Group-reading forms are modern descendants of the art of the mountebank, who could do a show anywhere at any time. Without this kind of flexibility and simple power over the audience's imaginations, the interpreter loses the real advantages of his art; and so, while we try to make use of whatever means we can devise to assist our audiences to the right experiences, we run the danger of going too far and usurping their imaginative functions. Therefore, we should repeat the best rule we know and apply it for all staging: *Do no more than absolutely necessary.* Good reading will force the audience to do the rest!

## GROUP READING IN THE CLASSROOM

Because group-reading programs need so little staging, they are ideal for classroom use. Two or three students of interpretative reading can work together in preparing ten- or fifteen-minute programs: collected scripts of various kinds of literature, short readers- or narrative-theater presentations of scenes from plays, short stories, or episodes from novels. Your instructor will undoubtedly welcome such creative efforts from you.

# Appendixes

# Appendix I
# The Major Books in Interpretation

Bacon, Wallace A., *The Art of Interpretation*, 2nd ed. New York: Holt, Rinehart and Winston, Inc., 1972.

Bacon, Wallace A., and Robert S. Breen, *Literature as Experience*. New York: McGraw-Hill Book Company, Inc., 1959.

Bahn, Eugene and Margaret L. Bahn, *A History of Oral Interpretation*. Minneapolis, Minn.: Burgess Publishing Company, 1970.

Beloof, Robert, *The Performing Voice in Literature*. Boston: Little, Brown and Company, 1966.

Brooks, Keith, Eugene Bahn, and L. LaMont Okey, *The Communicative Act of Oral Interpretation*, 2nd ed. Boston: Allyn and Bacon, Inc., 1975.

Coger, Leslie Irene, and Melvin R. White, *Readers Theatre Handbook: A Dramatic Approach to Literature*, 2nd ed. Chicago: Scott, Foresman and Company, 1973.

Doyle, Esther M. and Virginia Hastings Floyd, *Studies in Interpretation*, vols. 1 and 2. Amsterdam: Rodopi NV, 1972, 1977.

Geiger, Don, *The Dramatic Impulse in Modern Poetics*. Baton Rouge, La.: Louisiana State University Press, 1967, Chapter 1 "Toward a Poetics for Making, Seeing, and Saying."

Geiger, Don, *The Sound, Sense, and Performance of Literature*. Chicago: Scott, Foresman and Company, 1963.

Haas, Richard, *Theatres of Interpretation*. Ann Arbor, Mich.: Roberts-Burton Publication, 1976. (Two of your authors participated in the writing of this book.)

Haas, Richard and David A. Williams, *The Study of Oral Interpretation: Theory and Comment*. Indianapolis, Ind.: The Bobbs-Merrill Company, Inc., 1975.

Lee, Charlotte I. and Frank Galati, *Oral Interpretation*, 5th ed. Boston: Houghton Mifflin Company, 1977.

Lee, Charlotte I., *Oral Reading of the Scriptures*. Boston: Houghton Mifflin Company, 1974.

Long, Beverly Whitaker, Lee Hudson, and Phillis Rienstra Jeffrey, *Group Performance of Literature*. Englewood Cliffs, N.J.: Prentice-Hall, Inc., 1977.

Long, Chester Clayton, *The Liberal Art of Interpretation*. New York: Harper & Row, Publishers, 1974.

Maclay, Joanna Hawkins, *Readers Theatre: Toward a Grammar of Practice.*
New York: Random House, Inc., 1971.

Maclay, Joanna H. and Thomas O. Sloan, *Interpretation: An Approach to the Study of Literature.* New York: Random House, Inc., 1972.

Mattingly, Alethea Smith and Wilma H. Grimes, *Interpretation: Writer, Reader, Audience,* 2nd ed. Belmont, Calif.: Wadsworth Publishing Company, Inc., 1970.

Parrish, Wayland Maxfield, *Reading Aloud,* 4th ed. New York: Ronald Press Company, 1966.

Roloff, Leland H., *The Perception and Evocation of Literature.* Glenview, Ill.: Scott, Foresman and Company, 1973.

Sloan, Thomas O., *The Oral Study of Literature.* New York: Random House, Inc., 1966.

Woolbert, Charles Henry, and Severina E. Nelson, *The Art of Interpretative Speech,* 5th ed. New York: Appleton-Century-Crofts, 1968.

# Appendix II
# Anthologies of
# Literature

The following list of literary anthologies is organized here by title to suggest the great range of types of anthologies in their subject matters. It is hoped that one subject may suggest others to the student. This list is not intended to be all-inclusive or to indicate that these books are the best in any way.

*A Pedlar's Pack of Ballads and Songs, with Illustrative Notes.* Edited by W. H. Logan. Edinburgh: William Paterson, 1869. Detroit, Mich.: Reissued by Singing Tree Press, 1968.

*A Romantic Storybook.* Edited by Morris Bishop. Ithaca, N.Y.: Cornell University Press, 1971.

*A Southern Vanguard.* Edited by Allen Tate. Freeport, New York: Books for Libraries Press, 1947.

*A Treasury of Great Science Fiction, Vol. 2.* Edited by Milton Boucher. Garden City, N.Y.: Doubleday & Company, Inc., 1959.

*A Treasury of the World's Great Letters.* Edited by M. Lincoln Schuster. New York: Simon and Schuster, Inc., 1940.

*A Treasury of the World's Great Speeches* (Revised and enlarged edition.) Edited by Houston Peterson. New York: Simon and Schuster, Inc., 1965.

*American Folk Poetry: An Anthology.* Edited by Duncan Emrich. Boston: Little, Brown and Company, 1974.

*American Negro Poetry.* Edited by Arna Bontemps. New York: Hill and Wang, 1963.

*Best American Plays; 7th Series, 1967–1973.* Edited by Clive Barnes. New York: Crown Publishers, Inc., 1975.

*Black Short Story Anthology.* Edited by Woodie King. New York: Columbia University Press, 1972.

*Black Theater, U.S.A.: Forty-Five Plays by Black Americans, 1847–1974.* Edited by James V. Hatch. New York: The Free Press, 1974.

*By a Woman Writt: Literature from Six Centuries by and about Women.* Edited by Joan Gonlianos. Baltimore: Penguin Books, Inc., 1974.

*Come Back, Africa; Fourteen Short Stories from South Africa.* Edited by Herbert L. Shore and Megohelina Shore-Bos. New York: International Publishers, 1968.

*Concrete Poetry: A World View.* Edited by Mary Ellen Solt. Bloomington, Ind.: Indiana University Press, 1971.

435

*Confucius to Cummings: An Anthology of Poetry*. Edited by Ezra Pound and Marcella Spann. New York: A New Directions Book, 1964.

*Contemporary American Speeches: A Sourcebook of Speech Forms and Principles*. Edited by Wil A. Linkugel, R. R. Allen, and Richard L. Johannesen. Belmont, Calif.: Wadsworth Publishing Company, Inc., 1965.

*Contemporary Black Drama*. Edited by Clinton F. Oliver and Stephanie Sills. New York: Charles Scribner's Sons, 1971.

*Contemporary Drama: Eleven Plays*. Edited by E. Bradlee Watson and Benfield Pressey. New York: Charles Scribner's Sons, 1956.

*Contemporary Drama: Fifteen Plays*. Edited by E. Bradlee Watson and Benfield Pressey. New York: Charles Scribner's Sons, 1959.

*Drama: An Introductory Anthology*, Alternate Edition. Edited by Otto Reinert. Boston: Little, Brown and Company, Inc., 1964.

*Dylan Thomas's Choice: An Anthology of Verse Spoken by Dylan Thomas*. Edited by Ralph Maud and Aneirin Talfan Davies. New York: A New Directions Book, 1963.

*Eight Great Tragedies*. Edited by Sylvan Barnek, Morton Berman and William Burto. New York: New American Library, 1957.

*Eight Plays from Off-Off Broadway*. Edited by Nick Orzel and Michael Smith. Indianapolis, Ind.: The Bobbs-Merrill Company, Inc., 1966.

*Fairy Tales for Computers*. New York: The Eakins Press, Publishers, 1969.

*50 Great Short Stories*. Edited by Milton Crane. New York: Bantam Books, Inc., 1952.

*Flights: Readings in Magic, Mysticism, Fantasy, and Myth*. Edited by David Adams Leeming. New York: Harcourt Brace Jovanovich, Inc., 1974.

*From Darkness to Light: A Confession of Faith in the Form of an Anthology*. Edited by Victor Gollancz. New York: Harper & Row, 1956.

*Gentlemen, Scholars and Scoundrels: A Treasury of the Best of Harper's Magazine from 1850 to the Present*. Edited by Horace Knowles. New York: Harper & Row, 1959.

*Giant Talk: An Anthology of Third World Writings*. Compiled and Edited by Quincy Troupe and Rainer Schulte. New York: Random House, Inc., 1975.

*Gothic Tales of Terror: Classic Horror Stories from Great Britain, Europe and the United States, 1765–1840*. Edited by Peter Haining. New York: Tapling Publishing Company, 1972.

*Great American Speeches 1898–1963*. Edited by John Graham. New York: Appleton-Century-Crofts, 1970.

*Great Russian Plays*. Compiled by Norris Houghton. New York: Dell Publishing Company, Inc., 1960.

*Hero/Anti-Hero*. Edited by Roger B. Rolin. New York: Webster Division, McGraw-Hill Book Company, 1973.

*Images of Women in Literature.* Edited by Mary Anne Ferguson. Boston: Houghton Mifflin Company, 1973.

*Insights: A Selection of Creative Literature about Children.* (Selected and edited by the Child Study Association of America.) New York: Jason Aronson, 1973.

*Literature of the American Indian.* Edited by Thomas E. Sanders and Walter W. Peck. New York: Glencoe Press, 1973.

*Literature for Interpretation.* Edited by Wallace A. Bacon and Robert S. Breen. New York: Holt, Rinehart and Winston, Inc., 1961.

*Literature for Listening: An Oral Interpreter's Anthology.* Edited by Keith Brooks, Eugene Bahn, and L. LaMont Okey. Boston: Allyn and Bacon, Inc., 1968.

*Lyric Poems on Twelve Themes.* Edited by Charles H. Kegel and William J. Shanahan. Glenview, Ill.: Scott, Foresman and Company, 1970.

*Masters of Modern Drama.* Edited by Haskell M. Block and Robert G. Shedd. New York: Random House, Inc., 1962.

*Midland Humor: A Harvest of Fun and Folklore.* Edited by Jack Conroy. New York: Current Books, Inc., A. A. Wyn, 1947.

*Missouri Reader.* Edited by Frank Luther Mott. Columbia, Mo.: University of Missouri Press, 1964.

*Modern Satiric Stories: The Impropriety Principle.* Edited by Gregory Fitz Gerald. Glenview, Ill.: Scott, Foresman and Company, 1971.

*Modern Science Fiction.* Edited by Norman Spinrad. New York: Anchor Books, 1974.

*Modern Stories from Many Lands*, 2nd Enlarged Edition. Edited by Clarence R. Decker and Charles Angoff. New York: Manyland Books, 1972.

*Myths and Motifs in Literature.* Edited by David J. Burrows, Frederick R. Lapides, and John T. Shawcross. New York: The Free Press, 1973.

*Naked Poetry: Recent American Poetry in Open Form.* Edited by Stephen Berg and Robert Mezey. Indianapolis, Ind.: Bobbs-Merrill Company, Inc., 1969.

*Nebula Award Stories, No. 11.* Edited by Isaac Asimov. New York: Harper & Row, Publishers, 1977.

*New Directions in Prose and Poetry, No. 34.* Edited by J. Laughlin. New York: New Directions Publishing Corporation, 1977.

*Pegasus Descending: A Treasury of the Best Bad Poems in English from Matthew Arnold to Walt Whitman.* Edited by James Camp, X. J. Kennedy, and Keith Waldrop. New York: Macmillan Publishing Company, Inc., 1971.

*Plays of Our Time.* Edited by Bennett Cerf. New York: Random House, Inc., 1967.

*Poet's Choice.* Edited by Paul Engle and Joseph Langland. New York: The Dial Press, 1962.

*Prize Stories 1977: The O. Henry Awards.* Edited by William Abrahams. Garden City, N.Y.: Doubleday & Company, Inc., 1977.

*Reading Modern Poetry.* Edited by Paul Engle and Warren Carrier. Glenview, Ill.: Scott, Foresman and Company, 1968.

*Short Stories: A Critical Anthology.* Edited by Ensaf Thune and Ruth Prigozy. New York: Macmillan Publishing Company, Inc., 1973.

*Social Psychology Through Literature.* Edited by Ronald Fernandez. New York: John Wiley & Sons, Inc., 1972.

*Stories from the New Yorker, 1950 to 1960.* Editors of *The New Yorker.* New York: Simon and Schuster, 1960.

*Story and Structure*, 2nd ed. Edited by Laurence Perrine. New York: Harcourt Brace Jovanovich, Inc., 1966.

*The Antic Muse: American Writers in Parody; A Collection of Parody, Satire, and Literary Burlesque of American Writers, Past and Present.* Edited by R. P. Falk. New York: Grove Press, 1955.

*The Beat Generation and The Angry Young Men.* Edited by Gene Feldman and Max Gartenberg. New York: The Citadel Press, 1958.

*The Best American Short Stories 1976.* Edited by Martha Foley. Boston: Houghton Mifflin Company, 1976.

*The Black Poets.* Edited by Dudley Randall. New York: Buxtam Books, 1971.

*The Chicano; From Caricature to Self-Portrait.* Edited by Edward Simmen. New York: New American Library, 1971.

*The Fireside Treasury of Modern Humor.* Edited by Scott Meredith. New York: Simon and Schuster, 1963.

*The Forms of Fiction.* Edited by John Gardner and Lennis Dunlap. New York: Random House, Inc., 1962.

*The Living Underground: An Anthology of Contemporary American Poetry.* Edited by Hugh Fox. Troy, N.Y.: Whitson Publishing Company, Inc., 1973.

*The New Israeli Writers: Short Stories of the First Generation.* Edited by Dalia Rabikovitz. New York: Funk and Wagnalls, 1969.

*The Old West in Fiction.* Edited by Irwin R. Blacker. New York: Ivan Obolensky, Inc., 1961.

*The Poem in Its Skin.* Edited by Paul Carroll. Chicago: Follett Publishing Company, 1968.

*The Poetry of Black America; Anthology of the 20th Century.* Edited by Arnold Adoff. New York: Harper & Row, Publishers, 1973.

*The Political Imagination in Literature.* Edited by Philip Green and Michael Walzer. New York: The Free Press, 1969.

*The Rise of American Jewish Literature; An Anthology of Selections from the Major Novels.* Edited by Charles Angoff and Meyer Levin. New York: Simon and Schuster, 1970.

*The Short Story: Fiction in Transition.* Edited by J. Chesley Taylor. New York: Charles Scribner's Sons, 1969.

*The Story: A Critical Anthology*, 2nd ed. Edited by Mark Schorer. Englewood Cliffs, N.J.: Prentice-Hall, Inc., 1967.

*The Troubled Vision: An Anthology of Contemporary Short Novels.* Edited by Jerome Charyn. London: Collier-Macmillan Ltd., 1970.

*The Voice That Is Great Within Us: American Poetry of the Twentieth Century.* Edited by Hayden Carruth. New York: Bantam Books, 1970.

*The White Pony: An Anthology of Chinese Poetry.* Edited by Robert Payne. New York: New American Library, 1947.

*The World of Short Fiction: An International Collection.* Edited by Thomas A. Gullason and Leonard Casper. New York: Harper & Row, Publishers, 1962.

*The World Split Open: Four Centuries of Women Poets in England and America, 1552–1950.* Edited by Louise Bernikow. New York: Random House, Inc., 1974.

*The World's Best Short Short Stories.* Edited by Roger B. Goodman. New York: Bantam Pathfinder Editions, 1972.

*The World's Love Poetry.* Edited by Michael Rheta Martin. New York: Bantam Books, 1960.

*This Is My Best in the Third Quarter of the Century.* Edited by Whit Burnett. Garden City, N.Y.: Doubleday & Company, Inc., 1970.

*Today's Poets: American and British Poetry Since the 1930's.* Edited by Chad Walsh. New York: Charles Scribner's Sons, 1964.

*21 Great Short Stories.* Edited by Abraham H. Lass and Norma L. Tasman. New York: New American Library, 1969.

*Types of Short Fiction,* 2nd ed. Edited by Roy R. Male. Belmont, Calif.: Wadsworth Publishing Company, Inc., 1970.

*Wonders and Surprises; A Collection of Poems Chosen by Phyllis McGinley.* Philadelphia: J. B. Lippincott Company, 1968.

*Youth and Maturity: 20 Stories.* Edited by James Soulos. New York: Macmillan Publishing Co., Inc., 1970.

# Index of Authors
# and Titles

# Index of Topics